P9-CMU-865

titanium
ebay®

second edition

a tactical guide
to becoming
a millionaire powerseller

titanium
ebay®

second edition

Skip McGrath

ALPHA

A member of Penguin Group (USA) Inc.

ALPHA BOOKS

Published by the Penguin Group

Penguin Group (USA) Inc., 375 Hudson Street, New York, New York 10014, USA

Penguin Group (Canada), 90 Eglinton Avenue East, Suite 700, Toronto, Ontario M4P 2Y3, Canada (a division of Pearson Penguin Canada Inc.)

Penguin Books Ltd., 80 Strand, London WC2R 0RL, England

Penguin Ireland, 25 St. Stephen's Green, Dublin 2, Ireland (a division of Penguin Books Ltd.)

Penguin Group (Australia), 250 Camberwell Road, Camberwell, Victoria 3124, Australia (a division of Pearson Australia Group Pty. Ltd.)

Penguin Books India Pvt. Ltd., 11 Community Centre, Panchsheel Park, New Delhi—110 017, India

Penguin Group (NZ), 67 Apollo Drive, Rosedale, North Shore, Auckland 1311, New Zealand (a division of Pearson New Zealand Ltd.)

Penguin Books (South Africa) (Pty.) Ltd., 24 Sturdee Avenue, Rosebank, Johannesburg 2196, South Africa

Penguin Books Ltd., Registered Offices: 80 Strand, London WC2R 0RL, England

Copyright © 2009 by Skip McGrath

All rights reserved. No part of this book shall be reproduced, stored in a retrieval system, or transmitted by any means, electronic, mechanical, photocopying, recording, or otherwise, without written permission from the publisher. No patent liability is assumed with respect to the use of the information contained herein. Although every precaution has been taken in the preparation of this book, the publisher and author assume no responsibility for errors or omissions. Neither is any liability assumed for damages resulting from the use of information contained herein. For information, address Alpha Books, 800 East 96th Street, Indianapolis, IN 46240.

International Standard Book Number: 978-1-59257-842-9
Library of Congress Catalog Card Number: 2008937771

11 10 09   8 7 6 5 4 3 2 1

Interpretation of the printing code: The rightmost number of the first series of numbers is the year of the book's printing; the rightmost number of the second series of numbers is the number of the book's printing. For example, a printing code of 09-1 shows that the first printing occurred in 2009.

Printed in the United States of America

Note: This publication contains the opinions and ideas of its author. It is intended to provide helpful and informative material on the subject matter covered. It is sold with the understanding that the author and publisher are not engaged in rendering professional services in the book. If the reader requires personal assistance or advice, a competent professional should be consulted.

The author and publisher specifically disclaim any responsibility for any liability, loss, or risk, personal or otherwise, which is incurred as a consequence, directly or indirectly, of the use and application of any of the contents of this book.

Most Alpha books are available at special quantity discounts for bulk purchases for sales promotions, premiums, fund-raising, or educational use. Special books, or book excerpts, can also be created to fit specific needs.

For details, write: Special Markets, Alpha Books, 375 Hudson Street, New York, NY 10014.

This book is dedicated to my wife, Karen, who is affectionately known by our customers as the Shipping Goddess and has made hundreds of electronic friends throughout the eBay community. Every year when we exhibit at eBay Live, more people want to meet her than me. Karen is the reason behind our near perfect feedback rating. She answers every e-mail with patience and grace and always takes the customer's side of the problem into account. Besides that, she is the love of my life.

Contents

Part 4: Advanced Listing and Selling Strategies

Part 5: You Can't Grow Without Automation

Part 6: Beyond eBay

Part 7: Managing Your Business for Growth

Appendixes

Introduction

I still remember my first eBay sale. In fact, my first transaction on eBay was a sale. I'd spent two evenings in 1998 surfing around on eBay, but I had yet to buy anything.

I collect books on nautical and maritime subjects and had a duplicate book, *Sailboat Racing Strategy and Tactics*, which I had picked up in a box of books at a tag sale. It was a used book in good condition, and I had paid less than a dollar for it, so I decided to list it on eBay.

I listed it in a seven-day auction with a starting price of $1. I checked on it every evening when I got home from work, but after five days, I still had no bids. Because that was before eBay had hit counters that told you how many people had looked at your auction, I couldn't tell if anyone was even looking at it.

Finally, late on the fifth night, I got my first bid of $1. By the time I got home from work the next day, I had two bidders. The highest bid was up to $6.25, and I still had another day to go. About five minutes before the end of the auction the following day, another bidder joined in and pushed the book up to over $12. One of the bidders managed a last-second snipe and won the book for $14.25. Two things happened when that first auction ended. I made $13.25 profit on a $1 book, and I was hooked on eBay forever.

My wife, Karen, and I had previously operated an antique business in Millbrook, New York, before packing up and moving to the San Juan Islands north of Seattle, Washington, in 1996. Before we left, we sold off all the furniture in our shop and packed the smaller pieces in boxes to take with us. They were to be the start-up merchandise for a new shop someday.

Right after selling that first book, I went into the basement, opened one of the boxes, and took out a nice pair of brass beehive candlesticks, which still had the $89 price tag on them from our shop. I photographed them with my new digital camera, and my son helped me figure out how to upload the photos to web space on our family website.

I launched the candlesticks in another seven-day auction, and they followed almost the same pattern as the book, no bidding activity for the first five days and then bidders coming in one by one. Hoping a low starting price would attract lots of bidders, I had taken a chance and started the bidding at $29, which was below my cost. By the sixth day the candlesticks were bid up to over $75.

I can't remember the exact sequence, but again the bidding became hot within the last few minutes of the auction, and the candlesticks ended up selling for over $100, quite a bit more than I would have retailed them for in our shop.

When the auction ended, Karen and I looked at each other and had exactly the same thought: why do we need an antique shop? We can make money selling antiques from home—even in our pajamas!

Over the next year we sold several hundred items on eBay and lost money on only one item. Our feedback climbed steadily as we honed our eBay selling skills. And, yes, we occasionally found ourselves in front of the computer launching auctions or corresponding with bidders and buyers while still in our pajamas and having our first cup of morning coffee.

Today we still sell antiques and collectibles, but we've also expanded our business into books and new designer clothing. In 2003, I became a registered eBay Trading Assistant. (A Trading Assistant is someone who sells things for others on consignment. Today consignment selling is one of the fastest-growing business segments on eBay.)

More than 16 million people have sold something on eBay. Over 800,000 sell more or less full-time, and 2 million sell something on a fairly regular basis. Who are these active eBay sellers selling to? eBay buyers number over 125 million on 23 international eBay sites, including the newest one in India, a country of 500 million people. You can shop on any eBay site from any country in the world. Since starting on eBay in 1998, I have sold and shipped goods to more than 40 countries, including Malaysia, Jordan, South Africa, and Qatar. At the time of this writing, in mid-2008, eBay counted more than 185 million global registered users.

eBay ended 2007 with over $44 billion in gross merchandise sales, which is the total value of goods and services sold during the year. Yet eBay itself sells nothing but access to their platform. eBay does not sell a single antique or collectible, razor blade, or even digital camera, although over 10,000 digital cameras are sold on eBay during any given month. It is you and I who do the selling. If every eBay seller were an employee of eBay, the company would be the largest private employer in the world, larger than Wal-Mart and Lowe's combined.

How do you get your piece of this global marketplace? It is easy to sell an item on eBay. After you have registered and set up a PayPal account, you can list an item and launch it in three minutes. Millions of people do this every day. They are the occasional users and eBay hobbyists. The other category is the full-time eBay professional. It is difficult to get firm numbers out of eBay, but eBay observers and financial analysts estimate that about 800,000 sellers run either full-time or substantial part-time eBay businesses, listing several million individual items every single day.

eBay calls these people PowerSellers and awards them formal designations based on their monthly gross merchandise sales and the opportunity to earn fee discounts if they qualify with superior customer service ratings.

PowerSellers are eBay top sellers who have sustained a consistently high volume of monthly sales and a feedback rating of 98 percent positive or better. (There are several million-dollar-a-year sellers who are not PowerSellers because their positive feedback is less than 98 percent.) As such, these sellers rank among the most successful sellers in terms of product sales and customer satisfaction on eBay.

eBay has five levels of PowerSeller. Reaching the higher levels earns you access to e-mail and telephone support and invitations to special promotional programs eBay puts on throughout the year. The five levels are based on an individual's average gross merchandise sales for the previous three months or his average sales for the past twelve months:

Bronze	$1,000 month
Silver	$3,000 month
Gold	$10,000 month
Platinum	$25,000 month
Titanium	$150,000 month

Although there are plenty of books about selling on eBay, this one is designed to take the occasional or part-time seller through the PowerSeller ranks to reach the Platinum and even the Titanium level, as these are the levels where one can truly make a good living on eBay today.

Building a profitable eBay business shares many of the same requirements you'll find in any offline business, including the ability to control costs, manage inventory, market products, and service customers. But eBay also has specific requirements and unique strategies. And I have done my best to cover both areas because each is critical to your success.

The days of easy money on eBay ended by 2002 when its growth and success started attracting large corporations and experienced small and medium-size business owners.

In the early days of eBay, I could buy a lot of closeout designer blue jeans by the pallet load for under $5 a pair and sell them on eBay for up to $25 a pair. Today, many of the closeout companies who used to sell to me are selling the blue jeans themselves directly on eBay. Large operators can buy container loads of consumer electronics or toys directly from overseas manufacturers and put them on eBay at as low a price as you could get from a wholesaler in smaller quantities.

Does this mean you can't make money on eBay today? Not at all. It just means the game has changed. There are niches and opportunities in any market. Every competitor has a weakness, and opportunities to exploit them abound. You just have to know where and how to find them.

I also receive e-mail from readers who wonder if a person can still make money now that eBay has raised its fees. Well, my gas costs more; food costs more; and just about everything else costs more than when I started on eBay. Yes, the fees have steadily increased each year, but so have my sales and my profits. In January of 2008, eBay had another large fee increase, but my sales and profits in February through April were some of my best months ever since starting on eBay. Market and product research is important in any business, industry, or sales channel. This is doubly true on eBay. Learning how to research a product and find and exploit opportunities on and off the eBay platform forms a large part of this book and is essential to any successful eBay seller.

Another important requirement for success on eBay is automation. eBay's largest and most successful sellers list hundreds or even thousands of auctions a month, and I cover automating the auction process in detail.

I've been selling successfully on eBay for over nine years, and in this book I do my best to share all my strategies, tips, secrets, and techniques. I also share my mistakes, so you don't have to repeat them. In addition, I have reached out to the PowerSeller Community on eBay to bring you advice from some of eBay's most successful sellers. You'll meet Jay Senese of JayAndMarie, one of the highest-ranked sellers on eBay with over 900,000 recorded feedbacks. You will also meet Mike Enos, a Platinum PowerSeller and one of the leading experts on eBay product acquisition. These experts and others will offer comments and advice on their areas of expertise. Look for them in the gray sidebars throughout the book.

eBay is a business, and as with any other business, it takes time and practice to learn all the steps and techniques to be successful. Don't stress yourself out if everything isn't clicking the first time you try it. Nothing in this book requires a college degree or advanced business skills to learn, but you'll have to take the time to study and learn how the pros do it if you want to be successful.

Yes, you can still buy books for $1 that you can sell on eBay for over $14. And yes, eBay is still just as much fun today as the day I started.

Acknowledgments

I would first like to thank my agent, Marilyn Allen, who believed in this project and worked tirelessly to find a publisher. Mike Sanders, my editor, has shepherded this from concept to market. Mike is patient, helpful, and most importantly, has you, the reader, foremost in his mind. I would also like to thank the highly professional production staff at Alpha Books including Megan Douglass, production editor, and Nancy Wagner, copy editor.

My development editor, Ginny Bess Munroe, did a fabulous job of catching my mistakes, bringing order to sometimes chaotic text, and cleaning up some occasionally tortured prose.

My daughter-in-law, Lissa McGrath, an author and eBay seller in her own right, did the technical editing and fact checking and caught a lot of the little details that I often missed.

I owe a nod also to the very nice and professional folks who man the eBay PowerSeller support phones. Whenever I had an arcane technical question or needed clarification of a policy, they always had the answer at the tip of their fingers.

Finally, I would like to thank Pierre Omidyar, who started eBay, not for starting an online auction company but for proving to all the doubters that people are basically good and that complete strangers can trust each other to exchange goods and money with one another.

Special Thanks to the Technical Reviewer

Titanium eBay, Second Edition, was reviewed by an expert who double-checked the accuracy of what you'll learn here, to help us ensure that this book gives you everything you need to know about eBay. Special thanks are extended to Lissa McGrath.

Trademarks

All terms mentioned in this book that are known to be or are suspected of being trademarks or service marks have been appropriately capitalized. Alpha Books and Penguin Group (USA) Inc. cannot attest to the accuracy of this information. Use of a term in this book should not be regarded as affecting the validity of any trademark or service mark.

part 1

Organizing Your eBay Business for Growth

One of the things all successful eBay business owners share is a passion for organization and doing things by the numbers. I have interviewed dozens of Platinum and Titanium PowerSellers, and all of them have stories about how fast their business grew and how their business organization and systems couldn't keep pace, continually forcing them to update and reinvent systems and processes that weren't working. All wished they had taken the time to set up and organize their business from the beginning to accommodate the growth.

Organizing your business for growth starts with choosing your business name and creating your brand and carries through to the selection of hardware and software, your corporate organization, and the writing of a realistic business plan designed to carry your business from Silver to Gold to Platinum to Titanium levels.

This part takes you through the steps to set up and organize your business model, your systems, and your processes in a manner that will enable you to grow smoothly without interrupting your business flow later to reorganize.

chapter 1

Preparing Your Business for Growth

I know you are eager to dive right into the subject of high-powered selling on eBay, but good organization and a good business foundation are critical to the success of any business, and that goes for eBay as well. The way you organize and operate your business is essential to your success and will have a long-term impact on your ability to scale your business to the Gold, Platinum, or Titanium PowerSeller level.

PowerSeller Tip

eBay recently announced a new level of PowerSeller called the Diamond Level. This is for really huge corporate sellers with hundreds of thousands of listings for sellers who sell $500,000 a month worth of goods, and who have a minimum of 4.8 DSR across the board. Diamond PowerSellers will have the ability to negotiate listing fee discounts with eBay.

A well-organized business increases the number of wholesale suppliers who will work with you, lower your taxes, limit your liability, and increase your profits. Taking the time to do it right the first time will save you money and headaches later. As you go through the chapters in Part 1, some of them might not seem very important, but I encourage you to take the time to review them anyway. Even if you are an experienced offline business owner, take a look at these chapters; things are a little different in the online world and on eBay specifically.

Depending on your level of experience on eBay, you may have already accomplished many of the steps addressed in this section. Nevertheless, I suggest you at least scan or review each subject for new techniques you may have missed when you originally set up your business.

Although the goal of this book is to teach you how to run a large eBay business, you can't run a really large eBay business selling exclusively on eBay. The margins are just too small. In the early days of eBay there was far less competition—and the competition was less sophisticated than it is today. The average seller could command higher prices and make a larger margin on every sale than is possible today. Also, eBay's fees were much lower a few years ago. Today because there is so much competition on eBay, margins have eroded. This fact, combined with eBay's higher fees, has forced sellers to expand off of eBay into other venues such as Overstock.com, Amazon, and other web-based auctions and stores. Today the most successful sellers use eBay as a gateway or an advertising platform for their other selling channels both on and off eBay.

As you organize your business, keep in mind that it is impossible to run a large online business without a high degree of automation. Consider the math: the average successful auction on eBay ends with an item selling for approximately $60. Using this figure, if you are going to achieve gross merchandise sales of $100,000 per month, you will have to successfully close more than 1,600 auctions each month. ($100,000 Gross Merchandise Sales (GMS) divided by $60 Average Selling Price (ASP) = 1,666 auctions a month.)

And not every auction closes successfully. You might have to launch as many as 2,500 auctions to achieve 1,600 successful ones. That is an average of 83 auctions a day or 2,500 auctions a month. When you consider that launching an auction consists of taking a photo(s) and uploading it, selecting a category, writing a title and description, and scheduling the auction, you can see why it will be necessary to automate this function. Remember also that you need to complete each successful auction on the back end. This includes communicating with the buyer, receiving payment, shipping the item, and posting feedback.

But don't let these numbers frighten you. Hundreds of top sellers launch as many as 1,000 auctions a week, and several automated programs are available to help you do this. We cover these in detail in the section on Automation.

1.1 Get the Basics Right

All of this takes resources, including money, time, hardware and software, business services, shipping supplies, and perhaps even an employee or two. Some sellers are able to finance their growth with profits, but most of us need to raise capital to make these investments. In order for banks, wholesale suppliers, shipping companies, and other businesses to take you seriously, you need to run a well-organized business.

As we get into the next chapters, you will see how important your business organization is and how it affects your ability to deal with your business stakeholders. You simply cannot grow your business to a large level with a part-time business model, systems, and equipment.

1.2 Essential Systems and Services

One decision you will face fairly early is whether you can operate the business from your home or will need commercial space. If you are selling very small, yet expensive items, such as stamps, coins, autographs, high-end or rare collectibles, you won't need a lot of storage room and might be able to operate the business from your home. For larger items, such as electronics, apparel, books, or automotive parts, you will need a very large home or somewhere you can store, photograph, and ship large amounts of goods.

Unless you are going into the consignment business where you need walk-in exposure, you do not need space in an expensive retail area. Most cities and towns have small industrial parks in the outlying areas where you can rent secure space cheaply.

1.3 You Can't Do This Alone

If you are operating out of your home, you might be okay hiring a part-time employee. But most people are not comfortable having employees in their home. Along with the inconvenience, there is the issue of liability. Finding property and liability insurance for a business in the home can be difficult. Although some limited policies are available, it is much easier and cheaper to find insurance if you have a commercial address.

The decision to hire employees is simple. For every dollar you spend or invest in your business, you should get a return. Will having an employee enable you to launch more auctions? Will having an employee free your time to pursue activities that will make you money? Look at your activities. What makes you money: standing in line at the post office or taking photographs and launching auctions?

Many think frugality is a virtue, but frugality in business has its own place. Saving money on office supplies is frugal and can lower your overhead. Saving money by standing in line at the post office when someone could do that for you is not frugal—it's a waste of resources. For more on running an eBay store, see Chapter 47.

For more on hiring employees, see Chapter 59.

For more on automating your business, see Chapters 41 through 45.

For more on financing your business growth, see Chapter 6.

chapter 2

Naming and Branding Your Business

If you don't already have a name for your eBay business, take some time and care in coming up with one as you'll be putting that name on letterhead, business cards, and your business license, all of which are necessary elements to running a successful business. Of course, you *can* run an eBay business without these things, but you will never break through to PowerSeller levels without them.

2.1 Choosing a Business Name

If you are in one line of business only, then a specific name gives you credibility as a specialist. Some examples might be: Janie's Children's Apparel, Jason's Collectible Cards, Westwood Jewelry Sales, Nautical Antiques & Collectibles, Books and More, Import Motors Marketing, and so on.

However, if you are a general merchandiser or will be buying and selling different categories of products, you would do better with a more general business name. Some examples might be Southwest Marketing, Alley Trading, Auction Deals, Williams Associates, Northwest Marketing & Sales, or Summerdale House, Inc. These names could apply to almost any type of business and give you the freedom to describe your business as virtually anything you want. However, be careful of using the words Inc., Incorporated, Partners, Limited, and Ltd., as these terms all have specific legal meanings. For instance, it is illegal to call yourself a corporation if you are not incorporated. If you are going to become an eBay Trading Assistant (TA) or consignment seller, you might want a name such as *Consign-On-line* or *SellForYou*.

Figure 2.1

One eBay seller's memorable name was The Cabana Girl.

Besides a business name, you need to choose a memorable eBay username. Whatever business name you choose, make sure it can be easily worked into your username.

There are some great examples of successful sellers on eBay with specialized business names that have corresponding eBay usernames. One of the most famous is Jay Senese. His eBay user ID and his business name were the same: OneCentCDs. Jay became the largest seller on eBay offering used and closeout CDs by starting all his auctions at 1¢. So many people copied his success and cloned slight variations of his name that he finally gave up and changed it to JayAndMarie. (His wife Marie works in the business with him.) By that time Jay and Marie had become so famous that they essentially branded their own names. Some other business names that combine to make clever eBay usernames include …

Business Name	Username
Golf Time, Inc.	Golftime
Mr. Mobile Accessories	Mr_Mobile

Professional Car Parts	ProCarParts
Video Planet Sales	Video_Planet
Closeout Book Distributors	BookCloseOuts
Camera Auction Center	CamerasAtAuctions

Having a clever and memorable name will pay dividends as you grow your business. It will also enable you to brand your business across several platforms (eBay auctions, eBay Store, Web Store, and offline store).

2.2 Branding Your Business Name

Also give some thought to developing your brand. A brand consists of more than a name. It is, or can be, a combination of your business name, your eBay username, a logo, and the look and feel of your auctions and website. Brands are meant to build credibility in the customer's mind and to create a memorable impression that people will recognize when they return to your auctions, your eBay store, or your website. A brand will help you gain recognition on eBay and the web. It will help people remember you. When you think of branding, think beyond eBay. Eventually you will want a web store, so your brand should be capable of translating to other formats.

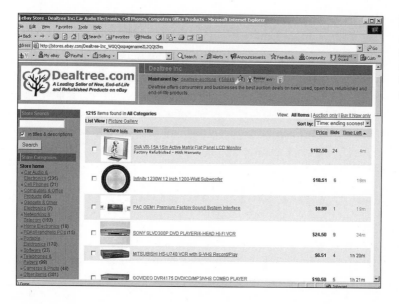

Figure 2.2
Dealtree.com has worked hard to build brand recognition among eBay customers.

PowerSeller Tip

The whole point of having a logo and a memorable name is so that satisfied customers can find you again and recommend you to others. If people remember your business name, website, and/or eBay username, they can go directly to your sales portal, thereby avoiding possible exposure to your competitors.

2.3 Creating an eBay Store Name

An eBay store is a place on eBay where you can sell merchandise at a fixed price and can list items indefinitely, as opposed to the one- to ten-day auction format. The listing fees are much lower than for auctions. As of this writing it costs only 3, 5, or 10 cents per month, depending on the selling price, to list an item in your eBay store (in addition to the monthly eBay Store subscription fee).

eBay gives you the freedom to create a name and a logo for your eBay store. You can create a banner at the top of your store or even design your whole store with your own unique look. As you are choosing a business name and a brand look and feel, think about how it will fit into a banner design.

PowerSeller Tip

Several web designers specialize in designing eBay store logos and banners. A search for "eBay banner design" on any eBay page will turn up several fixed price listings for this service. I have seen several great designs from these specialists that cost as little as $100, but you will most likely pay a little more for a comprehensive design that will work across your auctions and store and also have the ability to translate later to a website design.

2.4 Web Store and URL Selection

Virtually all large eBay sellers also have a web store or their own website where they sell the same or similar merchandise they sell on eBay. As well as your eBay username, you also want a memorable website name and URL. Long URLs are cumbersome, so think of something catchy and short. It might contain all or part of your business name or describe what you sell. You can find out if website

URLs are available for free at www.godaddy.com. Just type a URL you are thinking of using into the search box, and it will tell you if it is available. If it is, you can register it for less than $10 per year.

For more on building your brand on eBay, see Section 53.1.

For more on setting up an eBay store, see Section 47.1.

For more on establishing a web-based store, see Chapter 48 and Section 49.1.

For more on creating a website and reserving a URL, see Section 49.2.

chapter 3

Business Types

Three types of business structures are available to the small business owner in the United States and Canada today:

- Sole proprietorship
- Corporation (including limited liability corporations [LLCs])
- Partnership

Each business type has its own unique characteristics, advantages, and disadvantages.

3.1 Sole Proprietorship

A sole proprietorship is the most basic business structure in the United States. If you do not incorporate or form a partnership, the IRS will treat your business as a sole proprietorship. If you are in business with your spouse, you are still a sole proprietorship, even though both of you are in the business. If, however, you form an "informal" partnership with someone, the IRS will treat you both as sole proprietors.

When my wife and I had an antique business, we ran it as sole proprietors. We even ran our eBay business as sole proprietors for the first year. This category allows *almost* all the business expenses and deductions a corporation can get. Each year when you do your personal taxes, you file an extra form, called a Schedule C, with your taxes. A Schedule C is simply a form where you list your income and individual business expenses. If your income is greater than your expenses, you make a profit. This money is added to any other money you made from salary or any other income and is taxed at the normal personal income rate. If you suffer a loss, you can deduct the loss from your salary and other income.

3.2 Corporations

The IRS classifies corporations by how they pay taxes. If you choose to incorporate your eBay business, you'll need to decide how to classify your corporation.

The S-type Corporation (commonly called an S-Corp) is the most common corporation used by most small businesses in the United States today. An S-type Corporation does not pay any taxes on its profits. Instead, all the profit or loss flows through the corporation to the stockholders (that's you) and is taxed as ordinary income as opposed to earned income. This difference is important. Earned income includes things like salary, bonus, commissions, and you have to pay Social Security and Medicare tax as well as federal income tax on it. Ordinary income is income from sources other than salary, such as your corporate income, and is not subject to Social Security and Medicare taxes. You pay only the basic federal income tax on this income.

Here is how the IRS distinguishes S Corporations from general, for-profit corporations:

An S-Corp begins its existence as a general, for-profit corporation upon the filing of Articles of Incorporation. Once formed, a general for-profit corporation that has not requested "S Corporation Status" with the IRS will be required to pay income tax on taxable income generated by the corporation. In addition, any dividends distributed to shareholders may be subject to taxation as dividend income to that shareholder as well (hence the problem of double taxation that can occur in other types of corporation).

After you have formed the corporation, you may elect "S Corporation Status" by submitting IRS form 2553 to the Internal Revenue Service. Once this filing is complete, the corporation is taxed similarly to a sole proprietorship or partnership rather than as a separate entity. The income is now passed-through to the shareholders (you) for purposes of computing tax liability. Therefore, each shareholder's individual tax return will report their share of the income or loss generated by the S corporation. If you are the only owner, then 100% of the income of loss would be passed through.

Although there are significant advantages to incorporating, the primary advantage is limiting your liability. A corporation is considered a "person" under the law for purposes of contracting and liability. After you incorporate, the corporation will purchase inventory and sell the goods on eBay or your web store.

This liability protection is extremely important to the small business owner. Suppose you sell an electric scooter on eBay to someone who gives it to his child for Christmas. On Christmas Day, the child is running it in the street in front of his home. A wheel falls off, and the child crashes, injuring himself. It would be difficult for the parent to sue the Chinese company that made the scooter. He could, and probably would, sue the importer or distributor you purchased it from, but he could also sue you. Because it is virtually impossible for you to purchase product liability insurance (more on this in Section 8.2), you are now exposed to this liability. In this case, because you are incorporated, the lawyers would sue the corporation—not you personally. If they win, they could only attach the corporation's assets, not your personal assets such as your home and retirement funds. For this reason, most small business owners keep a minimum of assets in their corporation and a minimum of funds in their corporate bank accounts.

This is a simplified explanation of how incorporating protects you against personal liability. You must follow specific rules in how you set up and run your corporation to prevent a potential plaintiff from reaching through the corporation to attach your personal assets. If you don't maintain proper paperwork and files, if you commingle money from the corporation, or if you use the corporate debit card for personal expenses, you are opening yourself up to personal liability. Lawyers and creditors always try to pierce this corporate veil when they file a lawsuit against a small-business corporation. However, as long as you follow the rules, you more than likely will be able to protect your personal assets.

(Note: The discussions and examples provided here are simple illustrations for informational purposes only. Although I have years of experience owning and running small businesses, I am not an attorney, CPA, or licensed tax professional. I strongly urge you to contact an appropriate professional before making any decisions that could impact your legal or tax liability.)

Another advantage of incorporating is credibility. When you have a business name that ends with Inc., other businesses take you more seriously. Wholesale distributors will be more willing to deal with you. You'll more easily gain entry to wholesale merchandise marts and trade shows and find trade credit.

After liability protection, the greatest advantage of incorporating is the potential tax savings. One of the most significant tax advantages is the ability to reduce your self-employment taxes (Social Security and Medicare taxes). When you work for a company, your employer takes 7.65 percent out of your paycheck on your first $90,000 of income to pay for your contribution to Social Security and Medicare. The employer then matches this amount before sending it to the government, so the total tax is over 15 percent.

When you are self-employed as a sole proprietor, you are both the employer and the employee, so you have to pay the entire 15 percent in addition to your regular income taxes. When you incorporate, the corporation can "hire" you as an employee and pay you a salary. The IRS requires this salary be reasonable, but it can be much lower than the $90,000 maximum SSI taxable amount. (Your accountant can help you determine what a "reasonable" salary is for your corporation's income level.) For example, if you made a $100,000 profit in the corporation, you could pay yourself and/or your spouse a salary of $35,000 and take the rest of the money as dividends. This way you only pay the 15 percent self-employment tax on $35,000 salary instead of the full $90,000. This results in a tax savings of about $8,250 per year. You still have to pay the normal personal income tax on the combined income of your salary and dividends, but you don't have to pay Social Security or Medicare tax on the dividends.

One disadvantage of this method is your contribution to Social Security is lower. A lower contribution will result in your receiving lower Social Security benefits when you retire. However, you can greatly offset this if you place the $8,250 you save into a tax-advantaged retirement account. Social Security averages a 1 percent return over time, so if you earn even a small return of 4 or 5 percent a year on the retirement account, you will have more money to retire on than if you relied only on Social Security. Furthermore, when you place the $8,250 into a tax-advantaged retirement account, you don't pay taxes on the invested amount, and the investment accumulates tax-free until you reach retirement age.

Among several other tax advantages of incorporating, a common one is the office-in-the-home. If you keep an office at home even if you have another commercial office, instead of deducting the percentage of space and costs as a sole proprietor would do, you simply rent your office to the corporation. You can charge the corporation the same amount that equal space would cost if you rented space in town. Then on your personal taxes, you can deduct the cost of the office space as a business expense and take depreciation on that part of your home.

PowerSeller Tip

A car is usually a large expense for self-employed business owners. Instead of deducting business mileage on your car, the corporation can buy a car (or your car) and pay all the expenses such as insurance, gas, oil, maintenance, tires, and so on. This is much simpler than allocating a percentage of business use and keeping detailed mileage logs.

A corporation has more flexibility in setting up tax-advantaged retirement programs that allow you to invest your profits on a pre-tax basis. The amounts you are allowed to invest pre-tax are larger than an individual is allowed in a simple IRA. This is a great way to shelter your profits from taxes and set money aside for your retirement.

The two most popular pension plans for small, closely held corporations are the Keogh Plan and a Simplified Employee Pension (SEP-IRA). The SEP-IRA is simpler to set up and administer but does not allow you to contribute as much as a Keogh Plan.

A simplified employee pension SEP-IRA is a written plan that allows an employer to contribute to his or her own (if self-employed) or his or her employees' retirement without becoming involved in more-complex retirement plans (such as Keoghs). The SEP functions essentially as a low-cost pension plan for small businesses.

As of this writing, employers can contribute a maximum of 25 percent of an employee's eligible compensation or $40,000, whichever is less. Be careful not to exceed the limits; you will incur a nondeductible penalty tax of 6 percent of the excess amount contributed for each year in which an excess contribution remains in a SEP-IRA. A potential disadvantage of a SEP-IRA is that you must also contribute to any employees you hire.

A Keogh plan, a tax-deferred retirement savings plan for small corporations and people who are self-employed, is much like an IRA. The main difference between a Keogh and an IRA is the contribution limit. Although exact contribution limits depend on the type of Keogh plan you select, in general a self-employed individual may contribute a maximum of $30,000 a year and deduct that amount from taxable income. The limits for IRAs are much lower.

Like an IRA, the Keogh offers the individual a chance for his savings to grow free of taxes because taxes are not paid until the individual begins withdrawing funds from the plan. Participants in Keogh plans are subject to the same restrictions on distribution as IRAs, namely distributions cannot be made without a penalty before age $59\frac{1}{2}$ and distributions must begin before age $70\frac{1}{2}$. A Keogh requires a little more paperwork to set up, but any competent brokerage firm or financial advisor can do this.

PowerSeller Tip

One company that has made a specialty of setting up these plans and working with small businesses in other ways is Ameriprise (formerly owned by American Express). You can read about their services online at www. ameriprise.com. Just click the Investments tab. Even if you decide not to use Ameriprise, this website has some great information to help you understand your retirement choices. If you want to compare costs and services, most large insurance companies have services that set up these accounts. Additionally, most stockbrokerage firms also provide this service.

Another advantage of incorporating is that you can hire your children as employees. Instead of giving your children an allowance, hire them to help you with small tasks such as cleaning the office, washing the company car, helping with packing and shipping, and so on. In this way, the money you would probably give your children anyway becomes an expense for the corporation and reduces your taxable income. Be careful of paying them too much, however, or they could incur some tax liability. This is a good topic to talk over with your tax advisor.

Once again I caution you that I'm not a Certified Public Accountant (CPA) and I don't give tax advice. After you set up your corporation and meet with your attorney, you should hire a CPA who will explain the costs your corporation can expense, the deductions you can take, and the paperwork you need to fill out. Your CPA can also help you with quarterly tax returns and filing any state sales tax returns, as well as preparing your federal and state corporate and personal tax returns at the end of the year. Depending on the level of work a CPA does for you, these services will probably cost between $500 and $1,200 a year. However, when you consider how much you'll save in taxes, this professional help is well worth the investment.

The final advantage of an S-Corp. is the fact that you are less likely to be audited. The IRS has a separate compliance and audit division for corporations, and the IRS Corporate Audit Division has finite resources and can only do so many audits per year. Given their limited resources, they tend to go after the larger corporations where they can find larger amounts of money. This doesn't mean you are audit-proof—it just means that, statistically, you have less chance of being audited as a small S-Corp. than you do as a sole proprietor or a partnership. Again, your CPA can advise you if you are doing anything that would raise the "audit flag" with the IRS, and you can take the proper action to avoid this.

Always follow your CPA's advice. I have only been through one audit, but it was agonizing. My CPA was with me every step of the way, and in the end I actually ended up getting over $300 back. The IRS only disallowed one deduction for $45, but we uncovered more than $1,200 in expenses I had not claimed while researching through all our files and receipts. Nevertheless, I would have gladly let the IRS keep the $300 if I could have avoided the audit.

You can set up a corporation very simply online. One of the largest companies is Legal Zoom at www.legalzoom.com. Depending on the state you reside or incorporate in, the fees to incorporate will usually be between $100 and $300. If you use the link to Legal Zoom on the reader resource page at www.skipmcgrath.com/titanium, we have arranged a small discount for my readers.

You do not have to incorporate in your own state if their fees are too high. A lot of companies incorporate in Nevada or Delaware because these states have attractive incorporation laws.

3.3 Partnership

A partnership is created when you sign a partnership agreement and file your taxes with the IRS as a partnership. There are several types of partnerships, but none of them are really suitable to running an eBay-type business. Law firms and medical practices are the most common form of partnerships.

Partnerships have several drawbacks. For one, if you are sued, each of the general partners is personally liable. For another, if you and your partner decide to part ways, dissolving the partnership can be very messy. In addition, a partnership lacks the flexibility of a corporation and does not enjoy all the tax advantages. Finally, partnerships are considered high-value targets by IRS auditors and get audited on average three times more than corporations.

There are two basic types of partnerships: the General Partnership and the Limited Liability Partnership.

A General Partnership is a form of business entity in which two or more co-owners engage in business for profit. For the most part, the partners own the business assets together and are personally liable for business debts.

In the absence of a partnership agreement, the partners equally share the profits. A partnership agreement, however, can provide for a different method of sharing profits and losses.

Each partner is, jointly and severally, personally liable for the debts and taxes of the partnership. For example, if the partnership assets are insufficient to satisfy a creditor's claims, the partners' personal assets are subject to attachment and liquidation to pay the business debts. Each partner is also jointly and severally liable for a co-partner's wrongdoing or tortuous act (e.g., the misapplication of another person's money or property). This is a fancy way of saying you are liable if your partner does something wrong.

The other form of partnership is a Limited Liability Partnership (LLP), which is designed for businesses such as law firms or investment companies. In an LLP, there are general partners and limited partners. The general partners run the business and share all the liability. The limited partners only share in the profits and losses.

As I stated earlier, neither of these is suitable for an online sale and marketing business. They are primarily designed for accounting and law firms, medical groups, and investment companies that employ a large number of professionals.

3.4 Limited Liability Corporation

One additional type of structure, called a Limited Liability Corporation (LLC), is a hybrid between a partnership and a corporation. An LLC allows you to form a partnership with someone, yet enjoy the limited liability of a corporation. If you want to go into partnership with someone else, you might want to explore this avenue. Personally, I would always recommend becoming an S-Corp. An LLC, just like other forms of partnership, can be very messy to dissolve when the partners disagree over business issues or experience personality conflicts.

A final consideration is financing. As your business starts to grow and you want to expand, you might need to borrow money from a bank or seek investment capital. You will find the basic corporate structure works best as you have the flexibility to issue stock, bonds, or convertible bonds, which are popular with venture capitalists.

For more on how your corporate structure affects your taxes, see Sections 4.2 and 4.4 and Chapter 9.

chapter 4

Business Licensing and Taxes

Small business owners must deal with business taxes, licenses, and regulations at all levels of government. This can seem daunting at first, but in most states they are fairly simple to handle.

4.1 Local Business License

If you are running your business out of your home, you will most likely not need a local business license from your town or county (although some require it if your home is within city limits). Typically, local business licenses are designed for businesses where customers visit the business location. If, however, you open an office or take some space in a commercial location, then you might need a local business license.

Most towns charge a fairly low fee to get a basic business license. In my hometown, for example, the initial fee is $90 and $25 a year after that.

If you set up in a commercial location and get a local business license, you also need to meet local fire safety codes and adhere to regulations regarding signage and other local laws and safety regulations.

4.2 Federal Tax ID Number

If you incorporate or if you plan to hire an employee, you'll need a federal tax ID number, which is very easy to obtain by downloading a simple one-page form from the IRS website (Form # SS-4) at www.irs.gov.

Select **Forms & Publications** from the pull-down menu and then type **SS-4** to get the correct form. Simply fill out the form and mail it to the address on the form. It can take 4 to 6 weeks to receive your federal tax ID number in the mail. A faster way is to call the IRS toll-free number on the irs.gov website and request a number. The agent will give you your number right over the phone. For details, download the form "Understanding Your EIN" from the same Forms & Publications section on the IRS website.

EIN stands for Employer Identification Number, which often confuses people. Even though you do not have any employees, you are still technically an employer in the eyes of the IRS. So don't be confused, the EIN is the same as a Federal Tax ID number. Also don't confuse this with a state tax number, which we cover in the next section.

Use the federal tax ID number in place of your Social Security Number when you open bank accounts, apply for credit, or send invoices for your business. Use it to file your business tax return, and furnish it each time someone paying you money for services requests it.

4.3 State Sales Tax Number

If you live in a state that charges sales tax, you'll need a state sales tax number. States that do not charge sales tax, such as Oregon and Idaho, typically issue a business-use tax number that serves the same purpose.

PowerSeller Tip

Several bills designed to allow states to collect sales tax on out-of-state Internet transactions (including eBay sales) are floating around the U.S. Congress. One bill, which several states have adopted, does require Internet-based sales taxes to be collected and paid on out-of-state shipments; however, it exempts businesses that do less than $4 million in annual sales. eBay has been at the forefront fighting this legislation. Each year eBay takes 50 top sellers, one from each state, to Washington, D.C., and they roam the halls of Congress meeting with legislators lobbying against any form of Internet tax. In the United Kingdom, the government has not been successful collecting VAT (the UK form of sales tax) on individual eBay sales and sellers, but they are now collecting the VAT on sellers' eBay fees.

A sales tax number enables you to purchase merchandise for resale without pay-ing sales tax to the vendor at the time of purchase.

Whenever you sell something that is delivered to an address in your state, you must collect sales tax from the customer and remit the sales tax to your state's revenue department. Most states require you to file and pay your sales taxes quarterly, although in some states you must do this on a monthly basis.

You *do not* have to collect or pay sales tax on orders that you ship out of state.

State taxing authorities are cracking down on Internet sellers who don't pay their sales tax. Typically, state compliance officers pretending to be legitimate customers will purchase something low-cost from you or just send you an e-mail pretending to be a customer asking if you charge sales tax. If you don't charge the tax, they have you dead to rights, and you will be open to some serious fines—and in some states there can be criminal penalties as well.

PowerSeller Tip

eBay makes it easy to collect sales tax on in-state transactions. On the eBay Sell Your Item web page is a drop-down box where you put in the name of your state and the percentage of sales tax to collect. Then when an auction ends, if the buyer is located in your state, eBay automatically adds the amount of sales tax due to the auction and shipping amount. If your state requires you charge sales tax on the shipping and handling as well, there is a handy check-box to select to do this automatically as well.

You also need a state sales tax number to purchase wholesale merchandise. Most legitimate wholesale companies simply will not sell to you unless you have a sales tax number.

Getting a sales tax number is very simple. In most states the fee is very low, typically from $25 to $100, although some states require new businesses to put up a deposit as high as $500, which is usually returned after one year if the busi-ness pays its taxes on time.

Visit my website at www.skipmcgrath.com/titanium, and click the navigation link State Sales Tax. This will take you to a page where you can link to the websites of all 50 states, where you can get information and download forms. In most cases you can apply for a number right online.

4.4 Employment Taxes

We discuss the issue of hiring employees later, but this is a good place to address the tax issues. Even if you don't hire an employee, if you or your spouse is employed by your personal corporation, you will be subject to withholding and employment taxes.

The first type of employment tax is the Social Security and Medicare Tax mentioned briefly in Section 3.2. Employment taxes primarily finance Social Security's Old-Age, Survivors, and Disability Insurance (OASDI) program and Medicare's (HI) program. Tax rates apply to earnings up to a maximum amount of $97,000 in 2008. The current tax rate is 7.65 percent for an individual. This rate is matched by the employer (your corporation, or you, if you are a sole proprietor) so the total tax rate is 15.3 percent of any income you take as an employee. This tax is also colloquially known as the Self-Employment Tax. If you hire an employee, you will deduct 7.65 percent from her paycheck and match that with another 7.65 percent, and you must remit this amount to the IRS monthly.

The other employment tax is your basic federal income tax. You must deduct and pay to the IRS the federal income tax per the IRS schedule. (It is available on the IRS website at www.irs.gov. Searching the term *income tax schedule* will bring up links to the income tax schedules for the current year).

The IRS considers nonpayment of payroll withholding tax a serious offense. The fine is 100 percent! If you are more than 30 days late paying the IRS your Social Security, Medicare, and income taxes, you will owe them double the amount you failed to pay.

If you live in a state that has a state income tax, you'll also need to collect and pay this amount to your state. Other employment taxes you might encounter include state disability tax, unemployment tax, and worker's compensation tax or mandatory worker's compensation insurance contributions. Most states offer owners or officers of small employer-owned corporations a waiver from these taxes.

4.5 Taking Care of All the Details

Don't stress over these taxes too much. Although many new business owners wonder how they will keep up with all the paperwork, they have three ways to handle it. The first is to hire a Certified Public Accountant (CPA) to do it for you. Most small CPA firms have a bookkeeping department or work with a local bookkeeping service who will handle the payroll and payroll tax issues for you.

Another way is through your local bank. Most large regional and national banks offer a monthly payroll service that handles payroll, including filing and paying all the state and federal taxes for you.

The third way is to do it yourself using a software program such as QuickBooks or Peachtree Accounting Software. After you buy the software, you download the tax rates and payment schedules for your state, and the software accounts for them every time you write a payroll check. The drawback to this is that you must remember to do everything on time.

Personally, I would have someone else do it. If you are running a large online business, your time is worth much more than what you could pay a bookkeeper, and the risk of making an expensive mistake is minimized. Shop around for services. For example, our bank offers payroll services for free if we have both a personal and business account and keep a minimum of $5,000 on deposit.

For more on taxes and the eBay seller, see Chapter 9 and Section 54.1.

For more on hiring employees, see Section 59.1.

chapter 5

Business Equipment and Software

When I first started selling on eBay, I owned a simple digital camera and an Apple iMac. That was pretty much it for my business equipment. Pretty soon my wife and I were running over 100 auctions a month, and within a few months, we had ramped up our business and were running between 200 and 300 auctions a month. We rapidly ran out of computer power, so the first thing we did was add another computer—a new, more powerful iMac. We also switched from dial-up Internet service to DSL and invested in a newer digital camera. We then constructed a dedicated photo studio in one corner of the garage and a storage and shipping station in another. (My wife, Karen, had the older car of the two, so she got to park outside.)

One of the lessons we learned early on was not to skimp on our business equipment. If you bought this book, it was because you want to make the leap from eBay hobbyist or part-time seller to a full-time PowerSeller. One of the things this will require is an investment in professional-quality hardware, software, and communications equipment, so let's look at some of the equipment, software, and systems you'll need to scale your business to the next level.

5.1 Computers, Connections, and Faxes

We have always been partial to the Apple Macintosh operating system and computers because they're powerful, user-friendly, and very reliable. Unfortunately, most specialized software written for eBay and website applications today is Windows-based, and since you are going to use many of these applications, you'll want a computer with a Windows operating system. If you're a die-hard Mac user, you can load Windows on one of the newer dual-core Macintosh computers with Intel chips. However, this requires you to buy the additional operating system program as well as other software programs, which can get costly.

I find it necessary to have at least two computers. We use one for our day-to-day correspondence, running QuickBooks accounting software, and doing research, and we dedicate the other one to launching auctions. We have it hooked up next to our photo setup so we can seamlessly take a photo, upload it to our auction software, write the auction description, and launch the auction. Even if you are operating by yourself, it is much easier to have two computers: one dedicated to your auctions and transferring files and photos to your website, the other for correspondence and the managing of your business.

Our computer next to the photo setup is actually an older inexpensive laptop connected to a docking station with a large monitor so I can edit and really see the quality of the photographs before I upload them. I like having a laptop because I can take it with me when I travel and stay in touch with the office. We also go to a lot of wholesale trade shows. If I find a product I am interested in buying, I can hit the nearest Starbucks and go online to eBay or use my research tools to see if the product I am interested in is selling on eBay and how much it is selling for.

If you are going to buy a new computer or computers for your business, remember the basic rule of computer purchasing: *buy as much computer memory and power as you can afford.* This is not an area to skimp on; you don't want to waste time with a slow or unreliable computer. One factor to consider is the computer's display. I like the new flat-screen displays that come with most computers today because they are bright and easy to read and take up very little space on the desk. You'll be spending a lot of time in front of your computer, so a good display is a very worthwhile investment. Another issue is service. Unless you are highly skilled in computer operating systems and hardware, I recommend you purchase a service contract that includes immediate telephone support and next-day onsite maintenance.

You'll also need a fax machine. A lot of wholesale companies do not post prices on their websites; so when you contact them about their products, they will fax their price list to you. You'll also need to fax your sales tax certificates and other documents, such as purchase orders. Although the trend in business is toward e-mail, I find I use my fax machine several times a week in this business.

Finally, you cannot run a large eBay business with a dial-up modem. I prefer DSL because it costs less, but many people use high-speed cable if they already have cable TV. I cannot stress enough that time is money. Time spent waiting for pages to download can really add up to a long workday if you are launching and checking hundreds of auctions a week. I know dozens of big-time eBay sellers, and not one is still using a dial-up connection.

5.2 Accounting and Bookkeeping Software

We cover several specialized software applications related to listing and selling on eBay in the section on automation (Section 5.8). But you'll also need to invest in some basic software to run your business.

The obvious choice for general everyday business software is Microsoft Office. Office includes word processing (Word), spreadsheet (Excel), e-mail (Outlook), database (Access), Presentation (PowerPoint), and a web publishing program, which you can use to create newsletters, flyers, and even web pages (Publisher).

You need to protect your computer(s) from hackers and viruses, either of which can take over your computer and mine your sensitive data, such as credit card and other personal information, or crash your computer and destroy your hard drive. Norton, PC Tools, and MacAfee all make popular security and virus-protection programs.

It's also essential to have systems in place for backing up your data—especially your sales and accounting records. There are plenty of options available today. I use a web-based service, to which I upload my files periodically. Large companies including Apple, Microsoft, Yahoo!, and even some of the major computer makers such as Dell and HP offer such backup services. Alternatively, you can burn your data to CDs, or transfer it to an external hard drive, or use other hardware storage programs and devices, such as Norton Ghost or StorageSync. You can purchase automatic systems that back up everything on your computer while you work. Although they are very expensive, they might be a good solution because they put the least demand on your time.

You will also need general accounting software. Although several accounting software packages are available, QuickBooks has virtually become the standard for small businesses. Other popular packages include Peachtree, Cougar Mountain, MYOB, and Clarisys. QuickBooks can also do your payroll, write checks and invoices, keep track of your bills and payments, and run detailed reports to help understand your sales and operating costs. QuickBooks offers frequent web updates and an online backup service for securely storing your data.

eBay, PayPal, and several of the auction management services have modified their reporting systems so you can download data into your QuickBooks program.

PowerSeller Tip

If you sell different categories of product on eBay, create an account in QuickBooks for "eBay Income" and one for "cost of goods sold." Instead of lumping all your product purchases and sales into this one category, create a subaccount for each category of product under the main account. This way you can generate cost and sales reports by product category to help identify your least- and most-profitable products.

If you don't know a debit from a credit or an asset from a write-off, I recommend hiring a local bookkeeping service. When you look in the yellow pages, most of them will note in their ad if they use QuickBooks. In my experience, it is much easier to find people who know QuickBooks than it is to find people who are familiar with Peachtree or any of the other accounting programs. Bookkeepers tend to come and go—I've had three over the past four years.

A major advantage of using QuickBooks is that so many bookkeepers use and understand it. If you use QuickBooks and lose your bookkeeper, it's fairly easy to find a new bookkeeper with experience using the program, which will enable him to get up to speed on your business very quickly.

Make sure you set up your accounts correctly and, just as importantly, actually *use* your accounting program. It is extremely easy to write checks, pay bills, and allocate expenses to the correct account. Putting *all* your transactions into QuickBooks will save you hundreds of dollars at the end of the year when you prepare your taxes. All you'll have to do is print out an income statement and give it to your CPA. Because he has a complete income statement, it will cut the preparation time in half and save you money on tax-preparation fees.

Microsoft Office, a good anti-virus and security program, and an accounting program such as QuickBooks will cover most of your general software needs.

As we go through the book, I'll tell you about several specialized software programs for things such as image management, shipping and postage, website hosting, and managing your eBay auctions.

5.3 Photo Studio

In focus groups of eBay buyers, bad photos were the second-highest complaint after poor packaging and shipping. If you're going to be successful on eBay, you must develop the ability to take good photographs.

This will require at least a basic photo "studio" consisting of a tripod, a neutral backdrop, and a few lights. If you are truly going to rise to the Platinum or Titanium PowerSeller level, you'll need a slightly more sophisticated setup.

Simple table-top studio setups are available for under $250. If you're selling objects that are easy to photograph and smaller than a microwave oven, several solutions are available. If you are selling larger objects, you might need to put some thought into the setup and location of your studio. Clothing sellers will need mannequins or dress forms to display the clothes properly. If you are selling glass objects or jewelry, items that can be very challenging to photograph, you need special equipment.

PowerSeller Tip

Buy two digital scales and four measuring sticks. You will have at least two areas where you examine, pack, and write descriptions about your items. Make life easier for yourself, and have your tools handy.

—The Cabana Girl

Art and antique sellers might want to set up a larger backdrop of textured wallpaper to highlight their objects and buy a Persian rug on which to display their objects. You'll also need some dark cloth to highlight shiny or bright objects, such as those made of gold, brass, or silver.

Many items have difficult shapes to work with or can't stand on their own. Supplies such as tape, fishing line, museum putty, wax, clothespins, and other paraphernalia will help you position these items.

5.4 Lighting

Digital cameras work better using static light as opposed to flash. Shooting outside on a cloudy day or in the shade on a bright day works fairly well, but you can't always control the weather or the time of day you have available to shoot, so you need to purchase some artificial lighting.

But you don't need fancy professional lighting equipment. For small objects, a couple of gooseneck student lamps with at least a 75-watt bulb (100 watts is better) work fine. For larger items, use inexpensive clamp lights—available at any hardware store—that clamp onto practically any nearby object.

PowerSeller Tip

Several light bulb manufacturers, including GE and Sylvania, market bulbs that filter out the yellow rays in normal incandescent light bulbs. These create a more natural-looking light that matches the white balance setting on most digital cameras, resulting in better photos with correct color rendition.

You need two lights to fill in shadows, which otherwise can be very distracting in your photographs. You can also fill in shadows with a reflector; just place a piece of white cardboard or foam-core on the opposite side of your object to bounce some light into any dark areas. Visit the Auction Photo Resources link on www.skipmcgrath.com/titanium to link to an interactive lighting display where you can click on various lighting schemes and see the results in real time. This section also offers dozens of digital photography tips and resources.

5.5 Pre-Fabricated Photo Studios

If you don't want to build your own studio, one simple solution popular with eBay sellers is the EZ Cube from ezauctiontools.com (see Figure 5.1). The EZ Cube is a ready-to-use tabletop photo studio made out of a translucent nylon tent. You set your objects in the tent and shoot with either outdoor sunlight or indoor studio lights shining in from each side and will get almost perfect photos every time with no shadows or reflections.

The EZ Cube comes in four different sizes. The 12-inch unit is great for shooting jewelry and other very small objects, which are notoriously difficult to shoot. They also make 20-, 30-, and 40-inch models. All the models and discounted pricing are available at www.ezauctiontools.com.

EZ Cube also makes specialized accessories for shooting glass, coins, stamps, and highly reflective objects that are difficult to photograph. These products range in price from $55 for a simple light tent to $350 for a complete system with lights and colored backdrops.

If you are searching for this type of tent, you may also find some competitive models—some of them at very low prices. If you see these, be careful. Some of the very cheap light tents are pretty poor quality or they come with very low-power halogen lights. I have tried some of these and the results were not that good.

Several other professional studio setup systems are on the market. MK Digital, at www.mkdigitaldirect.com, sells a comprehensive line of professional studio setups with prices starting around $600 and going up to just over $3,000 for larger units. Their system comes with its own software for managing and uploading your images.

Figure 5.1
EZ Cube tabletop studio system.

5.6 Image Software

You do need imaging software to edit your digital photographs. Most digital cameras come with photo-editing software, and some of the photo studio setups on the market come with their own software, and these systems generally work fine for almost all applications.

Adobe Photoshop CS is probably the most powerful image-editing and management software on the market, but it is expensive and requires some training to use. Adobe also sells Photoshop Elements 3.0, a more user-friendly and less-expensive version of Photoshop CS. Imaging is one area where the Apple Macintosh shines. I know several sellers who keep an Apple laptop next to their photo studio and use Apple's proprietary software, iPhoto, or load their Mac with the camera's software. This way they can easily shoot, look at the photo onscreen, crop or rotate the photo, and upload it quickly and easily.

5.7 Shipping Station

Successful eBay sellers do a lot of shipping. Properly packaging and shipping your orders is critical from the standpoint of both customer service and costs. Your customers will expect their items to arrive securely packaged and in good condition. If not, they will complain—or even worse, leave you negative feedback on eBay. Shipping supplies are also a major expense for eBay and web-based sellers.

You'll need a dedicated shipping station. You might start with a large table and some professional tape guns, a scale, label printers, and rolls of blank newsprint and wrapping paper. You'll also need plenty of room to store bubble wrap and Styrofoam peanuts, as well as your boxes. If your shipping station is not situated near your operations computer, it can be very helpful to have a computer dedicated just to shipping. This way you can connect an electronic scale and label printer to the computer and load your shipping software or web-based shipping utility on the computer right next to your packaging station. Many eBay sellers simply buy an inexpensive secondhand computer for this purpose, because you don't need a lot of computing power for this function.

Shipping supplies are bulky and expensive. They take up a lot of room, tie up your cash while in storage, and are expensive to purchase and have shipped to you. So do some research to find supply vendors who meet three main criteria (in order of importance):

- They are geographically close to you, so shipping costs from them to you are minimized. It doesn't do you any good to use a supplier on the East Coast with great prices if you are on the West Coast, because your shipping costs will wipe out any savings. The other issue is time. When you need supplies, you want them quickly.

- They always have stock on hand and can ship to you the same or next business day. This way you can minimize your inventory of supplies on hand and order as you need them, which will free up your storage space and cash.

- They have low-price, high-quality products.

Notice I placed cost last on the list. That's because the first two items are of far greater importance. If a vendor is very close and can ship quickly, you'll save far more money than by negotiating a lower price with someone from whom you have to order a three-month supply of packaging peanuts. Besides, after you settle on a regular vendor, that vendor will usually extend greater discounts.

If a vendor is offering a lower price for larger quantities, try negotiating a time frame connected to the quantity. For example, let's say a company has a price break when you buy 1,000 boxes at a time. Ask if they will extend that price to you if you agree to buy 1,000 boxes over a three-month period.

Another way to save money on shipping and packaging supplies is with recycled boxes and materials, and companies using recycled materials are springing up everywhere. Several companies now sell recycled boxes, for instance. Check your local phone book or the yellow pages of the nearest large city. Just be careful to place a small order first to assess the quality.

Also, plenty of free shipping and packing supplies are available if you look in the right places. Although you definitely don't want to spend a lot of time every week going from store to store looking for used boxes, it might be worthwhile to visit several stores to see if you can make a long-term arrangement with them. Maybe you can arrange to show up at the store on the same day every week and pick up what they have.

I am acquainted with a lady who owns a gift shop in our town. Every Thursday I show up and take most of her boxes and all of her Styrofoam and bubble wrap. She was able to cut her recycling bill in half, so it's a win-win situation for both of us.

If you need small to medium boxes, contact gift shops, kitchen stores, and your local Radio Shack. If you need larger boxes, check with clothing and hardware stores. Stay away from food and liquor boxes. The post office and most shipping companies will not accept used liquor boxes, and food boxes are often stained and/or smelly.

PowerSeller Tip

The way you package your items is one key to your customers' satisfaction. Poorly packaged goods can lead to everything from additional costs in refunding, replacement of the original shipment, or negative feedback. Here are some packaging tips:

- For DVDs or CDs, whether movies, music, or software, use cardboard CD mailers.

- For clothing, use Tyvek mailers. Wrap the clothing in tissue paper, and then place it in these water-resistant, tear-proof mailers. Also, because these mailers are lightweight, shipping is cheaper than shipping clothing in boxes.

- For postcards, photos, stamps, or sports cards, you have a couple of good options. You can place the flat item between two corrugated pads and then slide that into a bubble mailer, or you can use StayFlat Mailers, which are difficult to bend and often come with self-adhesive strips.

- For glass and other fragile items, double boxing is your best protection against breakage. First, wrap your item in bubble wrap, and then place it in a box, leaving approximately two inches of space on all sides of your glass piece. Fill this void with packing peanuts or a void fill paper, such as balled-up blank newsprint or craft paper. Then place this smaller box inside a slightly larger one, and again fill the void space with Styrofoam peanuts or bubblepak.

5.8 Automating the Shipping Process

Packaging, addressing, and shipping can be very time-consuming. Anything you can do to automate the process will save you time and money. If you do your own shipping, that's time spent away from your most profitable activities, such as product research, listing auctions, and communicating with customers. If you hire an employee to do your shipping (a very good idea, by the way), you are paying him or her by the hour. So automating the process can really deliver dollars to your bottom line.

The first step in automating your shipping is to select a shipping carrier. Most eBay sellers use USPS Priority Mail for their smaller packages and one of the big three shipping companies—UPS, FedEx, or DHL—for their larger packages. If you plan to sell anything that weighs less than five pounds, I recommend you use USPS Priority Mail because it's fast, efficient, and costs less than the other services when shipping to a residence. UPS is competitive on small packages shipped to a business address, but most eBay buyers have items shipped to their homes. The other advantage of Priority mail is the free shipping supplies. You can order free boxes, tape, and Tyvek envelopes from their website that come stamped with the eBay logo. The lower cost to ship, combined with the free shipping supplies, make Priority mail hard to beat.

The USPS does not offer any software for shipping, but several third-party companies have stepped up to fill this role, including Endicia, Stamps.com, and Pitney Bowes. After investigating all three of these companies' shipping programs, I've found that Endicia (www.endicia.com) has by far the easiest-to-use software and handles the widest variety of packages.

They also offer discounts on scales, label printers, and supplies. Best of all, Endicia is a web-based solution. You open an account and simply go online and download the software. You can use your own laser printer, or Endicia will sell you an integrated scale and label printer so you can simply cut and paste the address from your payment notification e-mail into the field, put the package on the scale, select the type of postage (first-class, priority, parcel post, media mail, etc.), and hit Enter. Endicia calculates the postage and prints out a label with the address, postage, and delivery confirmation on it. The Endicia program can even automatically send a customized e-mail to the customer with the delivery information and tracking number. There is no faster way to handle USPS shipments.

For larger items, you'll want to select from USPS Priority Mail, UPS, FedEx Ground, or DHL. Each company has a website where you can go online and determine the cost to ship an item. I recently ran a cost comparison of over–five-pound packages on the websites of the UPS, FedEx Ground, and USPS Priority Mail. I entered three different size and weight combinations to three different destinations: one close, one in the middle of the country, and one on the farthest coast.

On average, FedEx Ground beat the other two handily when shipping to a residence. When shipping to a business address or if I used the faster services such as second-day air or three-day select, it was much closer, but FedEx Ground still won. The other advantage FedEx Ground has is package size. They will ship a larger dimension and heavier package than either of the other two companies. So if you are shipping larger, heavier items, this might be the only choice. (Note: all three shipping companies list their maximum package weight and dimensions on their websites.)

After you decide which company you want to use, simply go to its website and open an account. After you open your account and get an account number, e-mail the company and ask to be put in touch with your local sales rep. Be sure to explain that you are a large-volume shipper. When the sales rep contacts you, set up a meeting in person to negotiate volume shipping discounts.

All the big three companies offer automation software and label printing solutions. Although you can order equipment and materials online, order them through your sales rep instead, because he often has the power to comp some or all of their software and equipment.

You can get an automation setup for UPS, FedEx, or DHL similar to what Endicia offers for the Post Office (described earlier). The software is usually free, and the cost of the equipment can be free or discounted depending on the volume of your shipments. If you're shipping more than 500 packages a month, you'll be surprised at how interested these companies will be in your business and how willing they'll be to deal with you.

For more on accounting and bookkeeping software, see Section 54.1.

For more on eBay automated software, see Section 43.1.

For more on a photo studio and digital photography, see Chapter 46.

For more on shipping products, see Chapter 57.

For more on shipping policies, see Chapter 33.

chapter 6

Financing Your Growth

Making a six-figure income on eBay takes a substantial investment in inventory and equipment. And for most people this will require some type of investment capital or financing.

The amount of money you invest in your eBay business depends on how large and how fast you want to grow the business. Look at your present eBay business from the standpoint of how many auctions you are running and what you are realizing in gross merchandise sales per month. Then ask yourself these questions: What would it take to double my business? Or triple it? Or quadruple it? Business people, including eBay professionals, call the answers to these questions scalability.

6.1 Understanding Your Business Model

All kinds of business models exist on eBay. Some large eBay retailers sell thousands of low-cost items, such as CDs and books. They might make a large margin on each sale in terms of percentage, but the dollar profit per item is fairly small.

Others sell fewer, higher-priced items. In most cases, their margins are smaller in terms of percentage but larger in terms of dollars. For instance, if you sell antiques, you might only realize a 20 percent gross margin, but your average selling price might be as high as $2,000. The margin is small, but you might average a $400 profit per sale. If you sell 25 items each month at $2,000 a pop, your gross merchandise sales (GMS) will be

$50,000. At a 20 percent margin, you'll make $10,000 a month before subtracting your other costs, such as eBay and PayPal fees. (For the purpose of this discussion, we will ignore the fee costs and other direct expenses although you will need to factor these into your business and financial planning.)

Then there are the mid-range sellers. One PowerSeller of after-market automotive parts averages around $200 on each sale with about a 35 percent gross margin. He closes about 100 auctions a week, which translates into a GMS of $40,000 per month and a gross margin of $14,000.

If you sell books and your average selling price is $10, and you realize a gross margin of 50 percent on each sale, you would make $5 per sale before your other costs. If you close 1,200 successful auctions a month, your gross merchandise sales (GMS) would total $12,000, and your gross margin would be $6,000. If you wanted to triple your GMS, you'd have to do one of two things: raise your average selling price by finding more expensive products to sell or sell three times as many items. Or you could do a combination of both.

Now that you know your options for increasing sales, you must ask yourself several questions:

- Do I have a reliable source for the additional merchandise?
- How much money will I need to purchase the additional inventory?
- Do I have the time to launch the additional auctions, or will I need help (employees)?
- Do I have the systems, equipment, and technology in place to support the additional sales volume? If not, what do I need, and how much will it cost?
- Do I have the physical space to store the goods and the large amount of shipping supplies to support the high volume of merchandise I plan to sell? If not, how much will it cost to rent space?

After you've answered these questions, then you can calculate how much money you need to reach your objective.

6.2 Capitalizing Your Growth

Growing an eBay business to $1,000,000 a year will take a sizeable amount of capital. Because you'll need to be able to launch hundreds or even thousands of auctions per month, you'll need at least one employee. And with this kind of volume, you probably can't operate out of your home, so you'll need to rent space and furnish it.

It is possible to raise money before you start a business. However, raising money for a new, unproven start-up can be very difficult. I recommend you start your business and run it profitably at a lower level for at least a few months, which will demonstrate your ability to create a profitable business model and execute it. More important, it will give you credibility with bankers and other lenders and make the job of raising capital much easier.

Bankers, other lenders, and professional investors are far more willing to invest in an ongoing business than a start-up. After you prove a business concept and demonstrate your ability to execute it, raising capital through investment or debt financing becomes a matter of demonstrating the scalability of your business. (If I had *XX* dollars, I could grow my business *XX* percent.)

Three basic types of investment capital are available:

- Retained earnings
- Debt
- Investment (venture capital)

Let's examine each one.

6.2.1 Retained Earnings

All capital has a cost. Retained earnings are the profits from your business that you reinvest into your enterprise. If you're making enough money to reinvest your earnings, do so, as this is the cheapest form of capital you'll ever find. Also, the fact that you are reinvesting your own profits into the company makes your business look more attractive to lenders and investors. Just be sure to keep track of this amount, which is very easy to do if you're using QuickBooks.

6.2.2 Debt Capital

Debt capital is simply borrowed money. The advantage of borrowing money over finding an investor is you don't have to give up any ownership in your company. The downside is that banks and commercial lenders usually require collateral or that you personally guarantee the business loans or both.

A loan is a good solution when you require only a small amount of money and could pay off the debt if you had to without losing your home or going into bankruptcy. For example, if you borrow between $10,000 and $20,000 and then, for some reason, your business fails, the loan amount is small enough that a bank will work out a payment plan with you. If, on the other hand, you borrowed $50,000 to $100,000 or more, most banks will immediately foreclose on the loan the moment you default. An exception to this is when you have inventory to put up as collateral (see Section 6.5).

6.2.3 Investment Capital

Investment capital, also called equity capital, is money that you or someone else invests in your business in exchange for a share of the ownership or profits. Some budding entrepreneurs borrow money from, or find investors among, their own families and friends. There are two drawbacks to doing this. First of all, these people are not professional investors, and they will constantly be giving advice and interfering in your business decisions. Secondly, if something does go wrong, you could very well lose your friends and put stress on family relationships.

People who provide equity capital are typically called venture capitalists. They provide funding in exchange for a percentage ownership in the corporation or for a percentage of the sales or profits. Equity capital is expensive over the long term; however, sometimes it's the only capital you can find.

Of the two kinds of venture capitalists, the first are professional venture capital firms. Unless you are looking for over $1 million in capital and have a business model that shows your enterprise growing to over $5 million in sales, it is unlikely a professional venture firm would talk to you.

The second category of venture capitalist is known as an "angel" in the industry. Angels are usually local entrepreneurs who typically look for small ventures where they can invest amounts from $50,000 to $500,000 and see an opportunity to double or triple their investment within a year or two.

Angels rarely advertise but are most often found by networking. Start by talking with your banker, your lawyer, and the folks at your local chamber of commerce or county development agency. They will usually know who the angels are in your community.

You'll need a business plan and all the financial data you needed for bank financing, as well as financial projections for cash flow and profit and loss (P&L) for the next three years.

Unlike the professional venture capitalists, angels often become involved in your business. Most of them consider themselves smart and experienced and will want to share their knowledge with you as well as watch over their investment. Depending on just how smart she is and her personality, this can be a blessing or a curse.

6.3 Equipment Leasing

To grow your business, you'll probably need new equipment, such as computers, cameras and other photography equipment, copiers, and faxes. But rather than using your precious capital to purchase equipment, look into equipment leasing. Most business equipment has a residual value. Because of this, a lease will often have lower monthly payments than purchasing equipment on credit. For example, if you borrow $20,000 to finance an equipment purchase at a 10 percent interest rate for three years, your payments would be about $722 per month. Leasing the same equipment could lower your payments to less than $500 per month. At the end of the lease, you have a choice of purchasing the equipment for its residual value or simply turning in the equipment and buying or leasing new equipment.

Because computer equipment becomes obsolete very quickly, you might want to return any computers at the end of the lease. If you leased something with a long product life, you might want to exercise your purchase option since this would be cheaper than buying new equipment.

6.4 Financing Inventory

Borrowing money to finance inventory is called factoring, in the retail trade, and is probably the easiest type of credit to find. All you need to do is show a lender you are a successful seller and can turn the inventory over rapidly. The lender retains ownership, but not possession, of the inventory until you sell it. A typical contract might give you a $50,000 line of credit to buy inventory. The contract provides money to buy the inventory and list it on eBay or on your website. Each month, you file a report with the lender listing the amount of inventory sold. You then pay this amount to the lender with interest.

Here is an example: you have been buying electric scooters from an importer at a price of $90 each in lots of 50 and selling them on eBay for $150 each. At this price you are able to sell 25 units a month. The scooters have been selling so well that you decide to take out a loan to purchase larger quantities of scooters directly from the manufacturer.

You purchase $20,000 worth of electric scooters from a company in China. Because you are importing directly in container-sized quantities, you get a good price. Because you are able to buy the scooters for only $60 each, you'll make an additional $30 on each scooter.

The finance company charges you 1 percent interest per month on the outstanding balance of your inventory. You bought 333 scooters for the $20,000, and by lowering your price $10 under the competition, you can now sell 50 units a month. At this price you are still making $20 more on each scooter, but you can now sell double the amount you were selling before.

Before you took out the loan, you were making a gross margin of $1,500 per month on the scooters. Now that you have lowered your cost and doubled your sales, you are making $4,000 a month. At the rate you are going, you will sell all the scooters in about six months. During this time you will pay 1 percent per month on the $20,000 or approximately $1,200 total. You will make an additional $15,000 in gross margin for an increased expense of $1,200.

Admittedly this is a simple example. Inventory financing is slightly more complex, but the basic fact remains: if you don't have the money to invest in building your inventory, inventory financing is one of the best ways to scale your business to much higher levels.

Let me add one final caution on this subject. Do not purchase large amounts of inventory unless you know for a fact it will sell. Don't rely on your instincts. It can be tempting to buy products very cheaply when the product looks good to you, but you should always *test market a product* before committing to purchase a large quantity (see Chapters 11.3 and 11.4).

6.5 Finding Business Credit

Up to this point I've made it sound pretty easy to get credit. However, whether you're looking for inventory financing or general business credit, you'll have to jump through some hoops. Although lenders are eager to extend credit to good customers, they'll want to understand your business and the type of inventory you sell before they hand over any cash.

So start with a good system for maintaining data on your inventory; your lenders are going to want to know how old the inventory is, what its condition, cost, and average selling price is, and how fast it turns over. You should have a computerized system for maintaining your data and reporting the status of your inventory. The lender will want to see your sales history to ensure that the products are moving quickly.

Take good care of your inventory—your lender might want to inspect it from time to time. Keep inventory levels as low as you can while keeping up with your sales volume. Most of all, buy carefully so you're not stuck with merchandise that won't sell or becomes obsolete quickly.

Before approaching a lender, put together a basic financial package, which would consist of the following information and documents:

- Balance sheet. This financial report shows the status of a company's assets, liabilities, and owners' equity and gives a complete picture of the worth of a company.

- Income statement, also called profit and loss statement (P&L). The P&L is a summary of your revenues (sales), costs, and expenses during one accounting period. It shows how profitable a company is. (If you use QuickBooks, it only takes about one minute to produce a P&L statement.)

- Cash flow projections. These are estimates of the schedule on which money will actually move into and out of your company. Cash flow projections are very different from your income statements.

- Business tax returns. A bank or lender will most likely want to see your actual tax returns for at least the past year and sometimes for the past two or three years.

A lender might also want to see a business plan, which we cover in the next chapter.

6.5.1 Banks and Commercial Lenders

If you are seeking debt capital, the best source is usually a small local bank or community bank. Large national banks occasionally loan money to small entrepreneurs, but small community banks often specialize in these types of transactions.

Your own bank is the best place to start, because they know you. If you now use one of the large money-center banks and they don't want to work with you, you might want to change to a local community bank where you can develop a relationship. Loan officers in large banks are frequently transferred and promoted. Just when you develop a relationship, the person is transferred, and you have to start all over again. In smaller banks, the loan officers tend to stay in the same position for longer periods of time.

Start by approaching the commercial loan officer of your local bank. Bring your business plan and your personal and business financial statements. (If you are using QuickBooks, you can easily create a profit and loss statement and a cash flow statement). Your business plan should show how you will use the funds you plan to borrow and how this investment will increase your sales and profits and enable you to pay back the money.

As long as your business is profitable and shows consistent cash flow, your bank will probably loan you the money. If you are not profitable, you shouldn't be borrowing the money.

Finally, a new source of capital for small entrepreneurs has become popular in the past year. Pierre Omiydar, the founder of eBay, has invested in a company called Prosper at www.prosper.com. Prosper is a person-to-person lending company, which operates much like eBay in that you put a loan request (listing) on Prosper and people bid on a piece of it. If enough people bid on your loan to fully fund it, Prosper packages the loan and sends you the money. You make your monthly payments directly to Prosper, and they distribute the payments to the individual lenders. No collateral is required, and the rates are often lower than you can get from a bank.

6.5.2 SBA Loans

Another source of financing is a bank loan backed by the Small Business Administration (SBA). Most commercial banks offer SBA loans. These loans do not require collateral; however, even if you are incorporated, you might be required to personally guarantee the loan. The rate will depend on your credit history and how long you've been in business, though they typically vary anywhere from 7 percent to 12 percent. The rates are usually set as a percentage over the prevailing prime rate and are adjusted quarterly. In addition, the SBA charges 1 percent on top of the rate to guarantee the loan.

Because the SBA requires at least a two-year business history, these loans are not useful for start-up businesses.

6.5.3 State and County Development Agencies

Many rural counties have federally or state-funded development agencies that often have access to funds to attract companies to the area or to fund start-up companies that will create employment. Unless you plan to employ at least 5 to 10 people, they would probably not offer funding. However, if you employ at least a couple of people, they can often arrange training grants, property tax breaks, and other services useful to the small business. They often give training grants even if you will only hire one employee. A typical training grant is a salary supplement the agency pays while you train your employee. For example, if you wanted to hire an employee at $12 per hour, you would pay the employee the prevailing minimum wage, and the development agency would make up the difference until the employee was fully trained. Other programs might include free computer training for your employees at a local community college or tech school.

The best way to find these development agencies is to contact your local chamber of commerce.

For more on business plans, see Chapter 7.

For more on test marketing products, see Chapter 11.

For more on financing your business, see Chapter 7 and Section 16.2.

Writing Your Business Plan

A business plan is nothing more than thinking through your business model, goals, and sales projections and writing it all down. Your plan doesn't need to be highly detailed or sophisticated. You just want to cover the basics so you have a clear idea of what your business will look like and how you plan to grow it. If you already have an existing eBay business or an offline business you will be bringing onto eBay and the web, then you have a lot of the information you will need.

If you visit any large bookstore, you'll find many books dedicated to writing business plans. If you have the energy to wade through one of these—great! If not, you can follow this basic outline:

1. Write a brief description of your business. What business are you in? What do you sell? Who are your customers?

2. Describe your products either by type (e.g., consumer electronics, antiques, novelties, or collectibles) or specifically (such as expensive collectible watches, rebuilt computers, photography, and art books).

3. List the sources where you can buy these products.

4. Build a financial plan by answering these questions. How much will your products cost? What will you sell them for? What is your profit margin per sale? How many will you have to sell to make your target number of dollars per week/month? What are your fixed costs? (These are things such as computer payments, telephone, cable, or DSL service, ISP service, and so on.) What additional assets will you

need to build the business to this level (rent, employees, new computers, etc.), and how much will they cost? Do you have the capital you need, or will you have to find financing? If so, you will need to include the finance payments into your financial plan.

5. What is unique about your business? Do you have any special expertise or experience in what you are selling? How can you use this expertise to your competitive advantage?

6. How much money can you invest in your business? What will you spend this money on and how long will it take to achieve positive cash flow? (You will need cash flow projection spreadsheets to go with this section.)

7. How will you market your product in addition to eBay? (Will you use other auctions, a website, e-mail, flea markets, etc.?)

Do your best to answer all these questions. If you are married or have a partner, talk about this together and bat some ideas around. You will be surprised how the very act of performing this exercise clarifies your thinking and gives you confidence. If you are writing your business plan to raise money, keep it brief and to the point. Investors and lenders are busy professionals—they want just enough information to understand your business model and decide if it has a chance of success.

PowerSeller Tip

A good basic book for writing business plans is *The Complete Idiot's Guide to Business Plans* by Gwen Moran, available online or from most bookstores.

The Center for Business Planning at www.businessplans.org has several online resources to help you write, develop, and review your business plan. These include business plan software, free articles written by experts, and a web-based library of resources containing links to hundreds of sites offering research materials on every area of starting and planning a business.

How Investors Evaluate Your Business

If you are writing your business plan for the purpose of borrowing money or raising capital, you need to understand how potential lenders or investors will look at your financial plan. Financial professionals use several ratios to help them understand the viability of your business. Here is a list of the most popular ratios used according to the U.S. Small Business Administration:

- **Cash ratio.** A measure of the amount of cash available to offset current debt (Cash ÷ Total Current Liabilities). A ratio below .5 may mean you are having cash flow problems, possibly because of a significant backlog in accounts receivable.

- **Quick ratio.** A measure of the amount of liquid assets available to offset current debt (Cash + Accounts Receivable ÷ Current Liabilities). A healthy enterprise will always keep this ratio at 1.0 or higher.

- **Current ratio.** A measure of the degree to which current assets cover current liabilities (Current Assets ÷ Current Liabilities). A high ratio indicates a good probability the enterprise can retire current debts. A ratio of 2.0 or higher is a comfortable financial position for most enterprises.

- **Current liabilities to net worth.** A measure of the extent to which the enterprise is using creditor funds versus their own investment to finance the business (Current Liabilities ÷ Liabilities + Equity). A ratio of .5 or higher may indicate inadequate owner investment or an extended accounts payable period. Take care not to offend your vendors (creditors) to the extent it affects your ability to conduct day-to-day business.

- **Total liabilities to net worth.** A measure of the extent that the net worth of the enterprise can offset the liabilities (Total Liabilities ÷ Liabilities + Equity). Avoid a ratio greater than 1.0 because it indicates the creditors have a greater stake in the business than the owners.

- **Fixed assets to net worth.** A measure of the extent of an enterprise's investment in nonliquid and often overvalued fixed assets (Fixed Assets ÷ Liabilities + Equity). A ratio of .75 or higher is usually undesirable as it indicates possible overinvestment and causes a large annual depreciation charge that will be deducted from the income statement.

- **Fixed assets to total assets.** A measure of the extent to which fixed assets are financed with owner's equity (capital) (Fixed Assets ÷ Total Assets). A high ratio, .5 or higher, indicates an inefficient use of working capital, which reduces the enterprise's ability to carry accounts receivable and maintain inventory and usually means a low cash reserve. This will often limit your ability to respond to increased demand for your products or services.

For more on business plans and setting goals, see Chapter 60.

chapter 8

Insuring Your Business and Your Income

As small eBay sellers, my wife and I insured our inventory and equipment for the first few years through our homeowner's insurance. Allstate, State Farm, and most large property and casualty (P&C) insurers offer a business-in-the-home rider on a homeowner's or renter's insurance. These riders are usually limited to $5,000 or $10,000. As our business grew and we were storing larger and more expensive quantities of merchandise, we outgrew our business-in-the-home rider. A flood, fire, or theft would have resulted in thousands of dollars in losses.

Although we were still operating the business out of our home, we had to find commercial storage for our inventory. Most insurance companies will simply not offer large-dollar insurance policies on inventory stored in a private residence.

You also need inventory insurance if you are borrowing money to finance inventory. If you take out an unsecured loan, the bank or finance company might also require you to show proof of life insurance or even to purchase a life and disability policy from them that they could use to repay the loan if something happened to you. So let's review some of the types of business and personal insurance you will need.

8.1 Property and Casualty (P&C) Insurance

P&C insurance is just what the name implies. It insures property against any type of casualty or loss. Property can include your vehicle, a building, business equipment, and any inventory you have on hand. Loss can include virtually any type of loss, such as earthquake, tornado, hurricane, water damage from flooding or even a burst pipe, fire, theft, and conversion (conversion is a fancy term for fraud or employee theft).

You can purchase P&C insurance in two ways: you can go directly to any of the large commercial insurance companies (most of which are listed in your local phone book), or you can deal with an independent insurance broker. The advantage of dealing with a broker is that she will shop the market to find the best product for your particular situation. The other advantage of using a broker is advice. A good commercial broker is a wealth of information and a consultant in insurance matters. She will endeavor to make sure you have both adequate coverage and the lowest rates for your coverage.

Brokers are easy to find. Almost every village, town, or city in America has at least one. Some brokers specialize in P&C; larger brokerage firms offer a range of services including liability, life and disability, financial and business planning assistance, and more.

8.2 Liability Insurance

Most businesses buy liability insurance to protect themselves against a customer injuring himself at their business location. Typically eBay sellers do not have customers visiting their locations, but you will have other visitors, such as the copy machine repair guy, UPS drivers, and even the total stranger who walks by your business and slips on the ice you forgot to salt.

8.2.1 Automobile Liability

If you have a corporate vehicle or are using your personal vehicle for business use, you also need commercial automobile liability coverage. Your P&C broker can provide your liability insurance. In fact, liability insurance is usually provided as part of your basic P&C coverage on your building or your automotive policy. You also might be able to purchase an umbrella liability policy if you insure both your building and your vehicle on the same policy. This is a cost-effective way to purchase high volumes of liability insurance that covers all risks up to a certain amount, usually $5 or $10 million.

8.2.2 Product Liability

Unless you have a really large business grossing over $2 or $3 million a year, you probably cannot afford product liability insurance. A typical product liability policy has a very high deductible—often as much as $50,000. Rates can vary from a low of 1 percent of the value of the product you are selling for nondangerous products to as high as 10 percent or more for high-risk products. The latter would include any type of toy, baby items, children's clothing and accessories, any moving vehicle (scooter, bicycle, etc.), models, sharp objects, and other items likely to injure someone.

Instead of product liability insurance, small sellers (under $1 million/year) often rely on their corporate status to protect them. In many product liability cases, the plaintiff's attorneys are looking for deep-pocket defendants. Plaintiff's attorneys work on contingency fees, meaning they get a percentage of the settlement or judgment. If you run your business properly to prevent an attorney from piercing the corporate veil and you keep a minimum amount of assets in the corporation, a plaintiff's attorney will usually realize it isn't worth the effort to go after you. Having said that, let me stress once again that I am not an attorney, so check with both an attorney and your insurance broker if you have questions about product liability.

8.2.3 Offshore Asset Protection Trusts

A new area of protection becoming more popular is the Offshore Asset Protection Trust. Although several large companies set up and manage these trusts, this area is fraught with scams and fly-by-night operators. If your business grows to a very large level and you are interested in this type of protection, work with your attorney and CPA to find a stable, legitimate provider.

8.3 Life, Medical, and Disability Insurance

If you ever worked in the corporate world, you were probably used to the generous benefits your employer provided. Now that you are self-employed, you are that employer, so if you want generous benefits, you'll have to provide them yourself.

8.3.1 Life Insurance

First, you should have adequate life insurance to provide for your family in the event something happens to you. But as a business owner, you will also want to carry some extra insurance that your spouse could use to pay off any business debts or to continue to operate the business by hiring someone to manage it or to continue operations until the business is sold.

Most financial planners recommend that the minimum amount of life insurance you should carry is at least three times your annual income. I would also advise your carrying enough to pay off your mortgage if you have one, plus any business debts you have. Consult with an insurance professional to find the best policy for your needs.

8.3.2 Self-Employed Medical Insurance

Medical insurance is probably the most important type of insurance for people who own their own businesses, because getting sick or being injured can be very expensive. Hospitals and doctors will treat you without insurance, but you might not get the best care for your situation. If you cannot pay for your care, your account will be turned over to a collection agency or an attorney. And no corporate veil is going to protect you against this type of loss.

In most but not all states, the "Blues" (Blue Cross and Blue Shield), other insurance companies, and local HMOs offer policies for the self-employed. You can also contact the National Association for the Self-Employed (NASE) at www.nase.org. NASE is a nonprofit association set up to represent the self-employed in Washington, D.C., and it also offers association-style benefits such as health, dental, and other insurance products as well as association discounts on travel and other business products and supplies.

In most states, the NASE-contracted insurance companies offer traditional medical policies. However, some states have passed laws that guarantee coverage to every individual regardless of his current medical history or condition. In these states, NASE only offers scheduled plans which have very strict limits on how much they will pay for hospital stays, surgeries, and other services. (For example, a policy may limit payment to $300 a day for a hospital stay even though the hospital might charge $1,000 per day.) If you buy one of these plans, make sure you purchase adequate amounts (i.e., buy the higher schedules available) to cover a catastrophic medical condition.

Relatively new players in this arena are the wholesale buying clubs such as Costco and Sam's Club. These companies now offer self-employed health insurance to their members in most states. I recently investigated a policy from Costco and found it was quite competitive with my current policy.

Take the time to understand the costs and risks of the various policies you are considering. If you have a large family and you use medical care frequently, then it might be more cost-effective to buy a low-deductible policy. If, on the other hand, you are healthy, single, and rarely visit doctors, purchasing a high-deductible plan will be much more cost-effective.

In 2003, Congress passed legislation authorizing insurance companies to create Health Saving Accounts. HSAs allow you to set up a pretax savings account that you combine with a high-deductible medical policy. Each month you set aside an amount of money to pay for any medical bills you incur before you meet your deductible.

Because this money is being set aside on a pretax basis, it gives you an effective "discount" equal to your tax rate on each medical bill you pay. If you stay healthy and don't use the money, it accumulates tax-free until you retire. At that time you can use it to fund retirement medical insurance such as Medicare Gap Plans, or you can roll the money into your retirement savings account.

8.3.3 Disability (Income) Insurance

Disability insurance is nothing more than income insurance. It insures your income if something happens to you and you cannot work. Simply put, you are insuring your ability to get up every morning, go to work, and earn an income.

If you couldn't work, how would you pay your bills, buy food, and pay your rent or mortgage? Many people mistakenly think the government will take care of this if they become disabled, which used to be more true than it is today. In the mid-1990s, the Social Security Administration severely tightened the rules on disability claims. Before then, almost 90 percent of all disability claims were granted. After the rules were changed, that percentage dropped to under 50 percent. Also, a person must be totally disabled for one year before he can apply for benefits. After he applies, it can take the SSA up to six months to adjudicate his case and begin paying benefits.

Disability insurance is sold in increments that reflect a percentage of your monthly income. Typical percentages are 50 percent, 60 percent, and 66 percent.

You can buy short- to medium-term policies with durations of two, three, or five years, or you can purchase a permanent policy that will pay benefits until age 67 or even 70. You can also select an elimination period—a waiting period until benefits kick in. All these factors affect the cost. For example, a policy with a 180-day waiting (elimination) period will cost significantly less than a policy with a 60-day waiting period. If you have enough savings to get through a six-month disability, selecting a 180-day elimination period will significantly reduce your costs.

Disability insurance can be expensive. If you live in a state, such as California, that offers a state disability program, you might want to take advantage of that for part of your disability coverage. As an owner or officer of a small corporation, you do not have to participate in state disability programs, but you are usually eligible to. Whether you get state or private insurance, one advantage you have is that selling on eBay is considered a white-collar occupation, which tend to have lower rates than blue-collar jobs.

For more on insurance, see Appendix B.

For more on setting up your business as a corporation, see Section 3.2.

chapter 9

Taxes and the eBay Seller

Millions of small eBay sellers clean out their garages and attics and spend their weekends going to garage sales to find things to sell on eBay. Although all income is technically taxable and should be revealed, when you have a garage sale, no one expects you to fess up to the IRS and claim the income and pay taxes on it. Likewise, most occasional eBay sellers don't bother to state their income from eBay and pay taxes on it either. So are they avoiding taxes? Technically, yes, but the IRS is too busy to chase after these minor tax avoiders. That is not to say, however, that you couldn't get caught in a random audit.

If, however, you're going to be a professional seller, you must keep records of your sales and pay taxes on your profits. That's not to say you shouldn't do whatever you can, within the limits of the law, to reduce your tax burden. It is perfectly legal, moral, and ethical to do everything you can within the law to minimize your taxes. The U.S. Tax Code is very clear on this fact. You need to pay all the taxes you owe and not one penny more. You can do plenty of perfectly legal things to lower your annual tax bill, and you should do every one of them.

A detailed discussion of tax strategies is beyond the scope of this book, but I will try to provide some examples to make clear the importance of good tax planning and show just how much money you can save.

If you want to minimize your taxes, you need to develop a plan and follow it. The first thing you should do is sit down with your CPA and explain your business to him.

9.1 Tax Reduction Strategies

One of the most important tax reduction strategies to recognize is that a tax dollar deferred is a tax dollar saved. If you can legally delay paying taxes until a later date, you are saving money because you have the use of that money. For example, whenever you purchase equipment, the IRS allows you to write off all or a portion of the cost as an expense against your income. If you purchase a new computer on December 31 instead of January 1, you can take the expense against income in the current tax year instead of waiting a year to take the deduction. Taking the reduction in the current tax year will reduce your profits and thereby the tax you will pay on those profits.

When you purchase your inventory and how you account for it can affect your taxes as well. You'll need to select the "cash" method or the "accrual" method of counting your inventory value. Then you need to decide if you treat your sales from inventory as FIFO—First In/First Out or LIFO—Last In/First Out. Several tax-savings strategies are available that depend on which of these decisions you make, so discuss this with your accountant. To advise you of the best one, he will need to know how often your inventory turns over, what the value of your inventory as a percentage of your sales is, and how much inventory you tend to accumulate early in the year and dispose of late in the year. This is very important. If you are moving hundreds of thousands of dollars of inventory through your business during the year, the tax implications can be enormous.

Setting up a Keogh Plan or a SEP-IRA can also save you thousands of dollars in taxes each year. The tax savings can be so great that I've known businesspeople to borrow money to put into these plans near the end of the year to get the savings and then pay the money back after the end of the year. What you pay in interest for this short-term loan is far offset by the tax advantage. I discuss these two types of plans in Chapter 3.

9.2 Running Your Business to Minimize Taxes

Tax reduction categories are of two types: business expenses and business tax deductions. A business expense is money you spend running your business, including paying postage, purchasing inventory, putting gas in the company car, and paying a salary to an employee. A deduction is an expense you are allowed to take on your tax return after you have calculated your income minus expenses. Some popular deductions include charitable deductions and deductions for educational expense, attending an eBay seminar or buying this book, for example.

The first step in minimizing your taxes is to keep good records of all expenses and deductions. If you are spending money on business-related expenses out of your own pocket and you don't prepare expense reports to get the money back from your company, you're losing money. Although it is sometimes necessary to spend your own money, I find the easiest thing to do is to run everything possible through the company's books, and the easiest way to do this is with QuickBooks.

We have our corporate bank account set up in QuickBooks so we can write checks from our corporate account right on the computer. We also have a commercial checkbook where we can write checks, which we carry to trade shows and merchandise marts when we are shopping for inventory. When we're back in the office, we just enter them into QuickBooks. We also have a debit card tied to the corporate bank account, and we use that when paying for business meals, renting a car while traveling on business, buying gas for the company car, and so on.

The key to minimizing your taxes is to make sure that every single expense related to your business is accounted for in your profit and loss statement at the end of the year. Losing receipts and being sloppy with your bookkeeping can literally cost you hundreds, if not thousands, of dollars a year. Additionally, if you ever are audited, having those records on QuickBooks will save you hours of work preparing your records for the auditor.

PowerSeller Tip

And don't forget to account for sales tax on items you buy at retail to resell. We usually buy our goods from wholesale suppliers where we do not pay sales tax, but occasionally we will purchase a closeout lot of something from a retail store or hit a big sale at one of the outlet malls. And when we do, we pay sales tax. Almost every state has a procedure where you can recover this tax if you bought the item for resale. Usually it is no more than listing the taxes on your quarterly tax form and asking for a credit.

The other key to saving taxes is to maximize the use of your business funds. If you want a new digital camera, let the business buy it (as long as it will be used primarily for business-related purposes). Nothing says you can't borrow the camera to take some photos of the kids on Christmas morning.

In Chapter 3 we mentioned using your children in the business. If you have children, this is a great way to teach them something about running a business, having responsibilities, and getting paid for work. At the same time, you get to deduct what you pay them as a business expense.

If your children are very young (8 to 12), you might give them simple tasks such as cleaning your office, washing the company car, counting your inventory, and so on. As they get older, you can teach them to package your shipments and even use the computer to create your shipping labels. Once they are old enough to drive, they can take your shipments to the post office and run other errands. I once met a seller at eBay Live who sells games and toys and employs his kids as marketing consultants. They play with the games and toys and even get their friends' feedback on a new product before the seller buys a large quantity.

Another way to save money on taxes is to combine business travel with vacation. The IRS has some very strict rules about doing this, but they are easy to follow and can really reduce the cost of a vacation. For example, my wife and I went to Costa Rica a few years ago. While I was there I did some product research, and we purchased about $5,000 worth of inventory to sell on eBay. I could not write off my wife's expense, but I was able to write off a portion of my travel expenses against the business. I think that vacation cost us about $2,500 total, and I was legitimately able to write off about $1,100 against the business.

End-of-year tax planning can be a big issue for a business. The best thing you can do is sit down with your CPA in September and talk about your business plans related to purchasing equipment and inventory in the last three months of the year and work out a strategy.

9.3 Audit-Proofing Your Business

You can't really audit-proof your business completely because the IRS performs random audits. However, random audits are fairly rare; the real problem is the targeted audit. The IRS has certain secret parameters for small business and personal tax returns. These parameters are typically ratios or percentages of types of expenses and deductions related to the size and type of your business.

For example, if an advertising agency were to spend 10 percent of their income on entertainment, that would not be unusual because the advertising industry has to entertain their clients. If an Internet sales business spent 10 percent of their income on entertainment, that would probably trigger a red flag with the IRS. Your tax return would be kicked out to an examiner who would look it over with a fine-toothed comb to see if it warranted an audit.

Audits can take two forms. You could be selected for a general audit (a real nightmare), or the IRS could just audit one part of your tax return—in this case your advertising expenses. The examiner would ask you to provide detailed reasons and proof of all the entertainment expenses you claimed along with an explanation of the business purpose, the results obtained, copies of receipts, the name, title, and company of the persons entertained, and so on. If, after you provided this information, the auditor was not satisfied, she would probably order a general audit of your entire business. If the auditor thinks your activities were really egregious, the IRS can audit your taxes not only for this year but also back two more years as well. Believe me—you do not want to go through this.

The first step in audit-proofing your business is both a defense against being audited and something that will also help you if you ever are audited: keep good records!

The second step is to keep a good distance between your business and personal spending. Running a small business or corporation already has a lot of great tax advantages to it. Don't try to stretch them. Be careful of using corporate or business funds for personal expenses. Don't borrow and/or lend money back and forth between you and the business. Use your business bank account for business only. Don't take large cash advances that you can't cover with legitimate tax receipts for expenses or pay back. Most importantly, do not understate your income. Taking a business expense or a deduction that is later disallowed can result in paying back taxes with interest. Failing to claim income on your tax form is a crime punishable by fines and even imprisonment.

Don't send up red flags to the IRS. Yes, you can occasionally combine a business trip with a vacation, but if you fly off to your condo in Cabo San Lucas three times a year and go sport fishing, don't pay for the fishing boat with your business account and later claim you were trying out new fishing gear to sell on eBay.

For more on taxes, see Chapter 3.

For more on using QuickBooks and other accounting software, see Section 5.2.

For more on record keeping for taxes, see Section 53.1.

chapter 10

Setting Your Goals and Measuring Success

I know plenty of successful businesspeople who do not create formal written goals. But I know far many more who do—and on average these folks tend to be much more successful.

Written goals serve several purposes. Large goals serve as a vision of where you want to be in the future, and small ones provide the stepping-stones to get there.

To be useful, your goals should be specific and achievable. A goal such as "I want to become a millionaire within two years" is both vague and might be highly difficult to achieve unless you already have $800,000 in assets. A better goal would be : "I want to achieve Platinum PowerSeller status within one year and Titanium PowerSeller status within two years." If you want to relate your goals to income, you could set up steps such as:

1. Earn $5,000 a month by (date)
2. Earn $7,500 a month by (date)
3. Earn $10,000 a month by (date)

10.1 Designing Your Business

After you set your "big picture" business goals, you should set subgoals: a list of tasks you need to complete to achieve your first goal.

For instance, if you don't already have an eBay business, your first task should be to list all the things you need to do to set up and organize your business. These might include setting up your corporation and opening bank accounts, finding an accountant (CPA), buying computers and equipment, and finding suppliers for your products. Make a complete list of all these tasks, and treat them like goals. And remember to set completion dates for each task.

Don't forget you are designing your business. Remember to set goals related to branding and creating a "look and feel" for your business that is memorable to buyers. Go back to your business plan (Chapter 7), and use it as a guideline for creating your task list.

10.2 Setting Your Specific Business Goals

After you have completed your task-list goals, you'll want to set *specific business goals*. These involve determining how many auctions you will run and how often. You should also set your goals for reaching certain business metrics, such as conversions, sell-through rates, and average selling price. A metric is a measurement; conversion means a successful auction with a winning bidder. The conversion ratio metric is the number of auctions launched versus the number that close successfully. This is also referred to as your sell-through rate (see Part 7 for business metrics).

Your business goals should also include sales and profit goals by quarter and year, going out at least two years. The variables of seasonality and holidays make measuring sales and profits monthly too difficult to provide meaningful information. When you start making money, you'll have to send quarterly estimated income taxes into the IRS, so setting these goals up in conjunction with the tax calendar quarters will save you some work.

10.3 Measuring Success

An old business saying states: "If you can't measure something, you can't control it."

The purpose of having goals is twofold. First, you're setting achievable targets. Second, you can use them to measure your progress in hitting your big-picture goals. If you aren't measuring your success, you'll have difficulty spotting problems that will keep you from reaching it.

Goals have both a numerical value, such as dollars earned, and an accomplishment value, such as Completed Phase I of my market research. Both types of goals must also have a time value—the date they are to be accomplished—to be meaningful.

Goals can help you focus your activities to achieve your business plan. Remember these points to help you set and achieve your goals:

- Set realistic goals and subgoals (tasks), and write them down.
- Keep moving forward; never look back except to learn from your mistakes.
- Focus your energy; don't be distracted by other issues and businesses.
- Hone your skills; practice and experiment for success.
- Increase your knowledge; read everything you can find that relates to your business and your goals.
- Manage your time and your energy, but don't forget to set some time aside for yourself and your family or friends.
- Surround yourself with positive people. Don't listen to those who say you can't be successful.
- Most of all, have fun!

PowerSeller Tip

Good plans shape good decisions. That's why good planning helps to make elusive dreams come true.

—Lester R. Bittel, *The Nine Master Keys of Management*

For more on business planning, see Chapter 7.

For more on measuring your business metrics, see Chapters 55 and 56.

part 2

Product Selection and Pricing

eBay has over 30,000 categories and subcategories of products. Almost everything legal is for sale—and sells—on eBay, but many sellers fail to make money consistently. Invariably when I talk to these sellers, they blame their products. Although there are products that don't sell well on eBay, most often the problem lies with the seller's product strategy, pricing, and competition.

The most successful PowerSellers have learned hard lessons about the value of research and testing before committing their resources to a product. As they grew, they also learned the value of inventory management and control systems that warned them about looming product and pricing issues while they were still manageable.

This part examines the products that sell on eBay, the importance of finding a profitable niche, ways to find new product niches and the products to fill out the niches, how to analyze your competition, and how to develop pricing strategies for success.

chapter 11

Product Selection and Research

Since July 2000, I have published *The eBay Seller's News*, a monthly newsletter for professional eBay sellers. I get many questions from readers, but by far the most frequently asked one is: "What products are the most popular on eBay?" Other common questions include "What should I sell on eBay?" and "What products make the most money on eBay?"

Although the answers to these questions really depends on the kind of seller you are and how, where, and at what price you can buy your products, I can try to help you figure out the answers to these questions. In this chapter, I review several products and product categories that sell well on eBay, but the list is by no means complete—that's because eBay vendors sell millions of items on eBay in more than 50,000 categories and subcategories.

In addition, I discuss several product areas that are fairly easy for any eBay seller to enter. I'm not suggesting you enter one of these areas, although you certainly could. The purpose of this discussion is to demonstrate that people can make money in plenty of categories. Perhaps after reading about some of the possibilities, you will develop some ideas of your own.

PowerSeller Tip

eBay prohibits the sale of some items on its site, including firearms, lock-picking sets, alcohol, and Nazi memorabilia. For a complete list, go to the eBay Site Map, and click on *Rules & Safety*. On this page you will find a link to all *Prohibited and Restricted Items*.

11.1 Finding the eBay Sweet Spot

There is no single "sweet spot" on eBay. Sellers have created sweet spots throughout the site. The trick is to find your own sweet spot: the one product category where you can control your destiny and your profits.

To demonstrate the variety of items that turn a profit on eBay, here is a short list of some items I have sold myself and for others over the past nine years:

Eighteenth-century cherry desk

Set of six eighteenth-century coin silver spoons

50-year-old miniature Eskimo kayak

Dentist's chair and drills

Starbucks collectible mugs

Rachael Ray Chef's Knives

Studio photo lighting equipment

Espresso machines

Thousands of nonfiction books

New and used fishing equipment

Portable BBQ grills

BBQ tool sets

Firepit BBQ grills

Fendi and Prada handbags

Burberry umbrellas

Walrus oosik with an ivory handle

Barracks building from the Manzanar Japanese Internment camp

2002 Porsche Boxster-S

1.3-Ct diamond engagement ring

Ampex reel-to-reel tape deck

Ralph Lauren Polo tennis shoes

Nikon digital camera

Hasselblad camera body

Vintage 1985 Apple computer

Bang & Olafson stereo system

Six Steelcase office cubicles

A broken espresso machine (the buyer knew it was broken)

Veterinary CO_2 laser surgical system

Professional router table

Large lot of MG auto parts

Collection of Gund teddy bears

So what is the test of a successful product?

- A reliable source of continuing supply at a price where you can make an acceptable margin
- A minimum of competition
- High barriers of entry to new sellers
- A large-enough market to meet your sales targets
- A product that lends itself to spin-offs, multiple sales, repeat sales, and the ability to up-sell the customer accessories or complementary products

As we continue through this chapter, keep this list in mind. As you consider each product, ask yourself if it meets the criteria we listed. You won't always find a product that meets all these requirements, but it must always meet the first test: can I find a reliable supply at a price point where I can make an acceptable margin? If you fail this test, your business model is doomed.

11.1.1 Pick Your Passion

Choosing what to sell can often be overwhelming. My advice is to look at your own skills, hobbies, and interests first. If you're selling something you enjoy and are very knowledgeable about, that will come across to your buyers when they read your auctions.

If you currently own a retail store, gallery, or antique shop, simply research which of your products will sell well on eBay. I explain how later in this chapter.

Do you love cooking? Do you get into cookware and gourmet food items? Do you collect sports memorabilia? Start there. Perhaps you love to read and always wanted to own a small bookstore but could never afford the investment. You can start small on eBay with only a few dozen books and build your business from there. (Several Platinum PowerSellers sell nothing but books.) The same goes for art. You can buy art posters or prints wholesale from several distributors, and thousands of art prints and posters sell every day on eBay.

I once spoke with a dental hygienist who was struggling to find a product to sell. She had tried several categories with no success. I asked her if she knew very much about dental equipment. Of course she did! She now sells used dental equipment on eBay. When we last spoke, she was selling over $40,000 a month and had two employees. She has expanded into dental supplies and is just starting to represent a few small manufacturers of new equipment.

If you are a computer or software whiz, then look to the computer area for items to sell. Better still, write a software package or build a computer-related product or accessory and sell it on eBay.

PowerSeller Tip

Don't think that you need to limit yourself to a certain product theme. You can sell *anything* on eBay if priced right. My rule of thumb is this: if you can source an item for half of the regular price, and make a decent profit, then you can sell a ton of them on eBay! Don't be afraid to sell a mixture of new, used, closeout, liquidated, information product, etc.

—Mike Enos, PowerSeller and eBay Guru (www.platinumpowerseller.com)

Your business and product ideas are limited only by your imagination and, of course, the existence of a market. Whatever you decide to sell, become an expert at it. Read up on your products; talk to other merchants and collectors; research your competition; learn something about the history of your product; and study the manufacturers. Knowing your product category in depth will pay many dividends down the road.

Don't look for the quick kill, that one hot product that will make you rich overnight. If it exists, others will see the opportunity and start underselling you within weeks of your first offering. The same goes for fad products. Fads are by their nature short-lived.

Never sell a product you aren't enthusiastic about. If you don't believe in what you're selling and you aren't willing to stand behind your product, your online business will certainly fail. If you wouldn't buy the product for yourself or strongly recommend it to a friend or family member, then do not sell it on eBay. You might sell a few, but in the end you will not build a long-term business.

There is no question that some products sell better than others. Computer products and software are particularly hot sellers because almost all eBay users are *prequalified* for those products. In other words, the fact people are buying on eBay means they own a computer. Using a computer means they need hardware and/or software. Therefore, almost anyone buying on eBay is a potential customer for computer hardware, software, or accessories.

Anything kitchen-related also has a huge market on eBay. After all, everyone cooks at least occasionally. Cooking and gourmet-related items are very popular, and some sellers even sell specialty foods.

Sometimes the best products are the obscure or less obvious ones. Thousands of eBay sellers auction sports cards and collectibles, and that's the problem. Having so many sellers with essentially the same merchandise drives the price down, and you can't make a decent margin. However, if you look deep within this popular category, you can find the money-making products.

A long-time PowerSeller here in Seattle collects sports memorabilia. As he spent hundreds of hours scouring eBay for bargains, he realized right away that the market for common sports memorabilia was saturated and profit margins were too small, so he decided to look for only oddball and unusual items. He purchased a lot of 200 unused tickets from the Ali-Fraser fight (The Thrilla in Manila) and began auctioning them off on eBay one ticket at a time. The last time I saw him, he was still selling them at prices of up to $40 each, and he bought the whole lot for under $200. Now he goes to sports memorabilia auctions and shows and looks only for oddball or very unique items. The market for the things he sells is somewhat small, but because of the uniqueness of his merchandise, he commands obscenely high prices. Many of his items command markups of 500 percent or more.

When I first started selling antiques on eBay, I had some early challenges. I reasoned that lower-priced items or things that were hard to sell in a store would probably sell best, but that didn't work! So after a few tries, I switched to selling our more expensive, higher-quality items. Our sales took off, and we were getting bids 10 to 30 percent higher than we used to sell the items for when we had a store. If something doesn't sell well in a retail environment, it probably won't sell well on eBay either.

11.1.2 Create Your Own Product

Many sellers create their own product to sell on eBay. Some sell their own crafts and artwork, while others produce specialized software programs or other information resources. Because you are the manufacturer and totally control the cost and selling price of your product, this can be very lucrative.

Software is a huge seller. Think about it—every eBay user owns a computer. If you wrote a highly specialized application, you'd have a difficult time selling it to a software company because they're not interested in a product unless it can sell millions. But *you* could probably make a lot of money selling a few hundred or a few thousand copies on eBay and the other auction sites. For instance, the Pokémon collecting software has been very popular, although there is so much of it around, the price has fallen drastically. People collect everything, though. Just look at the collectibles selling on eBay, and write a database software program to help people keep track of and price their collectibles. (Even if you can't write software, you can often hire a programmer to create a simple software program for you. A good programmer can create a basic collecting program for just a few hundred dollars that you could use to potentially earn thousands of dollars.)

Or consider creating custom collectible price guides and selling them online. Although most of the major collectibles have price guides published by the major publishing houses, small, more niche-type collectibles or cult items rarely have a large enough following to attract major publishers. If you are familiar with such a niche, this is an opportunity to write a price guide or create a database program you can sell to collectors on eBay. Databases can be highly profitable because you can deliver your products electronically at very little cost or effort.

PowerSeller Tip

eBay used to allow the sale of digitally delivered information, such as software, eBooks, videos, and so on. However, they recently issued a policy whereby if you are selling a digital product, you must physically deliver it on a CD, DVD, or in print. Many sellers of digital information objected to this, but I found that by delivering a physical product, for example a video on a DVD or printing a book that I used to deliver as an eBook, I actually sold more and at higher prices.

Computer games are also big. The latest and hottest games are available from the master distributors, but you'll probably not realize the same price discounts that major retailers get and so won't be able to turn a decent profit. However, slightly older computer games are available very cheaply from closeout and surplus dealers. You can often find a computer game that sold for $49 last year for under $5 when purchased by the case. You can't get anywhere near the original price of $49, but you can often sell them on eBay for upward of $15 each.

Here is an example that's easy to replicate today. A few years ago, I purchased 500 surplus Hoyle Bridge and Backgammon computer games, all in their original wrappers. Each one still had the original $29.95 price tag on them. I paid $575 for the load plus $200 shipping, for a total cost of $775, which worked out to a unit cost of $1.55 each. I sold them on eBay over a three-month period at an average price of $14 each. That's almost an 800 percent markup for a product that someone else thought was junk.

Having warned you about the risks of following a fad, I must point out that eBay fortunes have been made on Furby toys, Pokémon cards, and Beanie Babies. These are being replaced by Harry Potter, Lord of the Rings, and WebKinz and will be taken over by new items by the time you read this book. There's nothing wrong with working the fads if you specialize in these types of products and know where and how to find a steady supply of them in small quantities. Just don't get caught with a large supply of inventory when the fad ends and prices crash, which has happened to thousands of unfortunate sellers.

11.1.3 Specialize in eBay Supplies

When Herman Levi went to California during the gold rush, he realized there were two ways to get rich: dig for gold or sell supplies to the miners. He chose the latter strategy and made millions selling blue jeans and other supplies to the thousands of miners passing through San Francisco. And you can use the Herman Levi strategy on eBay.

Start a business selling supplies to other eBay sellers. What do eBay sellers buy? They buy books and information, software, packing and shipping supplies, digital cameras, ink cartridges, and most of all, products to resell.

You can also sell supplies to eBay buyers. Card collectors buy cardholders and software to catalog them; doll collectors buy doll clothing and display cases; coin collectors buy coin holders. And the list goes on. Look at almost any eBay category, and you'll find some way to supply collectors with products to aid in their collecting.

11.1.4 Electronics

I get e-mails all the time from eBay sellers who want to sell the latest digital cameras, Blu-Ray players, video game consoles, stereo equipment, and computers. This is an excellent market on eBay, but *this is a very difficult business to enter.*

Large wholesale distributors for these products will not even talk to you unless you have a minimum $250,000 line of credit and can place orders for at least $50,000. If you don't have that sort of capital to start with, you can still play in this market by selling accessories. Take the iPod as an example. I once spoke to an Apple distributor about selling the iPod music player. They were happy to sell them to me wholesale with a minimum quantity order of 1,000 units at a wholesale item cost of $142 for the $199 unit. This would have required an outlay of $142,000 for the iPods plus shipping costs. When Apple stores were selling iPods for $199, iPods were selling on eBay for an average of $185. That works out to $43 a unit ($43 ÷ 185 = 23 percent margin). If you sold all 1,000, you would make $43,000 before eBay and PayPal fees.

This doesn't sound too bad. But what if you decided to sell iPod accessories such as earphones, speaker docking stations, cases, and so on? Accessories tend to have higher margins than the products themselves, yet they don't require such a large outlay of cash to purchase wholesale. Although a few large sellers were selling iPods on a margin of up to about 25 percent, other eBay sellers were selling accessories and realizing 100 percent markups. Of course, the ideal situation would be to sell both. Sell the iPod on eBay, and then upsell the accessory after the sale directly from your website.

The point here is that you can enter the market much more easily by selling the accessories than the units themselves. Instead of placing an order for 1,000 iPods for $142,000, you could buy a large amount of accessories for $5,000 and actually make higher margins. The higher margins will enable you to reinvest your profits in even larger purchases.

One of the largest sellers of cell phones on eBay started out selling used cell phones, then branched into accessories, and finally lined up a distribution agreement for the phones themselves. He now sells over $1,000,000 a month on eBay.

11.1.5 Used Merchandise

Hundreds of eBay sellers—many of them large PowerSellers—sell used goods they pick up at flea markets, garage sales, and thrift shops. Some of the best-selling used products are children's clothing, vintage clothing, western wear and cowboy boots, ice skates, athletic equipment, small appliances (Juiceman, pasta machines, food processors, mixers, and so on), old watches and estate jewelry, tools and equipment including heavy machinery, cars, boats, aircraft, motor-cycles and trailers, and more.

PowerSeller Tip

Few people strike gold when they're starting out selling used things, but all it takes is paying attention to what people want and are willing to pay for (through research and experience). I try to explain to new sellers that one of the rules of selling antiques and collectibles is that something that was high quality and expensive when it was new is more likely to increase in value than something that was cheap when it was new. Oddly enough, the very opposite is some-times true—cheap "throwaway" things that are relatively unique and scarce can often bring surprisingly good prices. You can train your eye to spot quality, but you have to have a "knack" to recognize the oddball things that someone will want (as opposed to the equally oddball things that NOBODY wants).

—Carol Hearn, eBay PowerSeller
(www.WanderingCreekAntiques.com)

Finding the quantities of used goods to support a large eBay business can be difficult, but it's by no means impossible, and hundreds of eBay sellers do it (see Part 3).

PowerSeller Tip

Only buy items that are in full working condition. Don't attempt to sell anything defective or broken unless you are selling it for parts—and be sure to make this fact very clear. It is critical to your success that you accurately describe all used items. In addition, take good photos, and be sure to point out any minor defects.

11.1.6 Used and Overstocked Books

Used books are big sellers on eBay, and this is a very easy business to start. Hundreds of sellers on eBay are making $2,000 a week and more selling used books. Some of the larger eBay used-book vendors are Platinum- and Titanium-level PowerSellers.

Unless you are an expert, forget about novels, literature, and rare expensive books. Any used bookstore owner will tell you his or her big money-makers are nonfiction books on art, photography, crafts, cooking, history, regional subjects, sports, cars, trains, aircraft, motorcycles, music, and children's books. The same is true on eBay. You can buy plenty of these books at garage sales, flea markets, and thrift stores.

The best books to sell are the large "coffee table" editions on movies, music, art, photography, transportation, and sports. I recently purchased a beautiful history of Porsche motorcars at a local thrift shop for $1 and sold it on eBay for $29. Browsing the closeout table at Barnes & Noble just after Christmas, I bought a brand-new marked-down *History of the Superbowl* for $5.99. It sold on eBay for $17.50.

PowerSeller Tip

Stay away from book club editions and series books, such as The Time-Life books, unless you have a complete set in perfect condition. I once found the complete Time-Life Photography series at a used bookstore for $65.00. I sold it on eBay for $122.00. That was less than I hoped to get, but still a nice profit. The problem with the large sets, however, is the hassle of shipping 24 heavy books.

Buy only books in good condition, preferably with an intact dust jacket. Never pay more than 35 percent of what you think they will sell for and no more than 20 percent of the original cover price. You can find plenty of books at garage sales and thrift shops for less than $2 that will sell on eBay for $10 or more. Stay away from books that would sell for less than $10; otherwise, you'll have to sell hundreds of books every week to make a decent income.

In addition to used books, tons of out-of-print and overstocked books are sold every day. These are the ones you see on the clearance table at Barnes & Noble. Wholesale book distribution companies are located in almost every major city. There are also websites and companies that specialize in overstocked books and out-of-print titles. (See Part 2, product sourcing section.)

A great way to find books to sell is to place a small classified ad in your local paper or classified advertising sites such as Craigslist.com and Kijiji.com. It might say something like this:

> Local dealer will pay top dollar for used nonfiction books in good condition. Call Kathy at 666-555-1111.

I once placed such an ad, and someone called me regarding his collection of more than 300 books. I bought the entire collection for $400, kept a few choice titles for my collection, and sold the rest for more than $4,000.

If you want to know what a book is worth before buying it, there is a new tool available from www.asellertool.com that allows you to check prices in real time from your cell phone or PDA.

You might also consider selling out-of-print and overstocked books. You can find wholesale book distribution companies in almost every major city as well as several online vendors. (See Part 3, on product sourcing, to learn how to contact these vendors.)

11.1.7 Closeout and Surplus Merchandise

Closeout or surplus merchandise is the staple of many large eBay PowerSellers. The opportunities to make money in closeout goods are great, but there are some pitfalls as well.

There are two kinds of closeout or surplus merchandise: returns and overstocks. Returns are goods the customer returned for some reason and could be something as simple as exchanging an item because it was the wrong size, model, or color. This category also includes "open box returns." These can include warranty returns or items that were blemished or broken in some way. Returns usually sell for less than overstock for this reason. If you buy a lot of returns, you might end up throwing half of the goods away because they are too damaged to sell on eBay.

Overstocks are called "shelf-pulls" in the trade. These goods didn't sell and were pulled from the shelf to make way for new merchandise. They usually have the original price tags on them and can be purchased for anywhere from 20 to 30 percent of their original retail price.

Shelf-pulls sell very well on eBay. In fact, most large eBay sellers of clothing, accessories, consumer electronics, books, and small appliances deal in overstock or surplus items. In general, you can realize a 50 to 100 percent markup on most surplus goods. Brand-name products and products in their original boxes or that are new with tags will command higher prices, getting you closer to the 100 percent markup.

PowerSeller Tip

Overstocked goods are usually sold by the pallet load. Pallets can be cheap to buy but expensive to ship. So when buying pallets, try to find a source geo-graphically close to you to minimize the shipping cost.

11.1.8 Remanufactured Electronics and Small Appliances

Manufacturers of almost every type of expensive electronic and mechanical merchandise offer "remanufactured" or "refurbished" goods, which can include computers, digital cameras, stereo and television equipment, and both small and large appliances. Remanufactured equipment and merchandise is typically goods that were returned by customers and, although not used, they could not be sold as new because the package was opened or some of the items were assembled. In some cases, refurbished items are warranty returns. Typically the manufacturers run these items through their normal quality-control process and then repair and repackage them. These goods are almost always offered with a full factory warranty.

This product category can support a very large and profitable eBay business, because the margins can be pretty good and the average selling prices are fairly high.

But how do you find them? The best way is to visit manufacturers' websites to see if there is a link to an outlet for these goods. Or you can e-mail manufacturers and ask how and where they sell their refurbished items. As a last resort you can call the company and ask for the purchasing department, and they will usually tell you how you can access these products.

Remanufactured products have been around long enough that savvy consumers looking for a bargain do not hesitate to buy them. They are big sellers on eBay. If you can find a good supply of remanufactured items, you will realize a steady source of profits on eBay.

11.1.9 Art, Antiques, and Collectibles

Name an item, and someone probably collects it. Did you know, for example, that people collect and pay big money for old eyeglasses? The catch is, where do you find old eyeglasses? You'll probably never see them at a garage sale; however, when you are at a garage sale, if the people having the sale are over 50, just ask them if they have any old eyeglasses or even old sunglasses lying around the house. You will be amazed how many people will come up with them. Antique or vintage eyeglasses sell on eBay in the $25 to $200 range.

The same is true of many more collectibles. Everyone knows that Elvis and Beetles memorabilia is highly collectible. The trick is to find the lesser-known things that most people don't think of. I have a friend who sells nothing but old fishing equipment and lures on eBay and sells over $4,000 a month. That doesn't sound like much money, but he usually gets a 500 to 1500 percent markup. He can buy an old fishing reel at a garage sale for $5 and sell it for $75. Other sellers do the same thing with vintage stereo equipment, old golf clubs and tennis rackets, and so on.

There are two keys to success for selling collectibles: knowledge and a good source of supply. You'll have to become highly knowledgeable about your particular category of collectibles. Knowledge will help you spot bargains and learn how to accurately describe your items. Collectible buyers appreciate buying from someone who is obviously knowledgeable because it gives them confidence in what they are buying and whom they are buying it from.

Finding a good source of supply for collectibles can be difficult. Selling newly manufactured collectibles is easier because you can buy directly from the manufacturer or distributor. Selling older, out-of-production collectibles is still feasible, but it could be hard to build a large eBay business because you have to spend a lot of time finding goods to sell, and the prices you can buy the items for will vary.

If you want to sell collectibles at the Titanium PowerSeller level, you'll have to sell a wide variety because the various collectible categories are too small to support a large-sized business. An exception to this is the sports card and memorabilia business that currently supports dozens of large sellers.

Some other categories, such as glassware, can also support a large eBay business, but once again, you'll have to do the research to determine which collectible categories are capable of supporting the size business you want to grow to.

Some eBay Selling Statistics

- More than 560 farm tractors and parts sell every day.
- More than 900 MP3 players are sold every day.
- A diamond ring is sold every 2 minutes.
- A book sells every 2.5 seconds.
- A car or truck sells every 50 seconds.
- A Ford Mustang sells every 39 minutes on eBay Motors.
- Used goods and merchandise will make up over one half of the $40 billion worth of merchandise that will sell on eBay in 2008.

11.1.10 Jewelry and Watches

The jewelry and watch market on eBay is big and getting bigger. This category probably has the largest number of sellers of any except sports cards.

The advantage of selling jewelry, especially high-end jewelry, is the high average selling price (ASP). Although the market is good for inexpensive costume jewelry, you have to sell thousands of items a week to make a large income. Jewelry made of gold, silver, diamonds, and other precious stones sells for a lot more money. In fact, if you research jewelry sales (see Chapter 12), you'll find the higher-priced pieces have a higher closing ratio than lower-priced items. As an example, I recently looked at diamond engagement rings. Rings of .5 to 1.5 carats selling in the $900 to $2,500 price range had a very low closing ratio—fewer than 20 percent of all auctions closed successfully. Rings selling for between $5,000 and $15,000 had closing ratios approximating 35 percent.

Another nice thing about selling jewelry is that suppliers are easy to find. You can import jewelry directly or buy from thousands of importers and manufacturers in the United States. There are major wholesale jewelry trade shows in most major cities at least twice a year.

The downside of selling jewelry on eBay is the competition. Jewelry can be expensive to buy and inventory, so make sure you have saleable merchandise before committing to a large purchase. This is an area where it pays to do very detailed research.

11.1.11 Business and Industrial Materials and Equipment

Business and Industrial (B&I) Equipment is the largest and fastest-growing category on eBay in terms of gross merchandise sales (GMS). This category includes a wide range of subcategories including agricultural and forestry equipment, construction equipment, health-care equipment and lab supplies, retail and food service equipment, industrial equipment and supplies, and office furniture, equipment, and supplies.

Here is a list of the major Business & Industrial categories on eBay. Each category has dozens of subcategories.

Agriculture & Forestry

Construction

Electrical & Test Equipment

Fuel & Energy

Health Care, Lab & Life Science

Industrial Supply & MRO

Manufacturing & Metalworking

Office

Packing & Shipping

Printing & Graphic Arts

Restaurant & Catering

Retail & Services

The advantage of the B&I category is the high average selling price of the items. If you are selling a piece of $50,000 farm equipment, a mere 15 percent margin will earn you $7,500 on one sale. I once sold an old German printing press for a company in Portland, Oregon, that had upgraded their equipment. A local auctioneer told them he thought he could sell it for $1,000. I visited the company, took some digital photos of the press, and made photocopies of the instruction manuals. I had to relist it several times before it sold, but it eventually sold for more than $11,000. I collected the money and took a 22 percent commission on the sale. Best of all, the buyer and seller worked out the shipping; I never touched the item.

This category is a natural for consignment selling. You can approach bankruptcy attorneys and find complete restaurants and businesses for sale. You can contact corporations that are growing and replacing equipment or downsizing and getting rid of equipment. There are farmers selling their old tractors, construction companies selling cranes and bulldozers, and doctors and dentists selling their used medical equipment. If you don't believe there is a market for these goods, do a search on one of the product terms and check the search box for completed listings. You'll see dozens, if not hundreds, of items selling for very large amounts of money.

11.1.12 eBay Motors

eBay Motors is a huge marketplace. More vehicles are sold on eBay Motors than on all the other automobile sales websites combined. If you're interested in pursuing this category, keep in mind that most states have regulations that prohibit you from selling more than three or four cars a year unless you have a dealer's license.

If you have an auto dealer's license or you can hook up with a small auto dealer, eBay Motors is one of the easiest categories to build a Platinum or Titanium PowerSeller business. You don't have to sell cars and trucks, though. Plenty of sellers concentrate on selling car parts, aftermarket accessories, auto-related clothing and personal accessories, automotive art, models, campers and trailers, and even old automotive books, catalogs, and advertising brochures.

Dozens of PowerSellers specialize in buying older cars (pre-1970) and breaking them up to sell the parts. I know someone who buys an old car and lists all the component parts on eBay until they sell. As soon as a part sells, he removes it from the car and ships it to the buyer. While I was working on this book, he had an older Pontiac GTO that was in horrible condition (rust, body and interior damage). Nevertheless, a lot of engine, transmission, brake, and electrical parts (along with some of the chrome and interior buttons and handles) were in perfect condition. He bought the car from an insurance company for $700 and got more than $4,000 for all the parts. It typically takes him about six to eight weeks to part out a car on eBay. After that he takes the hulk to the junkyard and starts looking for his next car. He once found a 1950s Plymouth for $400 that he sold as parts for over $7,000. He sold the windshield alone for $900.

PowerSeller Tip

Steve Lindhorst, one of the leading experts and trainers on eBay Motors, developed a system for eBay sellers to work with new and used car dealers to sell their cars for them. Steve has personally generated net incomes exceeding $5,000 a month using this method, which requires no cash or inventory investment on the seller's part. You can read about it at www.showroomsecrets.com.

Another great little book about eBay motors is *The Pocket Idiot's Guide to eBay Motors,* by my daughter-in-law, Lissa McGrath, available online and at bookstores.

11.2 Product Research

As noted earlier, my reason for reviewing all these potential sweet spots is to stimulate your thinking. Yes, you could sell any of the products I've just discussed, but I hope this review gives you some ideas of your own. Use this information and these anecdotes as a starting point for your own market research.

Research is one of the key tasks you can perform to grow your business and keep it profitable over the years. I've been selling on eBay since 1998, and I still spend one or two hours a week doing research. In the beginning, you should spend two or three times this amount of time if you want to be successful.

Research can tell you what is selling on eBay, how much it is selling for, what the seller's costs were, what headlines work, what kind of features to use, and so much more.

Start by writing down a list of sales categories, products, and product ideas that interest you. This will give your research some direction so you aren't wandering all over the eBay globe without a compass.

We're going to look first at research you can perform for free right on the eBay site itself. Then we'll look at some third-party research tools. I would advise investing in a three-ring notebook and a three-hole punch for this exercise. Take notes as you do your research, and print out the pages you turn up with results that interest you and put them in your notebook.

11.3 eBay Economics 101

An auction, and therefore eBay, is a pure marketplace. It is the essence of capitalism. Goods are sold, and prices are set, based on their true value in the marketplace at a given moment in time. I'm not going to teach Economics 101 here, but it is vitally important to your success on eBay that you understand this principal.

Three critical factors are related to the price an eBay seller can expect to realize for any given product:

- Supply and demand
- Product life cycle
- Competition

So let's look more closely at each of these factors.

11.3.1 Supply and Demand on eBay

The law of supply and demand is simple: the less the supply of something and the more demand for it, the higher the price someone will be willing to pay for it. And conversely, as the supply of something increases, the prices will fall.

I learned about the law of supply and demand when I was just a college kid. One summer I was lying on the beach and realized I had forgotten my sunblock. Not wanting to get burned, I walked more than a mile from my spot on the beach to a stall on the boardwalk where I bought a tube of overpriced sunblock. It only took a moment for me to realize that other people lying on the beach might pay even more if they didn't have to walk a mile.

At the time I didn't have any wholesale connections, so the next day I went to the supermarket and bought 50 tubes of the cheapest 15 and 30 SPF sunblock I could find. I walked up and down the beach hawking my sunblock for three times the price I had paid. I sold all 50 tubes within two days and made more than $200. Supply and demand: the market price of a product is determined by both the supply and demand for it. *On the beach, getting sunburned, no sunblock: demand is pretty high. The nearest shop is a 25-minute walk away: supply is pretty low. This adds up to one simple fact: price is pretty high.* I made more than $3,000 that summer working a couple of hours a day hawking sunblock.

In all fairness to economics professors around the world, the law of supply and demand is more nuanced than what I've just described, but my basic explanation captures the essence of it.

Here is a real-world example. Most of the diamond supply is controlled by a company headquartered in London called DeBeers. Several times a year, DeBeers invites diamond merchants to London to view diamonds. Each dealer is shown a predetermined quantity and quality of diamonds and told what the price is. The number of stones each dealer can buy is strictly limited. In fact, though, DeBeers has several years' worth of supply in their vaults and continues to mine more and more diamonds every year. Basically they control the supply so the market is not flooded with diamonds. In reality, emeralds are far rarer than diamonds, but there is no central organization controlling the supply, so a good-quality emerald tends to sell for about the same price as a similar quality and size diamond. If the supply were not controlled by DeBeers, diamonds would be far cheaper than emeralds.

How does supply and demand relate to eBay? The average eBay bidder is a bargain hunter by nature. That's why he's buying on eBay and not shopping at Nordstrom. If a buyer who wants a Tommy Bahama shirt types *Tommy Bahama Shirt* into the eBay search box, every auction for a Tommy Bahama shirt will come up. If the prospective bidder only sees a few shirts in his size, he'll bid a fairly high price to make sure he wins one. If, however, 20 or 30 shirts come up, the bidder will become more selective and more cautious in his bidding because he knows if he misses one, he'll get another chance. He might even place a low-ball bid on several auctions hoping to score a steal if one of them ends without a lot of bidding.

What does this mean to you as the seller when you are sourcing product to sell on eBay? It means you must pay attention to the law of supply and demand. Most eBay sellers will do the research to determine if the product is selling and what it is selling for, but they often neglect to research the supply. Besides finding out what a product is selling for, take the additional time to research the supply.

It is very important to look not only at the prices other sellers have realized but also at the price trend of a product over the past 30 days. Has the price been holding steady? If so, the supply is probably in equilibrium with the demand. But if prices are falling, look at how many listings there are. Have the number of individual sellers and the number of listings increased over the past 30 days? Are there more Dutch auctions for the product? (Dutch auctions are a favorite way for eBay sellers to dump inventory quickly. See chapter 24 for how Dutch auctions work)

Let's say your research shows that 300 units of Tommy Hilfiger polo shirts were listed on eBay in the past month. You calculate the average selling price of the shirts to be $35. What is going to happen if you buy a pallet load of 500 shirts from a surplus dealer and start selling them on eBay? You'll have more than doubled the supply. That's okay if you bought the shirts really cheap—at less than $10 each, for instance—because your increased supply could drive the price down to below $20.

You must always worry about what your competitors are doing. At the same time, you must be careful not to compete with yourself. If you are the cause of too much supply, you can drive prices down all by yourself.

11.3.2 Product Life Cycle

No product is eternal—unless, that is, you sell Bibles or old Frank Sinatra records.

There are two basic classes of products on eBay: antiques and collectibles and everything else. Antiques and collectibles, which include art, stamps, coins, Beanie Babies, rare books, and anything that appreciates in price over time, are priced strictly based on their demand at *any point in time*. In general, the price of most products in this category rise over time; however, we all know that some art, antiques, and especially collectibles go out of fashion, and when they do, prices for these items can fall precipitously.

The category of *everything else* includes just about anything else you can think of that is manufactured or produced today. This is the world of consumer goods: clothing, shoes, books, electronics, kitchen gadgets, beauty aids and nutritional supplements, furniture, tools, computers and software, cars and motorcycles, machinery, and farm equipment.

Virtually all manufactured products have a life cycle that starts when a product is first introduced. You can call this the *Introduction Phase* (IP) of a product's life. The length of a product's IP varies with the type of product and the level of consumer demand. An article of clothing might be in its IP during the season for that type of clothing. For example, bathing suits are usually introduced in department stores in March or April when stores start to show goods for the summer season. You could consider the IP for a bathing suit to last from March or April until Memorial Day. After summer starts, a bathing suit would move into its next phase: the *Selling Phase* (SP). By the beginning of August, the product would enter the final part of its life cycle: the *Liquidation Phase* (LP).

For nonseasonal products, the life cycle segments are about the same but are related to other factors such as when new models or a competitive product comes out. Some products, such as digital cameras, are frequently being updated and replaced with new models by the manufacturer. Companies such as Sony and Nikon come out with new models every three or four months. Until manufacturers stop introducing new models all the time, digital cameras will have a very short IP, perhaps as much as a few weeks, and a corresponding short SP of just three or four months before moving into its LP. A best-selling book, music CD, or video DVD might even have a shorter cycle life. These products can move from introduction to liquidation in as little as six or eight weeks. On the other hand, an automobile's life cycle is about nine months. Prices are pretty stable throughout the model year until about the nine-month mark. About three months before the new models come out, the manufacturer starts offering incentives, and the dealer cuts prices to clear inventory to make room for the new models. After the new model-year cars actually arrive, the dealer will really cut the prices of any prior-year cars still on the lot.

Why is this important to you as a seller? It turns out it's extremely important. *The price of a product is directly related to its position in the life cycle.* Both the retail and wholesale price declines fairly slowly within the early or Introduction Phase. For some really hot high-demand products, you will occasionally see buyers bid the price up above its Manufacturer's Suggested Retail Price (MSRP).

As time goes on, the price declines more swiftly until it hits the liquidation phase, when it drops off sharply. More importantly, the wholesale price drops more swiftly than the retail price. In the final period of the liquidation phase, wholesale prices can fall to or below 15 cents on the original (IP) retail dollar. Manufacturers and wholesale distributors sell in high volumes but work on fairly narrow margins. They must dump unsold inventory quickly once prices start to fall, or they find themselves in a loss position.

Traditional retail stores will start having sales toward the end of a product's season or as soon as sales of the product slow to clear out surplus inventory. After they lower the price to 50 percent of retail, they don't generally go any lower (except in retail clothing); instead, they will sell any leftover merchandise to a surplus or overstock dealer for anywhere from 10¢ to 20¢ on the original retail dollar. These dealers will in turn offer it to discount sellers such as dollar stores, flea market dealers, and eBay and website sellers at prices around 20¢ to 25¢ (or less) on the original retail dollar.

What you are selling and where it is in its life cycle when you buy it determines your selling price, and therefore profit, on eBay. During the introductory phase, supply tends to be low. If the product is hot (a lot of demand), prices will stay high until the supply, from both you and competitors, catches up with the demand.

PowerSeller Tip

What you *never* want to do is buy a product in the middle or just before the end of the life cycle. This is the eBay dead zone. By the time a product reaches its selling phase, the strong demand is over, more competitors are coming into the marketplace, and prices are about to fall. If you ordered a bunch of swimsuits in late April and they were delivered in May, you would only have a few weeks to get rid of them before everyone started cutting prices. Because you had such a large supply and a very short time to sell them, you would tend to list more auctions for greater quantity, thereby increasing the supply and basically competing with yourself by helping to drive prices down.

What kind of seller are you? Do you have the source of supply to buy new products directly from the manufacturer or the distributor when they first come out? If so, you can command high prices for new products during their IP. Or are you like many sellers on eBay, buying and selling products during their liquidation phase? You buy products at the end of their life cycles when the wholesale prices fall to bargain-basement levels and the products are sold to the bargain hunters on eBay.

Over the years, I have developed a set of "rules" that I use to analyze a new product or product category before deciding to sell it on eBay. It's really more of a checklist than a set of rules, but if you follow them, you will avoid costly mistakes:

- There are four levels of wholesale distribution: manufacturer, importer, distributor, and middleman. The closer you can get to the manufacturer, the less your product will cost. Never buy from the last level, the middleman, because it is virtually impossible to make money.

- Never buy a fad or short-lived product unless you are buying from the manufacturer or importer and the product is very early in its life cycle.

- Do not buy new or preintroduction products unless you are positive they will sell, based on the past history of similar products.

- Never buy a product during the selling phase (SP) or the early liquidation phase (LP) of a product's life cycle.

- Never buy a product if the quantity you are buying represents more than 10 percent of the available quantity in your marketplace.

- Never buy a liquidation-phase product unless it has a recognizable brand name.

Of course, there are exceptions to every rule, but be extra careful when you make them. Before you make any large investment in product inventory, always make sure there is a market for the product, you understand where the product is in its life cycle, and you know how much supply is available on eBay. This will keep you from having to liquidate your inventory just to get rid of it.

11.4 Market Research on eBay

To do market research on eBay, you need to know how to use the site's powerful search engine. If you want to know what price something has been selling for, search *completed listings*. Looking at an ongoing auction will only reveal what the current bid is. You want to know the actual selling price.

On every eBay page there is a **Search** box at the top of the page. Type in the item you're looking for, and you'll be brought to a page like Figure 11.1, which shows the results for a search of toy trains. Notice the drop-down box that allows you to sort your results by several criteria:

Best Match

Time: ending soonest

Time: newly listed

Price + Shipping: lowest first

Price + Shipping: highest first

Price: highest first

Distance: nearest first

Payment: PayPal first

Category

Figure 11.1
*eBay Search
Results for a search
of toy trains.*

Select the drop-down box of your choice. For our example, suppose you choose to search by **Price: highest first.** The page will refresh, bringing up all auctions for toy trains listed by the auction with the highest price. Unfortunately, the results bring up not only the items with the highest bids but also items with high starting prices, many of which have not received any bids.

This information is essentially useless in determining the worth of an item for two reasons. First, the seller may be asking an unreasonably high price as a starting bid. Second, even the items with bids are still in progress—unless you bookmark the auction and follow it to the end, you won't know the final bid amount.

If you scroll down the page and look in the left-hand column, you will see the view shown in Figure 11.2 in a box marked **Search options.** This feature allows you to refine your search further. If you check the box marked "Completed listings," results for auctions that have ended will come up. You'll still see auctions that failed to meet their starting bid mixed in with the successful auctions, but this is much more useful information. Now if you see an auction with a high starting price that did not get a bid or an auction that failed to meet its reserve, you may not know the exact worth of an item, but you do know it's not worth as much as the seller was asking. In addition, you can also see all the auctions for toy trains that ended successfully, and these auctions can give you an indication of your product's value.

Figure 11.2
eBay allows you to refine your search using the Search Options box on the left of the screen. Notice I've restricted my search to "Completed listings" and have included a price range of $50 to $200.

If you look again at Figure 11.2, you'll also see that you can type price ranges into the search criteria. So if you are looking for more-expensive collectible toy trains, you might want to put a price range that would capture only high-end auctions. On the other hand, if you are a toy seller, you may want to put a price range of $1 to $20 to eliminate the high-priced collectible trains.

Do not check the **Include title and description** box, because this will bring up every auction that has your keyword in the description, which could be thousands, depending on your keyword. For example, if you do a search for the keywords *old fountain pen*, checking the **Include title and description** box would bring up every auction with the word *old* or *fountain* or *pen* anywhere in the description.

Because using a single word for your search can return hundreds of auctions, you might want to narrow the search even more to get down to a more specific need. For example, suppose you are looking specifically for Omega watches as opposed to just any watches. You would want to use the *AND* keyword function in your search. In the search field, enter *Omega watch*. This will return a list of all results with the words *Omega* and *watch* in them and exclude all that do not contain both words.

If you are looking for items that include certain phrases or words that go together in a specific order, you can narrow your search even more. Suppose you are searching for teddy bears. If you put quotation marks around the two words *teddy bear*, eBay will return a listing of all auctions with the words *teddy bear* in them. The word *bear* must immediately follow the word *teddy* in the title listing, or the listing will not show up in your search.

If you are searching for items that might be listed under multiple words, you can use the **OR** keyword function in your search. For example, if you want to find all auctions that have in their title listing the words *cat* or *kitten*, then you would enter **(cat,kitten)** in the search field. This would return all auctions that have either the word *cat* or the word *kitten* in their listing. Make sure you type the parentheses and *don't* put a space between the comma and either word. You can also include other keyword functions. For example **crystal (cat,kitten)** will return all items that have crystal and either cat or kitten in the title. Note: there is a space between the word "crystal" and the parenthesis, but not after the comma between "cat" and "kitten".

eBay's search engine can also locate auctions with one word, but not another. If you are looking for watches but are not interested in Casio watches, use the AND NOT keyword function. In the search field, you would enter **watch –Casio**. This would return all results whose listings include the word watch, but exclude all listings that include the word Casio. Note: there is no space between the minus sign and the excluded word. Spending time playing with eBay's search feature until you are an accomplished searcher will put money in your pocket.

You can also use eBay's search feature to perform a lot of marketing research. If you are about to sell a new product, look at all the auctions for that product and related products, and analyze them. What can you do better? Can you improve on the listing title? How does the description read? Can you write a better one?

What about the photographs? Was it an RPA (reserve price auction) or did the auction start with a low bid or a high bid? Compare two auctions for the same or similar products. Which one got the most bids? You get the idea.

More than 80 percent of all people looking for products on eBay use the search feature. As we have just seen, you find products by typing in keywords. If you knew the most-searched keywords on eBay in any given category, you would know what people are looking for. If you know what people are looking for, you can use that information when deciding what to sell.

What are the popular keywords that people are searching? An easy way to find the most sought-after keywords is to visit eBay Seller Central at pages.ebay.com/ sellercentral.

This Seller Central page (see Figure 11.3) is a very valuable resource for eBay sellers. You can find a wide variety of information on the site, including teaching tutorials, information on top-selling items, and a monthly keyword research tool.

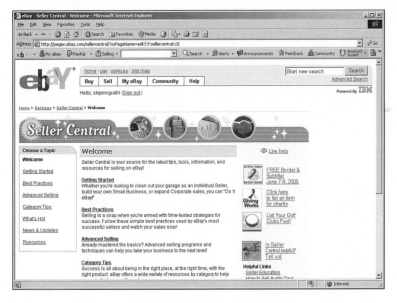

Figure 11.3
The Seller Central page on eBay.

If you look at the navigation bars on the left of the page, you will see two items related to research: **Category Tips** and **What's Hot.**

Figure 11.4
Seller Central's Category Tips feature.

Click **Category Tips** first, and you will see a list of the major eBay categories followed by category-specific strategies and resources, as shown on Figure 11.4. Take some time to explore this page, but for now, click **In Demand** under the **Jewelry** category.

Figure 11.5
Seller Central's results for Jewelry In Demand.

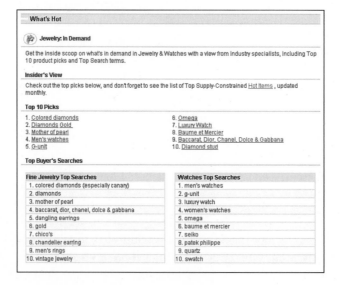

This will bring up a list of subcategories with the highest sell-through rates in the past month (Figure 11.5). It will also show a list of the top ten keywords for each subcategory—in this case, jewelry and watches.

Now let's explore the **What's Hot** feature. Find it on the left of your screen, under **Choose a Topic.** You will be presented with two options, **Merchandising Calendar** and **Hot Items by Category** (see Figure 11.6). The merchandising calendar presents a schedule for special eBay promotions, which we cover in Chapter 37. For now, click **Hot Items by Category.**

If you have Adobe Acrobat Reader installed on your computer, clicking this link will open your Acrobat reader. A report will open that lists every category on eBay with an associated *hot list* of the most-searched keywords in that category. Take a few minutes to print out the report, because this is a very valuable research and marketing tool. (I cover this report in Chapter 36 when we talk about keyword promotions.)

Figure 11.6
eBay's What's Hot page.

Look for the product categories and subcategories for the products you are selling or considering selling. Now do a search using the eBay search engine for the products that pique your interest. This will help you determine the price and supply-and-demand situation and lead you to your main competitors.

Although the eBay What's Hot report is free, it has two shortcomings. Because it's only published monthly, the information is always a little out of date. Also, the Adobe PDF file format does not allow you to drill down to get further information.

But for those of you looking for more current information in a format that's easy to search through, there's good news: third-party research tools are available that offer much more current information at relatively low prices.

11.5 Third-Party Market Research Tools

Several third-party market and product research tools are available to the eBay seller. Unfortunately, none of them are free, but all of them are reasonably priced and, in my opinion, a good value for what they deliver.

11.5.1 HammerTap Research

HammerTap has built a successful business supplying eBay buyers and sellers with auction management, launching tools, and research tools. HammerTap3, the latest release of their research tool, is very popular with experienced eBay sellers.

HammerTap3 is powerful software that can analyze any eBay market sector and produce detailed market research reports. You download the software to your PC and access the data by connecting to the HammerTap website. After you download the data and open the program, you are presented with several function tabs that will open to individual windows.

Unfortunately, I cannot show you screen shots of HammerTap reports because their user license prevents sharing data; however, you can see examples of the HammerTap website at www.hammertap.com. I contacted HammerTap and arranged a special discount for readers of this book. If you go to www. hammertap.com/skip, you will receive a $7.00 per month discount.

When you first go into HammerTap, click on the **Auctions** tab. This tab lets you scrutinize individual auctions to reveal winning eBay strategies based on data such as …

- Most popular.
- Starting price.

- Total sales.
- Auction duration.
- Average sale price.
- Average number of bids.
- Reserve auction sell-through rate.
- Which category items are listed in.

In Chapter 12 on competitive research, I examine the individual auction features of HammerTap in greater detail.

You can also perform competitive research on other eBay sellers. If you visit the **Seller**'s tab, you can access the following information:

- Sell-through rates
- Total sales
- Average bids per item
- Average sale price per item
- Most successful sellers

HammerTap also has a Reports page, which you can use to generate data about the auctions included in your research. This information helps you pinpoint specific eBay strategies to get the upper hand on auctions for a specific product or category. You can view information such as total sales in an eBay category, sell-through rates, ASP, Dutch auction statistics, and reserve auction statistics. You can analyze a particular item to see how much it might sell for, and you can find the best techniques for selling it. Find out how much your competitors are *really* selling in your marketplace. Some sellers list a lot but don't sell very much. Others have high sales with few auctions.

PowerSeller Tip

Your Sell-Through Rate (STR) is a very important measurement to track. The STR is the ratio of auctions that you list versus the number that close with a sale. Anything over 50 percent is considered good on eBay. (Over 65 percent is considered excellent.) If your STR is below 50 percent, you'll need to make a very high margin on each sale to remain profitable. STRs and other important business metrics are covered in more detail in Chapter 55.

HammerTap also enables you to strategize which categories would be best for your items by viewing bid data, sell-through rates, and average sales. You can easily increase your sales by knowing which items receive the most bids and which sell for the most.

eBay is a constantly changing marketplace. I like to follow the categories I sell in over time by periodically saving analysis reports to my hard drive and comparing them for changes. I can then continually compare my own activities by season and look for both positive and negative trends in my own selling activities.

11.5.2 WorldWide Brands Market Research Wizard

WorldWide Brands is a company started by Chris Malta, a successful eBay PowerSeller and website entrepreneur. Chris is also the product sourcing editor for eBay Radio and a frequent exhibitor at eBay Live.

WorldWide Brands offers access to direct wholesale sources and drop shippers. Their service is offered on two levels. Level one comes with all their wholesale information and a market research tool called Market Research Wizard (MRW). MRW is an eBay interface that scans eBay store sales for listings and prices that show you how much competition there is for a given product and what it is currently being offered for. Their upgrade product adds 20 hours of training videos on the wholesale industry.

The MRW is a program you download onto your computer that connects with the Internet and the eBay database. When you type a product name into the search box, in seconds it comes back with the market information related to that product. The data includes ...

- How much demand there is on the Internet for that product.
- How much competition you will be up against.
- What kind of advertising others are using to sell that product.
- Who your competitors are.
- How much your competitors pay for advertising.
- What the eBay auction listings and bids for your product are.
- What keywords your competitors are using.

At the end of the data, the wizard gives you a graphical chart that shows the probability of successful sales online. Interestingly, this is the only tool I have found that predicts product sales success both on the web through a web store and on eBay. You can download a free trial version of the Market Research Wizard at www.worldwidebrands.com/mrw/free_trial.asp.

For more on sourcing products to sell on eBay, see Chapters 19 and 25.

For more on competitive research, see Chapter 12.

For more on Dutch Auctions, see Chapter 14.

For more information on critical business metrics, see Chapter 55.

Competitive Product Analysis

Competition factors into everything you do on eBay. Almost every eBay top seller I know spends at least two hours a week looking at his competitors' auctions and analyzing their performance relative to his own.

Your research goal as it relates to products should be twofold. First, you need to determine if there is a market for a product on eBay. And second, you need to see if you can buy it at a low-enough cost and sell it at a high-enough price to make money.

12.1 Finding Your Competitors

In the early days of eBay, all you had to do was find a product at a good price and launch an auction. There was very little competition. For example, in 2001 the digital camera category had fewer than 1,000 cameras listed on any given day, and sellers enjoyed sell-through rates of over 50 percent. Today more than 10,000 digital cameras are listed every day, and conversion ratios in this category have fallen to below 30 percent. That means that on average you have to list your camera three times in order to complete a successful auction, which in turn means you will pay eBay three listing fees for each successful auction.

Does this mean you shouldn't sell digital cameras? Not necessarily. If you analyze the auctions for digital cameras, you'll find that although only 30 percent of auctions close successfully, some sellers are closing over 60 percent of their auctions. This is where it pays to analyze your competition.

Why is one seller closing a high percentage of auctions when another is not? What is he doing differently? What listing and pricing strategies is he using? All of this is very helpful information for you to know. Before I launch a new product on eBay, I always take the time to find all of my competitors, identify the most successful ones, and examine their auctions and listing strategies.

To find your competitors, you could do a search for completed listings and simply look at all the sellers, but an easier way is to use HammerTap (see Section 11.5.2). If you want to look beyond eBay to the whole World Wide Web, then you can use the WorldWide Brands Market Research Wizard (Section 11.5.3). You can search by product type (in this case digital camera) or by specific product (such as Nikon D70 or Canon EOS Rebel), and see who is selling them. If you sort the data by the most successful sellers by product, you can examine the auctions of each successful competitor.

12.2 Are Your Competitors Making Any Money?

The first question you should ask when you look at competitors' auctions is whether they are making any money. Using HammerTap, first look for the competitor with the highest conversion ratio.

Next, look at his average selling price (ASP); subtract the estimated cost of the product (you have to do some educated guesswork on this one) and the eBay and PayPal fees, and determine his profit margin. Is he making any money? If he is selling dozens of cameras a week and making only a 15 percent or less margin after fees, then his business is marginal because overhead and inventory carrying costs can easily eat up this small margin. If he is making a 25 percent margin but only selling a couple of cameras a week, he is making money on each of his individual auctions but not much money overall.

Now look at the most successful auctions to determine what is being done differently from other sellers with lower conversion ratios. Do they offer free shipping? Are they offering package deals that include a tripod and camera case? Do they start their auctions at a low price to attract early bidders? Are they using a reserve? How much detailed information do they provide about the product? Do they offer any type of money-back guarantee? What day do they start and end auctions? Do they use any eBay listing upgrades? What is their feedback score and positive percentage? List these and any other information that seems relevant.

Now move on to the competitor with the highest average selling price (ASP). Ask the same questions about this seller and write down your answers.

Now compare your auctions to theirs. What are they doing that you are not? Can you find a pattern? Factor in the costs of shipping, and determine whether the seller who offers free shipping is really making any more money than the one who is not. If a seller is getting a lot of bids by starting his auctions at a low price, does he ever get stung by having to sell a camera lower than his cost?

All this information is there for the taking—you just have to learn how to find it, analyze it, and apply it to your own situation.

12.3 Can I Make Money with This Product?

This is a question eBay sellers must constantly ask themselves. Unless you have found that one dream product and control its source of supply, you will always have varying levels of competition. And keep in mind that all of the other top sellers are looking at the same reports and using the same research tools you are.

The biggest mistake I see eBay sellers make is to purchase a product without first performing the necessary market research. Given the tools available, there is absolutely no reason to jump at a product offering, no matter how good it seems, without first determining whether you can make money selling it on eBay.

The last thing you can, and should, do is test. If you want to source your products at the lowest price, you'll have to buy in large quantities. But I will often pay more for a product to get a small quantity solely for the purpose of testing. I know going in that I probably won't make a lot of money buying at this higher price, but that's not the point. The reason for the test is to control my risk. If I buy a dozen of a given product and it doesn't sell at a profit, I have only tied up a little bit of money. But if I bought a pallet load and it didn't sell, I could be stuck with a large amount of unprofitable or even unsaleable inventory.

For more on researching your competition, see Section 15.2.

chapter 13

Pricing Strategies

How you price your products to get that first bid will have a great impact on your final selling price and how often you convert your auctions into sales.

There are several options—and just as many theories—as to the best way to price an item on eBay. One school of thought says to start all items at $1 with no reserve to create excitement and bidding activity. Others say you should always start your bidding at your cost to avoid the possibility of selling at a loss. And still others claim it's best to go ahead and start your auction at the minimum price you are willing to accept. We'll examine all these strategies, but I can tell you now, there is no one correct answer. You should base your strategy on the product you are selling, the demand for the product, and what your competition is doing.

Before we look at the various pricing strategies, you need to understand your costs. I spend more time on inventory and overhead costs in Chapter 16, but this information will give you a foundation to better understand your costs as they relate to selling both low- and high-priced items.

13.1 You Make Money When You Buy, Not When You Sell

I considered another title for this chapter: *Buy Low and Sell High*, which is actually a quote from the famous investor Bernard Baruch. Back when Wall Street was a wild, unregulated bastion of free enterprise, Baruch made $200 million before he turned 35.

Legend has it that one day in the late 1930s, Baruch was sitting on a park bench just outside the New York Stock Exchange eating his lunch, when a young trader sat down next to him. After some polite small talk, the young trader asked Mr. Baruch a very direct question, "Sir, you are the most successful trader on Wall Street. Would you be willing to share the secret of your success with me as I am just starting out and want to be successful?"

Bernard Baruch looked at him, thought for a minute, and then said, "Young man, the secret to my success is to always buy low and sell high."

This same advice holds true on eBay today. Here is the biggest secret of Platinum and Titanium PowerSellers: *you make money when you buy not when you sell.* If you can buy a product at the right price and if it has a market on eBay, you will make money on it.

eBay has two basic listing strategies. You can sell low-priced products in high volume, or you can sell higher-priced products in lower volume. Of course, there is a third strategy: you can also sell high-priced products in high volumes, but that is very hard to do and takes more capital than most of us can find.

There are risks and rewards to both strategies. If you are a high-volume seller of low-priced items, you will have to work much harder and longer to be successful. Just think, if you are selling a $10 item and making a $4 gross margin, you will need to close 100 successful auctions a week to make $400—and that's before your other costs!

13.1.1 Low-Price, High-Volume Selling

Some large PowerSellers specialize in low-cost items. Many of them have more than 2,000 auctions running at any one time and are closing from 100 to 300 successful auctions a day. To run this kind of auction you will need help— whether that's a spouse working with you or a full- or part-time employee.

How much you should pay for merchandise depends on what you're selling. When I buy any type of used or closeout/surplus merchandise that will sell for less than $100, I try to pay between 10 and 20 percent of the original retail price. For example, if I buy a pallet load of 200 surplus/closeout designer blue jeans from Liquidation.com, I might pay $4 a pair. Add another $2 for shipping, so my cost is $6 a pair or $1,200 for the whole pallet.

I expect that at least 10 percent of the merchandise on the pallet will be defective or essentially unsaleable. (Somehow this always happens no matter how careful you are.) That leaves me with 180 saleable pairs of jeans, so my cost is now $6.66 a pair.

Because these are designer jeans (Hilfiger, Polo, Gloria Vanderbilt, etc.), they probably carry a retail value of $39 to $49 a pair. Remember on eBay, however, I am not getting full retail; I'm looking to sell at the "quick sell" price. So let's say I start the auctions at $9.99 a pair and realize an average selling price of $24 a pair. That brings my total gross to $4,320 for the 180 pairs sold. Less my basic cost of $1,200, my gross margin is $3,120. Now let's look at the other costs:

eBay listing fees at 0.35 pair	$63.00
eBay Final Value fee (8.75 percent)	$378.00
PayPal Fees (est.)	$199.80
Box & packing material ($1 each)	$180.00
Total Additional Costs	$820.80 (rounded to $821)

I will assume I'll charge actual shipping, so that is a wash. Although in reality I could make as much as $1 per pair on shipping without gouging the client (see Section 33.1 and Chapter 40).

Take my gross margin of $3,120, subtract the other costs of $821, and I get a net margin (not profit) of $2,299. Divide that by the 180 jeans I sold, and I netted $12.77 per pair. That is pretty good. If it took me a week to sell the jeans, I'm making almost $2,300 a week before overhead costs. That is why I speak here of net margin—not profit. I don't make a profit until I pay (or subtract) my other costs, such as telephone bill, salaries, and general office expenses.

If I have a part-time employee helping out and I keep my other expenses low, I should be able to run my business for less than $500 a week. That means I would be looking at a net profit of around $1,800 per week. Of course, it might take more than a week to sell the entire lot. If it takes two weeks, I'm still making $900 week on the jeans alone. I should also have other auctions for other products going on at the same time.

I suggest you grab your calculator and go through this exact same exercise, but put in different cost points. What would I net if my cost was $9.75 per blue jean or $11.50? Determine the point at which my net profit is not worth all the work and other costs. That will answer the question at the beginning of this segment: how much should I pay for merchandise? I recommend you do this exercise now, before reading further, because it goes to the heart of a lot of the material I cover later in this chapter.

PowerSeller Tip

You can get a free auction fee calculator at www.ebcalc.com. This is a great tool for tracking and projecting your fees.

13.1.2 High-Price, Low-Volume Selling

Now let's look at the other scenario: selling high-priced goods in low volume. A few years ago, the U.S. Air Force sold off over 4,000 older model Palm PDAs on www.govliquidation.com, and individuals could purchase a minimum lot of 25. Even though this was an older model, there was still a market, but the average selling price was about half their original price, approximately $150 each. I watched that auction, and most of the lots sold for about $1,400 or about $56 each. If you were to sell all 25 over a two-week period at an average price of $145, you would gross $3,625. Less your cost of $1,400 + $100 for shipping, your net would be $2,125 or $85 a unit. Now I'll let you do the math to subtract the eBay fees (approximately $8 per item) and the PayPal fees of about 2.9 percent plus 30 cents per transaction (approximately $4.50 each). Shipping and handling material would be minimal because they all came in sealed boxes.

After you do the calculations, do them again to determine the highest price you would pay for these items where you could still make a *worthwhile* profit. Don't forget to subtract a percentage for your overhead. My nondirect overhead averages about 13 percent of my monthly sales, and you can use that figure if you don't yet have your overhead costs established.

The high-priced item route involves greater risk—you need to purchase large amounts of expensive merchandise. Now this is not a problem if you (1) have already tested the market and know it will sell and (2) have a *reliable* source of supply. Notice that I emphasize the word reliable. For example, will your supplier stand behind its merchandise if it is defective?

Most large PowerSellers are always on the lookout for new products and new sources of supply, but they tend to work with a small handful of suppliers at any one time. If you are going to have a steadily growing business, developing a strong relationship with these suppliers is critical.

13.1.3 Even Higher Price, Lower Volume

Now for the final exercise, let's go way up in value. Last year the wholesale club Costco (yes, Costco) was selling Cartier men's gold watches for $2,650. These watches retail at Cartier boutiques for just over $4,200. I called my wife at home and asked her to search eBay to see what that particular watch was selling for. She found one that had sold for $3,412 and another one that went for much less at $2,977. I averaged the two out and came up with a realistic probable selling price of $3,195. That would give me a gross margin of $545 per watch. I bought three watches and sold them over a three-week period. I did a little better than the average, because my three sales were $3,478, $3,290, and $3,410, which made my average sale $3,392. Less my costs of $2,650, I made $742 per watch.

Let's take a look at the costs per watch:

eBay listing and selling fees:	$117.14
PayPal fees:	$99.32
Total	$216.46

I made a gross margin of $742 per watch but only netted $525.54 on each watch at the end. My eBay fees were a little higher than normal because I used a reserve to protect myself on such high-priced items.

No one can tell you what to pay for something. You just have to test and do the research yourself to determine what to pay for any given item—and that research has to be based on how much you can sell it for.

Remember when researching items to sell on eBay, only use the search option for **Completed Listings.** The Completed Listings will show you all auctions that have closed, including those that closed but didn't sell. Better yet, also use Hammertap's research tool (www.hammertap.com/skip), which shows you the percentage of items that sold, the highest and lowest price it sold for, the average selling price, and much more.

13.2 Pricing Strategy #1: Low Starting Price

Now that we understand how to calculate costs and overhead, we can consider our pricing strategy. A large number of eBay PowerSellers believe that you should start all auctions at $1 with no reserve and let the market determine the final value.

The main advantage to this strategy is that low starting prices tend to attract more bids. If you were looking for a new Apple iPod on eBay and you saw one auction starting at $199 and another starting at $1.99, which one would you bid on? (All other factors being equal.)

Most people will bid on the lower-priced item. On a popular product, such as an iPod, a digital camera, or a brand-name piece of apparel, both items will sell for a good price, but the item that started lower will usually sell for slightly more, because a greater number of bidders will be vying for the item. So if you are selling an item you know is in high demand, the low starting price usually works out best.

PowerSeller Tip

No doubt, $1/No Reserve auctions can get *a lot* of action. Before doing this, though, check the recent history of the item. Does it normally sell for a price that you would be willing to accept? Is it commonly sniped at the last minute? If there is a risk of losing a lot of money on the item, be sure you can handle the loss and keep a close eye on how often you list the item.

As a rule, most eBay buyers find hidden reserve auctions frustrating and aggravating. If you are scared to death of losing money on an item, try starting your bid at the lowest price you'll accept instead.

You might get fewer bids, but at least you won't annoy potential buyers.

—Mike Enos, www.platinumpowerseller.com

The other advantage of starting an item at a low price is a lower eBay Insertion fee. eBay Insertion fees are determined by the listing price; the higher the listing price, the higher the Insertion fee. The Final Value fee is based on the final selling price of the item, so this is not a factor in your starting price.

The low-price strategy works well as long as you are selling an item that is in high demand. But what if you are selling an expensive piece of jewelry by a designer whom no one has ever heard of? If you start the item at a low price, you might not get enough bids to reach your cost. In this case you would actually lose money on the item. Instead, you might try to reserve a minimum price. As you're probably aware, eBay offers a feature called the Reserve Price Auction (RPA).

An RPA is an auction where you place a secret reserve price on an item. For example, suppose you are selling a very specialized piece of machinery. Your cost was $2,000, and you are hoping to sell it for much more. Because the market for this piece of machinery is so specialized, you are concerned that it will not get enough bids to reach your cost, so you place a $2,000 reserve on the item and start the bidding at a low price, such as $199, to attract attention. (It isn't really credible to start such a high-priced item at $1, although some sellers do this routinely.)

Whenever someone bids any price below your $2,000 reserve, their bid will be posted, but they will receive a message in their bid confirmation that says **Reserve Not Met.** New bidders coming to the auction for the first time will see the current bid price, and *Reserve Not Met* beneath the current bid price. Once the bidding reaches your reserve price, that line disappears and all future bidders will never know that there was a reserve on the auction.

This strategy has a couple advantages. First, you'll tend to get more bids because of the low starting price. This is important because items on eBay that already have bids tend to attract more bids. Any experienced eBay seller will tell you the first bid is the hardest one to get.

The other advantage is obvious: you don't have to worry about the item selling below your cost.

However, there are some disadvantages to using an RPA. For one, eBay charges a fee for the reserve in addition to the listing fee. If you listed an item at $199 with no reserve, the listing fee would be $2. But because you place a reserve on the item, eBay will charge an additional $2 reserve fee. On amounts over $199.99, eBay charges a reserve fee of 1 percent of the reserve amount up to a maximum of $50. So on a $2,000 reserve, this fee would be an additional $20. This can add up if your items end up not selling. Plus, your Insertion Fee is based on the reserve price, so your Insertion fee is $4 instead of $2.

The larger disadvantage to using an RPA is that many buyers do not like reserves, and some bidders refuse to bid on RPAs. They can clearly see if there is an active reserve on the auction before they ever place a bid, so some will just leave your auction as soon as they see the "Reserve Not Met" tag. You can't do anything about this except hope there are enough reasonable bidders out there to drive the price up to your reserve. There are no hard statistics on the percentage of people who will not bid on RPAs. Anecdotally, we know it is a significant percentage from eBay-led focus groups and postings on the various eBay message boards.

Some sellers think you will get more bids if you reveal the reserve amount, and I happen to agree. I go to Alaska a couple of times a year and buy very expensive Native American Eskimo art and artifacts that I sell on eBay. The market for these items can be very hot, but it is very small. I recently sold a beautiful antique Baleen basket for more than $2,000 that I purchased in a small native village for $700. I started the bidding at $199 with an RPA of $900. I placed the following statement in my auction:

> I don't like reserves and seldom use them. But my cost of this item was fairly high and the number of Baleen basket collectors is fairly small, so I have placed a reserve of $900 on this basket, which is well below its true value.

I actually received e-mails from people thanking me for showing the reserve amount. The basket attracted 14 different bidders and a total of 42 separate bids before it sold.

To summarize, low starting prices will attract more bidders and have the advantage of saving hundreds or even thousands of dollars in eBay fees over a year's time. But this strategy works best on popular items. If you are selling items that are not in high demand, it is better to use a cost-based selling price (see Section 13.3) or use a Reserve Price Auction. Personally, I have had more success with the Reserve strategy.

13.3 Cost-Based Starting-Price Strategy

A cost-based starting price is nothing more than starting your listing at your cost. The advantage is that you don't have to worry about losing money because the item cannot sell below your cost.

If your cost is a fairly low percentage of the usual final selling price for the products you are selling, this is a great strategy because potential bidders will recognize the difference between your starting price and the true value. I recently bought 12 dozen pairs of Ralph Lauren Polo tennis shoes for $18 a pair. The full retail price of the shoes was marked on the box at $97.95. I started the shoes at just above my cost at $19.99. It took about three weeks to sell the entire lot, and at the end my average price was in the range of $44 a pair—just over double my cost.

There is a slight fee disadvantage to listing at cost. In the preceding example, had I listed the shoes at a 99¢ starting bid, my listing fee would only have been 15¢. By starting the bidding at $19.99, my listing fee was more than triple at 55¢.

My primary concern was that I had so many different sizes, some of which are not popular. In fact, at least 10 pairs of shoes sold at their listing price of $19.99 and never attracted another bid. I made enough money on the other shoes to easily make up for not making any money on the other pairs. If, however, I had listed all the shoes at 99¢ and those six pairs sold for some ridiculously low price, my overall margin would have been much less.

I wish I could give you a formula for setting listing prices so they minimize fees and risk and maximize the final value, but it just isn't possible. Setting starting prices on eBay is somewhat of a black art; it just takes experience to develop a feel for what works. The best advice I can give you is to experiment. If you purchase a batch of identical or even similar products, try listing a few of them at different starting prices, both with and without a reserve, and see what works best. You might lose money on one or two items, but you just might maximize your return on the whole lot.

13.4 Buy It Now Pricing

eBay originally developed the Buy It Now (BIN) listing option to offer impulse buyers a chance to buy on eBay without waiting for an auction to end. BIN has been a huge success. At between 5¢ and 25¢ per listing, it's the biggest bargain on eBay. BIN has become so popular that eBay created a fixed-price auction where you set a BIN price and that is it. Because its price is fixed, it's not really an auction at all. You are just listing an item on eBay at a Buy It Now price. In the Fixed Price format you can not only set a fixed price, you can also list an unlimited quantity of items for the same fee.

How does Buy It Now work? The Buy It Now price is a price you determine that you are willing to take for the item you are selling at any time during the auction. However, the BIN price disappears after the first bid is placed (although eBay is experimenting with allowing the BIN price to remain visible on some categories. Because eBay's Best Match tends to favor auctions in the order of their ending time, most auctions on eBay do not attract bids until they have been up a few days. Therefore, your BIN price will usually be available until you get closer to the end of an auction.

Some bidders, who see your item and are interested in it, will often place a low bid just to get rid of the BIN price so they won't lose out to another buyer who might not want to wait for the end of an auction. When I am buying antiques and collectibles on eBay, I do this all the time.

BIN pricing tends to work best when you are listing your items with the cost-based pricing model. If you list your products at a low starting bid such as 99¢, you'll attract bids quickly, thereby killing the BIN price.

BIN pricing has a lot of advantages and really no disadvantages that I can tell. Running a successful eBay business requires you to turn your inventory over quickly and as many times as possible. Every time you turn your inventory over, you have more money to invest in more inventory, and this is how you grow your business. If you list all your items for seven days and they all sell, you're doing great. But let's face it, not every item sells. According to eBay, only 41 percent of all auctions result in a conversion (completed sale).

If you list your merchandise for seven days and a percentage of it sells within one, two, or three days using the BIN feature, then you are increasing your conversion ratio and turning your inventory over more often.

How should you set your BIN price? This is easiest when you are selling merchandise you are knowledgeable about and used to selling because you have a good feel for the price/value relationship. Keep in mind that the primary advantage of BIN is faster inventory turnover, so you don't want to set the BIN price at the high end of what your items usually go for. If I had an item that I bought for $10 and my selling prices ranged between $18 and $24, with $19.90 being the average, then I would set my BIN price at the average level. That would attract the most impulse buyers and result in more instant sales.

PowerSeller Tip

Another way to encourage bidders to use BIN is to offer them an incentive to do so. Around the holidays I usually offer free shipping with BIN orders. I simply add the estimated shipping cost to my BIN price. People who are shopping for Christmas gifts are usually in a hurry and looking for bargains. Also, eBay Best Match search favors items with free shipping for higher placement in search.

We once purchased a quantity of Fitz & Floyd Santa cookie jars just before Christmas. Our cost was $42 each. Normal retail (MSRP) was $129. I launched some of the jars right away in a three-day auction, and they all sold for around $85 each.

I only had a three-week window to move them so they would ship in time for Christmas, so I came up with the following strategy.

I live on the West Coast, so I calculated the shipping price to the East Coast, which was $9 via priority mail. I figured my average selling price was $82, so I simply added the $9 to the $82 and arrived at a BIN price of $91.

Then I launched the auctions and placed a BIN price of $91, with free shipping to any BIN customer. We put three individual auctions up every day in a series of three-day auctions. I purchased the eBay subtitle option. (This subtitle appears below the listing headline, and eBay charges 50¢ for this option.) The subtitle said "FREE U.S. Shipping for Buy-It-Now Customers."

We sold about one BIN cookie jar a day the first week. By the second week, as we were getting closer to Christmas, we were selling two a day. The final week, I put the remaining 33 units up in a series of one-day and three-day auctions, and almost half of them sold at the Buy It Now price.

BIN auctions have another benefit as well: when you do a search on eBay, the items come up in the order of those ending soonest. If you launch a BIN auction with a high starting price at the same time (within a minute or so) of a regular auction with a low starting price, bidders will see both auctions in close proximity to each other when they do a search. If someone sees a BIN auction with a starting price of $29 and another auction just above or below it on the search list where the bidding is around $9, they will get a "perception of value" from seeing the BIN auction, and that will tend to increase bids on the regular auction.

Then as bids on the regular auction get close to the $29 of the BIN auction, impulse buyers will be tempted to buy the BIN item now rather than wait for the auction to end. In other words, each auction supports the other one.

13.5 Second Chance Offer Strategy

In 2003, eBay introduced a new feature called the *Second Chance Offer* (SCO). Originally, the SCO was designed to offer the second-highest bidder the chance to buy at her losing bid price in the event the winning bidder did not pay and became what eBay calls a Non-Paying Bidder (NPB). The feature was very successful, and in 2004, eBay modified and expanded the feature so you could offer any under-bidder a second chance to buy in the event you have more than one identical item to sell.

Suppose you have an auction for a teddy bear and get the following bids:

Bidder	Amount Bid
Albert	$19.00
Betty	$21.00
Charlie	$22.50
Albert	$23.55
Betty	$24.55
Albert	$26.99
David	$33.55
Albert	$36.50
David	$39.25
Charlie	$42.50
Betty	$43.50

Betty wins the teddy bear at $43.50. Let's assume you are happy with any bid above $39 and that you have several identical teddy bears in stock. You can offer both David and Charlie a Second Chance Offer to buy a bear at the price they bid. David would get a bear for $39.25, and Charlie would get a bear for $42.50. Here is the best part: you would pay eBay the Final Value fee on all three sales, but you only pay the listing fee on the bear that Betty, the highest bidder, won.

Best of all, you have sold three items for a total value of $125.25 for the time and effort of placing only one auction.

The Second Chance Offer is pretty much automatic. When an auction ends, you simply click the link of the under-bidders you want to send an offer to, and eBay sends them a link to a special page where they click the **Accept** link if they want to buy. When they do this, a PayPal window opens up, and they just have to click to buy if they want to pay via PayPal. There are several advantages to the SCO. As already noted, you save money on eBay listing fees. Perhaps more importantly, you do not have to tip your hand, showing that you have more than one item, thereby preserving the perception of scarcity. Finally, you get to make multiple sales from one auction listing. In the preceding example, if your acceptable margin had allowed you to accept any bids over $36, you could have even had a fourth sale to Albert, who bid $36.50.

For more on pricing strategies, see Section 11.4, Chapter 15, and Appendix B.

For more on managing inventory, see Chapter 16.

For more on shipping see, Section 33.1 and Chapter 40.

chapter 14

Dutch Auctions

A Dutch auction is when you see an auction-type listing offering two or more *identical* items. eBay calls this a Multiple Item Auction, but most buyers and sellers still use the term *Dutch auction*, and I use the terms interchangeably here. In a Dutch auction the seller is offering multiple, *identical* items for sale. Unlike a regular eBay auction, Dutch auctions can have many winners.

When listing items using the Dutch auction format, you set the minimum price you are willing to sell for and specify the quantity you have for sale. The person who bids the lowest for the last available quantity sets the price for all winning bidders.

When someone bids on a Multiple Item Auction, he specifies the *number* of items he's interested in and the *price* he's willing to pay per item.

Winning bidders pay a price equal to the *lowest winning bid*. Winning bids are selected in order of bid price per item. For example, a bid for 5 units at $12 per unit is ranked above a bid for 10 units at $11 per unit. If two bids have the same price per item, the earlier bid is given priority.

Suppose you're selling cubic zirconium earrings. You have 10 pairs available and have set a minimum bid price of $9.99. Here's how such an auction might play out:

Bidder	Quantity Bid On	Bid Amount Per Item
A	1	$29.00
B	3	19.00
C	3	17.00
D	1	16.55

continues

continued

Bidder	Quantity Bid On	Bid Amount Per Item
E	1	15.95
F	1	14.99
G	2	13.50
H	3	11.90
I	1	10.50
J	3	9.99
K	1	9.99
L	3	9.99

At the end of the auction, the 10 highest bidders *by quantity* would win the item for what the tenth-highest bidder paid. In this example, bidders A through F would each get as many earrings as they bid on at a price of $14.99 because this was the price bid by the lowest successful bidder (F).

There were 12 different bidders and 29 total bids by quantity, but only 10 items were available. So only the bidders who bid more than $14.99 would win. Be sure you understand the concept before bidding on or listing a Dutch auction.

You can determine whether an auction is a Dutch auction by looking at the quantity information (see Figure 14.1). If more than one item is available, it's a Dutch auction.

Figure 14.1

Whenever you see more than one item listed in the "quantity" information for an auction, you are looking at a Dutch (multiple item) auction.

Vector Permanent Hair Removal Electrolysis NEW +FREE SH
FREE SHIP & $30 Cosmopolitan Virtual Make Over CD!

You are signed in

=*BuyItNow* price: US $199.99

Buy It Now >

Time left: **4 mins 22 secs**
5-day listing, Ends Jun-15-05 14:46:18 PDT
Start time: Jun-10-05 14:46:18 PDT
Quantity: 5 available
History: Purchases
Item location: 24 HOUR SHIPPING & CREDIT CARDS ACCEPTED!!
United States
Ships to: United States
Shipping costs: FREE - Standard Flat Rate Shipping Service (within United States)
Shipping, payment details and return policy

14.1 Dutch Auction Product Strategies

Not every product is a natural for a Dutch auction. First of all, realize that all the items must be identical. If you had a lot of one dozen Izod polo shirts, in order to sell them at a Dutch auction, they would all have to be the exact same size and color.

However, there are some exceptions to the identical rule. I once had a large lot of tektites. Space buffs and rock hounds collect these tektites, which are made when a meteor impacts the earth. The impact and the heat it generates turns the sand and dirt instantly into glass and spreads these glass pieces over miles of earth downwind from the meteor.

Each tektite is approximately the same size, but they come in all different shapes, and I had about 500 of them. It would have taken forever to list and sell 500 separate auctions, so I put them in a Dutch auction format where each bid was for a lot of 3 tektites selected at random. I set up several auctions with each one consisting of 50 lots of 3 starting at $9.99 per lot.

Apparently there are a lot of tektite collectors out there. The bidding became fast and furious, with many bidders bidding on five or more lots, and I was getting final value prices of over $25 a lot. (Later I learned why. It seems that tektites of the size and quality I was selling go for around $25 each in museum shops and nature stores.) In one of my auctions, one bidder bid $30 a lot for 25 lots.

You can also use Dutch auctions to sell wholesale lots. Let's go back to the example of the Izod polo shirts. If you purchased an entire pallet from a surplus dealer, you might end up with several hundred shirts. You could assemble lots consisting of one dozen each mixed lots that include shirts of different sizes and colors and sell the lots in a Dutch auction where you list one dozen lots at a time. Other eBay sellers will bid on the lots to break them up and sell the shirts in individual auctions. Of course, you can do this, too. I often buy a large quantity of goods to get the best price. I sell anywhere from one half to two thirds of the goods in a wholesale large-lot auction using the Dutch auction format. This strategy typically results in a fairly small margin, sometimes as low as 15 to 20 percent. I then sell the rest of the items individually and can realize margins as high as 75 percent because of the low price I paid. If you are going to do this, sell your individual items first before eBay is flooded with the high number of individual auctions from those who buy your wholesale lots.

14.2 Dutch Auction Listing Strategies

Dutch auctions tend to work best for common consumer products—electronics, computer parts and accessories, brand-name apparel and accessories, software and games, and information products such as "how to" and "make-money" books.

The minimum quantity for a Dutch auction is two items. However, it is somewhat impractical to sell only two items this way, and you will almost certainly get more by selling them individually. I generally don't use a Dutch auction unless I have at least 5 items, and 10 or 12 is even better. Be careful about listing too many items in one auction. Remember that you are trying to use the concept of scarcity to push up the prices. When I was selling the tektites, I did it over a three-week period in several auctions. Had I listed all 500 pieces in one auction, I never would have realized the high prices that I achieved.

If you start the bidding at a low price, you'll need to convince potential bidders of the value and/or scarcity in your item description. There are several ways to do this.

14.2.1 Make Sure Bidders Know the Retail Price

If I am selling an item that still has the manufacturer's retail price tag on it, I mention the retail price in the description and show a close-up photo of the price tag (see Figure 14.2).

Figure 14.2
When selling new items that still have the retailer's price tag on them, always include a close-up photo of the price tag in your auction listing.

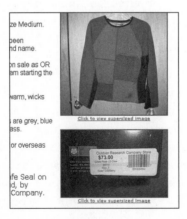

Earlier I told you about the wholesale lot of Ralph Lauren tennis shoes I sold. I found a web store that was selling the same shoes for almost twice what I was asking as a starting bid and placed a link to it right in my item description. Potential bidders could click the link and see what a bargain I was offering. Unfortunately, eBay no longer allows linking to off-eBay websites. To show the bargain, take a screenshot of the page that shows the product and the price and put a caption under the photo that says, "Here is what other websites are selling this product for." Or simply list the retail price and let the buyer do a Google search for it if they want to verify that price.

14.2.2 Maintain Sense of Scarcity

Let's return to the issue of scarcity. You might think that only economists understand the law of supply and demand, but I assure you that eBay bidders, a very savvy bunch, understand it as well. Think about when you bid for something on eBay. You type a keyword into the eBay search box for the product you want and up comes every listing for that keyword. If you want to buy a new digital camera and type in the keywords *digital camera*, you are presented with literally thousands of listings. This tells you there is an excellent supply of digital cameras on eBay and leads you to believe you can get a really low price. Now you narrow your search to a make or model you want. If you search for a make, such as Nikon, Kodak, or Sony, you still find hundreds of auctions. After you type in a specific model number, such as Nikon D-90, you'll finally have a manageable list to select from—probably between 50 and 200 items.

Now you start looking for your bargain. The really savvy eBayer will usually perform a Completed Listings search and see the price range of the auctions that have actually closed. This will give you the high and low ranges for that specific product.

When you start clicking the individual auctions, you'll notice two things. Some of the auctions will be Dutch auctions, and many of the auctions are listed by the same seller. If you see a seller with a large quantity of stock, you know this seller has plenty of inventory. If many auctions are ending soon and do not have bids, you can be sure that prices are, or soon will be, falling. If you really need a camera now, then you might bid. But if you are like a lot of people, you might decide to wait a week or two because prices are likely to fall even more.

Now that you know how savvy eBay bidders think, take this into account when listing your products. If you are selling digital cameras and have a large supply but are one of very few sellers of that particular model, you might want to sell them over a longer period of time. But if there is a large supply of the items you are selling, you should consider launching a number of auctions or even a Dutch auction with a starting price or a Buy It Now price at the lower end of the price spectrum so you can get rid of your cameras before the price falls further.

Digital cameras are probably a bad example simply because there are so many sellers. But no matter what you are selling, even if it is a niche market product, you never want to tip your supply hand. Recall my example of the tektites. Had I launched a Dutch auction with all 500 units, a lot of bidders would have realized I had a large supply and would not have bid until the last minute. Bidders know that auctions with a high number of bids create more interest and more bidding. Smart bidders will wait until the last few minutes of the auction to bid so they don't help drive up the price through their interest. However, when a bidder sees that the supply of something he wants is very low, he will often place a higher bid immediately to make sure he wins the item.

14.2.3 Launch a Standard Auction Along with Your Dutch Auction

The third technique I use to push bids on a Dutch auction higher is to place a Dutch auction for a quantity of the goods I am selling and launch a standard auction at the same time for a single item. However, on the standard auction I will list a starting price higher than the Dutch auction and an even higher Buy It Now price.

So let's review the three basic ways to drive bids higher on Dutch auctions. First, be sure to tell the seller the price or value of the item and, if possible, back this up with a photo of a price tag or a screenshot of a website that shows the higher retail prices. Second, control the quantities you list so you do not tip your supply hand. Finally, launch a standard or a fixed-price auction along with your Dutch auction that shows the items at a much higher price than you are starting off with in the Dutch auction.

14.3 Dutch Auction Pricing Strategies

When we looked at pricing regular auctions in Chapter 13, we discussed three basic strategies: starting at a low price such as one dollar, starting at a low price with a reserve, or starting at either your cost or the minimum you are willing to accept. The reserve price auction is not available on Dutch auctions, so we don't have to worry about that one. With a Dutch auction, you have the additional variable of quantity. This requires some additional caution on your part because you risk losing more money if you make a pricing mistake. Just as with a standard auction, a low price in a Dutch auction will attract more early bidders than a high price. This is important to keep in mind, because people are more willing to bid after they see another bid has already been placed. The good news is that, besides researching products (see Chapters 11 and 12), you can also research product quantities. To do this, look at the current auctions and see what quantities are available. Next, look at the completed listings and see how many products similar to yours have sold over the past week. This will give you a sense of the demand for the product.

HammerTap can help here, too, because the data table shows you how many of an item sold per auction listing.

14.3.1 Listing Your Products at a Low Price

If you have a low starting price and a very high quantity, you run the risk of dozens of bidders bidding at your minimum price. Making matters worse, after all the bids are placed, some items might not have gotten bids. Now you are stuck with selling to everyone at a ridiculously low price *and* having leftover inventory. If you have a large quantity of a high-demand product, it's usually best to list only a small batch of the product at a low price, so bidders will drive the bottom price up above the price you need to make a profit. You can repeat this process until you sell through your inventory. I would caution you, though, that this only works when there is real demand and the supply of similar goods is limited.

Remember one of the golden rules of selling on eBay: you always want to provide the impression of scarcity. Listing a large quantity of products at a very low price leads potential bidders to believe there is a large supply of a product available. It discourages impulse buyers and might make potential bidders wait until the end of the auction to see if they can win an item at your minimum price.

14.3.2 Listing Your Items at Cost

The other Dutch auction pricing strategy is to list your items at your cost or the minimum amount you are willing to accept. This strategy works best when you know you are selling a product that is in high demand. With this strategy, there is no risk that you will sell an item below its cost, but unless you are selling a really hot item, you might find it difficult to attract early bids.

After reading this, if you get the feeling there isn't really a perfect solution, you are correct. As I've said before, auction pricing, whether for Dutch or standard auctions, is largely a matter of experience and feel. Research helps, and I advise you to take the time to research not only prices but also quantities available, quantities sold, and the percentage of auctions that close for a given item you are trying to sell.

In the end, your pricing strategy is based on two factors, supply and demand. If supply is low and demand is high, you will always do better starting your auctions at a lower price and letting bidders drive the prices up. If supply is high and demand is medium, I recommend starting the item at your cost or a price that reflects your minimum acceptable margin. If demand is low and supply is high, set a price that will allow you to liquidate your inventory with the least possible losses.

Keep in mind, though, that sometimes supply imbalances can be temporary. If another seller suddenly comes onto eBay with a large supply and you are sure there is a continuing market for the product, wait him out. Don't wait too long, though, because cash is king, and you don't want to be stuck with nonperforming inventory.

For more on fixed-price auction strategies, see Chapter 40 and Section 44.2.

chapter 15

Niche Marketing Strategies

In the early days of eBay, the site was predominately used to sell collectibles, including sports cards, comics, toys, and Beanie Babies. In its first two years, almost every eBay seller was essentially working in a narrow product area or a niche.

A category is not a niche. For example, if you sell all kinds of toys, you are a toy vendor. If, however, you only sell action figures, you work in a niche. Selling only digital cameras used to be considered a niche, but today the digital camera market on eBay is so large that you would have to sell only one brand of cameras, such as Nikon, to be considered a niche in the camera market.

15.1 Benefits of Niche Marketing

Two primary benefits of niche marketing exist: sourcing and selling.

15.1.1 Sourcing

The more time you spend in a market or product category, the more knowledgeable you become about all the sources of supply for that market. And the more you know about a product itself, the more easily you'll be able to make better buying decisions.

When I was in the antique business, I sold a broad line of eighteenth- and nineteenth-century American antiques. Within that category, I specialized in the niche of early American woodworking tools. After a couple of years

I developed an expertise and a feel for the products; I could recognize makers, spot reproductions, and knew what tools were in high demand from collectors. After I developed the expertise, I could instantly recognize which products would realize the highest return, and my profits shot through the roof.

Remember our adage on pricing: you make money when you buy, not when you sell. As I gained knowledge about my niche, I became a more savvy buyer and was able to spot bargains. Plus, as word spread that I specialized in old wood-working tools, people with things to sell started seeking me out. At one point I routinely bought tools and sold them at markups of 200 to 300 percent.

When you decide to specialize in a niche of any kind, the first thing you want to do is become an expert in that area. Learn and read everything you can about it. Study the history of the product, and get to know the companies that manufacture the product and their distributors. The more you know, the better you will be able to buy.

15.1.2 Selling

The very fact that you are selling in a narrow market segment means you will have less competition and can therefore command higher margins. In addition, people prefer to buy from someone who is knowledgeable. For instance, Terry Gibbs is one of the largest and most well-known sellers of antique toys on eBay. People seek him out for his knowledge and his integrity. Everyone knows that when Terry describes a toy in one of his auctions, the description is accurate; he doesn't sell fakes or reproductions; and he will stand behind everything he sells. If you are selling something and you get a question, as an expert or a specialist you will be able to answer the question with the authority and detail that will give the bidder instant confidence and, more than likely, result in a bid.

Another selling advantage of niche marketing is the ability to accurately describe products in your auction descriptions. The added knowledge you have from being a specialist enables you to add more data and insider information that only a specialist would know. A potential bidder looking at your auction will have more confidence and perhaps bid more liberally than she otherwise might.

A final advantage of niche marketing is the ability to purchase inexpensive keywords in pay-per-click search engines we will discuss in Section 38.1. The very fact that you are working in a narrow niche means fewer people are bidding on the same keywords that you are.

15.2 Finding the Right Niche

Finding your niche is a matter of research and brainstorming. You might already have a hobby, interest, or life and work experience in an area that would make a good sales niche on eBay. This is where you should start. Work is always more fun—and usually more profitable—if you are doing something you like. If, for example, you enjoy computers, this is a great area in which to start your search for a niche.

Many people, even large companies, sell computers on eBay, so you would need a large amount of capital to compete. But the computer field has many subcategories, and there are many niches within these subcategories. Back up hard drives are a subcategory, but mini or portable drives could constitute a good niche. It takes a lot less capital to buy and build an inventory of flat-screen monitors than it does an inventory of complete computer systems. You could buy monitors in lots of 100 for what 20 complete computers would cost.

Another area might be all the little accessories, such as modems, wireless network hubs, cables and connectors, computer speaker systems, and so on, that one might need to go along with his computer.

Perhaps you like travel—specifically, you like to travel off the beaten path. Selling in the broad travel category can be daunting, but maybe you could work with a local travel agent and package adventure tours or specialty tours and sell them on eBay.

DVDs & Movies is a very large category crowded with hundreds of sellers. Yet several players within the DVDs & Movies category have found niches selling old movies, how-to DVDs, educational DVDs, documentaries, and so on.

The same thing goes for Music CDs and DVDs. Entering the broad music category could be difficult, and it would take a large amount of capital to compete, but you might be able to carve out a nice niche in jazz, folk, or alternative rock— or you could get very specific and sell something as narrow as bagpipe music or patriotic music.

Almost any broad category on eBay has subcategories, some of which are small enough to qualify as niches, and others in which you can find a niche. The key is that the niche you find must be active enough to generate large sales and not be crowded by hundreds of other sellers.

If you find a niche that is already dominated by one large seller, don't let that stop you if you think you have the ability to compete. By studying your competitor's auctions and policies, perhaps you can find a way to compete that doesn't require one of you to fail for the other to succeed.

After you have identified several potential niches that interest you, start your research. Use the eBay keywords report to see if people are searching the terms or keywords for the items you want to sell. Next, use the eBay search engine and HammerTap to determine the viability of the market. Using HammerTap, you can also further drill down into the categories you are interested in.

You might find a very profitable niche, but it may not be deep enough to sustain a large eBay business. It's no good to totally own a niche if the monthly Gross Merchandise Sales (GMS) is only $3,000. You want to look for a niche that will support a minimum of $25,000 a month in GMS—$50,000 is even better. Sometimes you can combine related niches. Going back to the computer example, you could sell monitors and keyboards. If you go into the automotive area, you could sell both performance exhaust systems and air-intake systems. These are two different products from different ends of the vehicle, but performance enthusiasts often buy these two components to improve the horsepower of their cars.

When you find a potential niche, ask yourself these questions to help decide whether it's viable:

- Is this niche large enough in terms of potential GMS to run a sustainable business? (Remember that it should have a minimum GMS of $25,000 a month.)
- Do I have or can I obtain the knowledge and expertise to work this niche?
- Does the product area interest me?
- Is the competitive situation in this niche manageable?
- Do I have a reliable and cost-effective source of the goods to supply my niche market?
- Are the margins for these products large enough to run a sustainable business?
- Can I expand the niche, or are there complementary products I can cross-sell and up-sell?

You don't have to totally own your niche to be successful, but you will need to be one of the handful of major players to have consistent, predictable, and long-term success.

15.3 Expanding and Maximizing Your Niche

After you find your niche and establish a position as the dominant player or at least one of the top two or three dominant players, you want to look for ways to secure and expand your market share. The techniques for doing this fall into several categories:

- Price control
- Depth and breadth of product
- Promotion
- Branding
- Customer service

Let's take a look at each one in turn.

15.3.1 Price Control

The main advantage of niche marketing is price control. Hopefully you have found a niche where there is little competition, which will enable you to command higher prices. However, be careful not to gouge customers. You want to build repeat customers, so you want them to leave every auction feeling they have scored a bargain.

You want to charge a price that is high enough to meet your margin objectives while being competitive with the other sellers in your area. But that doesn't mean you have to be lower. If you have a large inventory of products, many customers will come to you for that reason alone. Earlier we used the example of selling one type of music, such as folk music, within the Music CD category. If you have hundreds of auctions for different folk artists and albums, your auctions will be coming up almost every time a potential bidder does a search. Over time, folk music buyers will come to recognize your auctions, your format, and your username. If they buy from you and have a good experience, they'll be willing to pay a little more for the peace of mind they get dealing with you. That is one of the advantages of working in a niche.

A competitive price is one that is close enough to other sellers in your area that it won't chase potential bidders away. If, for example, you offer to combine shipping on multiple purchases and your competitor doesn't, you can get away with charging a higher price because the customer can still realize a savings.

If you are in a competitive niche and have the capital to purchase inventory in such large quantities that you can go far lower than your competitors, you can often make more money by selling at a low price in high volume, while driving any marginal competitors out of your niche in the process. If you don't have the capital to do this, then you'll have to secure your market share with other techniques.

15.3.2 Depth and Breadth of Product

If you're going to control or at least be a major player in any niche, you need to have enough product depth and breadth to serve your market and make it difficult for other players to compete with you. Depth of product refers to the quantity of each item you have on hand. Referring to our example of folk music CDs, you might only wish to inventory one copy of more obscure artists, but you'd want a good supply of the popular artists so you could always have at least one listed in your auctions or your eBay store. Breadth of product refers to the number of different artists and albums you carry. If you only list 20 different artists or albums, you don't have much breadth.

Another example might be automotive performance parts. If your niche is Ford Mustangs, you need to offer a wide variety of parts spanning several model years to achieve a breadth of products. If your niche is all 1990 to present Japanese cars, you'd only need to carry the most popular performance parts to achieve a broad product range.

You can take this example into almost any area. As a stamp dealer, you could specialize in only airmail stamps, but you'd want to carry airmail stamps from at least the dozen or so largest countries that issued them.

> **PowerSeller Tip**
>
> Having access to a breadth and depth of product can give you a controlling position in your chosen marketplace. Lacking depth or breadth enables your competitors to siphon off your customers.

15.3.3 Promotion

Promotion is another key to dominating your niche. I won't describe the specific promotional techniques here, as Chapter 36 covers that subject, but I want to explain why it's so important to promote yourself and your products.

eBay's special features can be expensive if you use them on a large number of auctions. For example, the **Bold** feature only costs $1, but if you launch 500 auctions a week using the Bold feature, you're spending $500 a week on bolding alone. Considering that even successful sellers close only 60 percent of their auctions, you are wasting $200 of that $500. Instead of using promotional features indiscriminately, use a special feature such as *Bold or Category Featured* on auctions for really popular merchandise—the ones you know will get a lot of eyeballs—or for products with a high sell-through ratio. Now promote your eBay store listings and your other auctions in the body (item description) of that auction copy. Invite readers to click to these other items with clickable HTML links embedded in your auction copy.

The single best promotional tool you can use is the eBay search engine. eBay's internal studies show that 80 percent of all items sold on eBay are found by bidders using the search engine. Because bidders type keywords into the search box that find the products they seek, it's essential that you learn all the relevant keywords for your products and use them in the auction titles.

Another way to promote your auctions is off of eBay. Lots of people, surfing the web looking for specific products, might eventually find their way to eBay but don't usually start there. Your eBay Store main page is basically a web page. As such, it can be indexed and found by search engines. If you have an eBay Store, use a search engine submission service to submit your storefront to search engines and shopping portals. You can also submit a single auction to a search engine, but this is often simply too much work for something that only lasts five or 10 days.

The field of submitting and promoting your website to search engines is very specialized, fast-changing, and the subject of numerous books; it is something you should discuss with your web master. If you are your own web master, you should set aside some time to study this important area.

However you decide to do it, do spend some time promoting your auction listings and your eBay Store. In sections 47.4 and 49.3, I explain how your website and your eBay Store can promote and feed off of each other.

PowerSeller Tip

It is a little-known fact that eBay will credit you 75 percent of the Final Value fee for any item sold in your eBay store when the buyer landed on one of your eBay Store pages from outside of eBay. For example, if you were selling old Joan Baez recordings and someone did a Google search and found your website with a link to your store listing and clicked through to it and purchased the album, eBay's technology will credit 75 percent of your Final Value fee to your account.

Some large eBay PowerSellers actually purchase pay-per-click services to drive traffic to their eBay Store in this fashion.

Another little-known fact is that eBay has an affiliate program. If you join the program (link from the eBay site map) and a person who has never bought on eBay before clicks your listing, registers on eBay, and buys his first product within 30 days of registering, eBay will pay you between $1–$50 (depending on the number of buyers you refer) . This is in addition to the 75 percent final-value fee credit. You can get the details and the complete eBay referral fee commission schedule at www.ebaypartnernetwork.com

15.3.4 Branding

Branding goes to the heart of your niche marketing strategy. If you're going to be the major player or even the dominant player in your niche, people have to recognize you. For this reason you might want to consider an eBay username that reflects the products you sell. Here are some examples:

One_Cent_CD

FolkMusicForYou

PerformanceCarParts

ElegantJewels

GreatOldToys

GadgetGalaxy

Art_Print_Warehouse

A memorable username is just that: memorable. People will recognize it when they see your auctions. If a buyer had a positive experience, he might search for your auctions instead of typing in a keyword to search for a product he knows you sell.

You want to create a template that shows the name of your business and "brands" your auctions with a standard look and feel. eBay has several standard templates, but they change these from time to time, so you would lose your look and feel whenever this happens.

If you use an auction management company such as Vendio, InkFrog or MarketWorks, these companies offer both standard and custom templates. However, I suggest you design your own because other clients of your auction management company will also be using the standard templates, which could cause confusion among buyers.

Auction templates are simple to design. Any competent web designer should be able to create a template for you for about $100. After you have the code, you can use it if you launch auctions directly on eBay or with any auction management company. This gives you the most freedom and the ability to change services any time you want without losing your branding.

15.3.5 Customer Service

The whole point of promotion and branding is to get the customer to remember you and, even better, to seek you out. Some customers remember who gave them a great price, but all customers remember who treated them to great service and a fun buying experience.

If you have breadth and depth of product, competitive prices, quick, friendly, and accurate communications, and delivery of the product as promised, customers will remember you. And that's the whole point of promoting yourself.

In Section 49.3, you learn about driving business from eBay to your website, which is where things really get profitable. Why? Because when you sell from your website, you're not paying eBay any fees. Every sale from your website nets you anywhere from 5 to 10 percent more margin on every sale.

If you meet or exceed your customers' expectations, you will find it very easy to drive customers to your website, where you can market to them in total freedom without eBay's fees and restrictive rules.

For more on product niches, see Section 11.1.

For more on keywords, see Section 38.1.

For more on promoting your website and your eBay store, see Sections 47.4 and 49.3.

For more on branding your niche, see Chapters 2, 44, and 53.

chapter 16

Managing Your Inventory for Profit

The inventory you buy to sell on eBay represents the largest financial commitment you make as an eBay seller. It also involves the largest element of risk. If you are going to be a large eBay seller, you have to carry large amounts of inventory. How you manage this inventory can be the difference between going Titanium and going bust.

16.1 Understanding Your Inventory

You must understand your inventory before you can manage it. The first thing you need to know is what and how much inventory you have. Have you ever been in a supermarket or drug store and seen people walking around with hand-held scanners for counting inventory? Large businesses know how critical inventory is to their profits, so they keep close tabs on it.

If you don't know what you have, you can't control it. If you only sell 5 or 10 different products, your task is fairly simple. You just need to know how many you have of each item. You can probably use a simple spreadsheet program combined with physical counting to track your quantities and your burn rate, or how fast you go through your inventory. If, on the other hand, you sell a wide variety of products, you need some form of automated system. There are two basic types: offline software (usually combined with a bar code reader) and online systems.

Software-based inventory systems are really designed for a retail store or warehouse environment. They work very well but are difficult to integrate into auction software or an online auction management system. For this reason, most eBay sellers rely on the inventory control modules available with the larger online auction management companies.

Most of the auction management companies, such as Vendio, ChannelAdvisor, MarketWorks, and InkFrog, are inventory-based. Instead of launching an auction, you first go into the system and create an inventory item. Each item includes the images you will use with the auction, a description of the item, the quantity on hand, your cost per unit, and a part number or SKU number.

When you launch an auction using one of these auction-management companies, a glance at your control panel will show you how many units you have on hand and how many are at auction or in your eBay Store. If an auction ends without a winner, the item is posted back to your inventory total. If it sells, it is deducted from your total.

You still have to perform occasional physical counts. After all, items can get broken, or you can make the occasional clerical or counting error. I think it's especially important to do a physical count as my inventory gets low. At least once a year, I manage to launch an item on eBay that I don't have. This is really embarrassing when the item sells, and I don't have one to ship, and usually ends up with me having to pay more (sometimes retail) to find one quickly to protect my feedback rating.

The benefit of online inventory control combined with an auction-management service is the convenience of handling both your inventory status and auction management all in one place and the level of automation it provides. The shortcoming is that these systems provide status but not true inventory management. Inventory management consists of understanding how well your inventory is performing and the ability to forecast inventory needs.

Besides the quantity on hand, you need to be able to analyze your inventory data in order to manage your stock. Some key things to consider are …

- **Burn Rate.** How fast are you going through your inventory?
- **Lead Time.** How long from the time you order does it take new orders to arrive?
- **Quantity/Cost.** What are the minimum and maximum quantities you can order and the cost implications of each?

- **Influence Factors.** Are there any seasonal trends in play? Is your burn rate the same now as it will be three months from now? Are there any economic trends in play or on the horizon that could affect your burn rate? Are there new products on the horizon that will kill sales of your current inventory?

Any item sitting on your shelf is costing you money in two ways: carrying cost and opportunity cost. Carrying cost is nothing more than the interest cost. If an item sitting on a shelf costs you $10, how much interest at current rates could you earn if that $10 was sitting in a savings account? If you finance your inventory, then your carrying cost is the interest you pay on that item each month that it doesn't sell. Opportunity cost is the profit you lose by having that $10 tied up in a nonperforming asset. If you have one category of product that sells very well and very quickly, then buy more of that product. The money you have tied up in nonperforming inventory is money you don't have available to buy products that do perform (sell).

Think of your inventory as the good, the bad, and the ugly:

- Good. You make money selling it.
- Bad. You break even or lose money selling it, but it leads to other profitable sales.
- Ugly. You lose money selling it, and it doesn't lead to other profitable sales.

Unless you closely monitor and analyze your inventory, you won't know which category your products fall into. Once again, if you only sell a few different items, this is very easy to stay on top of. On the other hand, if you specialize in selling folk music records and CDs, you might have hundreds of different titles. Staying on top of what is selling well and eliminating the slow-selling items can really make a difference in your profits.

Because not all inventory is the same, you have to manage it differently. I prefer the ABCD approach to monitoring and controlling my inventory. Simple and easy to do, it works like this:

- My A inventory is my most profitable inventory, the inventory that sells regularly and generates the highest margins. It might not be the best-selling product I have, but it is the most profitable.

- B inventory is the merchandise that has the greatest impact on cash flow. These are not necessarily the most expensive items I carry, but they could be. For example, if I sell a low-cost product that moves in high volume, then I need to carry a lot of this product. This might tie up quite a bit of my cash flow, because I have to purchase in large quantities and have a lot of stock in hand.

- C inventory is that inventory I need to have on hand because my customers expect me to carry it; it sells well enough to stock and is a manageable amount with a minimal impact on cash flow and opportunity cost.

- D inventory is everything else.

The A items fall into the category of the "good." These are the products you want to order more of and identify additional sales channels to move them through. If you are selling as many of these A items on eBay as you can, you might want to expand your sales efforts to Yahoo! and Amazon on the theory that if they sell well on eBay, they'll sell well in other places, too. Or maybe you put additional A items up in your eBay store to appeal to fixed-price buyers. When you identify an A item, work to maximize those sales.

You want to tightly manage and control the B items because they have the greatest impact on your cash flow. For example, if your supplier has a minimum order quantity of 500, you could try to work out a deal where you get the 500-unit price if you purchase 500 items over a 60-day period. This way you can order 100 items every two or three weeks so your cash is not tied up in inventory that takes three months to sell.

You need to manage the C items so you only carry the bare minimum of stock on hand. Even if you have to pay more to order smaller quantities, it's better to do this than to incur negative carrying costs and opportunity costs. I will gladly accept a smaller margin on these sales to free up cash to buy more A items.

D items usually fall into the category of the bad or the ugly. Try to sell off the bad items even if you make very little or no margin, and get rid of the ugly items at any price you can get.

16.2 Inventory and Cash Flow

Inventory, more than any other factor, has the greatest impact on an eBay business owner's cash flow. How you manage your cash flow will determine how fast you can grow your business.

The best way to control cash is to be careful of what—and how much—inventory you buy. Remember, when inventory is in storage, it is not making you any money, so plan what you purchase and how much of it you purchase very carefully.

QuickBooks gives you excellent visibility into your cash flow. You can pull cash flow reports daily, weekly, or monthly. Whenever you're about to make a large purchase, plug the amount into QuickBooks and run a report to see the effect it will have on your cash flow. Make sure you do not put yourself into a position where you'll run short of cash before the inventory starts generating sales.

One of the best ways to conserve cash is by negotiating credit terms with your suppliers. One mistake many people make is to constantly shop different suppliers, looking for the best deal. You might save pennies on the dollar with your purchase, but this will not endear you to your suppliers. When you ask them for favorable credit terms, they'll be less likely to grant them because they know next month you'll be buying from their competitors. I recommend that you establish solid relationships with reliable suppliers. If you pay a few pennies more for something but that supplier gives you 60 days to pay without interest, that is probably worth more than the few pennies you might save with someone else.

When you borrow money from your bank or a commercial lender who finances inventory, they have only one way to make money—the interest they charge you. A supplier has two ways to make money: on the goods he is selling you and by charging you interest on his credit terms. Because your supplier has another means of making money, you can often negotiate better terms with him than with your bank or commercial lender.

On the reverse side, many suppliers will give you generous discounts for paying cash. When you get a quote from a supplier, you will often see payment terms that look something like this:

2 percent Cash/1 percent 30/Net60

What does this mean? It means that if you pay your supplier cash on delivery, he'll give you a 2 percent discount. If you pay within 30 days, he will give you a 1 percent discount, and if you pay within 60 days, you just pay the full amount with no discount.

Now if you have plenty of cash flow and don't have to borrow to finance inventory, then you should take the 2 percent cash discount because you'll make an extra 2 percent on everything you sell. That can really add up over the course of a year. If, on the other hand, cash is tight, then take the net 60. You are getting 60 days of free money. If you can move most all the inventory within 60 days, you are essentially running your business on your suppliers' nickel instead of your own. These deals do exist, but they won't be offered to you if you continually shop your suppliers and make them compete against each other for your business.

16.3 Maximizing Inventory Turn Rates

Your inventory turn rate is how many times you sell through your inventory in a year. A mega-store such as Wal-Mart will turn its inventory over completely several times a year. As an eBay or website seller, you want to do the same thing. The more often you turn your inventory over, the more money you have to invest in more goods to repeat the process and to grow your business. There is no better way to improve your cash flow and boost your profits than by increasing your inventory turn rate. Inventory is not static, and everything sells at different rates, but let me use a static example to demonstrate the point, as doing so makes the concept easier to understand.

Suppose you sell expensive watches. Each watch costs $625. We will assume you have just enough cash to purchase 25 watches at a time. You sell the watches for an average selling price of $999 on eBay, and it takes six weeks to sell all 25 watches.

Your margin on each watch (before fees) is $374, or $9,350 on all 25 watches. Let's make the assumption that you could sell more watches if you lowered the price. For example, if you lowered the price to $925, you could sell all 25 watches in three weeks instead of six weeks. Your margin would drop to $300 per watch or $7,500 for all 25, but you would earn this $7,500 in three weeks instead of six weeks.

What is the effect over a year? There are 8.6 six-week periods in a year. So 8.6 × $9,730 (your original margin) works out to $83,678 per year. By lowering your price and accepting a lower margin per sale, you sell more watches in a year. There are 17.3 three-week periods in a year. So 17.3 × $7,500 = $127,750 per year. That's an increase of $44,072! Now admittedly this is a highly simplified example, but the point is important: if you can increase your turnover rate by lowering your price, you stand a good chance of making more money. Of course, this only works up to a certain point. You wouldn't want to sell your watches for $695 even if you could sell many more because your fees, overhead, and other costs would make this nonproductive. Besides, there is probably a limit to how many watches you can sell on eBay in any one-, two-, or three-week period.

The trick is to experiment to find the right balance between price and inventory turn while being mindful of the supply and demand situation. If you start selling too many watches at too low a price, you risk further eroding the price and eating into your profits.

Another advantage to faster inventory turn is pricing. The more times you turn your inventory over, the greater quantities you'll be purchasing from your supplier, and this will put you in a position to negotiate better pricing. The better pricing will somewhat mitigate the lower margins you receive by lowering the price of your product.

For more on inventory management, see Chapters 41 and 44.

For more on controlling cash flow, see Section 54.2.

chapter 17

The Drop Shipping Business Model

Drop shipping, one of the most highly debated subjects among eBay sellers, works like this. You place an item up for auction that you haven't purchased yet in the hopes that it will sell. If it sells, the buyer sends you the full (retail) price. You then send the supplier the lower wholesale price along with the buyer's address, and the supplier ships the product directly to the customer. You keep the difference between the retail and wholesale price.

I cover the types of manufacturers and distributors in great detail in Part 3, but you need to understand some basic wholesale concepts now to understand drop shipping. There are several levels of wholesale supply: manufacturer, importer, distributor, and subdistributors (also called middlemen and aggregators). The closer you get to the manufacturer, the lower the prices are but also the higher the quantities you must purchase. (However, there are exceptions to this, as you will see.) When you buy from an importer—or distributor in the case of domestic manufacturers— the prices will be slightly higher, but you can typically purchase slightly smaller quantities. When you get to a subdistributor or middleman, the price again goes up, but the quantity can get quite small—even as low as one unit.

Now that you have a basic understanding of a few of the key players on the wholesale scene, let's take a closer look at drop shipping.

17.1 The Drop Shipping Dilemma

What could be better than drop shipping? You take no risk, have no inventory to carry, and can launch hundreds of auctions for hundreds of products you don't have to purchase unless they sell. Right? Well, sort of. It is true you don't have to invest in inventory, but because you are essentially buying in very small quantities, you are dealing with a middleman who cannot afford to give you a truly wholesale price. Also, selling a product you don't have actual possession of involves some risk. What happens when you sell an item only to find out the supplier ran out during the week the auction was running and now you have nothing to deliver? This can earn you bad feedback, which can also impact the visibility of your other items in the Best Match search results.

The other factor is the eBay Insertion fee, which is a percentage of the starting price. The higher the starting price, the higher the fee. Unless an item is highly popular and in very high demand, you cannot risk starting your bid at a price lower than your cost of the product. Most drop shipping sellers start the items at their cost, which means they have to pay a higher Insertion fee. If you consistently list dozens of items listed at high fees and only a percentage of them sell, then the high fees will take a serious bite out of your margins.

PowerSeller Tip

In late 2008, eBay reduced the Fixed Price shipping fees to only 35 cents per month on most items, and you can list an unlimited quantity of items. You can also set your listings to relist automatically every 30-days. This reduces your risk of listing lower margin items and fits right into the drop shipping model.

Does all of this mean drop shipping doesn't work? Not necessarily. You need to solve two basic problems for drop shipping to work: finding products at a cost low enough to profitably sell on eBay, and controlling your eBay fees.

You can solve the first problem with a little bit of research. You'll need to perform extensive product research to find products to sell profitably using this model. First you need to research the selling side. What products are selling (that are available from drop ship suppliers), and what is the supply/demand situation? Because margins are typically lower when dealing with drop shipping suppliers, it is vitally important to find products with very little or no competition. You'll be looking for very narrow niche or unusual products that no one else is selling.

Here is an example. Swarovski crystal is very popular on eBay, being one of the highest-searched keywords on the site. Most people are searching for Swarovski crystal figurines and small crystal collectibles. I found a manufacturer that put a colored LED light into a piece of Swarovski crystal and put it on a pendant. The Jewelry category is very crowded, so I listed the pendants in the Swarovski Collectibles category, where collectors would see it. My cost on the pendants was $21 each if I purchased in quantities of 100, but the company would drop ship them individually for $24 each plus a $2 drop shipping fee.

I didn't want to risk $2,100 buying a large quantity because I wasn't sure they would sell. Other sellers were selling lighted pendants on eBay, but they were just glass or plastic and sold for less than my cost on the Swarovski units. So I decided to go the drop shipping route. I listed the pendants at $29 each in a series of five-day auctions, launching a new auction every two days.

I sold more than 40 of the pendants over a two-month period before the sales slowed down. My ASP for the first few weeks was over $44—an $18 margin per item—and about 70 percent of my auctions closed successfully. After two months, my ASPs started to fall, and my auctions began closing at a lower rate. I tried launching them in the jewelry category, but I only sold three or four. This was a perfect example of how drop shipping should work. Had I bought 100 pendants, I would have made much more money on the 40 pendants I sold, but as the novelty wore off and the sales slowed down, I would have sold the remaining pendants at a much lower price—doing a lot of work for very little money. Conversely, had they kept selling really well, then I would have the knowledge and confidence to go ahead and place a large order.

The key to success was finding a product that had virtually no competition and finding a location (the Crystal Collectibles category) where there were interested buyers and few competitors.

In this case I was dealing directly with the manufacturer of the product, so I was also getting a much better price than I could get from an aggregator.

17.2 Drop Shipping Aggregators

Drop Shipping Aggregators (DSAs) are essentially middlemen. These companies purchase products in small wholesale quantities (thereby not getting the best price), mark them up a small amount, and put them on a website for sale to eBay and other online sellers on a drop ship basis. There are dozens of these companies on the web, ranging from some very small, specialized companies to large operations that sell millions of dollars a year.

Some of the more popular ones include the following:

www.doba.com

www.dropshipdesign.com

www.megagoods.com

Most of these companies charge a membership fee to join or tack a special drop ship handling fee on top of the normal shipping and handling or both. To serve their market, they have to carry thousands of different products. For example, Drop Ship Design advertises that they carry more than 350,000 products. When you carry this many products, you simply cannot buy in the very large quantities that get you really low wholesale prices.

Here is an example of a product from a large DSA. Garmin GPS units are very big sellers on eBay, and I found a Garmin Nuvi 780 on a large drop shipping website. The retail MSRP was $899 for the complete kit, but this company was offering the same kit for $665. It's looking good so far. This particular company charges a $25 sign-up fee and a $4 drop ship fee on each product sold. In addition, they were quoting $22 for shipping and handling, which brought my total cost to $691

I searched the complete auctions on eBay and did a search for completed auctions for the Garmin Nuvi 780 and came up with about 200 different listings. The listed prices ranged from a low of $605 to a high of $999, *but none of them had sold at those prices.*

That's not to say that someone couldn't make money on these units. For instance, an online retailer not affiliated with eBay might be able to sell this particular GPS at a higher price on a website to someone who knows the normal retail is $899. But on eBay, where everyone can see all the auctions and all the products offered, I would never get a bid if I started my auction at my cost of $691. If I started at a lower cost and used a reserve price auction, I might get some bids, but it's unlikely the unit would sell for anywhere near a profit.

So where did the drop ship companies get their units? I did a little digging and found a light bulk wholesaler who was selling the same Garmin units for $545 in lots of 24 units and for $525 in lots of 48 units. The drop ship companies were probably buying at the lower unit rate of $525 and selling them for $665.

This example shows how difficult it can be to sell a highly popular and competitive product on eBay using the drop ship middlemen or aggregators. However, you can find products to sell if you take the time to find items that are not as popular and competitive.

Because I was already signed into the drop shipper's website, I spent some time looking around in related electronics and automotive categories. I soon found a digital automotive compass with barometer and altimeter that mounts on a car dashboard. The MSRP retail was $99 and the drop ship company was selling them for $42 + $4 drop ship fee + $6.90 shipping. My total cost would be $52.90. I looked on eBay, and no one was selling anything close to this particular item.

Because no similar products were listed, I didn't really know if it would sell, so I decided to launch an auction for one unit with a starting price of $49 + $6.90 shipping.

At the end of the 7-day auction, I had four bidders who placed 11 bids, and the compass sold for $82.55. This looked pretty good, so I launched another auction with a lower starting price of $19.99 to see if it would attract more bidders. The second auction brought in 9 different bidders, and the item sold for about the same price ($83.01). I made 46¢ more on the auction and saved 60¢ in eBay fees by listing at the lower starting price.

This told me there was a market for the compasses, but I continued to list them for a few more auctions with the drop shipper just to be sure. The auctions continued to work, and after three weeks I still didn't have any competitors.

It looked like I had a winner, so I called the manufacturer and got the name of their distributor. The distributor agreed to sell them to me in lots of one dozen for $38 each. This way I would be saving $4 per unit and the additional $4 drop shipping fee. With an Average Selling Price of $88, this gave me a margin of $50 per unit versus $42 by using drop shipping (plus I could take the small markup on the shipping, rather than giving it to the drop shipper). This was attractive enough to tie up cash in buying inventory. I continued to sell this compass and found a source for another less expensive compass as well. Over the next year I sold more than 300 auto compasses.

From these examples you can see how to use a drop shipping aggregator in two ways. One is to simply make money with no investment except the eBay listing fees. The other is to use it as a research tool before committing to purchase a large amount of inventory.

If you decide to pursue the drop shipping only route, you need to research and launch test auctions for dozens of products to find the ones where you can profitably sell at their higher wholesale price points. To create a large business would require a high volume of products and auctions going at any given time. You would also have to track your margins and fees very closely to ensure continued profitability.

In general, I am not a fan of the various middlemen drop ship companies as the work required to find a successful and profitable product is often too great to make this a consistently profitable activity. I do sometimes use these aggregators to test a product, but when I find a successful product, I then look for it in quantity.

17.3 Drop Shipping Manufacturers

Having just told you that manufacturers only sell in large quantities, I'm now going to back-pedal a little and talk about the few ways you might be able to convince manufacturers to drop ship.

But before continuing, I need to introduce a new player in the world of wholesalers: the manufacturer's rep. These commissioned salespeople represent manufacturers directly to retailers, thereby eliminating the distributor or middleman.

Large manufacturers such as Sony, Tommy Bahama, Dell, or Mr. Coffee deal only with large national distributors or, in some cases, even have their own captive distribution operations. They don't use manufacturer's reps, and they won't drop ship. However, smaller manufacturers—and reps who represent them—just might be willing to work something out with you. There are literally thousands of small manufacturers in the United States and Canada whose products range all over the map and can include virtually anything.

Finding manufacturers who will drop ship is well worth the effort and a better business model than dealing with middlemen companies.

Let me give you an example. When my wife and I were at the Seattle Garden Show last year, we found a fantastic solid steel fire pit and Bar-B-Q grill. We had had several of these in the past, which had broken, rusted out, or had smoke and sparks go all over the place. But this one was very well designed—strong enough to be indestructible. It had vents in the side to channel the smoke upward and a fine mesh top to trap the sparks. We bought one for ourselves and really liked it. Although the manufacturer's name was on the unit, it took me a while to locate him, but when I did, I immediately asked about drop shipping. It turns out that most of the stores he sells to only carry one unit in stock to show customers and take orders for him to drop ship. Drop shipping was 80 percent of his business.

So I decided to try them on eBay. In the auction description, I noted there were several designs and provided a clickable link to my eBay store. It was winter when we first put them up, but I still sold one or two units a week. Once spring came, I started selling five or six a week. I was the only one on eBay selling these units.

The fire pits sold for between $329 and $399 depending on the retail outlet. My cost, including shipping anywhere within the United States, was $200. The manufacturer had several different designs, so I put an auction up on eBay for one model and put the other six models in my eBay Store where the listing fees are much lower. I started them just below the lowest retail price at $279 with a Buy It Now price of $299, but I also charged $55 shipping and handling. Because the fire pits weighed over 50 pounds, no one was concerned about the high shipping charge.

Almost all of the purchases were at the Buy It Now price from my eBay Store. My margin worked out to around $154 per unit. At five or six units a week, this was a very profitable deal and the perfect example of drop shipping direct from a manufacturer.

The trick, of course, is finding the products and the associated manufacturers who will drop ship. Part 3 deals with locating manufacturers in great detail, but here I want to give you two ways you can locate manufacturers who drop ship their products. The first method is the Thomas Register, a company that has been publishing a five-volume printed guide to American Manufacturers for over 75 years. Almost every library has a copy, and it's sort of a giant yellow pages of virtually every product made in America. When I first used the Thomas Register over 20 years ago, it was only six or seven volumes, but today it has grown to 12 volumes. About four years ago the Thomas Register became available on the Internet at www.thomasregister.com. They call their Internet operation "ThomasNet."

Figure 17.1
ThomasNet welcome page.

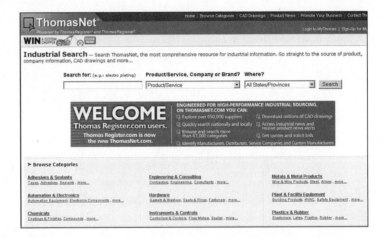

The first page lists primarily industrial categories. Some of these can be useful if you sell in the Business & Industrial category on eBay. For most other products you want to select the **Other** category, which will take you to the screen shown in Figure 17.2.

Figure 17.2
ThomasNet's Browse Categories page.

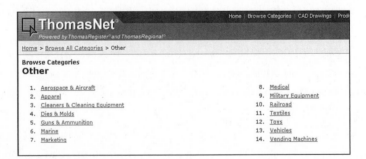

Note category 6, Marine. The boating and marine category on eBay is huge, with historically high sell-through rates, so let's take a closer look at that category. If you click **Marine,** it will take you to a list of product categories for virtually everything manufactured for the marine industry, from propellers to cup-holders (see Figure 17.3). When you click **category 29, Boats: Rescue,** you get a list of two companies that manufacture rescue and survival equipment for the marine industry (see Figure 17.4). The first one, Aviation Marine Specialty Products, has a website link.

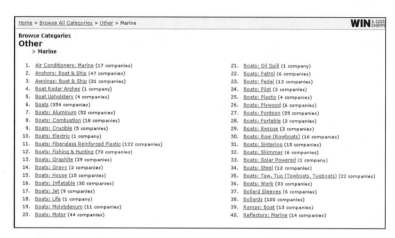

Figure 17.3
ThomasNet's Marine product categories.

Figure 17.4
Manufacturers of Rescue equipment listed on ThomasNet.

Clicking this link brings you to their website. If you look at the top of Figure 17.5, you'll see a list of the kinds of products this company makes. Now it is a simple matter to call or contact the manufacturer through their website and ask if they are willing to drop ship their products direct to your customers. Aviation Marine Specialty Products might or might not; I didn't contact them. But this illustrates how you can use the Thomas Register to find the small specialty manufacturers who will drop ship.

Occasionally you will run into a manufacturer who has not drop shipped in the past but is willing to consider the idea. I suspect that this manufacturer could be interested. They sell low-priced lightweight products, such as first-aid kits, that they probably would not be interested in drop shipping. But they also sell large, heavy, and expensive products, such as life rafts, which might be worthwhile for them to drop ship.

Figure 17.5

Using ThomasNet, you can find small specialty manufacturers who might be willing to drop ship products.

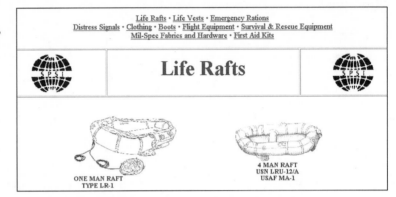

Small- and medium-size manufacturers are always looking for ways to increase their sales. The key to negotiating the deal is to convince them you are a large seller and can deliver a steady quantity of sales. A large number of uninformed people think eBay is just a place to trade collectibles and CDs. They have no idea about the millions of dollars a year in commercial, business, and consumer goods sold on eBay. If you educate them, you will have an opportunity to find new products to sell well before your competitors ever find them.

The Thomas Register is the most comprehensive solution to finding manufacturers for almost any product. Another way is to pay others to do the research for you.

Several companies sell directories of drop ship companies, but these typically include mostly aggregators and middlemen. However, Worldwide Brands' (www. worldwidebrands.com) Drop Ship Source Directory, which I introduced in Chapter 11, lists manufacturers who agree to drop ship. Worldwide Brands has a team of people who do nothing but research and contact manufacturers to determine if they will drop ship their products and if they are willing to work with eBay sellers. As of this writing, the directory lists more than 3,000 manufacturers covering over 500,000 products.

The interactive directory is organized by product, and you can do alphabetical searches by product or manufacturer. The site includes links to manufacturers' websites.

I have been using their service for over four years and find it well worth the money. If you go to the resource page for this book at www.skipmcgrath.com/titanium, there is a link where you can get a discount on their service.

For more on product sourcing, see Chapter 11.

For more on finding suppliers who drop ship, see Chapter 23.

For more on eBay fees, see Chapter 35.

chapter 18

Running Test Auctions

The primary purpose of running a test auction, which I've referred to several times in the preceding chapters, is to find out if there is a market for a product before you buy a large quantity. If you run an auction and the item sells, it's a pretty good indicator that there's a market out there. Just because you sell one item, however, does not guarantee there's a bigger market for your product.

I once ran a test auction for a very unique garlic press, and someone bought it with the Buy It Now price the first day it was listed. When I listed it again, it sat for seven days without a bid. Even worse, when I checked the hit counter, it had only gotten six hits during the entire week. I ran it one more time with a different headline, and the results were about the same. Not everything is suitable for eBay. This product sold very well in kitchen stores, but it was just one of those things that you had to touch and feel to understand. In the first auction, some eBay user who was in the market for a garlic press, or perhaps had seen one in a store, just happened to hit on my auction. Had I used that one successful auction to make a buying decision, I might have found myself sitting on several dozen garlic presses.

Recently I found a very unique battery-powered pepper mill. Most pepper mills you have to turn by hand or push a button to operate the powered one. But this unit starts grinding when you turn it upside down. And the top has a clever switch to adjust the grind size. But when I tested it on eBay

I got about the same results as the garlic press. I was going to give up when I decided that I should test it with a video showing how it operates. As Emeril says, "BAM!" It was a hit. So had I not taken the time to test it with video I would have missed out on a very profitable product.

You can also use test auctions to experiment with virtually any other part of selling on eBay, including helping to determine …

- Starting bids.
- Reserve amounts.
- Category and second category listing.
- Free shipping or not.
- Kinds of headlines (auction titles) for use.
- The use of eBay promotional features such as bold, highlight, and featured plus.
- Dutch auction quantities.
- Auction ending times and days.
- Using audio video or slide show photos in your listings.

Lately I have also been testing listings using the new fixed price fees and quantities mentioned in the previous chapter. This shows me if an item will sell in the fixed price format.

Whatever you're testing, take the time to accurately track and record your data. I set up an Excel spreadsheet with the information I want to track and then check my test auctions and update the data every day. To be really accurate, I check my auctions at the same time every day.

At the end of the auction, I record the hits, the number of watchers (this is located on your **My eBay Page**), the number of bids, and the final price. I also have a column to note if someone opted for the Buy It Now price.

Unless you are testing auction ending times, run your auctions to end at the same time. If you are testing which of two or more headlines is more effective, run the auctions simultaneously, but set them up so the auctions end several minutes apart and don't appear right under each other when someone does a search.

For more on running test auctions, see Section 34.2.

PowerSeller Tip

Don't confuse running a test auction with eBay's *Test Category.* A test auction is a real auction run in the appropriate category, where you are actually going to sell and deliver the product. eBay has a special category called *test auctions,* but this is designed for people who are experimenting with software tools, auction management systems, image management systems, and other technical issues. The purpose is for them to be able to see what something will look like when it launches on eBay. Most auctions in this category usually have a notice that says *This is a test auction. Do not bid on this item.*

part 3

Product Acquisition

This part is about how, what, and where to buy the products to sell on eBay.

Wholesale distributors, manufacturers, and dealers have their own language and terms. Learning this jargon can help you find your way through the wholesale maze.

Everyone looks to the web to source products, but some of the best wholesale opportunities are still offline. Learning how to get into and work a wholesale trade show or register at a merchandise mart are critical skills for any eBay seller. These places are where I often find that one unique product that no one else has.

The closer you can get to the source of a product, the more cheaply you can buy it. More and more eBay sellers are learning to import their merchandise direct from manufacturers in Asia. This can seem intimidating, but after you get some basics down, it's really quite easy. Another profitable tactic is drop shipping, but it has its perils. We take the mystery out of drop shipping and show you how to use this highly profitable sourcing tactic successfully.

chapter 19

Navigating the Wholesale Maze

Because you must learn to deal with several types of wholesalers, it is important to understand the differences between them, the markets they serve, and the way each operates. When you know who the players are in the world of wholesaling, your research will be more efficient, and you won't waste your time dealing with suppliers who simply will not deal with you.

This chapter introduces you to the various types of wholesale suppliers, teaches you ways to find and contact these wholesalers, and suggests some strategies and techniques you can use to deal with them. Later I will discuss several of them individually in subsequent chapters.

19.1 Master Wholesale Distributors

Also called national distributors, master wholesale distributors are the classic large wholesalers. They sign distribution contracts with a small number of manufacturers to distribute their product to regional distributors and large retail chains, although some will sell direct to retailers if they can purchase in large quantities. Most of them are national in scope, but you occasionally find some that operate in a protected geographic area.

Most national distributors are industry-specific. They carry a range of products related to one industry but seldom carry directly competitive products. For example, a national computer distributor would carry one brand of computer, one brand of monitor, and so on. A clothing distributor might carry one designer's product for men, another for women, another for handbags, and another for shoes, but none of them would be directly competitive with each other.

Master wholesale distributors are the most difficult of the wholesalers to deal with. They typically have very strict terms with regards to minimum order, or if they sell in small quantities, they require proof of creditworthiness and often require proof of a line of credit from your bank or commercial lender. These lines of credit can often be quite large—in the range of $100,000 to $250,000.

Until very recently, most master or national distributors required you to have a brick and mortar store before dealing with you, which is why some of the earliest sellers of computers and new consumer electronics on eBay were companies that also had storefronts. Lately, however, as more and more business has moved to the Internet, the master distributors have accommodated Internet sellers, but they still only want to deal with large sellers. If you have a line of credit, then you might be able to buy from these large distributors. Doing so could be very profitable because this is where you find the best pricing.

As a new seller, you might have a hard time finding these companies as most of them do not advertise their presence but are well known in their specific community. Rarely will you find them listed in the regular Yellow Pages.

But many large cities issue a Business-to-Business (B2B) Yellow Pages, so call the phone company for the nearest large metropolitan area and ask if they have this. If so, order one (they are free), as it is a valuable resource. Many wholesale companies, including the large national distributors, list only in the B2B Yellow Pages.

If you live in or near Los Angeles, New York, or Chicago (or if you have a friend or relative who lives there), try to get a B2B Yellow Pages from one of these cities. Most of the large national distributors are listed in one of these three books. For example, if you look under **software** in the New York City Yellow Pages, you will find only retailers, but the B2B Yellow Pages lists over a dozen software distributors. Another source for the B2B Yellow Pages is often your local library. Libraries in major cities usually carry the B2B Yellow Pages for most other major cities in the United States.

Finally, one way to find the large national distributors is to telephone the company whose goods you want to sell and ask them for the name of their distributor. I have tried e-mailing manufacturers from their website with this question and have never gotten an answer. But when I telephone the company, I have almost always gotten the information I need.

19.2 General Wholesale Distributors

General wholesale distributors often buy a variety of products directly from a number of manufacturers and importers. This type of distributor usually, but not always, specializes in a given industry such as fashion, jewelry, gifts, house and garden, consumer electronics, tools, and so on. Their products tend to cover a wide spectrum. Whereas a national distributor rarely carries competitive products, a general wholesaler might carry several brands of computers, accessories, software, and so on but would probably not exclusively represent any nationwide brands.

Some large national distributors sell directly to individual retail stores, but many of them only sell to the large chains and to smaller general distributors, who in turn then sell to the smaller retail outlets. If you go into a national chain store, such as Ritz Camera, in any shopping mall, it is probably getting its cameras from the national distributor. But if you visit Joe's Camera and Repair in Anysmalltown, USA, he is probably buying from a regional general wholesaler who is getting the product from a national distributor. For eBay resellers, these wholesale distributors are often much easier to deal with because they have reasonable credit terms and might have systems in place for dealing with eBay and other Internet businesses.

General wholesale distributors come in many sizes. Some are national in scope; others might only operate in a small geographical area. No matter their size or their scope, they are easy to locate and usually easy to deal with. You can find most of them on the web if you do a search. For example, when I searched **jewelry distributors** on Google, I turned up hundreds of them.

19.3 Manufacturers' Representatives

A manufacturer's rep is usually a one- or two-person business that represents both domestic and foreign manufacturers on a commission basis. If you are communicating with a manufacturer or foreign exporter, ask if they have a manufacturer's rep. Reps typically sell goods in smaller quantities than distributors.

When searching for manufacturers' reps, look in the Yellow Pages under **Manufacturers' Representatives**, and you will find a simple alphabetical listing. After this, most (not all) Yellow Pages have a Fast Guide that lists the reps by product category. For example, the Seattle Yellow Pages lists Electronics,

Food & Beverage, Hardware & Household, Marine, Packaging, Sporting Goods, and Toys, Gifts, & Novelties. Under each of these listings are manufacturers' reps that specialize in those products.

The listings don't tell you which companies the reps represent; you have to contact them and inquire about their product line. Your local gift or merchandise mart will usually have several manufacturers' reps showrooms where you can see their products.

Unless they are a very large company representing dozens of product lines, most manufacturers' reps do not have a website. They usually do business face-to-face by calling on retail stores or dealing with customers out of their showroom. I've always contacted reps at their showrooms, and the advantage of doing this is I can see the products and often purchase small sample quantities to test.

If you find a product you want to sell but cannot find a distributor, simply call the manufacturer (their name is usually on the box), and ask for the name of the rep in your area.

19.4 Liquidators, Surplus, and Closeout Dealers

Liquidators, surplus, and closeout dealers are a major supply source for thousands of eBay sellers. These companies specialize in buying excess stock from manufacturers, retail stores, and chains. There is no real difference between a liquidation, closeout, or surplus dealer, so for the sake of simplicity, we'll refer to them as closeout dealers.

In Chapter 16 I focused on the need to turn inventory over and get rid of excess or slow-moving stock. Retailers who sell clothing, sporting goods, and other seasonal items are always moving excess stock out of the store to make room for new products. Other products might be taken off the shelves simply because they are not popular or aren't selling fast enough. Technology products are constantly being replaced by new models. Whatever the reason, when stores have excess inventory, they usually call on closeout dealers to take it off their hands. Depending on the type of merchandise, these dealers might pay as little as 10¢ on the retail dollar (original MSRP) although they can pay as high as 25 percent for highly desirable goods, such as famous-name designer clothing and accessories.

Closeout dealers sell another category of goods called customer returns. When a customer returns an item, it is seldom still nicely packaged with all the tags in place, so a store cannot put it back on the shelf. Stores hold these products until they have enough of them to sell to a closeout dealer, who in turn sells the goods to resellers. Returns can cause several problems for the reseller. Additionally, when dealing with closeout dealers, you can encounter other problems, all of which I cover in Chapter 21.

19.5 Importers and Manufacturing Exporters

Overseas manufacturers and professional importers constitute another class of wholesale suppliers. Manufacturers who export their products directly typically work in very large quantities—in the thousands of units and/or container loads. Importers, as their name implies, import products from overseas manufacturers in a large quantity, such as 10,000 units, and break it up and resell it in smaller lots.

If you can afford to buy a container load of products, this is a great way to buy. You can't find a lower price. If not, then you may want to find an importer who could sell to you in a smaller quantity. You'd pay a slightly higher price, but it will still be at a price point where you should be able to make money.

Here's an example. Recently, companies in China have been making and selling the small Mini-RC helicopters that are popping up in stores and on eBay. Last year one popular model was selling for $29.95 in the shopping malls and for a little less on eBay. I saw these at a Shanghai Toy Fair the previous year. The manufacturer was offering them in 2,000 piece lots for $11 each, plus shipping. This was a larger quantity than I was willing to buy, so I asked the manufacturer's rep at the toy fair if he worked with any importers. He gave me the name of two importers in the United States. I contacted them and they were selling the units in lots of 144 (a gross) for $14.50 each, plus $75 shipping for the gross lot. Because a lot of issues are involved in importing, I cover this important subject in detail in Chapter 26.

For more on sourcing products, see Sections 17.2 and 17.3 and Chapter 23.

For more on negotiating with wholesalers, see Chapter 20.

For more on buying from closeout dealers, see Chapter 21.

For more on buying wholesale at auctions, see Chapter 22.

For more on buying from wholesale markets, see Chapter 23.

For more on buying from wholesale trade shows, see Chapter 24.

How to Negotiate with Wholesalers

Whole books have been written on negotiating tactics, but they all boil down to two main points. First, you must *know all the information that is at your disposal*; second, you must ask for something that is *within the other person's interest and ability to grant you.*

When I was much younger, I lived for several years in the Middle East where everything, including the price of milk, is negotiated. At first I struggled with the idea that everything was negotiable, and I overpaid for just about everything. After I made friends with local folks, they started teaching me how to negotiate. And in time, I actually found the process fun.

During the two years I lived in Iran, I purchased a number of beautiful Persian Rugs. Negotiating with the rug dealers could take place over several days with numerous visits to the dealer. Each session could last up to an hour or more and would involve drinking several cups of tea.

During these protracted negotiations, I had to know all the information that I could. This meant I had to know about the quality and type of rug I was buying, its value, how plentiful the supply of similar rugs was, and so on. I also had to ask for something the seller could grant. In this case, that "something" was the lowest price for which he would part with the rug.

The way to negotiate with wholesale suppliers and distributors is first to know *what* to ask for and then to ask. *You must ask!* Sellers will never volunteer lower prices, better terms, or lower quantities unless you request them. Remember, the person who is trying to sell to you probably needs the deal as much as you do.

Before you begin negotiations, collect all the information you can. You should have the catalog, price sheets, minimum quantities, payment terms, shipping policies, and so on. Next, figure out what you want—a better price, credit, better terms, free shipping, or smaller minimum order. Finally, ask for what you want. Always give a reason, and always ask in such a way that the seller *thinks* he will be doing you a favor if he agrees. Also, try to preempt his objections.

For example, if a seller has a minimum order of $5,000, you might say something like this. "Steve, $5,000 is a small order for you, but it's a big order for us. If your product sells well, then $5,000 is no problem for us. We can move a lot of product at your prices. But we are a small company, and we need to be sure our customers will like your product before committing to it. Would you sell us a minimum quantity of $500 for a market test so we can be sure it will sell before we go ahead?"

Notice that your statement recognizes his rules but asks for an exception. If you just asked for a $500 minimum order straight out, he would probably refuse. You have to give him a reason for accepting.

I have used this exact same technique to order small quantities from importers who have a $10,000 minimum order, and it works! Everything is negotiable— you just have to ask. But also keep in mind that it's the way you ask that is important. Humility, tact, and a sincere approach will give you an edge every time.

Many sellers focus on negotiating price when better terms might be more advantageous. Remember our discussion on seller financing in Section 16.2? In many instances, I will happily pay a slightly higher price if the seller will give me generous no-interest credit terms. This is almost as good as drop shipping. If I get 90-day, no-interest payment terms and can sell all or most of the shipment within that 90-day period, I am making money with no out-of-pocket investment.

So remember the key points to negotiating:

- *Learn everything you can.* Take the time to learn all the information you can about what you are buying. This includes competitive products, market prices, specifications and quality, the product's position in its life cycle, and the current supply and demand in your market.

- *Know what you want.* Do you want a lower price, smaller quantity, better credit terms, discounts on future orders, or quantity shipments spread out over time?

- *Ask for what you want.* Be polite and respectful; try to preempt any objections; and give them a reason for agreeing.

For more on product research, see Sections 11.4 and 11.5.

For more on running test auctions, see Chapter 18.

For more on sourcing products, see Sections 17.2, 17.3, and Chapter 23.

chapter 21

Buying from Closeout Dealers

As I mentioned in Chapter 19, closeout dealers go by various names, including liquidators and surplus dealers. There are literally thousands of closeout dealers in the United States and Canada. Some are very large national companies that buy surplus and returned goods from the large national department stores and chain stores; others are more regional. These smaller regional dealers buy from large local stores right down to mom-and-pop-size retail stores.

Some of the larger closeout dealers only deal in massive quantities such as a truck or container load. The smaller regional dealers will often buy a truckload of product from the large national companies, break it up, and sell it by the pallet load to individual dealers.

Before eBay, the most common place to find closeout merchandise was at flea markets, dollar stores, and some specialty retailers, such as overstock bookstores or clothing stores. Now eBay, ePier, eCrater, and other online venues such as Overstock.com are responsible for moving a very large percentage of the closeout goods available in today's market. Closeout merchandise is the single largest source of product on eBay today and is available in almost every category.

You can earn large profits with closeout merchandise if you buy carefully. Basically, you want to buy only desirable merchandise because not all merchandise sold by closeout dealers is truly closeout or surplus. The variety of goods carried can include several types of product. Some of these include:

- Seasonal goods.
- Store closing or bankruptcy merchandise.
- Obsolete goods replaced by newer products.
- Customer returns.
- Warranty returns.
- Seconds.

The best closeout merchandise falls into the first three categories on this list. Called *shelf pulls*, these products are still brand new and have the store tags or the manufacturer's price tags.

The last three categories—customer returns, warranty returns, and seconds— can be very problematic for the reseller and warrant a closer look.

Customer returns come in several varieties. Some, especially items returned in perfect condition with all the tags and packaging because of the wrong size, model, or color, are excellent items to sell. Returns always cost less than shelf pulls, so you can often get really great deals on these pieces. Sometimes returns come back in perfect condition, but without the tags or packaging. These are harder to sell, but there is still a market for them.

Warranty returns are more problematic because an item returned under warranty is usually broken or defective in some way. You should never buy a warranty return unless you are in the business and know how to repair the item.

Manufacturers' seconds are goods that are somehow flawed. They usually work but will typically have a small cosmetic flaw. These can be great items to sell as long as you carefully disclose the flaws to the buyer.

I have a niece who works for a company that manufactures expensive food smokers that retail for around $700. When I asked her if she could get me a discount because she worked there, she said she couldn't do that but suggested I buy a second. The company was selling a few units that had small flaws at half price plus free shipping. That got my attention, because these units are fairly large and the shipping alone was over $100.

So I bought one of the smokers, and when it was delivered, the outside, which is stainless steel, had a small dent about the size of a quarter on the side. That was it! That small dent saved me over $400! I called her back and asked about selling their seconds on eBay. We made an arrangement where she would send me a photo of the smoker that showed the damage or the flaw. I used the photos in my auctions, and we managed to sell three units over the next month at prices between $500 and $700, but with free shipping. The problem was the supply. The manufacturer didn't have a steady supply of seconds. However, large manufacturers who build in greater quantities often do have a steady supply of these goods. The trick is knowing the quality of the second. Just how damaged is something?

As the preceding example illustrates, sometimes seconds can be real money-makers, but it depends on the size and kind of flaws. Clothing is one area where you must be very careful. I have seen some seconds where the flaw was very small, and I would not hesitate to buy the item. I have seen others where the flaws were so apparent that I would be lucky to sell at my cost. In general, I would avoid buying seconds unless you can physically inspect each piece of merchandise or if the supplier will send it to you on approval, which is rare but does happen.

21.1 How to Find Closeout Dealers

Today almost all large and medium closeout dealers have a presence on the web. One of the easiest places to find closeout dealers is at the website www. closeoutcentral.com. Figure 21.1 shows the list of product categories down the left side of the page. This will take you to a page where you can view several suppliers by product category.

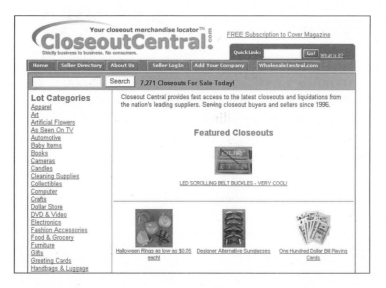

Figure 21.1
Closeout Central's featured closeouts.

If you click the link to *Baby Items*, it will bring up a page (Figure 21.2) that lists 57 matches for Baby Items.

Figure 21.2
Closeout Central's baby items.

Page:	1	2		
POSTED	**FOR SALE**	**SELLER**
03/23/05	2 Children's Airplane Spoons	SAV-ON CLOSEOUTS
03/23/05	Gerber Looney Tunes Juice Cup Tumblers / Holders	KML Sales Inc.
03/23/05	Diapers by the pallet!	Warehouse One
03/23/05	Baby Products	Canadian Home Liquidators Inc.
03/21/05	PAMPERS TYPE DIAPERS ONLY 10.3 CENTS EACH	AAA CLOSEOUTS SURPLUS SALVAGE LIQUIDATORS
03/21/05	FACTORY FRESH BABY DIAPERS ONLY 10.3 CENTS EACH	AAA CLOSEOUTS SURPLUS SALVAGE LIQUIDATORS
03/21/05	FACTORY FRESH BABY DIAPERS ,HUGGIES TYPE	AAA CLOSEOUTS SURPLUS SALVAGE LIQUIDATORS
03/21/05	BABY DIAPER BLOW OUT,LIQUIDATION	AAA CLOSEOUTS SURPLUS SALVAGE LIQUIDATORS
03/21/05	BABY DIAPERS SURPLUS & CLOSEOUT	AAA CLOSEOUTS SURPLUS SALVAGE LIQUIDATORS
03/21/05	BABY DIAPER FACTORY FRESH ONLY 10.3 CENTS	AAA CLOSEOUTS SURPLUS SALVAGE LIQUIDATORS
03/21/05	BABY DIAPER FOR EXPORT SPECIAL	AAA CLOSEOUTS SURPLUS SALVAGE LIQUIDATORS

This same page will not be available when you buy this book, but let's go a little further and see what turns up. When I click the second item on the list, Gerber Looney Tunes Juice Cups tumblers and holders, I get more details regarding the product (Figure 21.3). Let's examine this information.

Figure 21.3
Closeout Central's lot detail.

The first thing to look at is the name of the company and its contact information. Next check the price for the entire lot and the quality, which is new.

The entry entitled "FOB" tells you where the items are located—in this case, Buffalo, New York. These items are not that heavy, but for heavy items you want to find a supplier close to you to minimize the shipping cost. The shipping is listed as buyer's choice. I always prefer this because I can shop around for the best rate. Some sellers, however, will specify their shipping company and the cost. The "terms" line specifies the payment terms. Notice one of the terms is Credit. This company would probably not give you credit if this is the first time you purchase, but if you become a repeat customer, you might be able to negotiate credit terms with them.

Below the terms are the details or a description of what they are selling. In this case it says …

> Bottle Holders 24/8oz holders per case (21 cases available) Juice Cup
> Tumblers 24/4oz tumblers per case (20 cases available)

Now we need to do some math. There are 21 cases of bottle holders with 24 in each case, for a total of 504 bottle holders; and there are 20 cases of juice cup tumblers at 24 to the case, for a total of 480 tumblers. If you add up all the pieces, you would be buying a total of 984 pieces. Their asking price is $1,627.20. If you divide the quantity into the asking price, you come up with a unit cost of $1.65 each.

PowerSeller Tip

Licensed products such as Disney, Nickelodeon, and others are very popular sellers on eBay. The margin and low ASP on these items would not make them a leading candidate for an eBay auction, but they would make fabulous upsell products for an eBay seller who deals in baby items, which is a very large and successful category on eBay.

This dealer didn't tell us the retail price, so I did some research. I couldn't find any of these selling on eBay, but I did find them in a Yahoo! store. The tumblers were selling for $4.95 and the bottle holders for $3.95. These prices appear to be full retail, so you would most likely not get as much for these items on eBay.

If you sold them on eBay for 25 percent below retail, that would work out to $2.96 each for the bottle holders and $3.72 for the juice tumblers. So your potential gross margin works out to $1.31 on the bottle holders and $2.07 on the juice tumblers. And of course, we need to figure in shipping.

If you look back at the details screenshot, you'll see a **Make offer to purchase** clickable icon. If you click this icon, it will open a web mail page where you can send your offer to the seller. Just because the seller is offering the lot for $1,627.20 doesn't mean you have to offer that much. If you make a ridiculous offer, such as $500 for the lot, it will certainly be rejected. But if you offer something closer to the asking price, there's a good chance the seller will accept it or come back with a counteroffer (just like the "Best Offer" option on eBay fixed-price listings). Unless the price is really great and I don't want to lose out to another buyer, I usually make an offer that is 15 to 20 percent below the asking price. Most of the time, the seller will reply with a counteroffer that is 5 to 10 percent below the asking price. Even if you only get a 5 percent reduction, that is usually enough to cover the shipping.

Closeout Central only lists the closeout dealers who pay to advertise on their site. If you go to www.skipmcgrath.com/titanium, you'll find a list of closeout dealers, as well as a search box where you can search a term such as closeout, liquidation, or surplus, or you can narrow it down to a product-specific search, such as closeout apparel or closeout books.

You can do a search on the popular search engines such as Google and Yahoo!, but the problem with these searches is that many retail websites that sell closeout products will come up in the search, and you'll have to spend a lot of time searching through hundreds of listings to find the real closeout dealers.

Closeout goods are also available at wholesale auctions both online and offline. We cover how to buy at wholesale auctions in Chapter 22, but two of the largest online auctions are Via Trading at www.viatrading.com and Liquidity Services at www.liquidation.com.

21.2 Tips for Dealing with Closeout Dealers

When buying from closeout dealers, always make sure you know *exactly* what you are buying. In the case of the baby tumblers and juice bottles, I'd call or e-mail the seller and ask a lot more questions. First of all, I'd ask if the items still have the store or the manufacturers' price tags on them. I'd also ask about the product mix. Are all the glasses the same? How many different designs are there? What is the size and weight of the shipment? And so on.

If the products you are buying are not shelf pulls, you want to ascertain the quality of what you're buying. Are they seconds, returns, or warranty returns?

If you are buying anything that's large and heavy, review the shipping costs before you buy or bid. I always prefer to work with a dealer who will let me arrange my own shipping. Some unscrupulous dealers sell their goods at a low cost but make up the difference by padding the shipping or getting a kickback from their shipper.

If you don't know the company you are dealing with, ask for references. You can also post a message on the eBay PowerSeller boards asking if anyone has dealt with the company you are considering.

If you are not familiar with a product or if you are not sure about the quality, don't hesitate to ask for a sample. The company might ask you to pay for it, but they will usually refund the cost if you end up placing an order. After you have placed a few orders with the larger wholesale dealers, they'll usually send you free samples or ask only that you pay the shipping charge.

One final caution: closeout dealers sell all types of merchandise, including returns. Until you really know what you are doing, stick with new-in-the-box merchandise, preferably brand names.

For more on closeout dealers, see Section 19.4.

For more on product life cycles, see Section 11.3.2.

chapter 22

Buying Wholesale at Auctions

Auctions are the purest form of the capitalist system. It's a basic tenet of economics that something is worth what someone else is willing to pay for it. Auctions, whether they are on eBay, at Sotheby's, or in a cattle barn, are all basically the same.

Goods change hands without regard to their original value in auction markets. And the only price that matters is the one that bidders are willing to pay. Because this is the single most important concept of auctions, you must understand this concept if you are to be successful bidding at auctions. (This includes eBay.)

Auctions are an excellent place to find merchandise to sell on eBay or your website. Most people think of auctions as a place to buy antiques and collectibles, but almost everything is sold at an auction at one time or another. eBay, of course, is an auction, and just think of the thousands of different things that sell on eBay. In fact, eBay itself is a great place to buy stuff to turn around and sell at higher prices—right back on eBay!

You would be amazed at the number of people who buy items on eBay and turn around and sell them on eBay at far higher prices. Every day hundreds of items sell on eBay, ePier, OnlineAuctions.com, and U-bid at greatly undervalued prices. I once bought a collection of nautical books at an eBay auction for $4 each. The seller was selling them individually, and I had to bid on all 26 auctions to get the whole set. The set was missing two books, but I bought them elsewhere for about $10 to $20 each. After the set was complete, I sold it on eBay for over $700. The seller had no idea of the value of his almost complete set.

An amazing number of eBay sellers don't know how to write a title or item description or how to take decent photos, so the products they offer rarely sell for high prices. You can often buy items from them as the only bidder and turn around and resell them for a profit simply by properly marketing your auction.

Every day thousands of sellers are selling valuable products on eBay, ePier, eCrater, and Amazon (and many smaller auction sites)—but they don't know or understand the true value. These sellers are often amateurs who list products in the wrong category, don't describe them accurately, and often list them at a low starting bid with no reserve. Others, for some unexplainable reason, schedule auctions that end in the middle of the night when no one is awake.

PowerSeller Tip

If you're looking for something on eBay, sort the search results by *Time: ending soonest.* Then scroll to the bottom of the page or the next page to find items that end after midnight Pacific Time. Very few people are on eBay during the night, and you don't need to be up at that time to bid; just use one of the popular sniping programs to bid for you. These are programs such as the one available at www.auctionsniper.com where you enter the auction number and the maximum price you want to pay and the software will place bids for you during the last few seconds (this is called "sniping").

Here's an example. Suppose you collect Nantucket Baskets. If you do a search in the Collectibles category for **Nantucket Baskets,** you'll turn up dozens of items. But also try searching the term **baskets** from the front page, which searches all of eBay. A search for a general term such as **baskets** will usually turn up hundreds of auctions—but if you take the time to scroll down through the list, you'll probably find someone listing an expensive Cape Cod basket in the Household Goods category. I once saw one of these selling for $5 with no bids on it. The basket was worth over $200, and the same search also turned up a very valuable early Native American basket.

Besides eBay, local auctions can turn up lots of valuable products to sell on eBay. If you have any expertise in antiques and collectibles, you can go to local auctions and buy items that might seem expensive to you on a local basis but would sell for twice the price if given national and/or international exposure, which is what eBay and other electronic auctions give you.

When we were in the antiques business, we had a small shop in upstate New York about two hours north of Manhattan. Whenever I went to an estate sale or a small country auction, I learned to buy only the best pieces that were for sale. I might buy a nice nineteenth-century pine corner cabinet for $1,000, put it in our shop, and mark it up to $1,800. An antique dealer from New York City would walk in and ask for a 10 percent dealer discount, which we routinely gave. A week later our cabinet would be for sale in his shop for $2,900. This happened all the time.

Our shop had such a good reputation with three or four big-time antique dealers that they would call us every week and ask if we had anything new. I once sold a small Marquetry desk for $1,100 we had bought at a flea market near Albany for $300. It showed up a year later at a Christie's auction and sold for $2,400 to Leigh Kino, a famous New York antiques dealer who bought it with the plan of marking it up again. I have no idea how much he sold it for, but I suspect it was at least double what he paid.

The point is not how much we lost by selling too cheap but how much more you can get for goods when you have a large exposure. We could not command the high prices in a small town that a dealer in New York City could realize. But this was before eBay.

If you are dealing in any sort of antiques, art, collectibles, books, and so on, it is worth taking the time to carefully search eBay (and the other auctions) for prime examples of whatever you are looking for. It's amazing to me that thousands of eBay sellers don't know how to sell on eBay. They don't know how to correctly feature an auction, how to describe their product, how to place good images into their auctions, and how to draw customers to their auction. Clever bidders who really know their merchandise usually walk away with these sales for a song.

Small local auctions are your next best opportunity to find goods to resell. I don't do this type of business that much any more, but there is a large eBay seller in our town I see at every auction I attend. He always bids on any quality item that comes up.

And auctions aren't limited to antiques and collectibles. Local auctioneers are often engaged to sell the contents of entire stores, corporations, or restaurants that are going out of business. The town we live in is the center of sea kayaking in the Pacific Northwest. Every year a local auctioneer sells off the tour opera-tors' used kayaks because they buy new ones every season. My son, who is a kayaker, has bought several of these and turned around and sold them on eBay for a nice profit.

22.1 How to Buy at Live Auctions

An auction can be a very exciting and even an emotional experience. I am by nature a very competitive person, a trait that cost me a lot of money at auctions until I learned to control it.

It is very easy to get caught up in a bidding frenzy. This happens all the time at live auctions, but I've also seen examples of it on eBay.

One of the unfortunate facts of both live auctions and auctions on the web is the existence of auction shills. A *shill* is a phony bidder working in collusion with the auctioneer or the person who gave the auctioneer the merchandise to sell. Sometimes they form bidding rings. Their mission in life is to drive up the final price of each other's auctions. The legitimate buyer is the ultimate loser.

It is very hard to spot shills unless you go to the same auctions. If you are at an auction house for the first time you may not recognize anyone. But if you go to the same auctions repeatedly, you will often be able to recognize the shills.

Here are some tips for bidding and buying at live auctions:

- Arrive early and inspect the merchandise. Wear old clothes and bring extra layers; many auction houses are cold and drafty; some are even outside in tents.

- Carry a flashlight, a magnet (for checking brass), a small battery-operated black light (for spotting cracks and repairs), and a notebook. Also bring your sales tax number and plenty of business cards.

- Carry cash! Some small auction houses don't even accept traveler's checks. (I carry large amounts of cash in one of those passport wallets that I wear under my clothing).

- Be prepared to haul your goods away on the spot. Many auctions won't store goods until you return, or they'll charge you storage. Others will store goods for a specified period of time, such as two days.

- Sit toward the back of the room, so you can see all the bidders without turning around. I like to know who is bidding against me.

- Never make the first bid. This tips your hand that you are very interested in the item, and a smart auctioneer (or a shill) will notice that and work you over. Let someone else get the bidding started. I like to come in after at least two other people have bid.

- Make your first bid by raising your hand. Make subsequent bids by looking at the auctioneer and nodding your head. If an item goes past your bid limit, make the "cutting throat" sign with your hand, or move your head from side-to-side, which tells the auctioneer you are finished bidding.

- If the item is being bid in large units, such as $50 per bid, and is close to reaching your maximum, make the "half-bid" sign (a chopping motion with your hand to your arm)—this will add $25 to your bid instead of the $50 the auctioneer was asking for. The bids now move in $25 increments. This also has the effect of intimidating novice bidders into thinking the bidding has gone too high, and they will become more cautious.

- Pay attention and remember what your bid was. These auctions can move incredibly fast. If the people sitting around you are chatting and noisy, then get up and move. It is important to hear and to concentrate when you are bidding.

- If the bidding is moving too fast, just drop out. You can come back in when the bidding slows down. If you have been bidding, you can help slow down the bidding by hesitating when the auctioneer looks at you. Just look like you are thinking it over, and delay your bid by a few seconds. If you have been an active bidder, others will see this, and they will pause, too.

- Most of all, don't let your ego or your pride drive your bidding. Remember your preset limit.

22.2 Wholesale Dealer Auctions

If you have a deep desire to be mugged, you can take a walk in New York's Central Park after midnight, or you could attend a wholesale dealer auction. Okay, wholesale dealer auctions aren't quite that bad, but this is one place it pays to be careful.

Wholesale dealer auctions exist in most major cities. The goods they sell are usually a mixture of overstocked merchandise, slightly damaged goods, returns, lots of unclaimed freight, and various types of surplus. Plenty of pure junk is mixed in with some really great stuff. Some of my purchases at wholesale auctions have included the following items:

Hummingbird feeders	$0.85 each
Fuji disposable 35mm cameras	$10.00 dozen
Complete dinner set for 8	$32.00 set
Case of Ray Ban sunglasses	$46.00 case of 12
Black & Decker snake light	$70.00 case of 12
18-volt power drill	$12.00 each

Sometimes whole stores are liquidated. You'll also see a lot of restaurant auctions where you can get incredible deals on professional cooking equipment, dinnerware, and silverware. For example, I recently bought a slightly used, but still shiny, 15-gallon professional stockpot for $10 at a closeout auction that was also liquidating a restaurant the same day. Large professional stockpots cost over $100 at retail.

Attending a wholesale auction is a real education. You can find incredible bargains, but you must be very, very careful.

Here is my advice for attending a wholesale dealer auction:

- Never buy a "lot" of boxed, mixed merchandise. It has been picked over (called cherry picking in the trade), and all the premium goods have been removed. If the seller or auctioneer swears it hasn't been picked through, run the other way.

- Buy only new merchandise (*shelf pulls*). This is typically merchandise that didn't sell during the season or didn't sell well at all. Sometimes that means it was not a saleable product, but it could also mean the store just bought too much of it or another hotter product came along and the storeowner needed the shelf space.

- Be careful with items described as *returns* or *store returns*. Ask if they are *shelf pulls* or *customer returns*, because there will almost always be some damaged or nonworking items in a customer returns lot. It is okay to buy returns from established closeout dealers who will tell you the mixture. If you can buy returns at 10 to 15 cents on the dollar, you'll probably do okay because enough good stuff will be mixed with the bad.

- Stay away from freight-damaged goods unless you can visually inspect all the products in the box. Sometimes just the boxes are damaged. If you can open the box and look inside to be sure the goods are in good condition, then go ahead and bid.

- Don't buy anything at your first auction. Visit at least one dealer or closeout auction where you just observe. Look at the people; notice how they dress, how they act, which ones hang out together. Look at what the professional dealers are buying and the prices they pay. Take a small notebook, and jot down information to review later. You'll be surprised at what you can learn by just watching.

- Never buy merchandise you cannot physically and visually inspect. Buying goods at a closeout auction is a case of *caveat emptor* (buyer beware).

- Never buy *damaged returns* unless you are capable of repairing the items yourself.

- If something looks great but is not attracting any bids, leave it alone. Many professionals attend these auctions, and if they're not bidding, there is usually a reason.

22.3 Where to Find Closeout Auctions

The really famous closeout auctions are mostly in the Southeast, but almost every major city will have several smaller closeout auction houses. Look in the Yellow Pages under Auctioneers and Auction Houses. Read their ads, and look for words such as: Asset Recovery, Liquidation, Closeouts, Commercial Auctions, Surplus, Waterfront, Railroad, or Freight Clearance.

Contact each of the auction houses listed, and ask to be put on their mailing list. Every two weeks or so they'll send you a postcard in the mail announcing the date, time, and place of an auction, along with a description of the goods. Before wasting your time going to the auction, call them and ask them to send you a complete list of the merchandise for sale. Also ask how many sellers will be attending and how long the auction will last. Don't bother with small, short auctions. A great wholesale auction will have at least a dozen sellers or enough merchandise to last 6 to 10 hours. Some of the giant auctions in New York and the Southeast last the entire weekend.

Many of the hundreds of wholesale and closeout auction houses in the United States and Canada are now selling at web auctions. Here are a few of the more famous ones:

Maynard Auctions: www.maynards.com (several locations in Canada)

Queens Wholesale & Auction: 120 Vance St., Zebulon, NC, 919-269-6402

Boswell Trade Center: 105 South Adams St., Boswell, IN, 765-869-5516 (www.closeout-auction.com)

Harbor Warehouse: 2238 Cambridge St., Baltimore, MD, 410-918-1147

Armstrong Auctions: Caldwell, ID, 208-454-2910 (www.armstrongauction.com)

Myrtle Beach Auctions, Inc.: 5033 Dick Pond Rd., Myrtle Beach, SC, 843-828-4601 (www.myrtlebeachauction.com)

Some auction houses specialize in estates. These more traditional auction houses sell art, antiques, furniture, and so on. If you are in the antiques or collectibles business, then you already know about these kinds of auctions.

But if you are not knowledgeable about antiques and collectibles, you are taking a big risk buying at these kinds of auctions and hoping to resell on eBay. If you do deal in antiques and/or collectibles, estate auctions can be one of the best places to buy.

22.4 Wholesale Auctions on the Web

Closeout auctions on the web can be even more perilous than live wholesale dealer and closeout auctions, but they can also be highly profitable.

Unlike eBay, many of the wholesale auction houses don't have feedback and controls, so it's pretty much a case of blind trust. I have listed several of the wholesale or closeout auctions at the end of this section, but my personal favorite is www.liquidation.com. Most of the companies selling on Liquidation.com are legitimate wholesalers, surplus merchants, and closeout dealers. One of the largest is a company called Purplus—you'll see this name on quite a few auctions.

I have had one or two bad experiences on closeout auction sites that are worth mentioning. One was with a company that couldn't deliver the goods—and it took over four weeks to get my money back. Another was just a case of shoddy merchandise that was poorly described, but I had to donate almost half of it to the local thrift shop. Sometimes, when a deal sounds too good to be true, it is.

The best advice I can give you is to go with small orders only. On many of these sites, you often see the same product being sold by the same dealer at different starting prices. If you look closely at the minimum quantity, you'll see the difference.

A seller might offer a software package at a starting bid of $125 each on one auction. On another auction, he might offer the same software for $99 each. If you look at each auction separately, you will see that in the first auction, the minimum quantity is 5, but in the second (cheaper) auction, the minimum quantity is 25. In other words you can buy cheaper in volume. It makes sense, but it can be a bit confusing when you first look at it. Even though the price is a bit higher, I would advise paying a little more for the smaller order until you get to know the sellers and gain some experience.

Don't be afraid to e-mail the seller and ask questions about the product. The larger regular sellers don't want problems, so they will usually be honest with you. If you are buying something where the quality is important, offer to pay for a sample. As with wholesalers, they'll send you the sample for free if they believe you are a legitimate buyer but will usually ask you to pay the shipping.

One product line you see a lot of at the various wholesale auctions is older computer games, out-of-date software, and rebuilt or updated computers. You do need to be careful with these items, but you might be surprised to know there is great profit potential in many of the so-called obsolete products.

For instance, you can buy a pretty powerful computer updated with a lower-cost AMD chip for about $500. A similar performing new computer would cost over $1,200. If you buy these computers for $500 and sell them for $750 on eBay, that is a nice profit. There are users out there who are not afraid to take a chance on a refurbished product. There is even a great market for used equipment, as long as you stay with the higher-end products in good condition.

Government surplus and unclaimed merchandise auctions are also an excellent source of bargains. The postal service and customs are constantly running auctions around the country. (See the following list for information.) Also check with your local police or sheriff's department for auctions as many of them now run their auctions online.

Here are two of the major online wholesale closeout auction sites:

- www.ubid.com. This closeout auction sells items individually rather than in quantity. They also sell a lot of remanufactured goods. You can often find items here that you can resell on eBay.
- www.liquidation.com. We already covered this site, one of my favorites.

Here are some of the U.S. government auction sites:

- www.usps.com/auctions. U.S. Postal Service auctions sell unclaimed goods.

- www.gsaauctions.gov. The General Services Administration sells its surplus merchandise here.

- www.treas.gov/auctions/customs. The U.S. Customs Service runs auctions of surplus and seized merchandise.

22.5 Wholesale Auctions on eBay

A large number of closeout dealers are now selling on eBay in the Wholesale Lots subcategory that is located within most major product categories. These dealers are typically selling large lots by the case or the pallet load. For example, if you look at the Wholesale Lots in the Clothing, Shoes, and Accessories category, you might see something like Figure 22.1.

Figure 22.1

Shoes and Accessories category in Wholesale Lots.

I found 250 items listed in this category when I did this search. Notice the last item on the preceding screenshot, which is a 100-piece, New With Tag (NWT) lot of Ralph Lauren, Tommy (Hilfiger), Gymboree, and GAP infants' and children's clothing. When you click on the auction, it comes up with the description in Figure 22.2. I can't show all the information here, but the auction description contains photos of most of the clothing and a good representation of the lot.

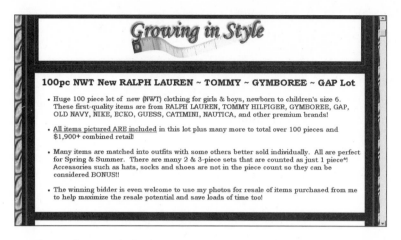

Figure 22.2
Information regarding New With Tag (NWT) lot.

This seller was selling 100 pieces of clothing. At the time I looked at the auction, it had 12 bids with the highest being $355. I followed the auction for the next three days, and it closed at $615.03. The seller was asking for $45 in shipping and handling, so that made the total lot cost $660.03. Because there were 100 pieces, the winning bidder ended up paying $6.60 per piece. This was in all probability a very profitable buy. I checked prices for several of the items using HammerTap and all the items I searched were selling for over $12 each; some items, such as the Tommy Hilfiger infant outfits, were selling for over $15 each.

Almost every major category on eBay has a subcategory for Wholesale Lots. Because we have a room in our home that is decorated in a nautical theme, I was looking for a print of a clipper ship. While searching on eBay, I found a seller who was offering a wholesale lot of 12 assorted clipper ship prints. I liked two or three, so I bid on the lot and won it for just under $50 or around $4 per print. When they arrived, I kept two of the prints for myself and sold the other 10 on eBay. They all sold at different prices, but the total was just over $200—a 400 percent gain, not counting the two prints I kept.

For more on buying at auctions, see Sections 25.3 and 25.4.

chapter 23

Wholesale Markets

Almost every large city in America has a place where wholesale distributors and manufacturers' reps set up showrooms for retail store owners and resellers to visit, look at the merchandise, and order products. Known in the trade as gift marts and/or merchandise marts, these marts showcase a wide variety of products, most related to the home and garden category. Larger home items, such as furniture, rugs, large art, and decorator pieces, are usually found in design centers.

23.1 Gift and Merchandise Marts

Gift marts and merchandise marts are some of the best places for a new seller to purchase goods for resale on the web or at auction.

First of all, you take less risk. You actually get to see and handle the merchandise you are going to buy, and only reputable companies are admitted to the center. In addition, wholesale merchants will often sell in small quantities because they're used to dealing with small local retailers.

When my wife, Karen, and I first started in the antiques business, we didn't have very much money, and our shop had very little merchandise. Antique shops attract a lot of browsers but very few actual buyers. We noticed that people would come in, look at our expensive collectibles and antiques, ask questions, engage in small talk, and leave without buying. They often had a slightly embarrassed look when they left.

One weekend we went to the 225 Merchandise Mart in New York City and came upon a company called Cape Cod Candles. I reasoned that everyone needs candles, and candles fit with antiques, so why not set up a display of nice candles in our store? It worked. Not only did our regular customers buy candles, but also the casual browser now had something practical to buy that only cost a few dollars. Within a few weeks we were generating several hundred dollars per week in profits from candles. Our cost was 50 percent of retail. Occasionally, Cape Cod Candles closes out a line or a color and sells these at 25 percent of retail.

The Cape Cod Company was wonderful to deal with. We could go into their shop in the gift center and shop just as if we were in a store—except we were paying wholesale. We sometimes bought only one or two of something. There was no minimum order, except on the box size (i.e., one box of 10 candles).

Gift centers have dozens, or even hundreds, of companies like Cape Cod Candles. In a typical gift center, about half of the companies are fairly small and might even be local companies. Almost every type of product is available from low-cost simple gifts to incredibly expensive gold and silver items, collectibles, linens, porcelain figurines, kitchenware, household accessories, dinnerware, china, and so on.

I have been using the terms *gift mart* and *merchandise mart* interchangeably, but there is a slight difference. Gift marts tend to be a little smaller and focus on gifts and small home decor items. Merchandise marts carry many of the same gift and home decor items but also have dealers in other areas, such as toys and games, kitchenware, light hardware items, and other things. The two biggest and most famous are Atlanta's AmericasMart and The Chicago Merchandise Mart.

The best thing about shopping in the marts is the constant turnover of merchandise. Every time we visit we see new things. August, September, and October are the best months to shop because they start showing what the hot-selling items for Christmas will be.

You don't walk out of the mart with your purchases. Instead, you place your orders and pay, and they ship everything, usually within three or four days. After you place three or four orders with the same company, most of them will extend you credit. After you have credit accounts with three or four merchants in the gift center, most of the other merchants will also give you credit.

Most gift centers in the United States are open Monday through Friday, from 9 A.M. until 5 P.M. Some of them are only open two or three days each week, so call ahead before going.

Although almost every major American city has a merchandise mart or gift center, you should make the pilgrimage to one of the larger cities, such as New York, Chicago, Los Angeles, San Francisco, Seattle, Atlanta, Dallas, Denver, or Miami. These cities have several gift centers. Whereas Pittsburgh might have a gift center with 100 merchants, New York has several centers with 200 to 300 merchants each. AmericasMart in Atlanta has 13 floors with more than 600 wholesale vendors.

I've included a list of a few of the larger marts and gift centers around the country. There are probably others that I am not aware of. If you don't see a mart listed for your city, look in the yellow pages under Gifts, Manufacturers, and Wholesalers. Occasionally the actual gift center will not be listed, but several companies all have the same address. This is almost always the gift center address.

Here is a list of the major merchandise and gift marts around the United States:

Bedford, MA

Northeast Market Center
1000 Technology Park Dr.
Billerica, MA 01821
(978) 670-6363
www.northeastmarketcenter.com

Charlotte, NC

Charlotte Merchandise Mart
2500 E. Independence Blvd.
Charlotte, NC 28205
704-333-7709
www.carolinasmart.com

Chicago, IL

The Merchandise Mart
200 World Trade Center Chicago
Chicago, IL 60654
312-527-7580
www.merchandisemart.com

Columbus, OH

Columbus Gift Mart
2000 Westbelt Dr.
Columbus, OH 43228
614-876-2719
www.thecolumbusmarketplace.com

Dallas, TX

Dallas Market Center
2100 Stemmons Freeway
Dallas, TX 75207
214-655-6100
www.dallasmarketcenter.com

Denver, CO

Denver Merchandise Mart
451 E. 58th Ave.
Denver, CO 80216
303-292-6278
www.denvermart.com

High Point, NC

International Home Furnishings Center
210 E. Commerce Ave.
High Point, NC 27260
336-888-3700
www.ihfc.com

Indianapolis, IN

Indianapolis Gift Mart
1220 Indianapolis Ave.
Lebanon, IN 46205
765-453-1687

Kansas City, KS

Kansas City Gift Mart
6800 W. 115th St.
Overland Park, KS 66211
913-491-6688
www.kcgiftmart.com

Los Angeles, CA

The L.A. Mart
1933 South Broadway
Los Angeles, CA 90007
213-749-7911
www.lamart.com

Miami, FL

Miami International Merchandise Mart
777 N.W. 72nd Ave.
Miami, FL 33126
305-261-2900
www.miamimart.net

Minneapolis, MN

Minneapolis Gift Mart
10301 Bren Road West
Minnetonka, MN 55343
952-932-7200
www.mplsgiftmart.com

New York, NY

New York Merchandise Mart
41 Madison Ave.
New York, NY 10010
212-686-1203
www.41madison.com

225 Fifth Avenue
7 W. 34th St.
New York, NY 10010
212-684-3200
www.225fifthavenue.com

New York MarketCenter
230 Fifth Ave.
New York, NY 10010
800-698-5617
www.230fifthave.com

The International Toy Center
177 Sound Beach Ave.
Old Greenwich, CT 06870
203-637-5466

San Francisco, CA

San Francisco Gift Center and Jewelry Mart
888 Brannan St.
San Francisco, CA 94103
415-861-7733
www.gcjm.com

Seattle, WA

Seattle Gift Center
6100 Fourth Ave. South
Seattle, WA 98108
206-767-6800
www.pacificmarketcenter.com

There are many places to buy wholesale—on the web, at auction, and so on—but gift centers are probably the best and most risk-free places to find goods to sell on eBay or on your website.

Merchandise marts and gift centers usually sell products designed for keystone pricing. "Keystone" is a wholesale term that means you can double the price of something to sell at retail. Unless you have something really unique, you will be unable to do this on eBay because people are looking for bargains—after all, that is the point of eBay. Therefore, you might only realize a 20 to 30 percent margin on goods from the gift centers and merchandise marts. This is okay as long as you are selling a good volume, turning your merchandise over often, and reinvesting the profits.

Keep in mind that it will be very hard to make a lot of money at a 30 percent margin if you are selling things for $10. When I visit a merchandise mart, I look for things that I can sell for $50 to $100 or more.

The final issue relating to gift and merchandise marts is gaining admission. These centers work very hard to keep the general public out, so you will have to prove you have a business. When you go to a mart for the first time, make sure to take your sales tax certificate, your business checkbook, business cards, and purchase orders. If you don't have purchase orders, you can buy preprinted ones at any office supply store. Simply have a rubber stamp made and prestamp them with the name of your business, or get ones you can print your name on using your computer.

23.2 Design Centers

Design centers are like the gift marts, except they deal in larger items, such as furniture and home accessories, lamps, candlesticks, tables and chairs, paintings, prints, frames, mirrors, ceramics, and so on. Some design centers have also started carrying patio furniture and garden sculptures. You probably will not be selling furniture on the web, but the design centers are well worth visiting for the many small things they sell.

Many of the design centers house small importers from Taiwan, the Philippines, Indonesia, and so on. These companies often sell small decorative items that make great eBay products. The design centers are often, but not always, located in the same neighborhoods as the gift marts, so you can almost always visit both on the same day.

You can locate design centers around the United States at www.dezignare.com/designcenter.html.

23.3 Jewelry Centers

Some of the larger merchandise marts, such as the San Francisco Gift Center and Jewelry Mart, have a jewelry section. Other large cities, such as Los Angeles, have their own separate jewelry mart. The jewelry marts house manufacturers, importers, reps, and distributors. If you want to sell jewelry on eBay, jewelry marts are the best place to shop. In many instances you can deal directly with manufacturers from Hong Kong and Italy, two places where beautiful jewelry is made.

The one difference between a jewelry mart and a gift mart is pricing. Prices in the gift and merchandise marts are usually fixed, and you cannot negotiate unless you want to purchase a really large quantity of something. In the jewelry marts, however, negotiating is the norm. The key to being able to negotiate successfully is to really know and understand what you are buying and what the prevailing prices are. This is why I would not recommend selling jewelry on eBay unless you have the knowledge and experience necessary or are willing to spend the time to learn everything you need to know to become successful.

For more on buying wholesale, see Chapter 19.

For more on finding suppliers offline, see Chapter 24.

For more on the art of negotiating, see Chapter 20.

Wholesale Trade Shows

Trade shows are my absolute favorite place to buy. First of all, I love to shop—and trade shows are a shopper's Mecca. New products are introduced at shows long before they hit the market. You can handle the merchandise, see and feel the quality, ask questions, and occasionally even get free samples.

24.1 A Sampling of Major Trade Shows

The best trade shows are in Las Vegas, Atlanta, New York, and Chicago, although you'll find good trade shows in almost every major trading city in the world.

24.1.1 The Chicago Gift Show

For general merchandise, one of the best trade shows is The Chicago Gift Show at the Chicago Merchandise Mart (The Mart) in Chicago, which is actually a collection of four shows that overlap. Don't let the word "gift" throw you—it encompasses hundreds of categories of merchandise. Some examples are gourmet foods, luggage, jewelry, watches, collectibles, trendy items (e.g., RC Stunt Cars, SpongeBob SquarePants, South Park, and so on), plush toys, specialty toys, executive gifts (e.g., Sharper Image), garden tools and accessories, household accessories, bed and bath, leather goods, country stuff, candles, handicrafts, fashion accessories, fountain pens, and so on. There is something for everyone at these shows.

The Mart is a huge facility that hosts trade shows all year around and also has many permanent wholesale dealers on the premises and in the surrounding area. The Mart also owns The Mart in High Point, North Carolina (furniture and home accessories), and the Design Center in Washington, D.C.

On the web go to www.merchandisemart.com for a complete listing of all their trade shows, locations, services, and registration info. Another source for trade shows is www1.buylink.com. Look under the **Resources** tab on the website.

Another huge show is the ASD/AMD Wholesale Merchandise show in Las Vegas held every March and August. It has over 4,000 exhibitors in three different convention halls.

24.1.2 The Las Vegas Consumer Electronics Show

The granddaddy of trade shows is the Consumer Electronics Show in Las Vegas. The show is held in January and is one of the largest trade shows in the world.

CES, as it's known in the trade, occupies all of the Las Vegas Convention Center, all the display space in the adjoining Hilton Hotel, and spills over to occupy space in four other hotels in town. (Many of the manufacturers hold lavish parties every night. Whenever you visit a booth, ask if they are having a party or if they have a Hospitality Suite. These are great places to meet people and score great gifts and free samples.)

Every type of consumer electronic device imaginable is on display at the CES, and the definition of "consumer electronics" is quite broad. There is even an "adult" section (walled off in its own area) for "adult devices and entertainment."

The CES show is about 50 percent manufacturers and 50 percent distributors and wholesalers. This is the place to make contacts, meet people one-on-one, and find out where you can buy the hot new products on display.

The biggest displays are obviously the large companies such as Sony, Hitachi, Panasonic, Dell, IBM, Microsoft, Hewlett Packard, Apple, and so on. Some of their booths cover 10,000 square feet. Employees of the manufacturers as well as dealers and distributors are present. Just ask the hostesses to introduce you to a dealer representative who will give you an opportunity to discuss your needs.

PowerSeller Tip

A great opportunity for eBay sellers is the hundreds of small companies located in the hotels, hallways, and fringes of the CES. These companies are seeking dealers, often for innovative new products. I absolutely guarantee anyone with an interest in any form of consumer electronics will find a great opportunity to buy something at one of these shows. When Tivo did their first show, they were located in a small, out-of-the-way location and would talk with anyone who showed interest.

24.2 Finding the Right Trade Show for You

Not all trade shows are giants like the Chicago Gift Show and the CES. There are hundreds of trade shows in Las Vegas, New York, Los Angeles, San Francisco, Atlanta, Miami, Portland, Seattle, Pittsburgh, Dallas, and Philadelphia. You can find them by checking with the convention bureau in each of these cities.

For example, in Las Vegas, the Las Vegas Visitors and Convention Bureau (www.lvcva.com/meetings/convention-calendar.jsp) lists upcoming trade shows for the next year. Enter a keyword in the search box such as "jewelry" and find a trade show for anything. You can also enter a time period, such as January 1, 2009 to March 31, 2009, and it will display every trade show scheduled during those months.

You can call a city's convention center or visitor's bureau and say "Hi, my name is Marilyn Smith and I am doing research on the trade shows that will be held in Pittsburgh this year. Would you mind e-mailing or faxing me your calendar of events at the convention center?" You will usually receive a response within the hour.

Some trade shows are so small (40 to 50 dealers) that they are not held in convention centers, but in hotels. You can find these smaller shows by reading the magazines of a given industry. Computer magazines routinely list or advertise information about upcoming trade shows. I saw an ad in a magazine called *American Quilting* for an annual trade show. Likewise, a friend of mine makes and sells artistic/collectible marbles. He attends about four glass-dealer and collector trade shows per year to sell his marbles.

And it doesn't matter what you sell—there is a trade show somewhere for any product. You can ask storeowners and dealers what trade shows they attend. You can check the website, or call the convention bureau in any major city and ask for a schedule of trade shows.

PowerSeller Tip

The ASD/AMD Merchandise Group (www.merchandisegroup.com) organizes some of the largest trade shows in the country.

Wand (www.wand.com) is an online global trade directory. After you register on the site, you can search for wholesale suppliers and find a trade show for virtually any product made.

24.3 Working a Trade Show for Profits

The real opportunity is to buy at trade shows. The manufacturers are there to promote; the dealers are there to deal. To be successful, however, you must look and act like a buyer.

You can't actually carry products out of the show. The dealers take orders (many have show specials that are usually great deals), and the products are shipped to your business address. Follow this advice to get the most out of a trade show:

- Wear dress-casual or corporate-casual clothes. Almost no one goes to a trade show in a coat and tie except the exhibitors. If you have a polo shirt with the logo of your company on it, that is perfect.

- Carry a bag or briefcase. By the end of the show you will be loaded down with samples, giveaways, and product brochures. And you need your hands free, so use a bag with a shoulder strap. Wear comfortable walking shoes. At a recent trade show, I could tell the real pros; they were pulling Rolling Bags behind them to hold all their brochures and catalogs.

- Make up a special business card just for trade shows. On it, use a different e-mail address from your usual one (use a third party e-mail such as those available through Hotmail or Yahoo!) and a post office box or private mailbox address. Almost every booth will be running some type of contest, and you'll want to use this business card to drop in the many fishbowls if you want to win something. If you use your regular e-mail address, by the time you attend a few shows, you'll be getting e-mails from hundreds of suppliers. I only give my real e-mail address to the suppliers I am really interested in. I still check my Hotmail address once in a while in the event I might find something there that interests me.

- Carry the following supplies:

  200 to 400 business cards (depending on the size of the show)

  A hand-held calculator

  Your business checkbook

  Professional-looking folder with a note pad inside

  Your sales tax number

  A few blank purchase orders

- Plan to stay for the whole show. It is silly to go to a three-day trade show and only attend a few hours.

- Always arrive the night before, and arrive at the trade show center the moment it opens. You'll beat the crowds, and you might get the first orders in for that hot product that's going to be in big demand. Also, if you are attending a show in Las Vegas, it's much cooler in the morning.

- Most trade shows have seminars in conjunction with them. Always attend these. You will meet people, make contacts, and usually learn valuable information about products and marketing.

- Enter every contest; drop your card into every fishbowl. First of all, you might win some really great prizes. You will also be put on mailing lists, which is actually good if you are in business, because you might receive free samples and promotions in the mail.

- Always register in advance for trade shows—the earlier, the better. First of all, you get a discount on the admission if there is an admission price. You also get offers for discounts on hotels, rental cars, and airfares; be sure to ask about them when you register.

  Another advantage of preregistering is that you get a professional, pre-printed nametag, and you don't have to stand in line to register when you arrive because your nametag and entry tickets are sent in the mail.

- Remember to bring plenty of documentation showing you are a legitimate business when you go to register at a trade show in person (business cards, commercial checkbook, purchase orders, and tax ID number).

- Many of the big companies throw lavish parties during the trade show. The names to invite are often taken from the registration list. So get your registration in at least six weeks in advance of the show, if possible, to be included in all of the activities and events.

24.4 How to Buy at Trade Shows

A trade show is a great place to buy. Most companies offer special "trade show" pricing if you place orders during the show. Ideally, you should go with a budget. You don't need cash, although you will need to be able to pay for goods before they are shipped if you don't have trade credit.

If you see something you want and don't have the money, just tell the seller you have already spent your budget, but you would like to place an order for later delivery (say three months) if he will still give you the special trade show price. This works about half of the time.

Don't be afraid to tell the sellers you are just a small operator selling at auctions and on websites. You will be surprised how cordial and helpful these people are. After all, they are salespeople, and they want to sell.

PowerSeller Tip

You might encounter dealers who won't sell to you unless you have a storefront. Here's how to handle that: thank the person you spoke with, and walk away. Go back to the booth the next day, and try to talk with someone else. Don't worry about being recognized; the people in these booths can't remember every conversation and person they speak with. Now just try and finesse the issue of a storefront. You don't have to lie, just act like a retailer with a store. If the issue doesn't come up, don't raise it. This technique will work about half of the time.

The other technique is to agree with the person and say that a lot of suppliers don't want to deal with eBay sellers because they undercut their retailers' prices. Then say that you will agree to sell at their minimum advertised price (MAP) if they will agree to work with you. I have actually used this technique to get a couple of exclusives.

You see a lot of totally new products at trade shows, and you want to be sure there is a market for them before you commit to placing an order. Fortunately, many of the larger trade shows have computer kiosks hooked up to the Internet where you can do research; otherwise, you'll need a laptop computer with Internet access. When you see a product that looks interesting, log onto eBay and go to the **advanced search** page. Type in the product, and click the box for **completed listings** to see if the product is selling on eBay and what sort of prices sellers have achieved over the past two weeks. If you use HammerTap, you can search back up to one year and see how the product did at the time of year you will be selling it.

24.5 Overseas Trade Shows

Major trade shows are also held in Europe and the Far East. Hamburg, Düsseldorf, London, Paris, Rome, Tokyo, Shenzhen, Taipei, Hong Kong, and Milan are major trade show centers. You can call, write, fax, or e-mail the convention bureaus (in English) and ask for a schedule of their upcoming trade shows.

If you're a book dealer, you already know about the major book fairs in Europe. If you deal in consumer electronics, you know about the Tokyo Electronics Show and the Shenzhen Consumer Electronics Trade Fair. If you are adventurous, these are great travel and business opportunities. And you can write off at least a portion of your overseas vacation against your taxes if you attend a trade show while you are there.

Far Eastern trade shows are the best. They give away tons of free samples and even small buyers are often invited to parties and out for special dinners. Placing even a small order will guarantee an evening of entertainment.

Overseas trade shows tend to be heavily attended by the actual manufacturers, and this is especially true in the Far East. These manufacturers typically want to sell in very large quantities. However, at the shows I have attended there is almost always an importer, agent, or manufacturer's rep available who can arrange for smaller-quantity purchases.

The foreign convention bureaus and associations organizing the shows almost always offer greatly reduced airfares and hotel packages to the shows. You will often even be met at the airport with free ground transportation if you register through the show management for your travel. I recently saw a trade show deal to China advertised at $999 including R/T airfare from Los Angeles or San Francisco, hotel, and daily transportation to the show.

In the next chapter you'll learn about Global Sources. Their website, www. globalsources.com, has information on almost every trade show in the Far East.

And don't worry about language. English is the universal language of commerce. Almost every trade show I have ever attended in the Far East and Europe had brochures and signs in both English and the native language.

In Chapter 26 I talk about direct importing. If this is a route you decide to take, then you'll really want to start attending the overseas trade shows, as this is where you can find the deals and the new products, well before your competition finds them.

24.6 Gaining Admission to Trade Shows

Much like the gift and merchandise marts, trade show management works very hard to keep ordinary consumers and nonbusiness people out of their shows. They aren't trying to make your life difficult for the heck of it. The vendors who exhibit demand this as they don't want to deal with the general public and they don't want nonretailers to see their wholesale prices.

Generally, if you are registered at your local merchandise or gift mart, you can just show that ID to gain admission to the show. If not, then you should arrive at the show with your full complement of business paraphernalia, which includes business cards, letterhead, purchase orders, a commercial checkbook with a bank account in the name of your business, and your sales tax number and forms. Don't be surprised if the people at the registration desk demand to see all of these.

The good news is that you only have to do this once. After you are registered, you will be sent preregistration forms every time a show comes to town. Most of the trade shows are put on by just one or two companies. After you are registered with both of them, you can preregister for any of their shows anywhere in the country.

For more on negotiating with wholesalers, see Chapter 20.

For more on importing, see Chapter 26.

chapter 25

Wholesale Sources for Art, Antiques, and Collectibles

The categories of art, antiques, and collectibles used to be the largest categories on eBay, but they have since been replaced by automobiles, apparel, electronics, and business and industrial goods. Nevertheless, thousands of eBay sellers are making excellent money in these categories—many of them at the Platinum and Titanium PowerSeller level. Most good-quality pieces in these categories sell themselves. The difficult part is finding the goods to sell.

One note before we get started: when I use the term *art* in this chapter, I'm not talking about new art that is commercially available from many wholesale suppliers and original pieces from artists themselves. Here I am talking about older art pieces, such as prints and maps, garden sculptures, and artistic collectibles such as scrimshaw ivory, Native American art pieces, and so on.

Vintage products are another popular type of product that falls within this area. These are items typically less than 50 years old that don't quite qualify as antiques, yet are collected by many people. Besides traditional collectibles, hot vintage categories include old tools, 1960s to 1980s–era electronics and photographic equipment, and vintage clothing from the 1960s and 1970s.

The term *wholesale price* doesn't really apply to the old art, antiques, and used-collectibles market. A wholesale price for an antique is any price you pay as long as it is less than you can sell it for. Unfortunately, very few wholesalers specialize in antiques and old collectibles. New collectibles that are still being manufactured are readily available, but older collectibles, like antiques, you must find the hard way.

Before starting on eBay, my wife and I were in the antiques business for over 12 years. Buying was by far the hardest part of the job. If we could find nice pieces at a good price, they seemed to sell themselves, but finding antiques at the right price was always a challenge.

Buying antiques and collectibles cheaply is where the real money is made in this business. (Remember: you make money when you buy—not when you sell.) Although I do list a few importers and wholesale antique dealers at the end of this chapter, there are several ways to buy antiques and collectibles far more cheaply than from these sources. Nevertheless, you can make money buying from the sources I list, though likely not as much as finding them on your own.

25.1 Garage and Yard Sales

Although it's seldom you ever find any rare or very expensive antiques at garage sales, this is where many dealers start. I have found hundreds of antiques, vintage items, and collectibles at garage sales. Admittedly, these were mostly items that would sell for under $100, but these items are the bread and butter of many small-town antique dealers and the right price range to sell on eBay. And if you are diligent, you occasionally make a nice score as I did recently when I bought a 1980s Nikon camera and two lenses for $150. It sold on eBay for over $1,100.

You can find good-quality art, antiques, and collectibles at garage sales if you use the right strategy. Although most of the items you find will be in the lower price category, some of these goods can realize high markups and occasionally you find that real treasure. My major finds have included a 1940s Bakelite bracelet that I bought for $1 and sold on eBay for just over $2,000 and an early eighteenth-century hand-colored map of New York harbor that I bought framed for $15 and sold for over $800.

There are some basic strategies to finding good antiques and collectibles at garage sales. First of all, pick your neighborhood. You will do best in neighborhoods where elderly people live because they have the most and oldest stuff.

Next are areas of more expensive homes. Watch the garage sale ads for words like *estate*. This means someone died or has been confined to a nursing home and someone is selling off his things. These are always the best kind of sales with the most saleable merchandise.

Use a map and plan your strategy by going to the best sales first. Always arrive early, just before opening time if possible.

My strategy is to scan the tables and pick up the first three or four good items I spot. If an item is in my hand, I don't have to buy it—I can always set it down after examining it, but no one else can snatch it up while I am holding it.

One technique, albeit a bit sneaky, is to visit the house the evening before. You will probably find the owners working in their garage setting up the sale. Walk up and say something like "I saw your garage sale ad and it said you were selling some antique tools. I collect antique tools, but I have to be out of town this weekend. I was wondering if I could take a look at what you have, if that isn't too much trouble." About half of the people will turn you away, but the other half will let you in. After you are in the garage, you can make an offer on anything you see.

A lot of people have stuff they don't know is saleable or just don't think to put it out at a garage sale. If you sell a certain kind of antique or collectible, always ask the people holding the garage sale if they have any. I know a fellow who sells old fishing lures, rods, and reels. He visits all the garage sales and just walks up to the homeowner and asks whether he has any old fishing lures. Invariably, many do and go get them. He gets to see them when no one else does.

It is tempting to buy anything you see that you know is cheap. But you need to shop selectively. Unless you are running an eBay junk shop, always look for the best merchandise. Also stay away from unusual items or what some people call white elephants unless you absolutely know the item has a market. Over the years I have bought a lot of "unique" items that sat in my shop, and later in my garage, for a very long time.

25.2 Estate Sales and Tag Sales

Formal estate sales are the source of some of the greatest finds in antiques and collectibles. They are a leading source of antiques for professional dealers.

Estate sales (and some tag sales) are usually structured events run by a professional hired by a probate attorney to dispose of a deceased person's furniture and accessories. I have found some great bargains at these formal sales, but the competition is stiff as they are heavily advertised to antique dealers.

The formal events are usually set up to give buyers a number. Buyers are let into the house in order, usually four or five at a time. I once went to a heavily advertised estate sale at 5 A.M., thinking I would get in line and get an early number. When I arrived, 20 people were already ahead of me. The only way to be assured of finding a bargain at one of these sales is to arrive early and get a low number.

Very few people who run estate sales are knowledgeable about all the items they are selling. You'll see many pieces, especially antiques, underpriced and many that are overpriced. (It sometimes pays to go back to an estate sale at the end of the last day when overpriced items are marked down and become more reasonable.) Because the organizers are not very good at setting prices, you can find some fabulous bargains. The problem is that you only have a few minutes to spot and select the bargains as the busier sales are moving people rapidly through the house.

This sneaky (but not illegal) trick can get you an advance look at an estate sale. When an estate sale is going on, the house is often for sale as well. A day or two before the sale, call the realtor whose name is listed on the sign, and tell him you're interested in seeing the house but can only do it today. If the realtor is busy, tell him you'd be happy to look at it on your own. Go to the house (with or without the realtor), and act like a prospective home buyer. While you are there, you can innocently chat with the people, look around, and spot the items you think you might be interested in. Now you know if it is worthwhile to show up at 5 A.M. to get an early spot in line. While you are there, you could even ask if you could buy an item you see. The top professionals will not sell to you before the sale, but sometimes one of the smaller dealers will.

Another trick to getting an advance peek at an estate sale is to volunteer to work at the sale. The sale organizers, who are running low-budget operations, need three or four people to dust, sort, mark, and tag the items to be sold. If you tell the seller you are trying to "learn the antiques business" and would be willing to work a couple of sales for free, you will probably be offered a spot. Now you'll have an opportunity to buy some of the items before the sale, as it is customary to let employees have the first crack before the doors open.

25.3 Local Auctions

Professional antique dealers get about one third to one half of their goods from auctions. When my wife and I were actively selling antiques on eBay, I could (and often did) go to a small-town auction on a Saturday and buy up to a dozen items. The next day I would list them for seven days on eBay. Almost always I'd make at least a 50 percent margin, and on many items I even doubled or tripled my money.

When you attend a small-town or country auction, as many as 200 people might be in the audience bidding. Most of them will bid on the lower- to medium-cost merchandise. The really prime pieces will only attract a few avid collectors or antique dealers. However, when you list these pieces on eBay, they are exposed to millions of people all over the world. I cannot say that I haven't ever lost money on a piece I bought at a local auction and sold on eBay—I have, but it's very rare. Even items purchased at auction for $10,000 or more can often be sold on eBay for a 10 to 20 percent gain. That is a small margin but a large dollar profit for one item. Having said that, although expensive antiques do sell on eBay, it can be very risky unless you really know what you are doing. The sweet spot seems to be art, antiques, and collectibles that sell in the $100 to $500 range. Pieces in this price range turn over much faster than either the cheaper or the more expensive pieces.

We covered auction buying earlier in Chapter 22, but remember these pointers when buying antiques and collectibles at an auction:

- Most important, arrive early and carefully examine what you plan to buy. Auction sales are final.

- Only buy premium items. Leave the mundane stuff for others. You'll make far more money on a really great piece in perfect condition than on something you see all the time.

- Never bid on anything that is cracked, broken, or flawed in any way that would detract from its value.

- Whenever an item sells for a really high price, the very next item usually goes very cheap. I don't understand the psychology of this, but I have personally witnessed it many times.

- If an auction is scheduled and the weather is really bad, always go! Bad weather can keep up to 50 percent of prospective bidders away from an auction, and less competition means lower prices.

- Never make the first bid, unless no one is bidding and the auctioneer cuts the opening bid down to a ridiculous price. I like to enter the bidding about halfway through.

- Never bid when more than three or four people are bidding at the same time. Adding to the bidding can start a frenzy that drives the price up. Wait until the action slows down.

25.4 Storage Locker Auctions

Storage lockers are a huge nationwide business. It seems that every town in America has at least one storage locker business, and hundreds of eBay sellers, most of whom are in the used-goods business, make a living just from storage locker auctions. You rarely find valuable antiques in storage lockers, but they can be a great source of vintage items, art, and collectibles.

By state law (in most states) storage locker owners must either hire an auctioneer or have the local sheriff conduct sales of goods left behind in abandoned storage lockers. (Most states allow the owner to sell the contents after 60 days of non-payment of rent.) The owners are not allowed to open the lockers and sell the goods individually—the locker contents must be sold "as is" as "a lot."

Large storage facilities auction from 5 to 10 units per month. Usually, if an auction company is doing the sale, they will schedule several sales the same day in different locations. I have followed the auctioneer from location to location, sometimes to as many as five per day. On one day I observed the contents of 22 units being sold from four different storage locker locations, all owned by the same company.

Typically very few people attend these auctions, and many who do will only bid up to $25 to $75 for the contents of a unit. These are usually flea market dealers. Stay away from the low-cost units, as they rarely contain much of value.

A storage unit auction usually works like this. The auctioneer or the sheriff's deputy will cut the padlock on the door and open it for about two minutes for people to peek inside. No one is allowed to enter the unit—you must look only from outside. (Carry a powerful flashlight because these units are usually dark or poorly lit.)

The bidding usually starts at about $10, and most of the units will sell for under $150. The handful of professionals will wait until they spot a unit that appears to have better stuff. A tip-off is boxes from a moving company. Most poor people move their own goods in U-Haul or supermarket boxes, but middle-class and upper-class people tend to use a van line or professional mover. The presence of several of these boxes usually means better-quality goods.

The better units usually sell in the $100 to $500 range. The most I've ever paid for a unit was $525, and the most I've ever seen a unit sell for is $790. In both cases the contents ended up being worth five to ten times that amount.

When the sale is over, you put your own padlock on the unit (carry a few with you to the sale) and go to the office and pay cash. They'll usually give you 72 hours to haul the goods off without charging you storage. Or if you want more time, you can just pay a month's storage—usually $25 to $75 depending on the size of the locker.

Now that you have bought the contents of the storage unit, what do you do with them? Come back the next day with your van or a pickup truck, and carefully unpack and sort the items into several piles as follows:

- Valuable items that you want to sell, such as any collectibles, glassware, art, small antiques, and accessories
- Good stuff that you don't personally sell but that has value. This could include electronics, good clothing, sporting goods, musical instruments, and so on.
- Useful, but essentially unsaleable, merchandise
- Trash

The first category you'll sell on eBay. The second category you can sell to a flea market dealer or second-hand shop.

The useful, but unsaleable category you can donate to the local thrift shop for a tax deduction. I once paid $115 for a storage auction where I netted over $700 from the goods I sold and a $210 tax deduction for donating the rest to the local Rotary Club thrift shop. The trash, of course, you just take to the dump.

Occasionally you'll end up with large items that are difficult to ship but still have some value. Because you probably don't want to bother selling these on eBay, you can list them on free local classified sites like www.craigslist.org or www.kijiji.com, which is owned by eBay.

The bonus that comes with purchasing storage locker contents is every once in a while you'll come upon something really valuable. I once found a collection of 78-RPM jazz records that I sold to a dealer for over $3,000.

Another time I bought a locker for under $300 that contained a collectible Fender guitar worth over $2,000 and a box of old candy dispensers that I sold on eBay individually for a total of $200. I also sold several other nice items in the locker for another $200.

Over the years I have found old football and baseball cards, collectible art glass, depression glass, a complete eight-piece setting of Liberty Blue dinnerware, silverware, old ironware platters, a trunk full of WWII memorabilia and an M-1 rifle, and a box of mountain-climbing rope, climbing shoes, and karabiners worth about $400. There was also a brand-new toilet, still in the shipping container, which now resides in our guest bathroom.

25.5 Advertising for Goods

Placing an advertisement in a major newspaper might be a little expensive, but this is by far one of the best ways to pull antiques and collectibles out of the woodwork. Make your ad specific; don't advertise for antiques in general. State your needs exactly; a photo of the types of items you are looking for works very well. And you will be amazed at the response you get.

I have a friend who deals in collectible fountain pens, some of which are worth more than $5,000. He told me his best finds come from placing a small display ad about two inches square in big-city newspapers. A recent advertisement read: "I Buy Old Fountain Pens for Cash," and it had a photo of a couple of old fountain pens. Depending on the paper, the ad could cost as little as $50 or as much as $1,000. He once placed an ad in *The New York Times* and received over 200 calls. He only bought about a dozen pens from the ad, but all of them were worth from $500 to $2,000 each, and he paid less than $2,000 for all 12 pens.

A company in Kansas City called The Antique Warehouse travels from city to city taking out full-page newspaper ads looking for antiques and collectibles. The ads are in sections, such as quilts, dolls, glassware, old toys, and so on, and each section has photos of the type of items they are seeking.

The ads don't use the words "Antiques Roadshow," but they give the impression that is what they are. The buyers set up in a hotel meeting room for the weekend, and people flock to see them. It's not unusual for The Antique Warehouse to spend $10,000 on advertising, but they might end up buying more than $200,000 worth of antiques and collectibles at 25¢ on the dollar. They then turn around and sell the items in their store and on eBay under a variety of user IDs.

This sounds like a lot of money for advertising, but you'd be surprised at the response they get. If you are trying to build a million-dollar-a-year business on eBay, this is a fast way to find valuable and expensive antiques to sell.

If you don't have a lot of capital, start small, reinvest your money, and you'll really be amazed at the results. It is important to specialize. People will come to you eager to sell and to talk with a "specialist" about their treasure. Offer no more than 40 percent of the "quick sale" value or about 25 percent of what the item would sell for in a retail antique store.

You should also place a small ad in local antique journals in the Item Wanted section. These journals are read by "pickers," people who travel to auctions, garage sales, estate sales, and even go door-to-door in rural areas asking people if they have any antiques to sell. When you get to know a few pickers, you'll have a steady supply of the items you are looking for.

Another free venue for advertising is the bulletin board in a supermarket and/or laundromat. Tack up a small sign on a card that says something such as:

> REWARD
> I pay cash for Antiques & Collectibles
> Call Ralph at 555-3333
> Top Dollar Paid for Old Vases, Glassware,
> and Silverware

You'll be amazed at how well these cards work. If you place 10 to 20 of these notices in various places around town (small towns are best), you will typically get three or four calls a week.

25.6 Antique Importers and Wholesalers

A few antique importers and wholesalers sell antiques and collectibles to dealers, and their prices are usually good enough to make money on. When we bought from these dealers for our antique shop, we would often net about 40 percent of our selling price. If you buy carefully, you should be able to do about the same or better.

PowerSeller Tip

If you have a choice, try to buy from suppliers who are geographically close to you to save money on shipping. Some dealers will briefly store items after you buy them, which enables you to buy the piece, photograph it, sell it on eBay, and then arrange shipment directly from the antique dealer to your customer, thereby avoiding the cost of shipping it to you.

Here are some of the more well-known wholesale antique dealers and importers in the trade:

- The English Antiques Warehouse (www.englishantiqueimports.com) are importers of fine (and some not-so-fine) antiques from Merry Olde England. They bring in several container loads every month.

- The Antique Warehouse of St. Augustine, Florida (www.antqware.com), imports antiques from all over Europe by the container load.

- ARK Antiques (www.arkantiques.com) is one of the largest importers of antiques. Located in New Jersey just across the river from New York City, they move so much inventory their website is seldom up-to-date, so it's best to call them. They will often send out photos and prices. They are very reliable and will accurately describe anything they sell you.

- Wholesale Antiques (www.exit3.i-55.com/~whlslant) in Ponchatoula, Louisiana, sells directly to dealers.

- Dynasty Antiques (www.dynasty-antiques.com) sells and exports fine Chinese antiques to dealers all over the United States. They are a very experienced and reliable company. Their minimum order is $1,000.

- Paul Antiques (www.greatstuffbypaul.com) sells and imports antiques from all over the world. He is one of the leading antique and collectible whole-salers in the United States.

- The Anderle Gallery (www.anderle.com) is a large importer and retailer of antiques and tribal art. The website prices are retail, so contact him for wholesale pricing.

- Thailand Trade Net (www.thailandtradenet.com) sells Asian antiques, wood carvings, and antique and reproduction furniture.

- Eastern Curio (www.easterncurio.com) is a large Chinese exporter of Chinese antiques.

- Boone's Antiques (www.boonesantiques.com/main.html) in Wilson, North Carolina, has over four acres of antiques from all over the world. You will have to call and identify yourself as a dealer to get wholesale pricing.

- Thomas K. Salese Antiques (www.tksantiques.com) has been supplying auctioneers, antique dealers, foreign clientele, and the general public with high-quality eighteenth- and nineteenth-century English and French furniture for 25 years. They also specialize in twentieth-century mahogany pieces. Their 7,000-square-foot showroom is constantly supplied with containers from England and France.

- Rosso Wholesale Glass (www.wholesale-glass-dealer.com) supplies antiques and collectibles dealers all over the United States.

- VVG Antiques (www.vvg-vietnam.com/antiques.htm) exports antique and ancient art objects from Vietnam and other parts of Asia. They have been supplying dealers in the United States and Europe for over 30 years.

- Monster time (http://www.monster-time.com) is a wholesaler of vintage wristwatches, including Bulova, TAG, Rolex, and Omega.

For more about buying and selling art, antiques, and collectibles, see Section 11.1.5.

chapter 26

Importing for Huge Profits

The idea of becoming an importer of goods to sell on eBay is at once frightening and intimidating. People fear getting cheated, running afoul of government import regulations, and dealing with people thousands of miles away who speak another language. Importing can be a scary proposition, but like almost anything else in life, when you know how to do it, it's not that difficult. Think about your first driving lesson, and now think about how you don't think about driving now; you do it more or less automatically.

The reality is that hundreds of successful eBay sellers buy and sell imported goods every day, and thousands more companies import and sell goods on e-commerce websites.

26.1 Why Import?

The benefit of importing is simple: it's the cheapest way to buy commercial products to resell. You are buying directly from the manufacturer, with no middlemen or distributors taking a bite out of your profits. People are often amazed to discover the markups involved after middlemen and distributors add their costs and profits.

Here is an example. Have you ever seen the popular family-band two-way radios that retail here in the United States for around $49 a pair? Manufacturers in Taiwan and China sell these radios in large quantities for as little as $9 a pair. Typically an importer buys them in large quantities at that price and sells them in smaller quantities to a distributor for $13 a pair. The distributor then sells them to a retailer in even smaller quantities for $20 a pair, who sells them at retail for $49 a pair.

If you import them directly from the manufacturer, you could undercut the retail price and sell them on eBay or your website for $39 a pair. If we assume shipping and customs duties and other import-related costs would add $1.50 to each pair of radios, your cost would be about $10.50 a pair. If you sell them on eBay for $39 a pair, your gross margin would be $28.50.

This example shows the huge profits you can make when you import directly. If you instead buy small quantities from the distributor who sells to retailers, you'd probably pay around $20 a pair, and your margin would fall to $19 on each sale instead of $28.50. Also, other sellers will be buying from the same distributor for the same price. So as the quantity of radios available on eBay increases, sellers will start dropping prices. Eventually the margins could drop to as low as $10 per unit or even less.

As this example demonstrates, buying in large quantities directly from overseas manufacturers gives you pricing power. You can lower the price to a point where you are still making an excellent margin and deny your competitors a decent margin, making it difficult for them to compete with you.

26.2 How to Make Money Importing

With a product as popular as family-band radios, you'd probably need to import directly or at the very least buy from an importer. As with any popular product, there is so much competition on eBay that you can't build a large business unless you have the pricing power. But importing takes a large investment. For family-band radios, you'd probably have to purchase 5,000 pairs to get the $9 price. That works out to $45,000 plus shipping and duties. If you don't have this kind of money, you will need to arrange inventory financing from one of the sources we discussed in Chapter 6.

However, you can import products that cost less. For instance, I have imported products in quantities of 1,000 units that cost less than $2 each. Do you remember the little butane pocket torches used for soldering? A few years ago they were selling on eBay for $9.95. Today you can find them on eBay for under $5. When I imported them in 2002, I was able to buy 1,000 of them at a landed cost of $1.77 each.

I didn't think I could sell that many on eBay, so I sold half of the shipment to several local hardware stores and hobby shops (more about this tactic later) in lots of 50 for $4 each. It took me about four months to sell the remaining 500 on eBay. At first I was able to realize over $9 on each torch, but within a month or so others had entered the market and had driven the ASPs down to around $7, which was still a very nice profit. If I had bought them from an importer or distributor at a higher price, say $3.50 each, I could still have made some money but not as much.

This brings me to another tactic you can use to import if you don't have the capital or inventory financing available to purchase large-dollar-volume items. Your primary business might be selling on eBay, but you have other ways to sell as well. In the example of the torches, because I bought directly from the importer, my pricing power was such that I could become both a wholesaler and a retailer. With some merchandise you can actually presell the products before you place and pay for the order. If your pricing power is such that you can show a retailer a product where they can realize a markup in excess of 100 percent, you will find it very easy to locate buyers. For example, when the torches were selling on eBay for just over $9, several of the retail stores I called on ended up selling them for $12.95. Because I was selling them for $4 each, they were realizing over 300 percent markups.

It can be difficult for a small entrepreneur to obtain supplier financing for a product that no one knows will sell. But after you have orders from existing businesses, getting credit becomes much easier.

Another tactic some eBay PowerSellers use is to simply find another eBay seller or a businessperson who is willing to split the order with them. Today even some companies will act as aggregators for other eBay sellers. You can find these people by placing requests on the eBay message boards in the Seller Central board.

You can also make money importing by becoming a wholesaler on eBay. As noted in Section 22.5, the Wholesale Lots subcategories are very active on eBay. A lot of sellers will buy a product in large quantities and basically become an import dealer.

I know one seller who deals in low-cost power tools he imports from China. He can buy one-inch impact power drills (used for drilling holes in rock or concrete) in China in quantities of 1,000 units for as little as $11 each landed cost.

He sells the drills on eBay for $19.99 plus $22 shipping. His shipping cost is only about $10, so he's making a total gross margin of $20.99 on each drill. He also runs an auction in the wholesale large lots category where he sells the drills in lots of one dozen for $14 each and has structured the shipping costs so he makes an extra $40 shipping on each lot. (Note: Some sellers still do this, but you could earn a low DSR score under eBay's new system.) In this instance his gross margin is $76 on each one-dozen lot sold. You would think this would result in everyone's buying from him and listing them on eBay to compete with him, but it doesn't. Most of his large lot sales are to store owners and flea market dealers. A few people buy them and turn around and sell them on eBay to compete with him, but because he is importing directly at the lowest cost, he has the pricing power to withstand the competition.

I see the same thing happening in the apparel category all the time. If you look at the auctions for designer blue jeans, you see many of the same sellers listing dozens of auctions for individual pairs of jeans as well as lots of 50 or 100 pairs at a time.

26.3 Locating Overseas Manufacturers

There are several sources for finding overseas manufacturers. One way is to simply go overseas and attend the trade shows (see Section 24.5). This way you can meet the sellers face-to-face, examine the product features and quality, and negotiate right on the spot. If you want to try importing without actually going overseas, you have several resources for locating products and manufacturers, but the best is Global Sources at www.globalsources.com.

26.3.1 Global Sources

Global Sources has a fantastic website that lists more than 50,000 companies in over 60 countries. In addition to locating manufacturers, you can use this website to research almost any type of product for price or specifications, find and register for overseas trade shows, get help with shipping and packaging, subscribe to several free magazines that feature new products, see travel offers, locate customs brokers and freight forwarders, and receive e-mail alerts for products you specify whenever a new product is introduced.

Go to the website, and take the visitor's tour. After that, you will be given an opportunity to register. I strongly recommend taking the complete tour first, as you will better understand the vast capabilities of this site.

When you register, you'll be asked a series of questions about the kind of items you import and your annual sales volume. If you are just starting out and don't have a track record, just make up some answers. Use your real shipping address, though, because this is where samples and shipments will be sent.

Many Asian companies still prefer to do business by fax, so it will be helpful if you enter a fax number. Some of them will ask you to fax them on your business letterhead before they will send you prices or samples. You will also receive a lot of e-mail after you register at Global Sources, so you might want to create a separate e-mail account (such as a free Yahoo! or Hotmail account) to avoid clogging up your primary account.

After you have registered, you can browse the various product categories, which are too many to list here, but they include Electronics, Gifts and Home Products, Hardware and Security Devices, Fashion and Fabrics, Telecommunications Equipment, Computers and Hardware, Jewelry, Timepieces, and Toys. You will also receive the *Global Sources* magazine, which has articles on new products and importing, trade show announcements, and advertisements from hundreds of companies, many of which don't have websites.

Global Sources is a great place to find and register for the overseas trade shows. They often have special travel packages to the shows. These are not advertised on the website but will be sent to you after you register for a show.

Check the Global Sources site on a regular basis, as they are constantly updating it with new featured products, closeout specials, special buying trips with subsidized hotel and airfare announcements, and all kinds of other news about international trade.

Most of the manufacturers sell only in large quantities, but you can sometimes negotiate to order smaller volumes. Also, if you search diligently, you can find many smaller manufacturers who will deal in small quantities.

When you get down to selecting products, photos will pop up with links attached for requesting more information, prices, delivery, and/or ordering samples.

Global Sources is the leading site for finding overseas manufacturers. Most of them are in Asia, primarily China, but companies from other countries are listed as well. The downside to Global Sources is that they feature mostly large companies that only sell in large volumes. This is perfect if you are playing in that market, but there are opportunities to locate other smaller, more-specialized suppliers through other routes.

Another large importing information site is Alibaba at www.alibaba.com.

If you would like to try importing in smaller quantities before diving into importing in a big way, check out www.globalsourcesdirect.com. This is a website operated by Global Sources that deals in smaller quantities, and you can pay for all your orders with PayPal.

26.3.2 Working with Commercial Officers

If you know that a certain type of product is manufactured in a specific country, you can contact the embassy for that country and simply ask for the commercial officer (CO) or trade consul. They manage and facilitate the import and export of products from their country. When you speak to a CO or consul, simply tell him what you are looking for, and he will get back to you with a list of companies that could supply your needs. In many smaller and developing countries these will often be small to medium companies that will be more than willing to work in small volumes. For instance, South and Central America, Asia, and Eastern Europe are filled with thousands of small cottage-type industries seeking to sell their goods abroad. You can locate any embassy in the world online at www.EmbassyWorld.com.

Some countries, including Australia and Ireland, have large Trade Commissions in the United States, which are separate from their embassies. For example, the Australian Trade Commission, Austrade (www.austrade.gov.au), has offices in several large cities in the United States. If you can contact them, they will help you locate product suppliers in their country who are looking to export to you. We recently found a company through Austrade who is supplying us with a unique barbecue grill that hooks into the trailer hitch on a car or truck for tailgating. The manufacturer has been looking for a distributor in the United States, but the barbecue market is very hard to break into, so he was delighted to sell to us.

Last year my wife and I visited Costa Rica to do some sport fishing. One of my good friends runs a nursery and also sells garden furniture and accessories. We were walking through a small Mercado and spotted some beautiful teak garden benches and tables. Costa Rica is one of the largest teak exporters in the world. The retail prices in the Mercado were about half of what these would sell for in the States, and I knew the wholesale prices would be even lower. Unfortunately, the seller refused to tell me how to contact the manufacturer (my high school Spanish didn't help). When we returned to the States, I told my friend about the furniture and showed him some digital photos I had taken. The next day I called the CO at the Costa Rican Embassy in Washington, and within three days I had a list of four manufacturers on my fax machine.

I didn't have any personal interest in importing teak furniture, but my friend contacted two of the manufacturers and ended up buying a container load of small garden benches, tables, and chairs. Even after shipping costs and duty, he was able to sell the furniture at a 300 percent markup. The company he was dealing with only had 10 employees and no website, so it is unlikely he could have found them without the help of the commercial officer at the embassy.

26.3.3 Visit the Country—Either Online or in Person

Another way to find these small exporters is to go to the website of almost any small country from Albania to Zimbabwe, and you'll probably find links to sites that list importing opportunities. For example, when my son was a teenager, he was looking for a cheap source of the then-popular Hacky Sacks, which are made in Guatemala. I did a search on Guatemala and found links to dozens of companies selling Guatemalan handicrafts. We imported three dozen Hacky Sacks, and he sold them to his friends at school. You can contact these companies, often by e-mail, and request catalogs and pricing information.

Direct importing requires a sense of adventure. If you like to travel and have that sense of adventure, an excellent way to get started importing directly is to visit the countries you wish to import from, much like I did in Costa Rica.

If you are really adventurous, you could go on a guided buying trip. The last time I looked at the Global Sources home page, they were offering a guided buying trip to Vietnam with low-cost airfares and rooms at the five-star Excelsior Hotel for $48 a night.

One nearby country that offers great opportunities for importing is Mexico. I know someone who used to go to Mexico twice a year to purchase sterling silver jewelry. He started small, but eventually was bringing back $15,000 to $20,000 worth of jewelry on each trip. He sold to stores and at flea markets, and his wife held jewelry parties in people's homes. He revealed that he was making a 400 percent markup on every retail piece of jewelry he sold and over 150 percent when he sold to stores.

I lost track of this fellow a few years ago, but I am willing to bet he is one of the many people selling Mexican silver jewelry on eBay today. You can do the same thing in almost any country as my friend did in Mexico. But be warned: you need a good head for business, a lot of patience, and a grand sense of adventure. The rewards for those who are successful are great: tax-deductible world travel and potentially huge profits.

No matter how you decide to import, just remember to research what you plan to buy before you purchase it. It is very easy to find beautiful things at great prices, only to put them on eBay and discover they won't sell.

26.4 Obtaining Sample Orders

One of the best ways to avoid getting stuck with merchandise that won't sell on eBay or your website is to buy a small sample quantity and test market it. Almost any manufacturer will either give or sell you sample quantities for this purpose. For example, when you are on the Global Sources website (see Section 26.2.1) and find a product you are interested in, you can click a link to request a sample. Most of the companies will send you samples of low-cost items for free if you give them your FedEx or UPS account number. For more expensive merchandise, they will usually offer to sell you a few pieces at or slightly above their normal wholesale cost.

Getting manufacturers to send you free or low-cost samples can be tricky. Unfortunately, there are people who routinely try to scam manufacturers into sending them free products, which makes manufacturers very skeptical. Some manufacturers will even send out a communication threatening to report you to the Federal Trade Commission if they think you are just trying to get free samples for your own use. If you get one of these, don't worry, it's not against the law to request free samples, and the Federal Trade Commission could care less. This is just a tactic some manufacturers use to discourage unsophisticated people who are trying to scam them.

If you actually want free or low-cost samples to evaluate, the first thing you have to do is create credibility. When you contact the manufacturer, be sure to write a professional, businesslike communication.

If you send an e-mail that says: "How much are your model XX-00 radios, and how many do I have to buy to get them?", they will probably ignore you. Instead try sending an e-mail or faxing them on your business letterhead a message that goes something like this:

Gentlemen:

Would you please send me two of your Model 100 Clock Radios for evaluation? We are preparing our fall selling lineup, and I would like one unit for evaluation and one for photography. Kindly ship by UPS second day air. My account number is 1234567.

Sincerely,

Jane Smith
Oakdale Novelties

The fact that you are offering to pay the shipping and furnishing your account number is the key.

Here is another approach:

Gentlemen:

I received the new product alert through Global Sources for your newest dive watches today. I would like to place a sample order for 25 pieces so we may evaluate the market for these interesting watches.

Kindly fax a pro-forma invoice to me at 202-555-6789. We do not mind paying a small surcharge for the sample order, and I will pay in advance by cashier's check or wire transfer to your bank.

Thank you,

Jason Jones
Jones Specialties

If you are successful getting 25 watches at the manufacturer's selling price, you can easily make money on the watches, plus evaluate the market to determine if you want to order a large quantity.

Notice that both communications used formal, polite language. This will help build your credibility.

Now I would like to add one word of caution. I once found a company in Taiwan that sold a very interesting line of hand tools. I sent a sample request for a few of their clever adjustable wrenches and gave them my FedEx account number. My communication must have really been credible because they sent me a sample of almost every tool they made—over 200 pieces—completely free. The only problem was that the FedEx bill came to over $600. That was a pretty expensive free sample!

26.5 Freight Forwarders and Customs Brokers

One of the things that scare people away from importing is the complexity of the rules, duties, and regulations. Type the word *importing* into any search engine, and you'll come up with hundreds of pages of information on The Harmonized Tariff Schedule, the ITC Interactive Tariff and Trade Database, Customs bonds, proof of origin, import quotas, and more. The simple fact is that there are thousands of rules and regulations to be followed, dozens of forms to be filled out, and a number of legal affirmations to be made every time you import something. How can you possibly learn everything you need to know to import? You can't! That is where freight forwarders and customs brokers come in.

26.5.1 Freight Forwarders

A freight forwarder is a company that works with you on the shipping end overseas to get your products from the manufacturer to the international carrier (ship or plane). They also follow your shipment and make sure it is delivered to your customs broker in the receiving country.

A freight forwarder can help you with packing, labeling (international goods must be labeled in a very specific way), and final delivery after your goods have cleared customs. Thousands of freight-forwarding companies operate around the world. Some specialize in specific goods, such as agricultural products or automobiles, while others are generalists.

Freight forwarders provide many other services as well. They can act as your agent to effect payment. Your bank holds the funds in escrow until your freight forwarder inspects and accepts the shipment. Only after they sign off will the bank release your funds to the seller. They can also arrange insurance, search carriers for the best shipping quotes, and quick customs clearance by using the U.S. Customs Remote Entry Filing Program. (Not all freight forwarders are compliant with the program. They must have the necessary software to interface with the U.S. Customs Service so they can enter all the data about your shipment before it leaves the overseas port. When this is done correctly, it allows customs to clear your shipment electronically unless they deem it needs to be physically inspected.)

Consider two things before selecting a freight forwarder. First, do they have an office in the country you are exporting from? It would not make sense to hire a freight-forwarding company with offices in Japan, Korea, and Hong Kong if you want to import goods from the Philippines. Fortunately, most of the really large freight-forwarder companies have offices in all the major exporting ports. Second, do they have an office in the major port you are clearing your goods through? If you are in Pittsburgh and your goods will clear through Seattle, then make sure the company you pick has an office in Seattle.

To find freight forwarders, just type the term "freight forwarder" and the city you're looking for. For example, *Freight Forwarder + Hong Kong.* This will get you listings of freight-forwarding companies that operate in Hong Kong. Some of the largest international firms include Serra International, Hankyu–U.S., Sanko, and Seaborne International.

You can also search for freight forwarders by country or product type at www. forwarders.com.

26.5.2 Customs Brokers

Customs brokers fulfill an entirely different role than freight forwarders do. Whereas freight forwarders help you pack and ship goods and arrange payment, insurance, and delivery, customs brokers help you chart the waters of government regulations, paperwork, and customs duties.

PowerSeller Tip

The average of all customs duties on all products imported into the United States is 2.3 percent. For a few products the duties can be as high as 15 percent, but these are a tiny fraction of all the goods imported. Most manufactured goods incur duties of less than 5 percent. When you consider that you are saving anywhere from 25 percent to 60 percent on the cost of your goods by importing, the tiny percentage paid to the U.S. Customs Service becomes irrelevant.

Customs brokers act as agents for importers, conducting customs business on their clients' behalf. Customs brokers, which can either be private individuals or companies, are licensed by the Customs Service, which is part of the U.S.

Department of the Treasury. They prepare and file the necessary customs entries, arrange for the payment of assessed duties, work to release goods in customs custody, and represent their clients in all custody matters.

Good customs brokers have a complete understanding of trade requirements and procedures and customs and tariff regulations. They might also assist you with advice on transportation options, types of carriers, and shipping routes. Additional services can include explaining exchange rates, arranging for appraisals, classifying products, and calculating duties in advance so you know what your costs will be. As you can imagine, the people who work for customs brokers have to be detail freaks. If they are very good at what they do, your shipment will sail through customs in a matter of hours. If not, your goods could be tied up for days. That's why it pays to shop around and always get references (and check them!).

Two of the largest customs brokers used by eBay sellers are A&A Customs Brokers (www.aacb.com) and Cleared and Delivered (www.clearedanddelivered. com). A&A exhibits each year at eBay Live and actively courts eBay sellers. They also operate duty-free warehouses in the United States and Canada where you can store your product in bulk, and they will drop ship individual items for you as you sell them.

Some companies offer both freight-forwarding and customs broker services. This can be very convenient as you only have to deal with one company for all your importing needs.

26.6 Ordering and Payment

The primary thing you need to know about ordering from overseas manufacturers is that you must be very specific. Spell out all the terms of your order in your purchase order, including the following:

- The exact model and/or part number you are buying, along with a description of the goods, for example, Model 1200 World Band Radio including 12 V recharger, with detachable antenna and one set of earphones.
- The exact quantity and package, such as 12 cases of Casio Baby G Watches packed 12 units to the case.
- The date the order will be shipped.
- The packaging (blister pak, individually boxed, etc.).

- The delivery date.

- The shipping method and/or carrier to be used.

- The payment terms, in detail, and any credit arrangements that you have agreed to.

- Any quality or regulation standards the items must meet (ISO standards, UL acceptance, etc.).

- The return policy, if any, for defective goods.

- The documentation the seller must provide, such as a clean commercial invoice that contains all information required by customs, certificates of origin, statement that no child labor was involved in the manufacture of the goods, etc.

There are a number of ways to pay for international shipments, but you'll probably only ever pay by bank wire transfers or international letters of credit.

The first and most common payment method is a simple bank wire transfer. You will often see quotes from overseas that show the payment type as T/T (telegraphic transfer), which is archaic shorthand for bank wire transfer. Large commercial banks with international departments have web-based systems where you can integrate document delivery with payment. For example, you send your bank the money to pay for the shipment along with instructions that they need to collect the commercial invoice and shipping bill of lading before releasing the money. You give your seller a web link where he can upload the documents. After the bank examines the documents and finds they comply with the shipment, they release the money to the seller. This method is used when you are dealing with sellers that you know and reasonably trust. For example, if I am importing electronic toys from a large Chinese manufacturer I've worked with before, I would use this payment method.

If you are dealing with a very small company without experience in exporting and you don't have anyone there to inspect the goods, verify the paperwork, or make sure you get what you ordered, you should use a payment system that offers more protection. This is where the International Letter of Credit (LOC) comes in handy.

An LOC is a formal procedure that enables you to spell out everything the seller must do before he gets paid. When you create a letter of credit, your bank is essentially acting as an escrow agent. Before the bank will issue the letter or credit, you first deposit the payment with your bank. The bank will hold the payment until all the terms of the LOC have been met. An LOC can either be paid "at sight" or within a specified period of time. At sight means that as soon as all the documents are delivered, the bank will release the funds. You could specify a period of time to include arrival and even inspection to make sure the goods you ordered were delivered.

I once imported a large quantity of goods from the Philippines where I included an inspection of the goods as part of the LOC terms. I had an agent in the Philippines actually inspect the goods as they were being packed for shipment to assess both the quality and quantity of what I was buying.

If you find yourself in a situation where you need an LOC, make sure your banker is knowledgeable and experienced. I would use a large commercial bank such as Citibank or Bank of America. These banks have full-time foreign trade departments staffed with experts who can assist you. Customs brokers are also knowledgeable in this area and can provide advice and assistance.

Having said all this, I can tell you that you will very rarely use a letter of credit. If you are dealing with manufacturers in Europe and Asia that regularly export goods to companies in the United States, they will know all the ins and outs of exporting and the correct documentation. These companies are looking for repeat business and are concerned with their reputation. Most of them can furnish references of other U.S. companies they deal with.

One other thing to be careful of when importing is getting stuck with items that have been recalled by the consumer product Safety Commission for safety reasons. Toys and baby items are highly susceptible to this. Some of the larger manufacturers will take recalled items back but many smaller manufacturers in the far east will not.

For more on importing, see Section 28.1.

For more on tax write-offs for work-related travel, see Section 9.2.

For more on identifying sources of imported goods, see Sections 24.5 and 25.6.

chapter 27

Obtaining Consignment Merchandise

In 2003, eBay created a category of seller called a trading assistant or a TA, who is a consignment seller or someone who sells goods for others in return for a commission or a fee. Consignment shops have been around for a long time, and it was natural that some of these shop owners would discover eBay and start listing their consigned items for auction.

eBay created the TA position to help people who don't know how to sell on eBay find sellers who'll sell their items for them. If you click the **Trading Assistant Program** link on the eBay Site Map, and then click **Find a Trading Assistant,** it will take you to a page where you can type in your zip code to find a local Trading Assistant (see Figure 27.1). This generates a list of Trading Assistants within a 50-mile radius of the zip code.

As the Trading Assistant program began to grow, a number of eBay entrepreneurs actually opened storefronts, and eventually several companies began as franchise opportunities. Some of the larger TAs included DropItOff and Auction Drop at www.auctiondrop.com.

Most of the eBay drop off store franchises failed for various reasons. Walk-in retail space is very expensive, along with the cost of advertising, employees, storage, insurance, and so on. In other words, it's a high-overhead business. When you add the overhead to the franchise costs and start-up fees, the business model just didn't work out. However, many people who started their own eBay drop off stores (i.e., non-franchise) have done very well. The key seems to be locating in an area where people can find you, yet not in the high-traffic and therefore high-priced retail areas.

PowerSeller Tip

Whenever I sell on consignment I always like to take possession of the merchandise. I have seen situations before where an eBay trading assistant sold merchandise and when the consignor found out how little it sold for they changed their mind. Now the seller is on the hook and you could earn a negative feedback for non-delivery. In cases of items that are too large for you to take and store, be sure and get an ironclad contract with the consignor.

Consignment selling can be very profitable, but one doesn't necessarily have to follow the retail model. The biggest expense and time factor in the consignment business is finding consignors with merchandise to sell. If you are going to sell something on consignment, to sell high-value or high-priced items is more logical than to sell dozens of low-priced items. If you are going to sell lower-priced goods, then you want to find consignors who can supply those goods in volume, such as retailers selling their surplus merchandise or an estate attorney liquidating an estate.

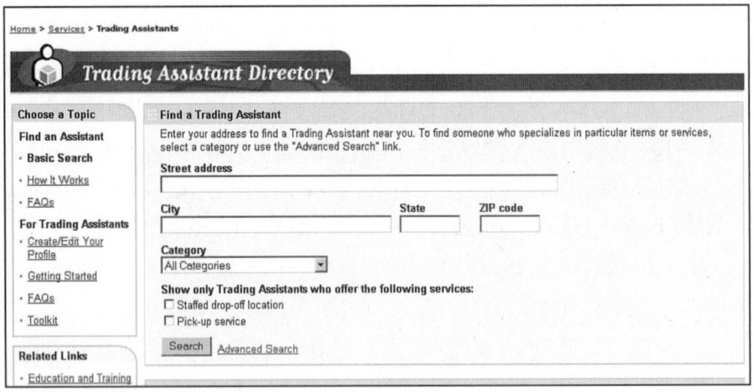

Figure 27.1
eBay's Trading Assistant search page.

Every city and town has plenty of consignment opportunities. Here is my top-ten list of consignment sources:

- Farmers who are looking to sell their used farm equipment rather than trade it in. Farm equipment is expensive, and farm equipment dealers rarely give good value on a trade-in.

- Construction companies with used heavy equipment to sell. Construction companies often buy heavy equipment to use on a large contract and then sell it at the end of the contract rather than carry it on the books until they get a new contract.

- Doctors, dentists, and veterinarians are always upgrading their medical equipment, and used medical equipment is a very large and active category on eBay.

- Corporations are often either downsizing or replacing equipment such as computers, copiers, PBXs, cubicles, and so on. This category is also very large and active on eBay.

- Manufacturing and printing companies are another source of used machinery. These companies are always upgrading and replacing machinery that still has a useful life.

- Cars, trucks, trailers, and campers are big sellers on eBay motors. Once again, people tend to get pretty low value when they trade their vehicle in. You can often get them a better price on eBay. Another opportunity is to approach local car dealers and offer to help them move their used cars on eBay.

- Retailers often have to move surplus merchandise. As outlined in Chapter 21, closeout dealers often pay retailers less than 15 cents on the retail dollar. You can often get 50 to 65 percent of retail on eBay, which leaves plenty of room for you to make a commission and still pay the retailer more than he would normally get.

- You can also sell current new inventory for retailers. Many small retailers would like to expand their businesses onto eBay but don't have the time, resources, or knowledge to do so by themselves. You can approach almost any retailer and offer to list and sell the goods on eBay for him.

- Attorneys are often called on to liquidate estates when someone dies, and bankruptcy attorneys have to find auctioneers to sell off the assets of bankrupt companies. eBay can almost always bring higher prices than either estates or bankrupt companies would realize with a local auctioneer.

You won't need an expensive retail location for selling these sorts of items on commission, but you will need a commercial address with a place to securely store, photograph, and ship the goods from. If you want to explore this market, you need the professional demeanor to approach businesses, so prepare business cards, letterhead, a simple flyer, and prewritten contracts and documents to support your efforts.

One of the best ways to find consignors is simply to become active in the business community in your town. Join the Chamber of Commerce, your country development center, and groups such as the Lions, Jaycees, and Rotary. This is where you meet the business people who can network you into opportunities.

Charities are another good source of consignment goods. Your local theater group or hospital is always trying to raise money. You simply get them to contact their members and donors and ask them to donate merchandise that you can sell on eBay to raise money for the charity.

One note of caution about consignment selling: several communities and even some states have laws that regulate consignment sellers. These laws are often related to regulations that cover pawnshops. Other states regulate and license auctioneers that sell for other people (as opposed to an eBay seller selling for himself or herself). Before you get into consignment selling, check the laws and regulations in your community, county, or state.

chapter 28

Wholesale Jargon, Paperwork, and Forms

The business of America is business. And business in America—and all over the world for that matter—is still conducted on paper. If you want to be taken seriously, you'll need to use the proper forms and learn some common buying and shipping terms. If you have ever worked in a retail environment, you've probably come across some of these forms, but the ones related to importing could be new. If you have only sold on eBay, you'll want to learn to recognize and use the forms that apply to you.

This is a very short course in the language of purchasing and an overview of some of the paperwork you will need to do business. You do not need to spend money buying or printing the various business forms. Several software packages (some selling for as little as $19.95) provide hundreds of business forms, including all those mentioned in this chapter. The forms can be customized with the name and address of your business and simply filled out and printed from your computer. Many of these forms (such as purchase orders) are also sold individually and in packages at office supply stores.

28.1 Wholesale Trade Business Forms

Here's a list of the most common forms you will come across when you buy wholesale from manufacturers and distributors:

- **Bill of lading (BOL).** This is the shipper's bill, which shows the method, cost, and timing of a shipment. If you shipped by air, a bill of lading is known as an air waybill.

- **Commercial invoice (CI).** This bill is for goods delivered or about to be delivered. The commercial invoice should essentially match the pro-forma invoice (see following description) with any changes you agreed to before placing the order. It should also match up with your purchase order.

  A complete commercial invoice will specify exactly the product, quantity, value, and a list of any special charges such as handling, packing, one-time set-up fees, and so on. If you are importing something, the invoice must also provide the eight-digit subheading code from the Harmonized Tariff Schedule of the United States. (This is usually provided by the exporter, or your customs broker can determine it for you.)

  The CI will also spell out the payment and delivery terms, warranties if any, and the return policy. If the terms on the invoice are different from those specified in your purchase order, do not accept the invoice until you resolve the issue (unless the new terms are acceptable to you).

- **Packing list.** This very important document is the list of goods, by quantity and description, that were packed in the box or shipment. Whenever you receive a shipment, you should always do two things. First, check the contents of the box against the packing list to make sure you got everything that was supposed to be in the box. Second, check the packing list against the invoice to make sure they match.

- **Pro-forma invoice.** Essentially, this is a quote from a seller to a buyer. It shows you what the invoice will look like and sets out the seller's terms. If you are buying a large quantity of something or buying something you want financing for, you should request a pro-forma invoice. This will enable you to see the seller's terms as well as the pricing and delivery data.

PowerSeller Tip

You can download free business forms at www.freebusinessforms.com.

- **Purchase order.** A purchase order is a form you use to purchase goods or services. It is a binding contract that contains the name and/or description of the goods you are buying, as well as the quantity, price, payment, and delivery terms. Many wholesale distributors and vendors will insist on a purchase order before they sell to you. Some vendors will supply you with a purchase order. If this is the case, read it very carefully, and make sure you agree to all of the terms. I think it's always better to use your own purchase order and write out the terms yourself.

28.2 Wholesale Jargon

Shipping wholesale involves a whole new vocabulary, and many of the terms used are not at all self-explanatory. This list gives you the main terms you will encounter when doing business with manufacturers and distributors:

- **CIF.** This stands for Cost, Insurance, and Freight. If someone quotes you a CIF price, that is the price delivered to your door.

- **FOB.** Free On Board is an archaic term for "This is my price at my shipping dock, packed ready for shipment. You pay insurance, freight, duties, and so on." If you are buying from a distributor in San Francisco and you get a quote that says FOB San Francisco, then that is the price before shipping. You would figure the shipping cost from the seller's warehouse in San Francisco to your location.

- **FAS.** These initials stand for Free Along Side. This is similar to FOB except that the seller will deliver the goods from his warehouse to the port or airport. After something is delivered FAS, you own the goods (if you have already paid for them) and are responsible for shipping them from that point on. An example of this would be if you told a seller to ship UPS to you using your UPS account number.

- *Force majeure.* This "act of God" clause typically states something like "Seller shall not be responsible for delays in performance caused by delays at manufacturing plants, in transportation, due to strikes, fires, floods, storms, war, insurrections, riots, any government regulation, order, act or instruction, or any other circumstances beyond the Seller's reasonable control."

- **Keystone.** This term means you can double the wholesale price to sell at retail.

- **MAP.** This stands for Minimum Advertised Price. Manufacturers are not allowed to set prices you can charge by law, but they can insist on the minimum price you can put in advertising. If you buy a product that has a MAP price, then that is the only price you can put on your fixed-price, eBay Store, or Buy It Now listings.

- **MOO.** This is not the sound a cow makes. It stands for Minimum Opening Order. This is the smallest order a manufacturer will accept as your first order. If you see the term MRO, that stands for Minimum Reorder. For example, on a manufacturer's price sheet you might see something like this: MOO$500/MRO$300. So your first order would have to be at least $500 and subsequent reorders could be as low as $300. MOO is dollars, MOQ is minimum quantity

- **Partner.** This is usually someone who is already registered and dealing with a wholesale company. This term is also sometimes used to denote an authorized reseller.

- **To-the-trade.** This term means a dealer will only sell wholesale to other dealers and retailers.

- **2%/30 or (Two percent/thirty).** These are credit terms. The numbers vary depending on the terms. It means a seller will discount his price by 2 percent if you pay within 30 days. You will sometimes see combinations of numbers such as 3% net, 2%/30, 1%/60. This means he will discount the price by 3 percent if you pay upon order or delivery, 2 percent if you pay within 30 days, and 1 percent if you pay within 60 days. Sometimes they don't show the % sign. On a price sheet at the bottom you will often see 3 net, 2/30, 1/60. Even without the % sign, it means the same thing.

For more on buying wholesale, see Chapters 19 through 25.

part 4

Advanced Listing and Selling Strategies

You've set up your business, found the killer product, and learned how and where to source it. Now you have to go head-to-head with over 800,000 full-time sellers, all vying for the same eyeballs and bids that you are.

How you list and sell and the techniques you use to promote your auctions and communicate with your customers can be the difference between success and failure in this highly competitive venue.

This part takes you through the strategies used by the pros to get their auctions seen, to get people to click on them, and to close the sale. We also show you how to build a great reputation on eBay and how to use customer service techniques to improve your Detailed Seller Ratings and earn fee discounts.

chapter 29

Building Great Feedback

eBay's feedback system is at the very heart of its phenomenal success. Ever since e-commerce began on the Internet, people have searched for a way to prevent being defrauded, and the feedback system is the solution to that problem. It isn't perfect, but eBay has an incredibly low rate of fraudulent transactions. According to eBay's Trust & Safety Department, fraudulent transactions average well below 0.1 percent of all transactions.

Although novice buyers often overlook the feedback for lack of understanding, veteran buyers *will* check your feedback before placing a bid. If they see comments such as "product not delivered," "slow shipping," and "poor communications," they probably won't purchase your merchandise. These are also the items featured in Detailed Seller Ratings (see Section 29.5).

If you want to be a successful eBay seller, you'll need a high positive feedback percentage, high DSRs, and lots of actual positive comments within your feedback profile.

Imagine a shopping mall where outside each store is a large board where customers post their comments about the store's products and customer service. And the store is not allowed to remove or change the comments, which are there for all to see before entering the store. Would you look at the messages before shopping at the store? Of course you would. Well, this is the role feedback plays on eBay. Everyone gets to see a review of your customer service and integrity *before* he places a bid on your item.

29.1 Understanding the Feedback System

If you are trying to scale a large eBay business, you've probably been using eBay for quite a while and already understand the feedback system. Nevertheless, many changes have occurred recently, and you need to thoroughly understand the rules so you can develop (or modify) your strategy to build and maintain a great feedback profile. I often see experienced sellers either breaking the rules or using selling policies that reveal a lack of understanding of the feedback basics.

Every eBay user has a feedback profile that includes basic information about the member, a summary of his feedback over the past 12 months, his Detailed Seller Ratings (DSRs), which are only displayed if the user is a seller and over 10 buyers have given ratings, and a list of actual feedback comments left by his trading partners from previous transactions.

Your DSRs and feedback are both important factors in how much visibility your items are given in the Best Match default search results order. So it's not just your reputation that's at stake—it's the visibility of your listings, too.

Only the winning bidder/buyer and seller can rate each other by leaving feedback. You cannot leave feedback on another eBay user unless it is related to a completed sale through eBay. In addition to rating a transaction positive, neutral, or negative, eBay members can also leave a short comment (up to 55 characters) about the seller or the transaction. The purpose of feedback is to give other eBay users an idea of what to expect when dealing with that member, and after the rating and comment is left, the feedback becomes a permanent part of the member's profile.

Prior to 2008, both buyers and sellers could leave a positive, negative, or neutral comment for each other. But in early 2008, eBay changed the feedback policy so that sellers may only leave a positive comment for a buyer, but buyers can still leave a negative or neutral comment for a seller.

You can view an eBay member's profile by clicking the number in parentheses next to his or her User ID (this is the member's Feedback Score). The Feedback Score represents the net number of positive feedback comments left for this user (by buyers or sellers) within the past 12 months. It is calculated by assigning a positive feedback comment +1, a negative comment –1, and a neutral comment 0. Figure 29.1 shows the Feedback Profile for an eBay seller. This member has a Feedback Score of 28,169, which constitutes 99.7 percent of his total feedback.

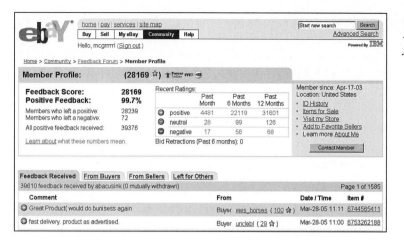

Figure 29.1
An eBay member's feedback profile.

This seller also has many neutral feedback comments, but these are not calculated in the positive feedback percentage. eBay toyed with the idea of counting neutral feedback the same as negatives in Spring 2008, but the uproar from sellers made them retract the change by the end of the summer.

Notice this member received a total of 39,376 positive feedback comments. eBay records all feedback comments but calculates only the original transaction and subsequent sales over a week after the original sale in the percentage and feedback score. The difference in the two numbers (39,376 and 28,169) is the number of repeat buyers within a week or buyers who purchased more than one item at the same time.

After a feedback comment is left, it is considered permanent and cannot be edited. However, the other party can leave a comment in reply as the user did in Figure 29.2.

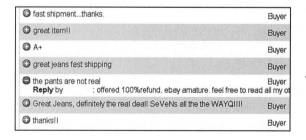

Figure 29.2
Feedback comments—note the reply to the feedback in the middle of the page.

eBay has announced that it will be releasing a system whereby members can remove or modify feedback comments after a dispute has been resolved or in cases where someone mixed up which seller he was leaving feedback for. It appears the seller will have to initiate the process and eBay has said it will monitor/limit the number of changes or removals a seller requests. eBay recently rolled out a system to do this on eBay.AU (Australia). That generally means they will test it there and eventually bring a revised version of the policy to the United States. Watch the eBay announcements boards, or check the Feedback Forum in the eBay Community pages to get the latest policy.

eBay members can be emotional about their feedback. If you run an honest business and deliver quality merchandise on time with good communications, you'll earn a highly positive feedback rating. But no matter how honest and sincere you are, you may still receive an occasional negative feedback. We all make mistakes. If you are a high-volume seller listing hundreds or even thousands of auctions per month, you will eventually make a mistake and send someone the wrong item or forget to ship something.

Most eBay buyers will send you an e-mail about their item before leaving you negative feedback. When you receive such an e-mail, you should bend over backward to fix the problem and apologize profusely, which will usually prevent the buyer from leaving negative feedback. Sometimes, though, no matter what you do or how hard you try, an unreasonable buyer will leave you a negative comment before ever giving you a chance to fix the problem. Invariably, when you look at this buyer's feedback profile, he is a complete beginner on eBay or has little or no feedback of his own.

You should also be aware of some additional policies regarding feedback. For instance, eBay does not allow you to engage in what it calls feedback solicitation. Here is what it says about feedback solicitation:

> Offering to sell feedback, buy feedback, or trade feedback undeservedly is strictly against eBay's feedback policies. Such activity is called feedback solicitation.

> Including the term *feedback* or any reference to eBay feedback in the listing title is considered feedback solicitation and the item will be removed. The only exception is if the term *feedback* is directly describing the item listed (such as part of a book title).

The other important feedback policy relates to feedback extortion. In its simplest form, feedback extortion is when someone threatens you with a negative feedback unless you do x, y, or z. For example, I once received an e-mail demanding that I ship a very heavy and expensive product for free. The buyer said right in the e-mail that she would leave me negative feedback unless I agreed. I reported it to eBay, and they suspended the buyer. But because I hadn't received payment for the item, I had to treat it like a nonpaying bidder and list the item again the following week.

eBay also prohibits milder forms of extortion, yet I hear examples of it all the time—even from experienced sellers. For example, a seller might include the following statement at the bottom of his auctions: "If you want me to leave feedback for you, then you must leave a positive feedback for me first. After I see your feedback comment, I will reciprocate." eBay doesn't police this very well, but when it is reported or they discover it, they will cancel your auction if it contains such a statement.

As a seller, waiting until you deliver a product and then waiting to see if someone leaves you positive feedback before you leave feedback is within eBay's guidelines, but you can't tell buyers that's what you are doing.

Frankly, there's not much point waiting since your only options as a seller are to leave positive feedback or don't leave feedback at all. I find I get a better response from buyers if I leave positive feedback when I ship the item.

Finally, a caution about the feedback you leave. Be very careful about what you say. Your words could get you sued. In case you're wondering, it has happened.

If a court were to find that your remarks constitute libel or defamation, you could be held legally responsible for damages to that member's reputation. Under federal law (the Communications Decency Act), because eBay does not censor feedback or investigate it for accuracy, eBay is not legally responsible for the remarks that members post, even if those remarks are defamatory. The Communications Decency Act protects eBay, but not the person who leaves the feedback, from responsibility for it.

If you suspect someone is violating the community guidelines, report it to eBay. eBay takes feedback extortion from buyers very seriously now that sellers cannot leave negative feedback. If eBay suspends the buyer, he will not be able to leave you negative feedback. If a buyer leaves you negative feedback and is later suspended from eBay, then eBay will automatically remove the offending feedback comment and recalculate your score.

Incidentally, if you receive a negative feedback and then even months later the buyer is suspended from eBay for any reason, that negative feedback will be removed from your Feedback Profile and Score.

29.2 How the Pros Build Feedback

Professional sellers consider their feedback rating an asset to protect just like their computers, cash, and inventory. Your feedback rating represents your reputation as a seller. If you sell high-priced products, it becomes even more important. When eBay did a study of how bidders use the feedback system, their research found that the higher the price of the item being bid on, the more often bidders checked the feedback rating before bidding. On really high-priced items (over $500), the majority of bidders not only checked the feedback rating, but they also took the time to scroll through the comments left by others before placing a bid.

The best way to ensure an excellent feedback rating is to deliver a quality product quickly, efficiently, and honestly.

After you have a decent feedback rating (i.e., over 100), you can tolerate one or two negative feedback comments. But until then, you should take the long view and remember you are trying to build a business that can generate thousands of dollars in income. Don't get all wiggy over a $9 item that someone was unhappy with. Unless you already have an excellent feedback rating, it's far better to return the customer's money rather than risk a negative comment, particularly because the buyer knows you cannot reciprocate with a negative, and their negative comment could make your other listings display lower in the Best Match search results.

If you are just starting out on eBay and want to build your feedback rating quickly, use some of these tips:

- Sell a low-cost item such as a baseball card or a stamp or a low-cost piece of costume jewelry for $1 each. You won't make much money, but you can sell dozens or even hundreds of items in a short time and quickly build your feedback numbers.

- In your confirmation e-mail, state that you post positive feedback for each buyer who pays quickly and give the link for your buyer to click to leave the feedback. This will help build your feedback rating, and your customers will appreciate it as well.

- Your e-mail signature should contain eBay's **Leave Feedback** link, which is www.feedback.ebay.com/ws/eBayISAPI.dll?LeaveFeedbackShow.

- An interesting statistic from eBay shows that only 40 percent of buyers bother to leave feedback. Many sellers add a personal touch by including a handwritten thank-you note with their order thanking the buyer for his business, encouraging him to contact them with any questions or concerns, and telling him that they left positive feedback for him. If you are running a lot of auctions, this could be a preprinted note you just sign and drop in the box.

- Customers sometimes forget to leave feedback due to the lapse in time between their last e-mail exchange and when they receive the product.

  So calculate the average shipping time to your customer, and arrange for an e-mail with your Leave Feedback link to arrive a day or two after he receives the merchandise. Your e-mail could say something like this:

  By now you should have received your new fly-reel.

  I hope you have had a chance to try it out. If you have any questions or any problems with your order, please e-mail me immediately.

  I enjoyed doing business with you and have left positive feedback for this transaction.

  Best regards,

  Jill Auctioneer

  P.S. If you would like to leave feedback about our eBay transaction, please go to www.feedback.ebay.com/ws/eBayISAPI.dll?LeaveFeedbackShow.

  Sending these well-timed e-mail reminders has increased my feedback response by at least 20 percent.

- Another way to increase your positive feedback quickly is to be overly generous in posting your feedback. If the buyer didn't send their PayPal payment until a week after the auction ended, so what? I still post a nice feedback comment. If someone cancels or doesn't follow through, I rarely bother leaving feedback since sellers cannot leave negative or neutral feedback. However, I do file an Unpaid Item (UPI) dispute to get my fees back.

  Ask yourself, "How many times have I misplaced an e-mail or forgot to send a payment immediately or had a family emergency?" Not all slow-payers are flakes; sometimes, people really do forget. Why create an enemy?

I remember the story of one poor lady who had a heart attack. Before her heart attack, her feedback rating was over 300, and all the comments were positive. While she was recuperating from her heart attack, several winning bidders, who hadn't heard from her, left brutal negative feedback comments. About a week after her heart attack, the woman's daughter sent out e-mails explaining the situation. Unbelievably, several of the buyers didn't believe her and continued to send abusive e-mails and complaints to eBay. It took copies of her surgery report and a letter from her doctor to get the negative feedback comments removed (for more on fixing negative feedback, see Section 29.3).

When someone leaves negative feedback on you, you have an opportunity to respond. When I want to bid on something, I always read the feedback details if the seller has more than one negative feedback. I once read a negative comment from someone whose order was wrong and late. The seller's response was, "I screwed up! It doesn't happen often, but this one was my fault." I was so impressed by the seller's honesty that I didn't hesitate to buy from her.

29.3 Fixing Negative Feedback

Getting eBay to remove a negative feedback comment is extremely difficult. eBay's policy on feedback removal states that negative feedback will be removed if …

- eBay is provided with a valid court order finding that the disputed feedback is slanderous, libelous, defamatory, or otherwise illegal.
- The feedback comment contains profane, vulgar, obscene, or racist language or adult material. Inflammatory language, such as "fraud, liar, cheater, scam artist, con man," etc. is strongly discouraged but will not be removed. But for example, using an ethic slur or calling someone a Nazi would be cause to have the comment removed.
- The feedback comment contains personal identifying information about another member, including real name, address, phone number, or e-mail address.
- The feedback makes reference to an eBay, PayPal, or law enforcement organization investigation.
- The feedback comment contains links or scripts.

- Negative feedback intended for another member will be considered for removal only in situations where the member responsible for the mistaken posting informs eBay of the error and has already placed the same feedback for the correct member.

- Feedback was left by a person ineligible to participate in eBay transactions, according to Section 1 of the eBay User Agreement, at the time of the transaction or the time the feedback was left.

- Feedback was left by a member who provided eBay with false contact information and could not be contacted. In general, the transaction period is 60 days from the end of the listing or 30 days from the date the feedback was left, whichever is longer.

- Feedback was left by a member who bid on or purchased an item solely to have the opportunity to leave negative feedback for the seller, with no intention of completing the transaction.

If you are left feedback by someone under one of these conditions, contact eBay through the **Contact Us** link on the eBay Feedback Forum Page.

29.3.1 Mutual Feedback Withdrawal

eBay discontinued their Mutual Feedback Withdrawal program in the spring of 2008 in conjunction with the change in policy preventing sellers from leaving neutral or negative feedback for buyers. And it will be introducing a new program that will allow buyers to change or remove a feedback rating. However, as of this writing, the full details have not been released.

You may have heard of SquareTrade Dispute Resolution. Unfortunately, this program was discontinued at the same time as the Mutual Feedback Withdrawal program ended.

29.4 Feedback and the Nonpaying Bidder

Dealing with nonpaying bidders is really a pain. You don't get very many of them, but when you do, the nonsense and time spent dealing with them is a major aggravation. Fortunately, you do have some recourse.

When a bidder doesn't pay, you can file an Unpaid Item dispute with eBay. This will sometimes be enough to get the bidder to pay for the item. If not, after seven days, you can request a credit on your Insertion and Final Value fees. PowerSellers will also receive a credit for their featuring fees (bold, Featured Plus, Buy It Now, etc.).

The problem is that in either case, the nonpaying bidder can, and usually does, leave you a negative feedback.

First, let's review how the policy works, and then I'll show you a shortcut that can save you time and aggravation and reduce the risk of getting negative feedback.

1. **The seller files an unpaid item dispute.**

   Sellers can report an unpaid-for item up to 45 days after the transaction date (i.e., the date when the buyer commits to buying the item and the seller commits to selling it). Usually the seller must wait seven days after a listing closes to file an unpaid item dispute. However, in the following exceptional cases, the seller can file a dispute immediately:

   - At the time of the filing, the buyer is no longer a registered user of eBay, or

   - The buyer is from a country to which the seller has indicated he will not ship, in the "shipping and payment details" section of the listing. (Regions to which the seller will ship are listed on the View Item page for the item in question.)

   In these two cases the buyer will receive an Unpaid Item strike (an eBay term for a bidder who doesn't pay for an auction). Each time he doesn't pay, he gets another strike, and the seller can close the dispute immediately and request a Final Value fee credit without any additional steps.

2. **eBay contacts the buyer.**

   After the seller files an Unpaid Item dispute, eBay sends the buyer an e-mail notification and displays a pop-up message if the buyer signs in within 14 days of the filing. The e-mail and pop-up message will provide details on one of the following situations:

   - A friendly reminder to pay. The e-mail and pop-up message will remind the buyer that payment has not been received, along with simple instructions on how to respond or how to pay for the item. If the buyer does not respond to the e-mail or pop-up message within seven days, the seller may file for a Final Value fee credit. The seller also becomes eligible for the Relist Credit. (If the relisted item sells the second time you list it, eBay will credit one of the Insertion fees back to your account.)

- A mutual agreement indication. While filing the Unpaid Item dispute, if the seller indicates that a mutual agreement has been reached with the buyer not to complete the transaction, eBay will ask the buyer for confirmation through an e-mail and pop-up message.

- If the buyer confirms the seller's statement about mutual agreement not to complete the transaction, the buyer will not receive an Unpaid Item strike and the seller can request a Final Value fee credit.

- If the buyer disagrees with the seller's statement on mutual agreement, the buyer will not receive an Unpaid Item strike, and the seller will not receive a Final Value fee credit. The dispute will be closed immediately after the buyer responds, and the seller will not be eligible to refile an Unpaid Item dispute for that transaction.

- If the buyer does not respond to the e-mail or pop-up message within seven days, then the seller will be able to close the dispute. The seller can file for a Final Value fee credit and the buyer will receive an Unpaid Item strike.

3. **The buyer and seller communicate.**

   The buyer is presented with several response options to communicate with the seller:

   - *I want to pay now.* Simply paying for the item will close the dispute. For listings where PayPal is available, the buyer just has to pay via PayPal and the seller can close the dispute.

   - *I already paid.* If payment has already been made, the buyer may provide details of the payment to the seller for review. The seller can then choose the appropriate option to close the dispute.

   - *Communicate with the seller.* The buyer and seller can attempt to resolve the problem by communicating directly through the eBay website. eBay will provide a message area where the buyer and seller can communicate with each other without relying on e-mail. The seller can close the dispute at any time by choosing the appropriate closure option.

4. **The dispute closes.**

   The seller can close the dispute after the buyer has responded at least once or if the buyer does not respond within seven days. The seller has several options to close the dispute:

- **We've completed the transaction and we're both satisfied.** With this option, the seller does not receive a Final Value fee credit, and the buyer does not receive an Unpaid Item strike.

- **We've agreed not to complete the transaction.** With this option, the buyer does not receive an Unpaid Item strike; the seller can file for a Final Value fee credit; and the item is eligible for the Relist Credit.

- **I no longer wish to communicate with or wait for the buyer.** With this option, the buyer receives an Unpaid Item strike; the seller can file for a Final Value fee credit; and the item is eligible for the Relist Credit.

A dispute can be open only for 60 days after the transaction date (i.e., the date when the buyer commits to buying the item and the seller commits to selling it). If the seller has not closed the dispute within 60 days, it will be closed automatically. When a dispute is closed automatically, the seller does not receive a Final Value fee credit, and the buyer does not receive an Unpaid Item strike.

Here is a simple way to solve this problem. Normally eBay requires that you wait seven days to file an Unpaid Item dispute and then another seven days before you can close it and get a refund of your selling fees. If you look closely at the Unpaid Item form, there are several buttons you can check for the reason for filing the form. One of the buttons says **Auction cancelled by mutual agreement.**

Now the trick to making this work is to place the following text at the end of each auction description:

> By bidding on this auction, you agree that if you have not paid for the auction or contacted the seller to arrange payment for this auction within seven days from the end of this auction, then this auction is cancelled by mutual agreement and neither party has any recourse against the other.

What does this mean? Well, if the buyer doesn't answer his or her e-mails or claims he didn't bid on the auction or it was some kind of mistake, then you go to the Unpaid Item Form, check the box that says the auction was cancelled by mutual agreement, and essentially the auction never happened.

eBay will send an e-mail and an alert to the bidder asking him to click a link to confirm the mutual agreement. In most cases the bidder will do this, as he probably does not want to pay for the auction. If he does, eBay will immediately credit the Final Value fee (but not the Listing Upgrade or Feature fees unless you're a PowerSeller) to your account. If you're not a PowerSeller, you won't get the feature fees credited back, but you may get the Relist Credit. If you relist the item and it sells the second time, eBay will credit you one of the insertion fees. The item must sell the second time for you to get this credit.

If the buyer does not respond to the mutual agreement e-mail, then you simply go back and file an Unpaid Item dispute and follow the procedure on that eBay page.

Both parties are able to leave feedback even if the auction is cancelled through mutual agreement. However, although it could happen, buyers tend not to leave negative feedback if you go through the mutual withdrawal process since they won't get an Unpaid Item strike.

One final note about feedback: there is a tab on your feedback profile labeled **Feedback left for others.** Not only will your prospective bidders see what other people say about you, but also what you say about other people. I like to see what kind of feedback sellers leave for other people. In the end, it is all about honesty and customer service. If you are honest in your item descriptions and give good customer service, your feedback rating will climb rapidly.

For more on building and maintaining great feedback, see Section 44.2 and Chapter 45.

29.5 Detailed Seller Ratings (DSRs)

Remember that board outside the store for previous customers to leave comments on? Well, now imagine if that had a summary of the most important aspects of the sales transaction at the top. This is the concept behind Detailed Seller Ratings or DSRs.

DSRs are four areas that are considered the most important to buyers. They are:

- Item as described
- Communication
- Shipping time
- Shipping and handling charges

In addition to leaving a feedback comment, buyers can rate the seller on each of these four key areas.

The rating is from one to five stars, and DSRs are completely anonymous so the seller has no recourse if a buyer leaves malicious DSRs. All you will see is the average DSR for that area, not the individual ratings left by each buyer.

To continue as a seller on eBay, you must maintain a rating of 4.3 on each of your DSRs. If you have over 10 DSR ratings over a 30-day period, eBay uses your 30-day average. If you have less than 10, they look at your 12-month average. If one of your DSR averages (whichever way they calculate it for you) goes below 4.3, you will be blocked from listing any more items.

Now this isn't as scary or final as it sounds. First, if you currently have items listed when your DSR average goes below 4.3, your auctions will still continue to run. So if the DSR ratings from those buyers brings you back above 4.3, you will be reinstated as a seller (so bend over backward to get 5 star ratings from each of those buyers!).

If you don't have any other items listed, you'll have to wait for lower DSRs to fall off your profile. Remember, DSRs are only on your record for 12 months. So if you had a really low DSR score from a buyer 10 months ago, when that drops off in two months, your DSR average will go up. As soon as it goes above 4.3 (based on your 12-month average), you will be able to list items again.

A lot of sellers overworry about the 4.3 DSR. In fact, when eBay instituted this rule, less than 4 percent of all sellers were affected. So as long as you pack your items well, ship them quickly, and communicate well with customers, you shouldn't have to worry about your DSR scores.

DSRs also factor heavily in the Best Match search order, so it's important to receive high DSRs in all four areas. If you average 4.7 or higher in all of your DSRs over the last 30 days and you've had three DSR ratings over the same period, you can get "raised" promotion in the Best Match search results. This is important since it is the default search results display order.

To get and maintain this DSR average, you need to be very clear in your description about shipping costs, when you ship, how you ship, etc. The multiple e-mails I've suggested will help you with the communication DSR, too.

Many buyers misunderstand shipping time and think of it as the time from when they paid to when they receive the item. On eBay UK, this DSR is named differently as dispatch time, which is far more accurate. Buyers should rate you based on the time from when they paid to when you shipped the item, but that's not always the case. This is another reason to always use a fast shipping service.

I recommend using USPS Priority Mail and always including delivery confirmation (free if you print your postage online) so the buyer can see when you shipped it and an estimated delivery date. (Plus delivery confirmation is necessary for you to be covered under PayPal's Seller Protection Policy.)

A buyer who pays for Priority Mail shipping and receives the item four days after he won it will generally give a higher rating for the shipping time than one who waited seven days for parcel post. You may have shipped both parcels the day after they paid, but buyers usually think in terms of when they receive the item, so the longer wait often gets a lower DSR.

If you're a PowerSeller, DSRs and feedback in general are critical to your business success. These examples show why you should strive to get 4.9 or even 5.0 on all DSRs and a high positive feedback percentage.

- PowerSellers must maintain a 4.5 average over all DSRs for the previous 12 months to keep their PowerSeller status.
- PowerSellers must maintain a 98 percent positive feedback percentage to keep their PowerSeller status.
- PowerSellers with an average of 4.6 on all of their DSRs over the last 30 days receive a 5 percent discount on their Final Value fees. If the DSR average is 4.8, the discount is 15 percent. If it is 4.9, the discount is 20 percent. That's a huge incentive!

DSRs are not the only factor that determines the Best Match order. Also included are the buyer satisfaction rating and the shipping cost (offering free shipping gets you bonus points on this one).

The buyer satisfaction rating is determined by DSRs, Feedback Score, and buyer disputes filed with eBay. A one- or two-star DSR rating will reduce your buyer satisfaction rating (the levels are Good, Needs Work, Poor, and Unacceptable) which has a knock-on effect to reducing your Best Match promotion level.

As you can see, DSRs, feedback, and customer satisfaction are all tied together. Thankfully it's not guesswork to see where you place in each of these standings. The Seller Dashboard in My eBay shows you exactly where you stand.

As you can see in Figure 29.3, your current DSRs are shown on the right side. You can choose to view your 30-day or 12-month averages compared with eBay's averages or your 30-day compared with your 12-month averages. This means you have no surprises when it comes to the end of the month.

Figure 29.3
The eBay Seller Dashboard.

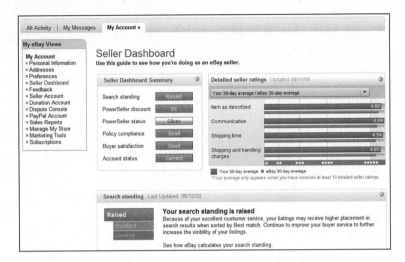

The Seller Dashboard also shows you what level promotion you have for Best Match (Raised, Standard, or Lowered). You can drill-down to see exactly what is affecting it, so you can improve in those areas.

Likewise, if you're a PowerSeller, the Seller Dashboard will show your Final Value fee discount and how it is calculated so you can strive to improve to get the higher discounts next month.

Remember, Best Match and the PowerSeller fee discounts are based on the last 30 days, not 12 months. Your positive feedback percentage is based on the last 12 months, so if you do get a negative feedback, it will only affect your score for 12 months, not indefinitely.

Keep an eye on your DSR levels. If any of your DSR's 30-day average is approaching 4.5, or even 4.4, you need to change something in your business quickly to get some 5-star ratings and increase that DSR. Offering faster shipping (or simply upgrading to priority mail without charging the customer extra) is a great way to get higher DSRs on the Shipping Time and Shipping and Handling Charges. Make sure to show the shipping cost on the postage label if it is higher than the buyer paid.

At the moment, you can only see your overall score. However, in 2009 eBay plans to roll out a new Seller Dashboard where you will be able to see all of your ratings—how many stars were given for each transaction.

You can find more about the Seller Dashboard at www.pages.ebay.com/help/myebay/seller-dashboard.html#tips.

chapter 30

The Auction Title: Headlines to Hits

Successful eBayers know how to write an item description (sales pitch) that hooks a browser's interest and then reels him in with just a few sentences. The first part of your eBay sales pitch is the auction title (what eBay calls the Item Title), often referred to as the headline, which should immediately focus a potential customer on your auction. If you get a bidder to click on your headline, you have won half the battle. Remember, unless someone actually clicks your headline, he won't read your auction (item description), and you'll never make a sale.

The headline is the single most important item in your auction. When a bidder performs a search or clicks a category, he is presented with a page listing about 40 auction headlines. The potential bidder scans the list looking for something that catches his attention. Making your headline stand out in this list is critical to your auction success.

A headline is nothing more than a collection of words designed to stop your potential buyer's eyes from scanning and linger long enough to click your auction. To achieve this, a headline must …

- Be compelling.
- Be concise.
- Describe a benefit.
- Use the correct product keywords.

30.1 Keywords in Titles That Sell

The single most important criteria for headlines is the use of relevant keywords. According to eBay, more than 80 percent of bidders find items on eBay by using the Search feature. People search for goods by typing in the names of the product they are searching for. You want your headline to be as exact as possible, yet also contain general keywords to make it come up in the greatest number of searches. Look at this headline:

JOE MONTANA SIGNED FOOTBALL JERSEY FROM 1982 SEASON -NR

This is an excellent headline for several reasons. First, it exactly describes what is being offered and indicates there is no reserve (NR). Second, it is very keyword rich. This headline would come up in a search for the following terms:

Joe Montana

football

football jersey

Joe Montana signed

eBay allows 55 characters in an auction title. This one uses all 55.

Here is another example of a good keyword-rich headline:

TRUE RELIGION DESIGNER BLUE JEANS, SIZE MEDIUM 34 WAIST

A woman searching for designer blue jeans might type in several combinations of keywords such as: blue jeans, designer blue jeans, True Religion (a popular brand name), blue jeans medium, blue jeans 34, true religion jeans, and so on. Any of those keyword combinations would cause this auction to come up in a search. This headline also uses all 55 characters.

Sometimes you need to describe the condition of an item:

CLANCY SIGNED 1ST EDITION ~ HUNT FOR RED OCTOBER, FINE

The word fine tells the buyer this book is in perfect, like-new condition, a quality every book collector searches for.

Notice that I use all caps in my headlines. All caps stand out better than a combination of upper- and lowercase headlines.

PowerSeller Tip

The use of all caps is somewhat controversial because some people claim this amounts to electronic shouting as is done in e-mail or on chat rooms. However, I have personally tested the use of all caps, and my listings with all caps always get more hits than those without. This may not be true for all products, though, so I suggest you perform your own test.

Because people are searching for products by keywords, it is extremely important that you use correct spelling. If you are selling a Staffordshire plate and spell it *Stafordshire*, your auction will not come up when bidders use the eBay search feature to find Staffordshire items.

Having said this, if there is a popular misspelling (is it Sketchers or Skechers?), you should use both to catch the many buyers who misspell the word without realizing it. A search for Sketchers produced 598 results, which seems fairly decent until you search for the correct spelling, Skechers, and get 4,357 results. Most buyers who search the misspelling would never realize because of the number of results they would get. Your strategy should be to use both spellings to catch buyers searching both terms. This does work. Recently I was selling the Rachael Ray line of chef's knives. I launched an auction where I misspelled Rachael as Rachel. The auction sold at a good price and I kept relisting it that way with very good results.

For an extra dollar, you can choose to bold your auction title. An extra dollar for a listing fee might sound like a lot, but eBay's research shows that a bold listing increases bids by an average of 25 percent. The bold listing fee has the highest return on investment of any eBay feature except gallery listing (Section 36.4) at 25¢.

30.2 Power Words in Titles That Sell

Years of research in the direct marketing community have proven that certain words have the power to make people act. If you have room in your title after including all the relevant keywords, include one or more *hot-button* words, words that are proven to increase interest. Here are some of the best-performing hot-button words:

RARE	NEW
LIGHTLY USED	BEST VALUE
SECRET	VINTAGE
TOP-SELLING	UNIQUE
BEST-SELLING	SEXY
LOVE	UNBELIEVABLE
FREE	SUPER DEAL
HARD-TO-FIND	UNUSUAL
AWESOME	BEST _____ ON EBAY

Be reasonable and accurate with your choice of words. Remember: your credibility is on the line. If a headline makes a seller click on your auction and it's immediately obvious the bidder is being misled, he will click off immediately.

eBay used to allow headlines that did not mention an actual product. You used to see headlines such as "My pet lizard thinks I'm crazy," or "My wife almost fainted when she saw these." These are no longer allowed. All auction titles must mention the specific product for sale.

PowerSeller Tip

Do not use tricky symbols or other cheesy ways (such as L@@K or lots of !!!!!!) or unusual combinations of lower and uppercase letters to attract attention to your auction. Such tactics immediately turn off potential customers and make you and your business look unprofessional.

Keywords in headlines have always been important. But in 2008, eBay rolled out its new search engine that defaults to Best Match. Since eBay made this change, using the correct keywords people search for has become even more critical. Your headline must mention relevant keywords people will use in their search. To increase your auction hits, you should also be able to answer "Yes" to at least one or two of the following questions.

- Does it arouse curiosity?
- Does it specify a product in detail?
- Does it mention or imply a benefit?
- Does it use a hot-button word?
- Does it solve a problem?
- Is it compelling?

For more on auction titles, see Sections 36.1 and 36.2.

For more on Gallery listings, see Section 36.4.

For more on describing your products, see Chapter 31.

For more on keyword advertising, see Chapter 38.

Descriptions That Drive Bids Through the Roof

eBay is a platform built on trust because it's a place where complete strangers sell to each other. Without trust the platform won't work, and sellers will have no customers. Therefore, the first goal of your auction description must be trust and credibility. Your auction description must inspire confidence. If your item descriptions are too far-fetched, use wild or silly adjectives, or make outrageous claims, you will sow doubt in your readers' minds.

One way to inspire trust is to accurately describe your product, including any shortcomings. If a product has a flaw, mention it. If the product is new, but the box is damaged, tell the prospective buyer about this. If a product is perfect except for a small scratch, explain the situation and show potential bidders a photo of the scratch.

31.1 Making a Sales Pitch

It's up to you to provide an enthusiastic and energizing description that will make your potential buyer feel like he needs your product. The item description is your sales pitch. Before you start writing the sales pitch, decide who you are writing to. If you are selling baby clothes to new moms, your item description will be quite different than if you are selling a money-making product to entrepreneurs. Look at your niche market and try to picture your customers. What are their likes and dislikes? What are they looking for? How old are they, and what kinds of jobs do they generally hold? What are their hobbies and interests? What makes them tick? Do they have a lot of disposable income? Are they seeking quality or a bargain—or both?

A successful sales pitch appeals to the self-interest of the customer. When writing a sales pitch, understanding the psychology of your customers counts more than writing ability. Remember: you want to appeal to the type of customer who will be viewing your auction.

eBay and all the auction-management services now have HTML editors that enable users to add boldface and italic type, bullet lists, and change text size and color and more features without knowing HTML. Use these features to make your auction more attractive and easier to read, but use them sparingly. I do *not* suggest giant letters and distracting features such as blinking, animations, and other "cheesy" items (unless you are selling a really cheesy product).

31.1.1 How to Structure Your Copy

The very first item in your item description should be a clear statement of precisely what you are selling. Suppose you are selling a brand-new Canon EOS Digital Rebel XTi 10.1 mega pixel digital SLR camera with a Canon EF-S 18-55 mm zoom lens, full factory warranty, and the following accessories:

- Leather carrying case
- Heavy-duty tripod
- 1-gigabyte high-performance memory card
- Compact flash card reader
- Cleaning kit

Because you want no confusion about what the bidder is about to bid on, you must include this information in the first paragraph of the auction. If bidders have to scroll through the whole auction to find out exactly what is included, you risk their clicking away and looking for another seller.

After the basic product overview, move into a full description of the product. I like to list any specifications, sizes and weights, or any features that help the reader understand what he is buying fairly early in the product description, usually before the third or fourth paragraph.

Among the information you should include are …

- Model or part numbers.
- Specifications.
- Brand names/manufacturers' names.
- Country of origin.
- Packaging.
- Size, weight, color, shape, etc.
- Age and specific condition.
- History and provenance.

Next, talk about the product's benefits. Tell the reader why he will enjoy and/or benefit from your product.

Be careful not to confuse *benefits* with the product *features*. For example, "This lovely teddy bear has yellow eyes," describes a feature. Look at this description with the benefits in italics: "This *unique* teddy bear *will bring delight* to your child. *Her eyes will light up* and *she will squeal with excitement* when you tell her, 'I got it just for you honey.'"

Here's another example: "This *unique* bagel slicer *is rugged*. It *will not break*. Its foam-lined handle is *soft* and *will not slip*, even if wet, and *is sized* for a woman's hand." In this product description, "foam-lined" is a feature. "Will not break," "will not slip," and "sized for a woman's hand" are benefits. You use features like "foam-lined" to describe benefits such as "will not slip."

Finally, fully disclose any flaws. You can put a positive spin on any shortcomings, but mention them honestly. This will increase your credibility and trustworthiness and the number of bids you receive. Here is an example:

> This circa 1940 HO tank car is in very good condition and still in the original box. The box is a bit worn and faded but is in pretty good condition considering it is over 60 years old. Best of all, it still has the original price tag on the box, showing it sold for $1.29.

In this example you should include a photo of the box so the buyer can see just how worn it is.

31.1.2 Copywriting Tips

A complete guide to writing winning advertising copy would be as long as this book. Rather than reinvent the wheel, I point you to your local library, where you can find many good books on the subject of advertising copy writing and direct response copy writing (which is what your auction description is). But until you get a chance to read those books, these keys can help you write a good auction description:

- Organize your thoughts and information before you start writing.
- Use action words and active verbs, because the goal of direct response copy is to get people to act. (Using active verbs instead of passive verbs is the most critical aspect of advertising copy writing.)
- Use short, simple words.
- Keep your sentences short, the shorter the better. If you write a sentence longer than ten words, follow it with one with fewer than five words. Short sentences command attention, so use them to describe your most important benefits.
- Use short paragraphs and/or bulleted lists.
- Use pronouns: you, me, I, she, him, and so on. *You* is the most powerful pronoun, so begin or end many of your sentences with the word *you*.

A word of advice: if you cannot write well, get some help! You don't have to write like Hemingway, but you should write clearly and concisely.

Bidders notice misspelled words and tortured grammatical contortions. If you're not confident in your writing skills, ask your friends and family for help. Take a writing class at your community college. Hire an English student to work with you. Your copy doesn't need to be brilliant, but it does need to be readable.

Prepare your copy in a word processing program such as Microsoft Word that has a grammar and spelling checker, and use those features! After you've done all this, paste your copy into the HTML editor in your eBay or auction manager listing tool.

Remember that more than 80 percent of bidders use the **Search** feature to find items they are looking for, so make sure the keywords in your auction title are spelled correctly. If not, the search option will not bring up your auction, and you'll get fewer bids. If you don't believe me, perform a search on the word *jewelry.* Now perform a search using the spelling *jewlery.* It is amazing how many people misspell this word. (This is a great way to find items on eBay that you can win at a low price because not many other bidders will find the item in their keyword search.)

31.2 Power Words and Emotional Appeal (You can't sell a diamond without the sparkle)

Power words such as *new, sexy, secret, bargain, hot,* and so on catch people's attention and work on their psychological hot buttons. Just do not exaggerate your claims, or you'll quickly lose credibility.

Make an emotional appeal to your prospective bidder. I like to do this by using words to create romantic or exhilarating images in people's minds. My wife occasionally sells expensive designer goods on eBay from companies such as Burberry, Prada, Fendi, Chanel, and Versace. After she describes the item, she tries to create a little romance in the customers' minds. Last year she had some great Fendi mirrored sunglasses. Here is one of the lines from her item description:

> Imagine pulling up in front of New York's Tavern on The Green in your Porsche Boxster and getting out wearing your hot new Fendi sunglasses. You will be able to see all the eyes on you, but they can only wonder what mystery your eyes hold.

Although my wife bought the sunglasses at an overstock price of 70 percent off of retail, she ended up getting almost full retail on the entire collection by the time they had all sold. I am willing to bet very few of her buyers own a Porsche or even knew where Tavern on The Green is, but that's not the point. When they read her description, they conjured a scene in their own minds that matched their own circumstances, and it probably didn't involve driving up to Burger King in their Ford Taurus full of kids.

Here is another example. One of the products we sell on eBay is an expensive fire pit. After I describe all the features, I explain the benefits, such as the spark arrestor, which prevents sparks from jumping out when a burning log pops, and the cut outs in the side, which drive the smoke up and away from people sitting nearby. Then I go on to describe what it's like to sit around the fire on a chilly evening snuggled up to my wife with a glass of Merlot in my hand.

Don't worry about whether your word picture matches your readers' situations—they'll modify your description to make it match their setting. Take my fire pit example: if someone doesn't have a deck, he will imagine himself taking the fire pit camping and using it in the woods or beside his RV—whatever his personal situation is.

Of course, you can't romance everything. If you are selling ink cartridges, there isn't a lot you can do. But you can describe almost everything else in a way that will spark your readers' imaginations.

Motivators other than romance appeal to people. Among the biggest motivators—especially among eBay users—is saving money. People will often spend money in the hopes of saving money. That is why the wholesale clubs like Costco and Sam's Club are so successful. People will spend $15 to buy a giant jar of mayonnaise because they reason that 10 smaller jars of mayonnaise would cost $25 if bought individually.

If I can't think of enough benefits, I will often do a web search for the product to see if I can find any advertising that others have done. You don't want to plagiarize the consumer advertising, but you can get ideas from it.

31.3 White Space and Bold Face

One of the most frustrating things I see on eBay every day is auction descriptions in small type that just go on and on in one long paragraph. Figure 31.1 is a screen shot from an actual auction. How could anyone make sense of this?

People tend to scan the page looking for something that grabs their attention. Instead of one long paragraph, use a series of short paragraphs, typically just three or four sentences each. Make lists, use bullets, and highlight important information with boldface type. Just don't overdo it with the bold. If every other word is bold or all caps, you lose the impact.

By using short paragraphs and lists, you create white space in your auction. This makes it easier for people to scan the page to find the information they want.

Digital Rebel XT Camera Specifications Camera Type Camera Type: Digital AF/AE SLR Recording Medium: CF card Type I and II Image Format: 0.87 x 0.58 in./22.2 x 14.8mm Compatible Lenses: Canon EF Lenses including EF-S Lenses (Focal length conversion factor: Equivalent to approx. 1.6x indicated focal length compared to 35mm format) Lens Mount: Canon EF mount Image Sensor Type: High-sensitivity, high-resolution, single-plate color CMOS sensor Pixels: Approx. 8.0 Megapixels Total Pixels: Approx. 8.2 Megapixels Aspect Ratio: 2:3 (Vertical:Horizontal) Color Filter System: RGB primary color filter Low-pass Filter: Fixed position in front of the image sensor Recording System Recording Format: Design rule for Camera File System (JPEG) and RAW. Exif 2.21 compliant Image Format: JPEG and RAW (CR2) File Size: JPEG: (1) Large/Fine: Approx. 3.3 MB (3456 x 2304), (2) Large/Normal: Approx. 1.7 MB (3456 x 2304), (3) Medium/Fine: Approx. 2.0 MB (2496 x 1664), (4) Medium/Normal Approx. 1.0 MB (2496 x 1664), (5) Small/Fine: Approx. 1.2 MB (1728 x 1152), (6) Small/Normal: Approx. 0.6 MB (1728 x 1152); RAW: Approx. 8.3 MB (3456 x 2304) Folders: Automatic setting File Numbering: (1) Continuous numbering, (2) Auto reset Image-processing Parameters: Standard parameters plus up to three custom processing parameter sets and monochrome can be set Interface: USB 2.0 Hi-Speed White Balance Settings: Auto, Preset (Daylight, Shade, Cloudy/Twilight/Sunset, Tungsten light, White fluorescent light, Flash), Manual (Custom: read off photo quality gray card or white subject) Viewfinder Type: Eye-level SLR (with fixed pentamirror) Coverage: Approx. 95-percent vertically and horizontally (against JPEG Large) Magnification: 0.8x (-1 diopter with 50mm lens at infinity) Eyepoint: 21mm Dioptric Adjustment Correction: -3.0 - +1.0 diopters Focusing Screen: Fixed Mirror: Quick-return half mirror (Transmittance: reflection ratio of 40:60, no mirror cut-off with lenses up to EF 600mm f/4) Viewfinder Information: AF points, AE lock, FE lock, AEB in progress, Flash ready, Improper FE lock warning, High-speed Sync, Flash exposure compensation, Red-Eye reduction, Shutter speed, Bulb, FE lock, Processing data, Built-in flash recycling, Aperture, Exposure level display (Exposure compensation, Manual exposure level, AEB

Figure 31.1
Don't make the mistake of writing an auction description like this!

Figure 31.2 shows an auction for a very important and expensive historical collectible. This flag signed by four presidents was being auctioned for over $10,000. You would think the seller could do a better job of designing the auction description to make it easier to read. Remember, credibility is everything. Does this item description inspire credibility?

********** ITEM DESCRIPTION **********

ONE OF A KIND PRESIDENTIAL HAND-SIGNED AMERICAN FLAG WITH CERTIFICATE OF AUTHENTICITY! SIGNED BY FOUR (4) PRESIDENTS AND THEIR FIRST LADIES! ... PLUS SENATOR EDWARD "TED" KENNEDY AND VICE PRESIDENT WALTER MONDALE! Exceedingly Rare One of a kind Large American Flag HAND-SIGNED BY PRESIDENT RONALD REAGAN & NANCY REAGAN, JIMMY CARTER & ROSALYN CARTER, GERALD R. FORD & BETTY FORD, GEORGE BUSH SR. & BARBARA BUSH, VICE PRESIDENT WALTER MONDALE AND SENATOR EDWARD "TED" KENNEDY! This One of a Kind Museum Piece measures approx. 8 X 12 1/2. with a wooden flag pole and Gold Pinnacle. PURCHASED FROM RIBBONS OF HOPE, A NON PROFIT CHARITY THAT WAS RESPONSIBLE FOR HAVING THIS RARE PIECE HAND-SIGNED BY EACH OF THE PRESIDENTS AND FIRST LADIES! THE FLAG IS ACCOMPANIED BY AN OFFICIAL CERTIFICATE OF AUTHENTICITY FROM FROM THE CHARITY ITSELF. This is one of the last items Signed personally by Ronald Reagan before loosing his ability to do so. THE CHARITY SPENT MANY YEARS AND A LOT OF MONEY COLLECTING THESE SIGNATURES IN PERSON. A one of a kind Museum Piece!

Figure 31.2
An expensive product gets lost in this confusing description.

If a product has a long list of specifications or features, break them up into several short lists by category, and give each category a heading. For example, you might first list the physical specifications (size, weight, and so on), follow with a list of the electronic specifications, and end with a list of the features.

The other major auction killer is reverse out type. A reverse out is when you feature white or light-colored type on a dark background. It might look artistically cool, but it is very difficult to read. If you are selling anything to people over the age of 40, don't use reverse out type. As people age, their eyes need more light and greater contrast to see well. An older person will have a very difficult time reading yellow type on a black background.

Type size is another factor. If you are selling body jewelry to teens, they can probably see the standard small-size type that eBay uses in their auctions. But if you are selling products that someone older might want to buy, go for the larger type. There are two ways to increase the type size in your auctions. If you are using HTML, start your auction description with the HTML command <font size +1>. Inserting this command in your auction description will increase the font size in your entire auction description. If you are using an HTML editor in your auction management system or in the eBay *Sell Your Item* form, then you can just select the font-size button and increase your font by at least one size. If you are not sure, just use the *Medium* setting.

31.4 Increase Sales with a Call to Action

There's a salesman's adage that says "If you want to make the sale, you have to ask for the order." I cannot tell you how many times I have seen a salesperson go through a perfect product presentation and then end it with, "Well, what do you think?" Would you take the time to write a perfect auction description only to end it with a sentence that says, "Well, what do you think?" Wouldn't something like "Place your best bid now so you can enjoy a sizzling steak on your new barbeque this weekend" be better?

I always end my auctions by asking for the bid. This is known as a *call to action* in the direct marketing industry. Think of all the direct marketing pieces you have received in the mail over the years. They all end with something such as "Don't let this once-in-a-lifetime opportunity pass you by. Call now!"

The same thing is true in your auctions. I have tested this extensively. Whenever I add a call to action, my auctions experience almost a 20 percent increase in the number of bids, and my final values average about 12 percent higher.

If your auction description is very long, you can actually put several calls to action in your auction. As you are writing about the benefits, use phrases such as "don't miss out on this fabulous eBay bargain, bid now." Then always put a final call to action at the end.

If you have additional items listed at fixed-price auctions or in your eBay store, you can also use a call to action to drive them there. When you do this, make sure you use a clickable link right in the call to action.

Here are some of the call-to-action phrases I have used in my auctions. With a little imagination you can probably come up with many, many more:

- Don't lose out to a sniper—Buy It Now.
- Don't lose out to a sniper; place your best bid now.
- This _____ could be sitting in your home this weekend. BID NOW.
- You will be heartbroken if you lose this fabulous eBay bargain to another bidder. Place your best bid now.
- Don't wait for the bidding to end; <u>click here</u> to visit my eBay store where you can Buy It Now.
- You might be busy when the auction ends, so just place your best bid now to win this fabulous …

Remember that you can't make a sale unless you ask for the order.

31.5 How to Kill Bids

Why would you want to know how to kill a potential bid? So you don't do it by accident. I am continually amazed by some of the statements I see in auctions that seem designed to turn away bidders. For the past two years I have been keeping a file of the ones I come across. Here are some of the best—or should I say worst—policy statements I've seen in eBay auctions, all taken from actual auctions. The spelling and grammar errors are theirs, not mine.

If you are not going to pay then don't bid me. I will chase you down and find you if you win this auction and don't pay me.

Don't bid unless your feedback is at least 25. I don't deal with eBay cherries. I will cancel your bid if you have less than 25 feedbacks.

Yes I am making money on the shipping. What did you expect me to do, ship it at my cost.

please bid good price on my cd because I am very poor and need money bad and right away. i only take money order or put cash in evelope and mail right away and i will be nice to you in feedback and god bless you too if you are a nice person.

I only ship on Thursday. If your payment arrives after Thursday noon then you will have to wait a week until I ship again. If you dont like this then dont bid.

I charge the correct shipping cost plus a $5 handling fee to cover my time for wrapping and standing in line at the post office. Do not bid if this is not okeydokey with you.

I only take money order, cashiers check or Western Union transfer. PayPal is a screw job. They want to charge me a 3% fee on every deal. If you send a personal check I will just throw it away so please don't bother.

i am selling this as is just the way it is i do the best to tell you condition and so i do not want your bid if you do not agree it is as is and that is happy for you. please pay me very quickly and leave good feedbacks and i will do same for you.

My shipping policy: I ship everything by priority mail on Monday and Friday. I charge the priority mail rate plus $2.00 to pay for box and packing material. I don't guarantee anything. If you want insurance the extra cost is $5.00. I know it doesn't cost that much to insure a package but I have to wait in line and fill out forms at the post office and keep the forms until a claim is made and that is a big pain but I will do it for $5.00.

(From the same seller above) My Returns Policy: No returns for any reason except if I send you the wrong item and then you need to send me a photo of what you received so I can be sure before your return it.

Whenever I see one of these statements I copy/paste it into a file I have been keeping. I also take a moment to check the feedback. Invariably, the sellers who post these ridiculous statements have a high negative feedback rating themselves. I cover the subject of shipping, payment, and return policies in Chapter 33.

For more on describing items, see Chapter 33 and Section 44.2.

For more on writing your shipping and payment policies, see Sections 33.1 and 33.2.

chapter 32

Credibility Equals Sales

In Chapter 31, I stressed the importance of writing credible auction descriptions, but building credibility goes much further than what you say in your auctions. If you are going to build a successful eBay or Internet business, you have to create an overall professional image. People will judge you in many ways. It starts with the look and feel of your auctions, how and what kinds of photos and images you use, your writing style—both in your auction and your end of auction e-mails—and how you package and ship your merchandise.

32.1 Keep Your Auctions Clean

The look and feel of your auction is the first impression a potential bidder/customer has of you. When you launch an auction, give some thought to how it will look to someone who doesn't know anything about you. As I mentioned in Section 31.3, make the font large enough for anyone to read easily. Keep your paragraphs short, with an extra space between them to make it easy for readers to scan the entire description.

Next come your images. Your photos should be clear and easy to view, with close-up shots where necessary to show any important details. If you are selling new products you can often find stock photos of them on the manufacturer's or distributor's website. In general these photos are probably copyrighted, but it's usually okay to use them in your auctions if you are an authorized reseller of a product. However, I prefer to also show a photo of the actual product you're selling, either in or out of the box, so a potential bidder knows exactly what she's bidding on. I think this enhances your credibility with the buyer.

If you are selling a new (unused) product in the original box (NIB) or an item that is new with tags (NWT), then show a close-up of the price or other information on the box or the tag. If your product has a designer logo or other well-known mark, show that, too.

eBay and the various auction-management software programs and online systems give you the option of placing your photos at the top, left, right, or bottom of your auction. If you know how to use HTML, you can also place images right into your description and have the text wrap around them, although this option can be time-consuming and probably isn't practical if you are launching large numbers of auctions for different products.

I prefer to put my photos at the top of the auction or on the left or right side. This way the viewer sees the photo right away. Placing photos on the top-left or top-right will enable viewers to see the photos at the same time they are reading your description.

Both eBay and all the auction-management tools on the market support the use of pre-designed auction templates. Dozens of designs are available, but it is important to pick one that is appropriate for what you are selling.

Figure 32.1 shows a template that works really well for selling antiques, western items, or anything vintage. Now look at the effect (Figure 32.2) when I use a completely different template for the same auction. Both templates are attractive, but the first one is more appropriate to the product.

The various systems and software on the market also make it easy for you to create your own template. If you are selling in just one class or category of product, consider designing a template that reflects the kind of products you are selling. If you have an eBay store, eBay also enables you to design the look and feel of your store. Many sellers also sell their products on their websites. If you do this, be sure to carry the same design theme through all of your sales channels. That way, when a customer visits your different sales portals, she will see the same professional image. This will not only help brand your image, but it will also project the image of a professional reliable business. This gives you credibility.

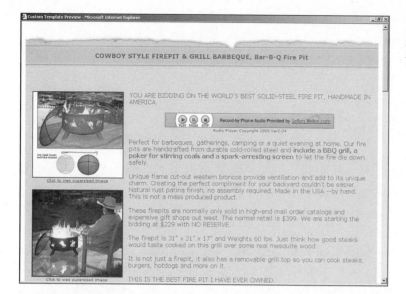

Figure 32.1
A template appropriate for vintage/western items.

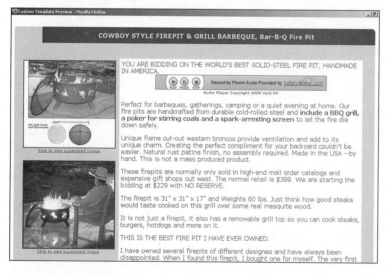

Figure 32.2
A more modern-looking template.

Finally, avoid any gimmicks that detract from your image and your selling proposition. This includes animated gif images or banners, pop-ups, spinning dollar signs, dancing cartoon characters, and those irritating mouse-overs. Many people find these gimmicks tacky and are put off by them.

The Internet has replaced direct-mail marketing as a prime spot for fraud and fast-buck operators. With direct mail, a fast-buck operator had to invest quite a bit of money in printing and mailing pieces to get a decent return. With the advent of the Internet and e-mail, it became possible to reach millions of potential victims with virtually no costs involved. This simple fact, and the vast amounts of spam computer users receive every day, makes people naturally suspicious of online commerce.

32.2 Trust and Safety on eBay

The good news is that eBay has succeeded in creating a platform where millions of users feel safe making purchases. Yet a small percentage of people have unsatisfactory experiences on eBay.

One of my newsletter readers e-mailed me for help. He had bid over $3,000 for a plasma TV on eBay from a seller who had a perfect feedback rating of over 100. The seller asked him to send a certified check or money order, which he foolishly did. After he mailed the check, the seller stopped answering e-mails and, of course, the TV never showed up.

A little investigation would have shown two things. Even though the seller had over 100 feedback comments, virtually all of them were from his buying, not selling. And when I clicked on the auctions connected to the feedback posts, they were for very cheap items. When I pulled up the profile, the seller had been registered on eBay for less than a month.

Basically this seller set up an account, spent some money in order to get feedback, and then launched dozens of auctions for expensive electronic items he did not possess and had no intention of buying or delivering. I spoke to the trust and safety people at eBay. They closed his account immediately and notified the police. It turned out the credit card he used to register was false and his address was a rented box. They wouldn't tell me how many people he'd scammed, but they did admit it was several. Privately, another source at eBay told me this seller made thousands of dollars in the week or so that it took for his scam to be uncovered and him be shut down.

Although such cases of out-and-out fraud do occur now and then, the problems most consumers have on eBay have more to do with lazy or shoddy sellers or sellers who either grossly or subtly misrepresent their merchandise. This can take the form of sellers who don't disclose slight shortcomings in the product up to those who sell out-and-out fakes and knockoffs.

32.2.1 eBay Trust & Safety Tools

eBay, and their online payment subsidiary PayPal, offer several tools to help buyers determine if they are working with an honest seller. When you register on eBay, you have to put up a credit card to verify your identity. The problem is that plenty of phony and/or stolen credit cards are floating around. There are even Internet sites where you can buy credit cards. They are preloaded with a fixed amount of money like a store gift card and look just like a normal charge card. You don't need to show an ID to get them, but they are good enough to get you registered on eBay.

Understanding the limits of credit cards, eBay came up with a system to further verify the identification of members. ID Verify establishes your proof of identity so others can trust you as their trading partner. The process takes about 10 minutes to complete and involves updating your information over a secure connection and answering a few questions. When you're successfully verified, you will receive an ID Verify icon in your feedback profile. eBay charges $5 for the service.

Here is how it works. When you click the ID Verify link in the eBay site map, a page comes up where you enter your personal information. Then you are transferred to a secure connection through Equifax. It brings up a page with questions for you to answer based on your credit report, such as the loan holder for your mortgage or the monthly payment for your car loan. The address you registered on eBay is also verified against the address on your credit report. If you answer the questions correctly and your addresses match, eBay will then place the ID Verify icon next to your User ID in all of your auctions (see Figure 32.3). This is valid until you change your registered address or telephone number. If you don't pass the ID Verify process, you do not get charged the $5 fee (if you do pass it is just charged to your eBay account).

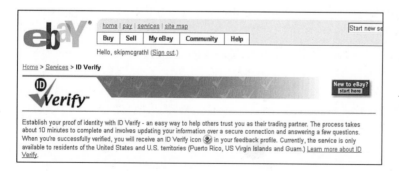

Figure 32.3
eBay ID Verify Page, showing the icon that will appear next to your User ID when you are successfully verified.

The other service that marks you as a trustworthy seller is PayPal's Verified User tag. If you are not already verified, there will be a link on your PayPal account balances page to click to start the process. You fill out a form giving PayPal the name and account number of your primary bank account. PayPal then makes two deposits to your bank account—usually a very small amount, such as 4¢. PayPal will send you an e-mail telling you that they have made the deposits. You then call your bank (or look it up online) and determine the amount of the deposits and inform PayPal via an online form on their website. If your information is accurate, PayPal will put the words PayPal Verified next to your name when they make a payment.

PayPal offers eBay buyers who pay with PayPal a buyer protection program. But there is one catch. To use the buyer protection program, the seller must be PayPal Verified. If you are PayPal Verified, eBay will place a small banner in your listing that tells buyers that this item is available for PayPal Buyer Protection.

32.3 Third Party Trust and Safety Tools

Other trust and safety tools are available to the eBay seller. The two most recognized are SquareTrade and Buysafe.

You can access SquareTrade from the eBay site map under the Safe Harbor Rules & Safety Listing, or just go to www.squaretrade.com. The SquareTrade program is somewhat similar to eBay's ID Verify, but they also insist you meet other standards and agree to dispute mediation.

All SquareTrade Seal Members must have their identity and/or contact information verified as a prerequisite to being approved for the Seal. Figure 32.4 shows the SquareTrade seal as it appears at the top of an auction description.

Figure 32.4
SquareTrade Seal.

When you click the SquareTrade seal in a seller's auction, the information shown in Figure 32.5 comes up.

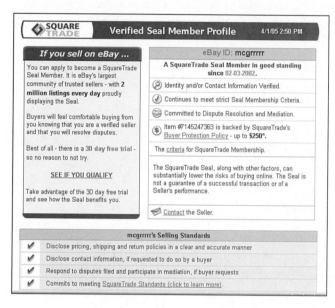

Figure 32.5
SquareTrade User Information.

SquareTrade uses a range of tools to ensure that they verify the contact information and/or identity of each Seal Member. According to SquareTrade, these tools include …

- Third-party databases (e.g., Equifax).
- Physical letter in the mail with a unique code—the Seal Member has to receive and return.
- Fax of a utility bill or other official documentation identifying the applicant and their contact information.
- For businesses, a Dun & Bradstreet # or an IRS Employer EIN.

SquareTrade Seal Members then have to maintain certain standards to retain their Seal. You can learn more about the seal and sign up at www.squaretrade.com/pages/ebay-seal-overview. (Squaretrade also offers a warranty program for electronic products. If you sell any type of consumer electronics, you may want to look into this as a way to earn extra income on your sales.)

The other popular online trust and safety tool is buySAFE. buySAFE is essentially a bonding service. After you qualify for their program, they will put a seal on your auctions. (See Figure 32.4; the buySAFE seal is located just below the

SquareTrade seal.) This seal tells prospective bidders that you are bonded up to the amount of money specified. Depending on the volume of your auctions, the length of time you have been on eBay, and your credit score, the buySAFE bond will vary from $5,000 up to $25,000 and is underwritten by a major insurance company.

When a buyer clicks the buySAFE seal, he is taken to an information page about the seller, as seen in Figure 32.6. If you also sell on a website, you can use buySAFE there as well.

Figure 32.6
*buySAFE User
Information page.*

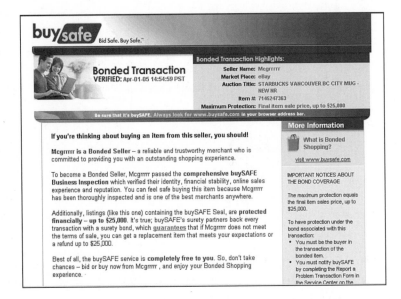

If you decide to sell expensive goods such as $900 digital cameras or $1,500 laptops, then the small cost to enroll in the SquareTrade and buySAFE programs is well worth it. buySAFE has performed research that shows conclusively that sellers offering items over $1,000 in value realize a 17 percent greater sell-through rate and achieve on average 4 percent higher values than sellers with similar items who do not use buySAFE.

eBay is a business that directly rewards honesty, sound ethical business practices, and professionalism. Any time spent on building a professional image will add to your sales and profits.

For more on building credibility with bidders, see Chapter 2 and Section 44.2.

For more on building credibility using your auction descriptions, see Chapter 31.

chapter 33

Policies That Sell

Every eBay auction has a place for the seller to enter information that is standard for each auction. Some of the standardized information sellers enter includes their shipping policy, return policy, warranty information, and occasionally a money-back guarantee. The policies you elect to use and how you describe them will impact your ability to get bids and make sales. They also help you attract repeat customers.

33.1 Your Shipping Policy

eBay users are acutely aware of shipping costs and shipping policies. As a matter of fact, shipping issues are one of the leading causes of negative feedback comments. These can range anywhere from "I never received the item," to "The item was poorly packaged and broken," and the occasional "He charged me $13 to ship an item that only cost him $3 to ship."

In 2007, eBay rolled out their newest addition to their feedback system, The Detailed Seller Rating (DSR) feature described in Chapter 29. Two of the four ratings are related to shipping. Your DSRs can affect your search position, so having clear shipping policies and communicating them to your buyers is critical to your success.

The best defense against receiving a negative feedback or a low DSR for shipping-related issues is, first, to pack and ship professionally and always use a tracking service and, second, to spell out your shipping policy and charges very clearly. More importantly, in your auction description, always direct the reader to your policy with words such as "please read my shipping policy very carefully." When I state my shipping charges in the item description I even put them in boldface type.

Make your shipping policy very clear, and include the following information:

- Which method you use to ship
- How soon you ship after receiving payment
- How much you charge for shipping
- Whether you charge a handling fee
- Whether you provide or offer insurance

33.1.1 How to Charge for Shipping

You have three ways to charge for shipping on eBay:

- Offer free shipping
- Charge the actual rate to that buyer's location (with or without an added handling fee)
- Charge a fixed rate to all buyers

Free shipping is only possible when you can receive enough margin to absorb the cost. There is no question that free shipping can help you get more and higher bids, but the bids might not always be high enough to cover the additional cost.

The ability to offer free shipping is a factor of the size and weight versus the selling price. If I am selling a very expensive postage stamp or baseball trading card, then I can afford free shipping. The steel fire pits I sell weigh 55 pounds and are the maximum size that can be shipped by a shipping service. If I offered free shipping on those, I'd have to raise the price from $219 to over $300.

A lot of eBay sellers prefer to charge the actual shipping cost. If you use UPS or USPS, eBay has made this very easy by offering a shipping calculator that is automatically included in your auction description, as shown in Figure 33.1. Potential bidders can plug their zip code into the calculator and determine the shipping cost for each of the shipping services you offer before they actually bid. You can also add a handling charge to the calculator that will automatically add a fixed dollar amount to each calculation.

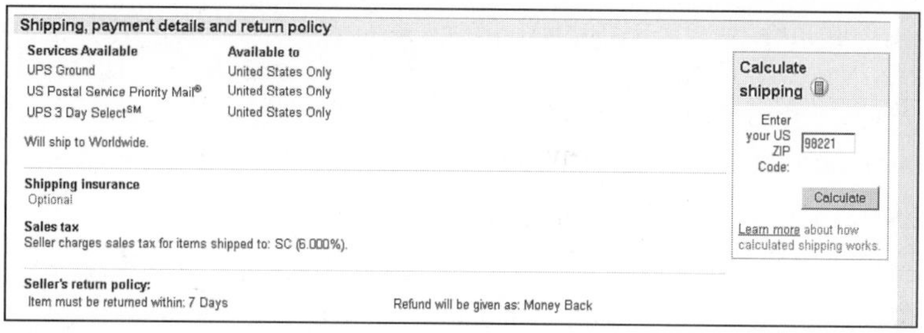

Figure 33.1
eBay Shipping Calculator.

The last method is fixed-price shipping. In fixed-price shipping you calculate the shipping charge to a preset destination. For example, I live on the West Coast. So I precalculate the shipping cost to a point midway across the country such as Chicago. If I ship past Chicago, I lose a little money on the shipping. But when I ship to someone closer, I make money. This way it averages out.

The advantage of a fixed shipping rate is that it shows on the search results page even when the buyer isn't signed in. If a buyer can compare your item's total cost to your competitors and see that your shipping charge is lower, you are more likely to get him to click through to the auction. If you use calculated shipping, the buyer must be signed into his eBay account for the calculated shipping cost to display here (if he is not signed in, it will just say *see description* instead).

Whichever method you use, always spell it out clearly in your auction description and disclose any handling charges. I believe it helps to explain why a seller uses a handling charge. In my auctions, I use the following statement: "We add a $2.00 handling charge to the shipping cost. We use only new high-quality packing materials to make sure your item arrives safely. The handling charge is necessary to cover the cost of these materials." Buyers will more likely accept paying extra charges if you take the time to justify the charge.

The last item in your shipping policy is when you ship. I use the following statement in my shipping policy:

We ship the same business day your payment arrives. Our cut-off time for shipments is 2 P.M. Pacific Time. Otherwise it will go out the next business day. We ship via USPS Priority Mail with delivery confirmation. This typically takes two to three business days to most locations. We will send you an e-mail when we ship your purchase with the delivery confirmation number and a link to the USPS website where you can track your shipment.

Notice that we ship every business day. Because we use Priority Mail for most of our shipments, we can even ship on Saturday. Priority mail is fast, offers delivery confirmation, and gives you one extra day per week to ship. People like getting their purchases quickly, and this usually shows in the feedback comments and DSRs they leave.

Many large eBay sellers only ship on specific days. Although this is more efficient, I don't recommend it. Consider what can happen when an auction closes on Sunday evening and you ship on Tuesday and Thursday. If the buyer's payment arrives after your Tuesday cut-off time, the package won't even go out until Thursday, a full four days after the auction closed. If you are shipping Priority Mail, the buyer would get her item as early as the following Tuesday, but if you use UPS, it might take an additional day. That is a total of 10 days after the end of the auction! This is a sure way to get a low DSR score for Shipping Time.

The chance to sell a customer an additional item is important to any eBay seller's profitability. Part of your business plan should be to build a loyal and happy customer base so you can sell them additional items later both on and off of eBay. Why make a buyer's first experience less than satisfying?

33.2 Payment Policy

The advent of PayPal has made payment very safe and convenient for most auction sellers. PayPal is responsible for over 80 percent of all auction payments.

As with shipping, it is very important to spell out your payment policy in advance so there is no misunderstanding.

I use this payment policy in my auctions:

> We accept and prefer PayPal. We also accept major credit cards.
>
> If you are new to eBay and have questions about our payment policy, please e-mail us through the **Ask seller a question** link at the top of this page. We will be glad to assist you with your transaction.

33.3 Return Policy

The next most important information buyers look for is your return policy. When you are listing an auction, eBay serves up a box for you to enter your return policy. Always fill this out, as eBay's new search engine scores auctions with return policies higher in the default *Best Match* search results order. However, the information you enter in this box appears at the very bottom of the listing page. Therefore, I also like to reiterate the return policy right in my auction description where buyers can see it more easily.

Your return policy is largely determined by what you sell. If you are selling product returns, seconds, or almost any used goods including books, records, CDs, and DVDs, you will want to explain that these items are sold *AS IS WITH NO RETURNS*. Most buyers will accept this if you fully and completely describe the item you are selling, including a full description of any flaws or shortcomings.

With mechanical or electrical items, you need to tell buyers, if you know, whether or not the item works. One large Seller on eBay sells nothing but consumer electronic returns and warranty returns. He has a large boldface disclaimer in his auctions that he buys these returns by the pallet load and cannot test each item and that you are taking a chance when you buy it. His policy is absolutely no returns. Despite the warning, he sells hundreds of items a month. However, his feedback rating is terrible. I think it was in the eighties the last time I looked.

Even though he warns people in large bold letters they might be getting an item that might not work and states this again in the end of auction e-mail giving them a chance to back out, a lot of buyers still leave negative feedback comments. What is really amazing is that people actually lie and leave posts such as: Seller promised new & delivered broken item in opened box.

I only sell used items occasionally. When I do, I use the following return policy:

> I have done my best to accurately and faithfully describe this item and will stand behind it. If you receive an item that is not exactly as described, please contact me before returning the item. I promise to work out a solution to your liking.

If I do make a mistake, I will, of course, accept the return for a full refund. But many times you can work out an alternate solution. If the buyer believes you made an honest mistake, he still might want to keep the item if you make a gesture such as refunding his shipping charge.

When I am selling new merchandise, I am more liberal. After all, if someone is buying something that is NIB (new in box) or NWT (new with tags), that is what she expects to get. If a buyer contacts me and says something is wrong with her item, I will almost always ask her to return it for an immediate refund.

My return policy for new merchandise is as follows:

> Your complete satisfaction is my top priority. Please inspect your purchase carefully when you receive it. If there is anything wrong, please contact me immediately, and I will ensure you get an immediate replacement or a refund if a replacement is not available.

Notice that I do not automatically offer a refund. There are people out there who suffer from buyer's remorse. This is seldom a problem with small purchases, but a handful of buyers on eBay get on the computer late at night after a few glasses of wine and go on a bidding lark. Later, when the bills come due, they start looking for ways to back out.

33.4 Money-Back Guarantee

Offering a money-back or unconditional guarantee is very controversial among eBay sellers. For the past five years I have sold my books on eBay and our website with an unconditional 90-day money-back guarantee. My return rate during that time has averaged about 1.5 percent and has never exceeded 2 percent. I've never tested my selling proposition without the guarantee, so I have no way to prove how it affects my sales. Instead, I have relied on years of research from the direct marketing community that shows that a money-back guarantee can increase sales anywhere from 20 to 50 percent. Every direct sales or marketing copywriter I have read or spoken to swears by the money-back guarantee.

I have also used a money-back guarantee whenever I sell anything on eBay or my website where there might be some doubt in a customer's mind. For example, we sell famous-name designer clothes and accessories. There are so many fakes and knockoffs selling on eBay that I guarantee our merchandise is genuine or I will refund the full purchase price. We have sold hundreds of designer items and so far have only had one customer claim something was not genuine. Even though it was, I refunded her money rather than get into an argument that could result in a negative feedback. That transaction cost me a few dollars in fees, but I'm sure I have made dozens of sales that I would not otherwise have made without our guarantee.

We also offer a no-questions-asked guarantee on our expensive fire pits if the customer is not happy for any reason. $219.00 + $55 shipping is a lot of money for a fire pit. By offering a guarantee, I transfer the risk from the customer to myself. We have one competitor on eBay selling the same fire pits from the same manufacturer. He undersells us by $20 but doesn't offer a guarantee. We sell five or six units a week whereas he sells one or two.

We have sold over 150 of these fire pits as of this writing, and so far only one has been returned. A woman was buying it for a surprise birthday present for her husband. When it was delivered, she realized she had nowhere to hide it and didn't think she was strong enough to move it and set it up and asked us to take it back. That order cost me $55 shipping to return, but I was able to resell it to someone else, so the loss was minimized. Yes, $55 plus the eBay and PayPal selling fees is a lot of money, but remember I am outselling my competitor three to one and getting $20 more for each unit.

Having said all this, I would not automatically assume that offering a money-back guarantee is right for every product. But for many products where the customer senses a degree of risk, a money-back guarantee might be enough to turn potential bidders into actual bidders.

For more on shipping methods, see Section 5.8.

For more on feedback and Detailed Seller Ratings, see Chapter 29.

For more on communicating policies, see Chapters 41, 42, and 44.

chapter 34

Best Times to Start and End Auctions

The best auction duration and times to start and end an auction is a very controversial subject among eBay sellers. Although there is no single right or wrong answer, let me offer some tried-and-true guidelines for establishing your auction length and end time.

34.1 How Long?

eBay offers five auction duration choices: 1-, 3-, 5-, 7- and 10-day auctions. One theory is the shorter the auction the better, because people don't like to bid on auctions that have a long wait until they end. Impulse buyers will definitely seek out shorter auctions. This is especially true if you are selling common products that are always available on eBay (such as jewelry, clothing and leather goods, digital cameras, MP3 Players, designer brand-name goods, popular collectibles, and so on).

If you are selling hard-to-find items or something of a very collectible nature as opposed to an easily available product, you want to expose your auction to as many people as possible over the longest period of time. Collectors tend to be more careful and will shop diligently for specific items for their collection. For items of this nature, I recommend the 10-day auction.

eBay has two promotional tools called Homepage Feature and Featured Plus (see Chapter 36) that will feature your auctions prominently at the top of search pages, but they are fairly expensive promotional tools. If you use either of these features, you should also consider a 7- or 10-day auction to spread the feature cost over a longer time period.

Different types of people shop at different times. You need to end your auction during a time when your target audience is online.

More people are on eBay during the evening and on weekends than during the day. Young people are usually out Friday and Saturday nights, but they are home and often on eBay during the after-school hours from 3 to 6 P.M. Older folks who stay home spend a lot of time on eBay during the day and on Saturday evening because it's usually a lousy TV night. (The most popular prime-time TV shows are on Monday through Thursday evenings.) If you are selling a product such as ink cartridges or shipping supplies to a business, these people usually buy during the day.

Here is a general rating of the best and worst days to end an auction, but there are exceptions:

Day	Rating	Comment
Monday	Fair	A lot of people surf eBay at work. After the weekend, they need their "eBay fix." Monday evening is also good, the best evening of the week after Sunday evening.
Tuesday	Worst	Tuesday receives the lowest number of bids on eBay.
Wednesday	Poor	Wednesday is not quite as bad as Tuesday.
Thursday	Fair	Thursday is not a bad time to end an auction in the spring and summer, because people who go away for the weekend will bid on Thursday before they leave.
Friday	Good	Friday before 6 P.M. can be a good day for students and young people.
Saturday	Good	Weekend days are usually better than weekdays.
Sunday	Excellent	Sunday evening is the time of highest bidding activity on eBay. If your auction ends about 11 P.M. Eastern time, you will maximize your bidding activity.

Whenever you launch an auction, always think ahead and ask yourself what is happening 1, 3, 5, 7, or 10 days (depending on the length of your auction) from now. Don't launch an auction that will end on a holiday weekend when no one is home or during the Super Bowl when everyone is in front of his television.

Don't forget your market. Although the evening is generally the best time to end an auction, it really depends on whom you are selling to.

PowerSeller Tip

The auction duration you select is closely related to what day your auction will end. For instance, I prefer to launch my 3-day and 10-day auctions on Thursday evening so they end on Sunday evenings. Between 4 and 6 P.M. Pacific time (7 to 9 P.M. EST) seems to work best for me, but you should experiment based on the types of products you are selling (eBay time on eBay U.S. is Pacific time).

Another factor to consider when deciding on the duration of your auction and what day to end it on is where your auction will appear. When a bidder performs a search or goes to the listing page for a category, he is given the following choices for viewing the auctions:

- Best Match (this is the default search unless the buyer changes it)
- Time: ending soonest
- Time: newly listed
- Price + shipping: lowest first
- Price + shipping: highest first
- Price: highest first
- Distance: nearest first
- Payment: PayPal first
- Category

If I am selling a product that is in fairly high demand and that people routinely search for, I like to list a series of three-day auctions every other day starting on Thursday. A three-day auction will show up near the top on the first day in Newly Listed and then at the top again just two days later in Ending Soonest.

This way I have a product near the top of the search results every day. This also helps you take advantage of a recent eBay search change where they no longer show duplicate items on the same day. If you are selling multiple identical items, listing them each on different days will help them appear in search more often.

34.2 Testing Auction Ending Times

As with almost anything on eBay that you have control over, it pays to test auction ending times. Although early Sunday evening is considered by most to be the best day and time to end an auction, I often get great response on other days.

When I am selling something for the first time, I run the auction to end Sunday evening. If it sells and I decide to invest in inventory, I run identical test auctions on other days. I am often surprised that the same auction will do just as well on the so-called "poor" ending days.

Lastly, I also check the best auction ending days and times in HammerTap to confirm this. For some reason there are some products that consistently do well on the so-called poor days.

For more on how to research the best auction-ending times, see Sections 11.4 and 11.5, and Appendix B.

For more on eBay promotional tools, see Chapter 36.

chapter 35

Is eBay Eating Your Lunch?

After the cost of inventory, eBay and PayPal fees are the largest expense for the eBay seller. Selling, or Final Value Fees, are incurred only when an item sells on eBay. However, every time you list an auction, you incur a listing (Insertion) fee, which you pay even if the auction ends without a sale, although you might be eligible for a Relist Credit if you choose to relist the item. We'll talk about this a bit later.

To recoup your listing costs, you need to spread the listing fees of the unsuccessful auctions over your successful auctions. Total up your listing fees (include both successful and unsuccessful auctions), and then divide this dollar amount by the number of successful auctions. This is the true cost to list an item on eBay.

Some of the top sellers on eBay have monthly eBay fee bills as high as $20,000. Even medium-size eBay sellers pay fees ranging from $3,000 to $5,000 a month. When you are spending this much in any expense, you need to pay attention and do everything you can to control and reduce this cost. If you spend $20,000 a month in fees and can reduce it by 10 percent, that works out to a savings of $2,000 a month or $24,000 a year. That's enough to hire an employee or make monthly payments on a new Ferrari.

35.1 Understanding Your eBay Fees

eBay has several types of fees. Understanding how eBay calculates their fees is essential to learning to control them. The various fees fall into the following categories:

- Insertion Fees: the cost to post an item for sale
- Final Value Fees: the cost to sell an item
- Fees for Listing Upgrades, such as Bold, Highlight, International Exposure, and so on.

The fees are different for Auction-Style and Fixed-Price listings. Also different fees are based on the category.

Note: eBay changes (raises) its fees occasionally. The fees listed in this chapter were accurate when this edition went to press. You can see the current eBay fees at this link: pages.ebay.com/help/sell/fees.html.

35.1.1 Listing Fees

Listing fees for Auction-Style listings are broken down into three categories: Insertion fees, Buy It Now fees, and Reserve fees.

Media items (books, music, DVDs & movies, and video games) have a different (lower) Insertion fee for the first three fee bands.

eBay Auction-Style Listing Insertion Fees

Starting Price	Insertion Fee Media Items	All Other Items
$0.01–$0.99	$0.10	$0.15
$1–$9.99	$0.25	$0.35
$10–$24.99	$0.35	$0.55
$25–$49.99	$1.00	$1.00
$50–$199.00	$2.00	$2.00
$200–$499.99	$3.00	$3.00
$500 and up	$4.00	$4.00

The Buy It Now fee applies only to auctions that add the Buy It Now option. The Buy It Now price must be a minimum of $1.

Buy It Now Fees

Buy It Now Price	Fee
$1–$9.99	5¢
$10–$24.99	10¢
$25–$49.99	20¢
$50 or more	25¢

Reserve Fee

Reserve Price	Fee
$0.01–$199.99	$2
$200 and up	1 percent of reserve price (max. $50)

Fixed-Price listings have a fixed Insertion fee no matter how many items are for sale within that listing or what the list price is. They also run for 30 days as standard and can be set to auto-renew every 30 days with the Good 'Til Cancelled (GTC) option.

For media items (books, music, DVDs, movies, and video games), the Insertion fee is 15 cents. For all other items sold in a Fixed Price listing, the Insertion fee is 35 cents. It doesn't matter if the price is $5 or $500, the Insertion fee is the same.

35.1.2 Final Value Fees

You are charged a Final Value Fee only if something sells.

Final Value (Selling) Fees for Auction-Style Listings

Closing Price	Fee
$0.01 to $24.99	8.75 percent of the closing value.
$25 to $1,000	8.75 percent of the first $25 + 3.5 percent of the balance over $25.
Over $1,000	8.75 percent of the initial $25, + 3.5 percent of the value $25.01 to $1,000, + 1.50 percent of the remaining closing value.

Final Value (selling) Fees for Fixed-Price Listings

Closing Price	Computers & Networking	Cameras & Photo	Electronics & Video Game Systems	Books, Music, DVDs, Movies, & Video Games	Parts & Accessories	Clothing, Shoes, & Accessories	All other categories
Item not sold	No Fee	No Fee	No Fee	No Fee	No Fee	No Fee	No Fee
$1.00–$50.00	6.00%	8.0%	8.0%	15.0%	12.0%	12.0%	12.0%
$50.01–$1000.00	6% of first $1–$50 ($2.94), plus 3.75% of remaining balance	8.0% 4.5%	8.0% 4.5%	15.0% 5.0%	12.0% 9.0%	12.0% 9.0%	12.0% 6.0%
$1000.01 or more	6% of first $1–$50 ($2.94), plus 3.75% of value $50.01–$1000 ($35.62) plus 1% of remaining balance	8.0% 4.5% 1.0%	8.0% 4.5% 1.0%	15.0% 5.0% 2.0%	12.0% 9.0% 2.0%	12.0% 9.0% 2.0%	12.0% 6.0% 2.0%

This example shows how the Final Value Fee is calculated for an Auction-Style listing:

> If an item sold for $1,250, you would pay 8.75 percent of the initial $25 ($2.19), plus 3.5 percent of the next $975 ($35.12), plus 1.5 percent of the remaining $250 ($3.75). Add up $2.19 + $35.12 + $3.75 to get your total final value fee of $41.06. This works out to a final value fee of 3.28% ($41.06 ÷ $1,250 = 3.28%).
>
> The Insertion fee for a Multiple Item (Dutch) Auction is based upon the opening value of your items.
>
> The opening value is the starting price multiplied by the quantity of your items. The maximum Insertion fee for a Multiple Item Auction is $4.00.
>
> The Final Value Fee for a Dutch Auction is determined by taking the Final Value Fee of the lowest successful bid and multiplying it by the number of items sold.
>
> For Fixed-Price Listings, the Final Value Fee is determined not just by the closing value but also by the category.

Let's look at the difference between Auction-Style and Fixed-Price Final Value Fees. I am using the "all other categories" Fixed-Price Final Value Fees, which are the second highest.

Comparison of Auction-Style and Fixed-Price Final Value Fees

Item Price	Auction-Style	Fixed-Price
$20	$1.75	$2.40
$45	$2.89	$5.40
$100	$4.82	$9.00

As you can see, the Final Value Fees are considerably lower for Auction-Style listings. However, the upfront cost is much less for Fixed-Price listings which means your risk is less, and you can sell more items with fewer Insertion fees. Also, remember I am using one of the higher Final Value Fees for Fixed-Price listings. Depending on the category, they could be four or more percent lower than this.

35.1.3 Fees for Listing Upgrades

eBay offers several optional upgrades designed to make your listing stand out and place them where more potential bidders will see them. I discuss these options in greater detail in the next chapter, but here is a quick rundown of their prices:

Feature Fee	Feature Fee
Gallery Plus 35¢	Border $3
Listing Designer 10¢	Highlight $5
Item Subtitle 50¢	Value Pack 65¢
Bold $1	Gallery Featured $19.95
Scheduled Listings 10¢	Home Page Featured $39.95
10-Day Duration 40¢	Quantity of 2 or more $79.95
Gift Services 25¢	List in Two Categories (double the Insertion fee and all listing upgrade fees except scheduled listings and Home Page Featured).

Two other traditional listing upgrades now have tiered fee scales. These are Featured Plus and Pro Pack. Pro Pack is a combo-pack including Bold, Border, Highlight, Gallery Featured, and Featured Plus.

Featured Plus Fees

Starting Price	Fee
$0.01–$24.99	$9.95
$25.00–$199.99	$14.95
$200.00–$499.99	$19.95
$500+	$24.95

For Multiple Item listings, the fee is the opening value multiplied by the quantity available. The maximum Featured Plus fee for Multiple Item listings is $24.95.

For Multiple Item listings, the fee is the opening value multiplied by the quantity available. The maximum Pro Pack fee for Multiple Item listings is $34.95.

Pro Pack Fees

Starting Price	Fee
$0.01–$24.99	$19.95
$25.00–$199.99	$24.95
$200.00–$499.99	$29.95
$500+	$34.95

International Site Visibility is an optional upgrade for sellers who want their items to appear in the main search results on international eBay sites that they ship to. The fees are tiered based on the starting price.

International Site Visibility Fees

Starting Price	Fee
$0.01–$9.99	10¢
$10.00–$49.99	20¢
$50.00+	30¢

The Business and Industrial category on eBay is often used to sell very expensive machines and materials. eBay has developed special fees for this category.

Business & Industrial Category Specific Fees

Insertion Fees	$20
Reserve Fees	$5
Final Value Fees	1 percent of the closing value (maximum fee $250)

PowerSeller Tip

There are several free eBay/PayPal fee calculators. I like the one from http:// auctionfeecalculator.com/us_ebay_fee_calc2.html. This tool allows you to plug in the listing type (auctions, fixed price, Dutch, etc.), any promotional fees, feature fees, and the expected final value, and it calculates and projects the total fees for you. This tool even includes a break-even calculator. Auction Fee Calculator also has links to calculate fees for all of the various eBay international sites.

35.2 Understanding Your PayPal Fees

PayPal fees are based solely on the value of the payment you receive. Depending on your volume and the size of your account, PayPal's domestic fees range from 1.9 to 2.9 percent (based on monthly volume) plus a flat fee of 30 cents per transaction. Cross-border/currency transactions are a little higher.

You can't do much to lower these except sell higher volumes. Once you go over $25,000 per month, PayPal will offer you a lower base fee.

PayPal Domestic Fees

Monthly Sales	Fee
$0.01–$3,000	2.9 percent plus 30 cents
$3,000.01–$10,000	2.5 percent plus 30 cents
$10,000.01–$100,000	2.2 percent plus 30 cents
Over $100,000	1.9 percent plus 30 cents

For PayPal's cross-border fees add 1 percent to each of the fees in the table.

35.3 Optimizing Your Auctions to Reduce Fees

Now that you understand eBay's various fees, let's take a look at how you can reduce them.

If you look at the eBay fee tables in Section 35.1.1, you will notice that, for Auction-Style listings, the fees rise at certain listing price break-points. Price your item's minimum bid at just below the breaking point in the fee structure. For example, if you hope to get $30 for an item, start the bid at $24.99 (Insertion fee $0.55) instead of $25 (Insertion fee $1.00). These savings may seem small, but if you are going to launch hundreds or even thousands of auctions a month, the costs will really add up quickly.

If you are selling at a Dutch auction or a Fixed-Price listing, look at the Final Value Fees to determine where to set your price. Setting your price just below the breaking point in the fee structure can save you considerable amounts of money over the long term. Remember, auctions and Fixed-Price listings have different Final Value Fees as well as different Insertion fees.

If you are selling popular items that always get good bids and sell well, then it makes no sense to start them at a high price. Whenever I have an item that almost always sells, I start it at 99¢, which incurs the lowest Insertion fee for auctions, or I sell it at Fixed-Price.

If an item doesn't sell, you may be eligible for the Relist Credit if it sells the second time. Many people think this is a "free relist"; it is not. You still pay the Insertion fee for the relisted auction; however, if it sells the second time, eBay refunds the Insertion fee you just paid. If it does not sell the second time, you do not get the Relist Credit. So you will have paid two Insertion fees and still have the item unsold. You do not get the Relist Credit if you choose to relist it a third time, even if it does sell this time.

The other thing you can do to control fees is to close a higher percentage of your auctions. You do this by eliminating slow-moving items. If you must carry a slow-moving item, carry it in your eBay store where the Insertion and Final Value Fees are lower (see eBay Store fees in Chapter 47).

For more on pricing strategies, see Chapter 13.

For more on controlling your eBay fees, see Section 29.4 and Chapters 43 and 44.

chapter 36

Promotion, Promotion, Promotion

eBay offers several ways to promote your auctions, most of which cost money. In Chapter 35 I showed you the cost of these promotions in terms of their related eBay fees, and in this chapter I tell you which ones work best and show you how to determine their potential return on investment (ROI).

Just because eBay says a certain promotional tool will increase your sell-through rate or final values, it doesn't mean it will. eBay's research numbers are an average taken over thousands of auctions; not every auction achieved the desired result. You won't really know if a certain promotional tool works for your specific product unless you test it. If you are selling a highly specific product in a fairly small niche, you might not need any promotional tool at all.

36.1 Keyword-Rich Titles

We already covered this feature in Chapter 31, but I want to reiterate the importance of keyword-rich titles. Given that over 80 percent of eBay buyers find items to bid on by searching, keyword-rich titles are the single most important form of promotion—and they are free!

36.2 eBay Subtitles

For 50¢, eBay lets you add a subtitle to your auction listing. A subtitle is a second title that appears in slightly smaller print just below your auction title on the eBay search results page, and can provide descriptive information about your item that buyers will see when browsing categories or viewing search results. It enables you to add information that doesn't fit in the title field but would be of interest to potential buyers viewing a list of items.

The words included in the subtitle are not searchable when buyers conduct a basic search. However, the subtitle will be searchable if the buyer checks the box *include title & description*, although eBay bidders seldom do this because it brings up too many results.

I find that subtitles also make your listing stand out somewhat from the other listings around it.

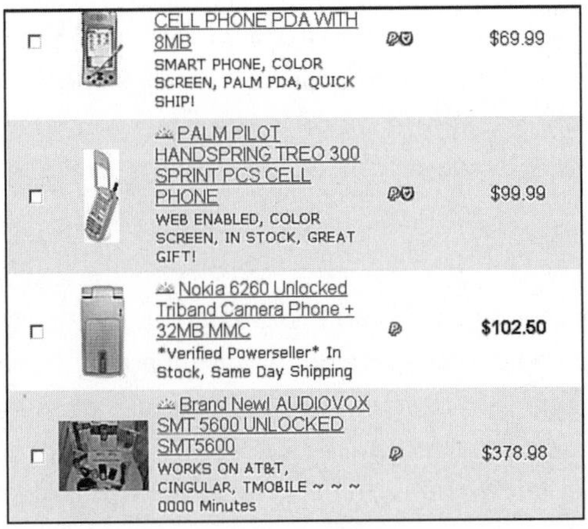

Figure 36.1
An eBay listing
with a subtitle.

36.3 Bold and Highlight

You can add the bold feature to any eBay listing for $1. The bold feature shows your auction title in boldface type to make it stand out (see Figure 36.2). eBay's own research has shown this feature increases final prices by an average of 25 percent. As long as you are selling an item that will sell for over $10, this is the single best promotional tool in terms of ROI. I use the bold option in almost all of my auctions.

You can highlight your auction for $5. Highlight is similar to bold in that it makes your auction stand out (see Figure 36.2). When you select this option, it places your auction title and gallery picture within a purple-colored highlight band. However, using highlight without bold makes it somewhat difficult for the bidder to read your title, so in effect this option costs $6 when you add the bold.

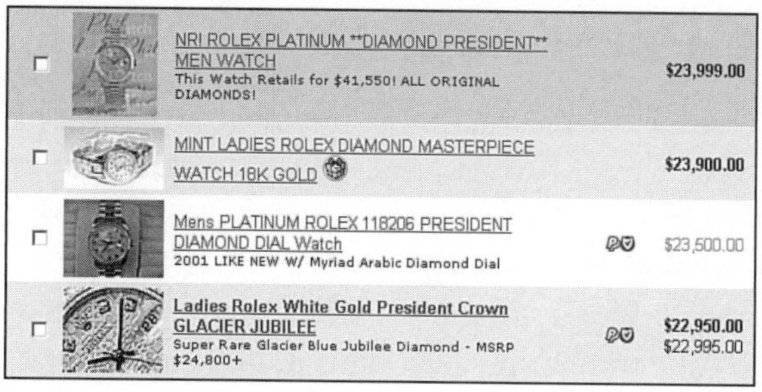

Figure 36.2
eBay listings using the bold and highlight features.

I am not a big fan of highlight and don't use it unless I am selling an item I expect to reach at least $100 and that has a high closing ratio. eBay hasn't announced any research statistics on this feature, which tells me it probably doesn't work that well or they would have.

36.4 eBay Gallery

Because it's free, the eBay gallery feature is the least-expensive promotional tool you can use. It places a small thumbnail photo on the search results or browse page next to your auction title. Many eBay bidders will not click an auction unless they see this photo, so I consider this feature mandatory. eBay's research shows that a gallery photo increases bids by an average of 11 percent. I expect it is much higher than this now since eBay made this feature free.

36.5 Featured Plus

Whenever an eBay user performs a search or browses a category, a list of items featured in that category comes up first. To include your item on this list, you must opt for the Featured Plus feature. This is a high-performing tool, but unfortunately it costs $9.95–$24.95 (based on the starting or reserve price on the listing).

I only use Featured Plus on very high-priced items to make sure they get high visibility. Featured Plus is also very useful for Dutch auctions where you might be selling a lower-priced item but a large enough quantity to offset the cost. eBay reports that Featured Plus items are 28 percent more likely to sell and have an average 12 percent higher final value or selling price.

36.6 Home Page Featured

The Home Page Featured auction is the most expensive promotional tool at $39.95 for a single item listing and $79.95 for a Dutch (multiple item) listing. Home Page Featured auctions rotate onto the eBay home page. It is important to point out that eBay does not guarantee either that it will rotate through or what time it will happen. Home Page Featured is a bit of a crapshoot, but it works most of the time. Your best odds of getting on the front page are if your auction ends on one of the less-popular days. If your auction ends on Sunday evening, a popular auction-ending time, your chances of getting featured decrease dramatically.

I once had an auction ending on a Thursday night where my item rotated onto the home page about an hour before the auction ended. I got over 250 hits in that last hour and the item sold for almost double what I normally received.

36.7 Other Features

The other two features eBay offers are 10-day Duration and Gallery Featured.

The 10-day Duration option costs 10¢. I always use this option if I am paying for any of the other features (except Bold), because I want to extend the life of the auction to get the most out of the special feature.

Gallery Featured is the option to have your image featured at the top of the gallery view (for category or search results), and costs $19.95. It also includes Gallery Plus, which enables the buyer to mouse over your thumbnail picture on the search results page (in list or gallery view) and a much larger version of the picture will appear. I have never used this option, and eBay has never released any research statistics on it. The only use I could think of for this feature is if you are selling a visually stunning product, such as a painting, expensive antique, or a beautiful Persian rug.

For more on promotion and upselling, see Chapters 44, 46, and 51 and Section 49.3.

chapter 37

Increase Your Sales with Free Promotions

Besides the fee-based optional features, eBay also offers free promotions. These usually take the form of special promotions around the holidays or themes that are tied to special events, such as the NCAA tournament, the opening of baseball season, or the Super Bowl. eBay also features hot product categories, which are promotions posted on the eBay home (main) page along with navigation links that appear on some browsing and search pages. The theme promotions and hot category promotions are selected by eBay and appear on the eBay home page. For example, if eBay selects designer sunglasses as a hot category, an icon will appear on the front page that, when clicked, will open up all the auctions for designer sunglasses.

The promotional front-page links get a lot of traffic and can increase visibility and hits to your auctions. If you know eBay will feature a product or category you sell in during a certain time, it pays to launch more auctions for those products during the promotion. If you visit Seller Central and click on *Merchandising Calendar*, it will take you to a page that gives the schedule for upcoming promotions.

37.1 eBay Holiday Promotions

eBay often runs special promotions tied to holidays such as Christmas, Thanksgiving, Valentine's Day, or Mother's Day. The promotions take various forms—for example, around Christmas, eBay often runs a free-shipping promotion. It places a link on the eBay home page that a buyer can click to search for any product for which the seller is offering free shipping. As a seller, you do not have to have the words *free shipping* in your title as long as you elected to use the eBay shipping options when you launched your auction and checked the free shipping box. If a buyer uses the free-shipping link to the search engine, only those auctions that offer free shipping will come up when the buyer does a product search. eBay announces free-shipping promotions in its daily announcement, which you can link to from the bottom of any eBay page.

Figure 37.1
eBay Home Page showing Hot Product Promotions.

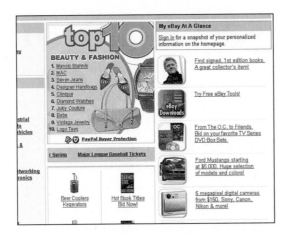

eBay also takes advantage of holidays by featuring a link on the main page to gifts that are appropriate for the season. For example, they might put a graphic of a heart and the words *Valentine Day Specials* with links to various categories of gifts—such as jewelry—that are appropriate to the season or the special day. Unlike the free-shipping specials, there is nothing you can do to get selected for these listings except to be listed in the appropriate category. Because you never know which categories eBay will select, around the holidays it can be useful to pay the extra $1 fee for the List In Two Categories option (you pay two Insertion fees and double most of the listing upgrade fees excluding the feature fees). This will list your auction in two categories as long as both categories are related to what you are selling. For example, you can list a piece of handmade jewelry in both the Jewelry category and the Craft category.

37.2 eBay Product Category Promotions

eBay also selects both specific products and product categories to promote on the home page. In Figure 37.1 there is a picture of former president Bill Clinton with a link beside it that says: "Find signed, 1st edition books. A great collector's item!" Below that is a photo of a videotape and DVD from the TV show *The O.C.*, and other links to Ford Mustangs and digital cameras. Each of these promotions has links to all auctions featuring the items being promoted. Once again, eBay doesn't tell sellers when it runs these unannounced promotions, so you can't really plan for them. However, they typically leave these links up for one or two weeks at a time, so it pays to check the eBay main page every day to see what they are promoting. If you have an item in the relevant category, you can launch an auction for it.

If you have a product that's similar to the featured category, you might be able to get away with launching an auction in two categories, one in the correct category and one in the category being featured. For example, if you are selling ladies' shoes and eBay is featuring designer clothing, you could also list the shoes in the designer clothing category because ladies who buy blouses also buy shoes. But if you try to list designer jewelry as designer clothing, eBay might see that as spamming the category and cancel your auction.

Another eBay front page promotion typically features highly searched terms. If you take another look at Figure 37.1, you can see the **Top 10 Beauty & Fashion** banner. Within it are links to hot search terms such as MAC, Seven Jeans, and Juicy Couture. Although you can't do much to take advantage of this promotion if you don't have the products to sell, you should keep close watch on what is being promoted because when your products are being promoted, you might want to launch more auctions or search your inventory for products to launch that fit the category.

If you have a drop-shipping supplier who carries a broad range of merchandise, this is a great way to work the system. For example, Figure 37.2 shows NASCAR items featured on the eBay home page. You could check with your drop-ship company for NASCAR–licensed merchandise and launch an auction. Because you are not investing in inventory, your only risk is the eBay Insertion fee. The risk will likely be offset by the increased number of hits your auctions will get from being linked to the eBay home page.

Figure 37.2
Example of an eBay product promotion on the eBay home page.

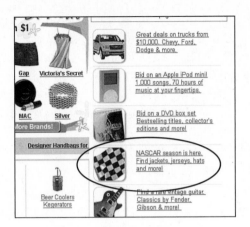

37.3 eBay Cross Promotions Feature

eBay offers a great free service that helps you cross-promote your auctions. Go to **My eBay** and click on **Marketing Tools** in the left sidebar. Click **Edit** next to **Cross-Promotion Defaults.** Here you can create rules for which items eBay features when a user bids or wins one of your items. If you have an eBay Store, you can also specify items you want to cross-promote at the bottom of your auctions, as shown in Figure 37.3. eBay's cross-promotion defaults first to items with the same keyword in the name and second to items in the same category. It takes very little time to set up rules to promote and upsell buyers to the products that match the best, or that you're trying to sell.

Figure 37.3
NASCAR collectibles are hot. When potential bidders scroll to the bottom of this auction for a Dale Earnhardt Jr. beer cooler, they see cross promotions for four other Dale Earnhardt Jr. items.

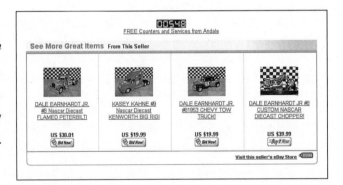

37.4 Gift Services

The eBay Gift promotion is free, but you have to spend 25¢ on eBay's Gift listing option to be eligible for it. If you select this option, it will place a gift icon next to your listing. When buyers see this icon, they know you agree to gift-wrap and ship the item to a gift recipient. You should also indicate in your auction description that you offer gift shipping, and tell readers what you charge for this service. By selecting this option, your auctions will often be linked to features on the home page when eBay runs their gift promotions. For example, eBay often runs home page features such as *Gifts under $25*. If you have selected the 25¢ gift option (see Figure 37.4), your auctions with starting prices or current bids under $25 will be selected for this free promotion.

When you look at Figure 37.4, notice the checked boxes that offer **gift wrap/ gift card, Express Shipping,** and **Ship to gift recipient.** When you check this, it does not mean you will provide these services for free.

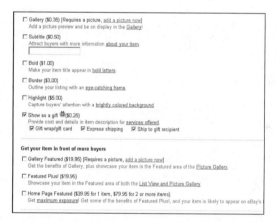

Figure 37.4
The Gift option selection box on the eBay Sell Your Item page.

Around Christmastime I often check the gift options in my auctions and then place the following statement in my auctions:

> We will happily gift wrap your purchase and send it directly to your recipient. We charge $5 for gift wrapping, including placing a card inside with a short message from you. If you would like express shipping, please e-mail us the address you would like your gift shipped to, and we will give you a shipping quote.

This way we make a little extra money on the gift-wrapping service, and I usually add a couple of dollars handling fee when I ship Express mail.

In addition to Christmas, eBay frequently runs gift promotions around Mother's Day, Father's Day, and Valentine's Day. Remember, the best way to take advantage of eBay's home page promotions is to check the home page every day and check your announcements folder on your My eBay Page for announcements about special promotions.

For more on promotions and upselling, see Chapters 44, 46, 49, and 51.

chapter 38

Building a Customer Mailing List

If you take Marketing 101 in college, one of the first things you learn is that it is easier and cheaper to sell to an existing customer. No matter what business you are in—be it setting up auctions on eBay, selling from a website, or operating a retail store, it costs to obtain a customer. With a retail store it may be the cost of advertising. On eBay it is the fees you pay to list and sell your items. But this is a real cost. If a customer buys from you once and is happy, it is likely he will buy from you again. And if you can sell to him directly without paying fees to eBay, that next sale and any subsequent sales will be more profitable. We talk about selling to your existing customers from a web store or your own website in Chapters 48 and 49, but here let's concentrate on how to build a mailing list of your existing customer base, which can become one of your most valuable assets. In Section 49.4.1 we talk specifically about how and why to market your list, but here our focus is building and maintaining a list.

38.1 List Management

You might think e-mail list management is simple—just keep a list of e-mail addresses and mail to them—but it is not that simple. One of the big issues today is unwanted e-mail or spam. Several states have passed very strict laws to combat spam, and the federal government now has a law called the can-spam statute. Both of these can result in serious fines and penalties and even jail time for serious offenders. And eBay will cancel your account if they get many complaints that you are spamming your eBay customers.

They have no problem with sending the occasional e-mail to a customer about a product or a promotion you are running. All of the anti-spam laws allow companies to contact their own customers within reasonable limits including contacting your customers and asking them if they would like to "opt-in" to your customer list, which is the best.

Once a customer has agreed to allow you to send him e-mail (opting-in), then you can market to him as often as you want.

38.2 Building an Opt-In List

The easiest and safest way to build an opt-in list is to use a third party e-mail list management company. I use a company called Aweber (www.aweber.com), but there are two other popular companies:

Constant contact   www.constantcontact.com

Topica   www.topica.com

What all these companies do is give you a web-based platform to manage your mailing list. I am familiar with Aweber, so I have listed some of their features below. The other services offer similar features, but Aweber is less expensive.

- Send e-mail newsletters. Aweber allows you to create newsletters in text or HTML format and schedule the mailings at scheduled dates and times.

- Set up multiple mailing lists. For example, if you sell several different categories of product, you can just set up different lists for each category.

- Create a signup form. Aweber gives you the simple HTML code you can paste into your website builder that will create a form to sign up for your newsletter.

- Positive confirmation. When someone subscribes, Aweber sends her a confirming e-mail. When the customer receives that e-mail, she must click on a link in the e-mail to confirm her subscription. If she does not do that within 48 hours, the link expires, and she will not be added to your list.

- Create Auto-Responders. An auto-responder is nothing more than a message that is sent out automatically to someone who takes a certain action. For example, you can set it up so if someone subscribes to your list or makes a purchase, he will get an automated thank you message.

38.3 Promoting Your List

You can promote and build your list in several ways. The first thing to do is invite your customers to join your list. The fastest way to build your list of existing customers is to offer them some incentive for doing so. Depending on what you sell, you could come up with some type of discount coupon or free shipping on your first order. The other thing you can do is offer some type of electronically delivered information product.

Here is an example. One of the products we sold during 2008 was the Rachael Ray line of chef knives. I created a simple 15-page eBook, delivered as a PDF file called *The Care and Handling of Good Knives.* It was basically information I researched on the web and put together that showed knife care, safety, and sharpening. When I sold a knife, I offered customers a free copy of the eBook if they joined my mailing list.

If you set up a web store or a website as we discuss in Chapters 48 and 49, one of the things you should do is place a sign-up box on your website with an invitation to join your list or newsletter (see below) and offer the customer a copy of your eBook, video, or coupon if he joins.

38.4 Creating and Building a Newsletter List

Online newsletters are very popular. If you sell products in a specific niche, this is a great way to capture customer and future customer names. For example, if you sell some type of photographic equipment, you could publish a monthly online newsletter with digital photo tips. If you sell children's toys, you could write a monthly newsletter about toy safety or reviews of hot toys. Basically, if you sell products where people are likely to come back and buy more of the same or other related products and accessories, then you can offer some type of newsletter.

There are two ways to send out a newsletter. Using Aweber or one of the other services, you can set up a special list for your subscribers. When you want to send out a newsletter, all you have to do is log into your account and click on the link to broadcast a message. At this point a box will open where you type your content. Then you save the content and select a time and date to send it out to your list.

The two methods to use are sending content directly to your readers where they read it as an e-mail or posting the newsletter content on your website and simply e-mailing a link where the reader clicks to read the content. I prefer the second method because it brings the readers to my website, which has two benefits:

- It increases traffic to my site. This helps the search engines rank my site higher and will help increase organic traffic to my site.

- Having readers already on my website increases the chances they will look around and buy something while they are there.

If you are not a prolific writer or have trouble finding content for your newsletter, there are two methods you can use. First search the web for bloggers, writers, or experts on your topic, and invite those people to write articles for you. In exchange you will give them a link back to their site.

The other method is to look for free content. Dozens of sites offer free articles on a wide range of subjects. Simply search the term *free articles* on a popular search engine such as Google, Yahoo!, AOL, or MSN. When you perform such a search, you will return a number of websites that offer free content in the form of articles. Most of them will ask you to register, and you need to read their rules for using their content. Once you do this, simply use the search box on their site to find articles that relate to your readers. Then just copy the article and paste it into your website or newsletter. These sites require that you link to the name of the author and his website in return for using his content.

For more on promoting your product niche, see Section 15.3.3.

For more about promoting your eBay store, see Section 47.3.

For more on setting up and promoting a web store or your own website, see Chapters 48 and 49.

For more information about marketing to your list, see Section 49.4.1.

chapter 39

Getting from Google and Yahoo! to eBay

Both Google and Yahoo! offer pay-per-click advertising programs based on specific keywords. You purchase keywords on a pay-per-click basis that links bidders from a web search directly to a specific auction or store or to your list of auctions. When you join these programs, you are given the opportunity to bid on keywords that, when clicked, will generate a short advertisement that you create. When someone sees your ad and clicks it, he will be taken directly to your auction or eBay store listing.

Google calls their advertising program Google AdWords; Yahoo! calls their program Yahoo! Search Marketing. Often these ads are linked to an eBay auction, as in Figure 39.1. When I performed a search for *antique toys*, Google brought up several ongoing eBay auctions that matched the keywords. But if you look to the right of the page in Figure 39.1, you see a row of text ads under the term Sponsored Links. Sponsored links are nothing more than pay-per-click (PPC) keyword searches.

One of the ways eBay promotes your auctions is by purchasing keyword listings on Google. eBay buys popular keywords based on their knowledge of what people are searching for. When someone clicks the sponsored listing, he is taken to a search results page on eBay just as if he had searched the term *antique toys* using the eBay search engine.

Figure 39.1
Google ads show-ing links to eBay.

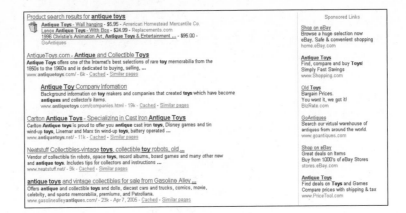

39.1 Buying Keywords Directly from Google and Yahoo!

But you don't have to go through eBay to have your listings appear on Google's or Yahoo!'s results pages. You can also purchase a keyword on Google or Yahoo! and have it link to your store or even a specific auction. Purchasing your own keyword on Google or Yahoo! can result in significant discounts of payments, as described here:

- Fee discount. If you set up the links to your eBay Store pages with the correct referral codes, and a buyer using that link then purchases something from your eBay Store, eBay will credit you 75 percent of the Final Value fee for that item. The referral code is either **?refid=store** or **&refid=store** and is tagged onto the end of the page URL. Which referral code you use depends on which page you land your customer on.

- eBay has an affiliate program they call the Partner Program. Under this program eBay will pay commissions to partners that drive traffic to eBay from non-eBay sites (e-mails, your newsletter, website, pay-per-click advertising, etc.) when these users register on eBay and take actions such as bidding or buying something.

  eBay has different payment schedules for different types of results. They will pay a percentage of the final value fees they earn when a sale is made and they pay for active registrations—what they call new active confirmed registered users (ACRUs). You earn money at different tiers based on the number of ACRUs you recruit and a bonus on the total number.

If you are going to advertise your auctions on Google or Yahoo!, then it pays to sign up for the eBay's partner program so you can take advantage of the discounts and payments. You'll find a link to the eBay Affiliate Program at the bottom of the eBay main page. After you're signed up, all you have to do is add your affiliate linking code to any links you have on web pages or blogs so everyone who bids, buys, or signs up as a new user will earn you money and reduce your eBay fees. Besides providing links to your own listings, you can link to other listings, other categories, and even get a linked eBay search box to put on your website.

Popular keywords such as *eBay* or *wholesale* are very expensive—as much as $1.50 per click. Some web-savvy entrepreneurs do nothing but buy keywords for obscure products that people might be searching for in the hopes of driving someone onto eBay and making money on it. Look at Figure 39.2.

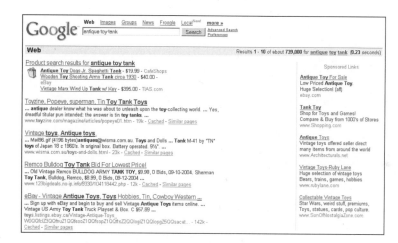

Figure 39.2
Results for a search for "antique toy tank."

When I searched the term *antique toy tank*, it brought up a sponsored listing in the top position that says:

> Antique Toy for sale
> Low Priced **Antique Toy**
> Huge selection (aff)
> eBay.com

The tip-off here is the *(aff)*. Google insists that anyone using keywords to drive traffic to any affiliate location identify themselves with either the word *affiliate* or the abbreviation *aff.*

39.2 Posting Pay-Per-Click Ads on Google and Yahoo!

Google is now the largest and most used search engine on the Internet, with Yahoo! well behind it—but still popular with millions of people. You can easily access both Google and Yahoo!'s pay-per-click advertising. Find Google Adwords at www.adwords.google.com and Yahoo! Search Marketing at http://searchmarketing.yahoo.com.

Creating an ad in Google Adwords takes only a few minutes. The first thing you do is pick the countries you want your ad to appear in (see Figure 39.3). I usually pick the United States, Canada, United Kingdom, and Australia because my ads are in English, and I don't want to pay for clicks when someone in Zimbabwe does a search.

Figure 39.3

Create Google Ad page.

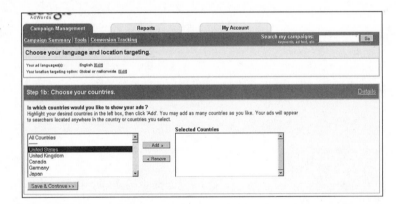

Next write your ad, as shown in Figure 39.4. Notice you are very limited in the number of characters you can use, so be both very specific and clever.

The first line is your headline. When I first tried the system, I used all caps for my headline, but Google doesn't allow this and rejected the ad. Also notice that there are two URL lines. The first is the display URL, which is the URL people see; the second URL is the actual URL of the page that will open when someone clicks the link. In this case I linked the ad to my eBay store.

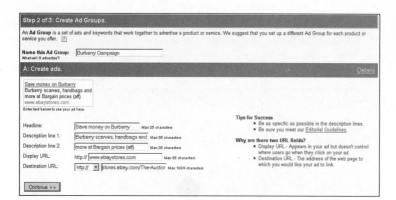

Figure 39.4
Write Google ad copy.

After you save this page and click **Continue,** you are taken to a page where you can select your keywords, as in Figure 39.5. You can see the keywords I entered.

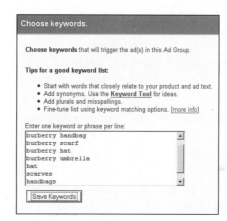

Figure 39.5
Google keywords selection.

After you enter the keywords, Google takes you to a page where you can estimate your traffic. Figure 39.6 shows you what they came up with.

The first thing you have to do is elect a maximum CPC you want to pay. I selected $1. If you look at the first keyword, *Burberry*, you will see that Google estimates it will generate 1,200 clicks a day at an average CPC of $0.67 per click. The cost per day would work out to $800.54 and my ad would appear in the average position of 1.6. This tells me two things. The keyword *Burberry* is very expensive, and if I'm going to spend $800.54 per day, I will have to sell a lot of Burberry merchandise. I sell Burberry merchandise on eBay when I can get it, but it can be hard to come by in large quantities. The other keyword *handbag* is also very popular, and therefore expensive. At $5,546.91 per day, I would need to be Macy's to sell enough handbags in a day to cover that cost.

Figure 39.6
Cost-per-click estimates for the selected keywords.

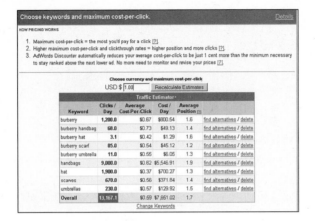

What this page does not show you is that you can set a daily budget. If you were to set a daily budget of $50, you would get clicks until your $50 was used up. Nevertheless, I would probably delete the *handbags* and *Burberry* keywords because I just couldn't find enough inventory to support those keywords. The other keywords all look very reasonable, but I would still only use the specific ones for the products I have in stock. With a budget of $50 per day, I could expect some very targeted traffic. And remember, some of that traffic would result in fee discounts and affiliate commissions that would help pay for the keyword searches.

Keyword advertising can be very profitable, but test your keywords very carefully. You can track the sell-through from a keyword click by looking at your eBay account statement at the end of the month to see how many referral credits you earned and on which products they were earned. Track the number of hits, bids, and sales during both weeks and compare them to see if the increases are worth the investment.

For more on using keywords in titles, see Chapter 31.

For more on keyword advertising, see Chapter 38.

chapter 40

Making Money with Free Shipping

Everyone loves something for free. In fact *FREE* is one of the most powerful words used in advertising copywriting. I've been using free-shipping promotions for over two years, and it has worked very well. Typically, when I offer free shipping in an auction, I see an increase in both the number of bids and the final value. We all know that nothing is really free, and buyers certainly know the cost is built into the selling price, but it doesn't seem to matter.

In late 2008, eBay changed the search results to feature listings with free shipping higher than those without when bidders and buyers use the default Best Match search results. There is also a search function buyers can select that shows Price + Shipping, highest and lowest first.

40.1 Pricing Your Merchandise for Free Shipping

How you price your merchandise for free shipping depends on what you are selling. Obviously, offering free shipping on large and/or heavy items, which are very expensive to ship, doesn't make sense. A free-shipping strategy works best for merchandise that you can ship via USPS, UPS, DHL, or FedEx Ground. In general, that means that the item must weigh less than 60 pounds and be no more than 70 inches around, although there are some exceptions to that rule.

Where you are located geographically also factors into your pricing. Being from Washington State, I am in the worst possible location, with the exception of Alaska or Hawaii. Sixty-five percent of the country's population lives east of the Mississippi River, and 50 percent lives in the states bordering the East Coast. Most of my shipments go to the East Coast, five or six zones distant from where I live. Because shippers' prices are based on zones (see Figure 40.1 for an example of UPS Ground Residential delivery rates; the last three columns are for shipments to Alaska, Hawaii, and Puerto Rico), a seller in Harrisburg, Pennsylvania, has a tremendous shipping advantage over me because such a large percentage of the U.S. population lives within one or two shipping zones of his location.

Figure 40.1
UPS Ground delivery rates by zone.

Domestic

UPS Ground
GUARANTEED DAY-DEFINITE ONE TO FIVE DAYS*

Zones	2	3	4	5	6	7	8	44†	45†	46†
1 Lbs.	$6.13	$6.30	$6.51	$6.78	$7.13	$7.25	$7.41	$22.86	$22.86	$30.15
2	6.23	6.62	7.28	7.41	7.95	8.14	8.53	25.53	25.53	32.82
3	6.29	6.93	7.64	7.91	8.49	8.77	9.48	27.89	27.89	35.19
4	6.46	7.18	8.02	8.43	8.99	9.28	10.09	30.37	30.37	37.67
5	6.78	7.29	8.40	8.83	9.39	9.76	10.71	33.33	33.33	40.63
6	7.00	7.54	8.55	9.09	9.67	10.14	11.07	36.57	36.57	43.87
7	7.37	7.78	8.75	9.41	10.01	10.50	11.60	39.23	39.23	46.52
8	7.66	8.04	8.99	9.63	10.33	10.98	12.33	42.06	42.06	49.35
9	7.88	8.27	9.18	9.88	10.58	11.58	13.13	45.16	45.16	52.46
10	8.15	8.33	9.39	10.15	11.03	12.41	14.02	48.01	48.01	55.30
11	8.43	8.72	9.57	10.37	11.50	13.30	15.03	50.99	50.99	58.28
12	8.68	9.02	9.79	10.61	12.02	14.19	16.12	53.49	53.49	60.79
13	8.97	9.31	9.95	10.85	12.60	15.10	17.21	55.84	55.84	63.14
14	9.16	9.60	10.15	11.10	13.30	15.97	18.31	58.40	58.40	65.69
15	9.35	9.91	10.33	11.36	14.00	16.86	19.40	60.77	60.77	68.07

In my case I assume that over 60 percent of my shipments go to zone 6, 7, or 8 and the other 40 percent go to zone 1, 2, 3, or 4. If I'm going to offer free shipping on an item, I use zone 4 as my average and calculate the shipping cost accordingly. This means I will lose a little money on shipments that go to the East Coast and make a little money on those that ship to the West.

I'm okay with this situation because, remember, I am usually getting a slightly higher final value on my auction because of the free shipping. In test auctions I have seen final values go as high as 25 percent higher when I offer free shipping, although the average is more like 12 to 15 percent. As long as my shipping cost is lower than 12 percent, which it usually is, I am making money.

Here is an actual example of an auction where I tested the free-shipping promotion. I launched an auction for a pair of Outdoor Research, Polartec WindBloc Trousers. My cost on the trousers was $45 from the Outdoor Research factory store where I bought 10 pairs on a closeout sale. The normal MSRP was $185.00, and they were new with tag (NWT).

I calculated the shipping to zone 4 at $7.90, which I added to my starting price of $45 to get a listing price of $52.90. However, I decided to list them at $49.99 to stay under the next break in the listing fee. This saved me $1.20 in listing fees. The trousers ended up selling for $114.20. I had seven bidders and 22 total bids.

The following week, I launched another pair also at $49.99, but this time without free shipping. I quoted the same shipping cost, $7.90, as a fixed-price shipping quote. I ran the auction with the same parameters: same ending day and time, identical title, listing, photos, and so on. This pair received only 14 total bids from three different bidders and ended up selling for $101.04, a difference of $13.16. If you subtract the shipping cost of $7.90, I made an additional $5.26 margin on the auction with free shipping even though my costs were higher.

Armed with this experience, I sold the remaining seven pairs—these were great trousers, so I kept one pair for myself—with free shipping over the course of the next three weeks. The lowest price I received was $109.03, and the highest price was $121.50.

Obviously, offering free shipping works. My wife sells Swarovski crystal jewelry. These sell in the $50 to $95 price range, are very small, and cost very little to ship. It is ideal to offer free shipping for this type of product. I almost always offer free shipping on any product that weighs less than five pounds and will sell for at least $35. If you use Priority Mail from the post office, you get free boxes; but if you are shipping with another carrier, don't forget to calculate the cost of your package and packing materials.

A lot of buyers look for free shipping, and remember that eBay often runs free-shipping promotions (see Chapter 37). Using free shipping for products that are appropriate will almost always make you more money.

Don't forget to put the words *Free Shipping* into your auction title. If you don't have the room, use the abbreviation *FS*. You can also place the words *Free Shipping* into the eBay subtitle, but don't forget that eBay charges you an extra 50¢ for subtitles. You must also always check the free-shipping box in the Sell Your Item form. This identifies your auction to eBay as a free-shipping auction and gives it higher visibility in the Best Match search results, and makes it eligible for free shipping searches and promotions.

40.2 Use Free Shipping to Drive BIN Sales

In Chapter 16 I talked about how Buy It Now (BIN) sales can help you turn your inventory over rapidly and thereby increase profits. You can also use the free-shipping strategy to increase your BIN sales, thereby speeding up your inventory turn rate.

The strategy is basically the same as for auctions, but there are a few little twists you can do. When I launch an auction with BIN, I put a notice along these lines in the shipping information of my auction description:

> Shipping for this item is $7.90 to the United States via Priority Mail. If you live in Canada or overseas, please e-mail me for shipping information prior to sending payment.

> If you use the Buy It Now feature to win this auction, I will ship it for free to any U.S. destination. If you live in Canada or overseas, I will give you $7.90 credit toward the shipping price. But remember, the Buy It Now price disappears after the first bid is placed.

Remember the idea is to move merchandise out as rapidly as possible. So you want to set your BIN price at the average selling price you usually get for the particular item you are selling, plus your shipping cost. I do find, however, that I can also add an extra 3 to 4 percent when I am selling in the pre-Christmas season because people are in a hurry and more willing to pay higher prices to be sure they get something.

If you have more than one of the same item, you can set up two auctions: one auction-style at a low starting price and the other as a fixed-price listing with just the BIN price. Launch both auctions simultaneously so they will show up near each other when someone does a search for Time: ending soonest. This way, potential buyers see both listings.

After the low starting price auction begins to get bids, the price will rise to near the BIN price. There is always a buyer who will want the item and not want to risk losing it at auction, and he will hit the BIN button to purchase your fixed-price listing immediately. Once again, don't forget to put the words *Free Shipping* in your title or subtitle.

40.3 Using Free Shipping to Generate eBay Store Sales

If you have multiple quantities of identical or similar merchandise, you can use free shipping to generate fixed-price sales from your eBay Store. This is even more profitable because listing fees in your eBay store are less than in the eBay auction or fixed-price formats. (See Chapter 47 for eBay Store fee information.)

If I have an item up for auction and also have the same item or even the same category of item in my eBay Store, I'll put a notice like this right in my auction description:

> FREE SHIPPING FROM MY EBAY STORE
>
> You do not have to wait for this auction to end to buy your _____ . I have several of these in my eBay store for immediate purchase with Free Shipping to any U.S. destination.

The words *eBay Store*, underlined in the preceding paragraph, would be a clickable link to my eBay Store. This way the potential customer does not have to navigate back to the top of the auction and hunt for the eBay-generated link to my eBay Store.

You can, of course, use the same notice to sell something from your eBay Store without offering free shipping, but I've found my store sales are much greater when I do.

For more on shipping strategies, see Chapters 17 and 33 and Section 5.7.

part 5

You Can't Grow Without Automation

As an eBay seller, your most important resource is your time. You have two kinds of tasks: high-value tasks that make you money and low-value tasks that need to be done but don't add anything to the bottom line. High-value tasks include sourcing products and creating auctions. Low-value tasks consist of sending out payment requests, packing boxes, and sending shipping notices.

Anytime you can automate any part of the routine processes, you've freed up your time to concentrate on the high-value tasks that make you money. If you automate enough, it can be like hiring an extra employee.

Almost every part of the eBay transaction—from taking photos and launching auctions to communicating with the customer and posting feedback—can be automated to some degree.

This part covers the types of processes that can be automated and the variety of offline software and online web-based solutions available to the professional seller.

chapter 41

Automating for Profits

Large professional eBay business owners launch hundreds of auctions per week. As you know, launching an auction consists of taking and uploading a photograph of the item, writing a title and an item description, selecting a category to enter, selecting any special feature or marketing options you want to use, setting a starting price, and scheduling the auction for launch at an appropriate time for the product category. All this is impossible to do in large volumes without some degree of automation.

Automation is an incredibly complex area with dozens of choices and no one good solution. Instead, the solution depends on what you are selling, your average price point, and the market you are targeting. Selling low-cost items such as books or CDs requires an entirely different system than you would use to sell high-priced jewelry or apparel. And there's even more work to do after the auction closes successfully. You need to communicate with the buyer, calculate the shipping cost, collect the funds, track the shipment, and post feedback for the buyer.

41.1 The eBay Selling Process

There's no question that automation can save you time, and therefore money. But it's important to regulate the amount of automation you use and to use it appropriately. You don't want your customers thinking they are buying from a robot.

In this chapter, I want to explain the automation options available to eBay sellers. But before looking at the options, let's take a closer look at the steps in the eBay selling process and consider which of these steps might be appropriate for automation. You can then use this as a framework to help you decide how much or how little automation you need for your business.

1. Selecting merchandise to sell is the first step in launching an eBay auction. I haven't figured out a way to automate this yet, and I doubt I would want to.

2. The next step is either taking a photo of the merchandise you are going to sell (preferred) or using the stock image provided by eBay for certain items, or if you have their permission, from the manufacturer. There are several things you can do to speed up this process. The first is to sell large quantities of identical merchandise (subject to the laws of supply and demand) so you only have to photograph an object once to generate many sales.

   You will also want to use image editing software to name, crop, save, and upload your photos to whatever image management software or web service you decide to use.

3. Creating a listing is probably one of the most time-consuming tasks an eBay seller faces. This is definitely an area where you'll want to use some automation. I discuss software and web-based solutions in Chapters 43 and 44. These systems enable you to create templates that show off your auction visually and contain standard language for your various policies such as shipping, payment, and returns. If you sell similar but not identical merchandise, you can write and save text to the templates that describes the merchandise in general terms so you only have to add the unique or specific data.

4. Scheduling an auction is a very important task to automate, because you can't always be near your computer to launch the auction so it ends at a specific time. For example, I often want my seven-day auctions to end on Sunday evening, but I don't necessarily want to work Sunday evenings. Both the software and web-based programs enable you to create inventory items as prewritten and predesigned auctions that you can launch at a scheduled time and date. In fact, the best systems enable you to launch recurring auctions, meaning that you can set them to always launch your auction at the same time every Sunday evening. (Note: eBay charges 10¢ to schedule an auction. If you are launching hundreds of auctions a week, this can get quite expensive. All the auction management services I discuss offer this service for free. The savings are usually enough to pay for their service.)

5. Answering questions from prospective bidders is another time-consuming task, but this is where you really want the human touch to come through, so I don't recommend setting up auto-responders with FAQs, although it's certainly possible to do that. What I do instead is keep a file of prewritten answers to typical questions and use them when possible, although I always use the person's name and add a personal note or some specific information to personalize the message.

6. Communicating with the winning bidders is one of your most important tasks. If you communicate quickly and provide them with all the information they will need to complete the sale, it will speed up receiving your payment, allow you to ship faster, and increase your feedback rating. Fortunately, eBay and PayPal have become automated to the point where the end-of-auction notice that now goes out has a link for PayPal account holders to just click the message and pay immediately. But this is where it can get tricky.

   In Chapter 33, I pointed out the merits of using a fixed shipping amount versus a calculated shipping amount. I think using a fixed shipping amount is a huge time-saver for both the buyer and the seller and leads to much less confusion when dealing with new eBay members.

7. Shipping eats up a lot of time, and anything you can do to automate this process will bring you large dividends. Three elements of this process can benefit from automation: the actual wrapping and packaging, applying the postage or shipping charges and labels, and delivering the goods to the shipper. You can't really automate the actual wrapping and packing of the merchandise into boxes unless you order them that way from the supplier. Some suppliers will do this, however, and if your supplier does, it's usually worth the small extra charge. What you can do to save time, however, is set up a professional shipping station with all of your supplies organized for quick access. Hiring someone to do the shipping is not really automation but can be a huge time-saver.

   Calculating and applying the postage or shipping charges and labels is very easy to automate. If you are using the Post Office, several companies, including the USPS itself, offer solutions (see Chapter 42). If you ship with a carrier such as UPS or FedEx Ground, they offer software and printers integrated with a scale to automate the process of calculating shipping charges and printing labels.

Last is the issue of delivering the shipment to the shipper. If your shipments are preprinted and registered using an automated system that is linked to the Postal Service System, you can simply drop off the goods, usually at the back entrance to the Post Office, where they have a place for volume shippers. If you are shipping Express Mail or Priority Mail, the Post Office will even pick up your shipments at your location for free. UPS, DHL, or FedEx Ground will pick up your shipments for free if you open an account with them.

8. The final step is posting feedback. This is fairly easy to automate, as almost all of the automated systems—both software and web-based—are capable of posting feedback.

PowerSeller Tip

If you plan on selling several items at a time, automating your process is an absolute necessity. I currently use Vendio. I import text files via their inventory importer, attach photos (all done locally on my machine) then launch to eBay and/or my website. All my e-mails are automated, i.e., Winning Bidder Notification, Payment Received Notice, Payment Reminders, and so on. The automation gives my clients immediate attention and saves me hours of work.

—from NY Baglady

Automating these functions will save you time, and therefore money. Always remember you want to spend your time on high-value tasks, those that are making you money. You are not making any money standing in line at the Post Office or downloading photos from your website into your auctions one at a time. You are making money when you're doing research, looking for new products to sell, communicating with customers, and writing great titles and descriptions.

41.2 Automating the Upsell

The only item I didn't cover in the preceding list is the upsell—doing what you can to sell additional products to your buyer as part of the original sale. I devote a full chapter to the art of the upsell—see Chapter 51—but it's worth spending some time on how to automate the process. An upsell, or cross sell, as it's sometimes called, is nothing more than offering the customer an additional product that you can ship at the same time as the product he originally purchased. Generally this is done by offering a discount or a savings on shipping.

As I pointed out in the introduction, you have two basic ways to automate the auction-launching process: online web-based systems and offline software. The ability to conduct an upsell as part of the check-out process is pretty much owned by the web-based systems. I have not yet seen a software solution that is very good at performing this process.

41.3 eBay Sniping Software

eBay sellers also buy on eBay. In fact, I often purchase merchandise to resell from eBay's wholesale large lots categories. The problem is I don't have the time to sit in front of the computer and follow auctions and try to snipe an item at the last minute.

Sniping is the art of winning an item by putting in a low minimum bid at the very last second. You can do this manually by opening two or even three windows on your computer containing the same auction. About 30 seconds before the auction ends, you place a bid for the minimum amount plus 3¢ over the current bid. Now load the next higher increment bid into the next window and the next one into the third window. Submit your bid in the first window, 10 seconds later hit bid in the next window, and about three seconds before the auction ends, hit the last window. You don't have to worry about raising your own bid, because eBay will not let you bid against yourself. But if you were to place a high proxy bid and there were other bidders out there, eBay would take your bid up to the maximum proxy amount if your initial bids were below other proxy bidders. By sniping you win the item at the last second and can often get it at a lower price than you would have had you placed a high proxy bid. If you do a web search for the term sniping software or sniping service, you will find several companies that offer automated sniping tools. We cover two of them below.

The problem with this method is twofold. First, you need a really accurate computer clock that is exactly synced to eBay's time. And then you need to be at the computer when the auction ends. I don't know about you, but I am just too busy running my business to do this. Fortunately, several automated sniping programs on the market will perform this task for you. I use one called Bidslammer (www.bidslammer.com), and another popular one is Bidnapper (www.bidnapper. com). They both work very well. The difference is that Bidnapper is a monthly flat service fee with unlimited snipes. With Bidslammer you pay a fee for each snipe plus a small percentage of the winning bid. If you bid on a lot of auctions, then Bidnapper is cheaper in the long run. But if you only use the service infrequently, you'd be better off with Bidslammer.

For more on automating your shipping process, see Chapters 5 and 42.

For more on auction management software, see Chapter 43.

For more on auction management services, see Chapter 44.

For more on upselling, see Chapter 51.

chapter 42

Automating the Shipping Process

Shipping is one of the most important areas to automate because it's very time-consuming and a low-value task. Additionally, if you manually address labels and enter data, it's easy to make a mistake. As noted in Chapter 5, most eBay sellers ship via UPS or the U.S. Postal Service (USPS), although FedEx Ground is gaining ground against UPS with eBay sellers. The other player in the market is DHL, but I don't cover them here because few eBay sellers use them.

42.1 USPS Systems

The USPS offers a small amount of automation right on their website at www.usps.gov. You can purchase postage and print labels (with or without postage) and add delivery confirmation for Priority and Priority Mail International (see Figure 41.1). The system is fairly basic but works just fine and will speed up your label printing. Additionally, delivery confirmation is free if you print it from the website, whereas if you stand in line for it at the post office, delivery confirmation will cost you 65¢ to 75¢ on every package.

The other advantage of preregistering the postage and delivery confirmation is that you can drop off your shipments at the back door or bulk shipping window of your local Post Office. The USPS requires that any package over one pound in weight be physically handed to a postal employee, so you cannot just drop your preaddressed packages into a mailbox. At most Post Offices, if you print out a prepaid label on all the packages, you can take them to the back door and ring the bell. When a postal employee comes out, you hand over the bins containing the packages.

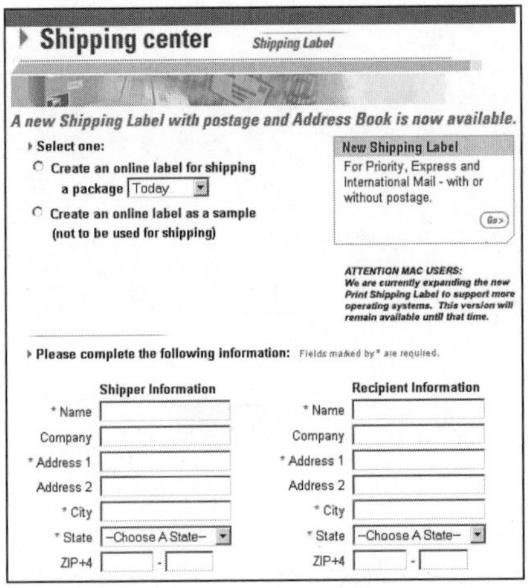

Figure 42.1
USPS postage printing page.

One of the disadvantages of the Post Office system is the inability to migrate or paste shipping addresses. Because the web entry field has the name and address components in separate boxes, you cannot just paste a name and address in. This can lead to errors because you have to enter the data manually.

42.1.1 Using Endicia for USPS Shipments

A better labeling system for USPS shipments is available from Endicia (www. endicia.com; see Figure 42.2). Endicia has by far the best solution, the easiest-to-use software, and handles the widest variety of packages. They also offer discounts on scales, label printers, and supplies.

Best of all, Endicia is a web-based solution. You open an account, go online, and download the software. You can use your own laser printer, or you can purchase an integrated scale and label printer (see Figure 42.3) so you can cut and paste the address from your payment notification e-mail into the field, put the package on the scale, select the type of postage (first-class, priority, parcel post, and so on), and hit enter. Endicia calculates the postage and prints out a label with the postage and delivery confirmation on it. The Endicia program can even automatically send a customized e-mail to the customer with the delivery information and tracking number. There is no faster way to handle USPS shipments.

Figure 42.2
Endicia Internet Postage website.

Figure 42.3
Endicia scale and printer.

Endicia works with both Windows and Macintosh operation systems. The software integrates very nicely with eBay and PayPal information to save you time and prevent errors caused by having to retype shipping information. As with the USPS website, delivery confirmation through Endicia is free.

Endicia allows you to add third-party insurance right on their website when you are entering the postage information, which helps you save money. Rather than buy expensive insurance from the Post Office ($1 per hundred of value), you can purchase insurance from a private carrier such as Discount Shipping Insurance (DSI). DSI only charges 55¢ per hundred of value on tracked shipments. (For more on insurance, see Chapter 57.)

Other Endicia features include integration with almost all the major auction management software systems and online auction management companies discussed in the next two chapters.

Endicia is cheaper than leasing a postage meter and will usually result in having your mail delivered faster because it electronically bar-codes your labels so they are ready for the USPS automation system.

A new feature of the Endicia Premium membership, which can really save you headaches, is called Stealth Postage. Professional eBay sellers know that you must charge a small handling fee on top of the postage to help cover the cost of your time and boxes and packing materials. But a large number of eBay buyers get upset when you charge them $4 for shipping and handling and they receive a package with only $3 postage on it. Stealth Postage creates a label with postage that the Post Office equipment can read but without the printed postage amount showing on the package label. Therefore your buyer has no idea what you actually pay in postage.

Some other unique features Endicia offers include the following:

- Print a shipping record, invoice, or receipt on the same page as your shipping label. Show customer, package, or reference data on the label itself.
- Save on Return Shipping Labels. Avoid $625 in annual USPS accounting/ permit fees for Merchandise Return service. Instead, you can print prepaid return shipping labels for your customers through your Endicia postage account.
- Endicia Premium includes special online transaction reports that list address and delivery data for all traceable packages. One glance through the listing will show your delivered, en route, and undeliverable packages. Special navigation buttons let you sort your package listings by date, address, mail class, postage amount, or delivery status.

Endicia can also help you with branding. Their system enables you to print your logo on your labels and envelopes and creates marketing postcards with tailored messages. You can customize multiple layouts and use them as templates. This means you are no longer tethered to a single envelope with your logo or a sticker on it. You can customize different envelopes for different mailings.

As of this writing, the flat fee for joining Endicia is $9.95 a month or $99 a year. The Endicia Premium plan is $15.95 per month and includes Stealth Postage, integration with leading auction management systems, and the ability to print return labels.

42.2 UPS Systems

The United Parcel Service, the number-two shipping solution after the USPS, have been very aggressive in promoting themselves to eBay sellers. UPS has made co-marketing deals with eBay and always exhibits at eBay's annual convention, eBay Live. In fact, they always have the largest booth at this convention. Because of the volume of shipments eBay sellers do, UPS offers them a discount of between 25 percent and 35 percent depending on their volume when they sign up for UPS through the link on eBay. And, at eBay Live 2008, eBay and UPS announced that once you obtain PowerSeller status, UPS will offer a further discount of 23 percent. Here is the link to open an account: http://pages.ebay.com/ups/whychooseups.html.

UPS adds a residential delivery charge, which makes them fairly expensive for many eBay shipments unless you are getting the discounts. UPS will give you substantial discounts of their premium services such as next-day and second-day air. But they will not discount their three-day select and regular ground service unless your shipments are in the thousands per year.

If rates are the downside to using UPS, their shipping systems are the upside. UPS offers both software and web-based shipping services, and both systems are incredibly sophisticated. You can download software into your computer that links with the UPS online management site. Besides the ease of printing labels and entering the package into the system, you get advanced tracking, reports, and signature capture.

UPS Online Tools are easy-to-install application programming interfaces (APIs) that add an advanced level of customer service and functionality to your auction-shipment automation or e-commerce website. The tools are free to download and come with e-mail customer support.

Easy-to-install tools such as UPS Tracking let your customers track packages worldwide without leaving your website or eBay. The tracking tool is a very useful feature which can help you …

- Improve customer service. Give your customers the ability to track any package shipped via UPS—any time, anywhere in the world.

- Increase customers' time on your site. Increase impulse buying by bringing your customers back to your e-commerce site by putting UPS Tracking at their fingertips.

- Reduce costs. Decrease customer support phone calls and reduce returns by making your shipping more efficient.

- Let your customers track their shipments right from your e-commerce site using your reference or order number.

- Add eBay site and website functionality. Your customers can shop, ship, and track from one location.

- Give customers peace of mind. Give your customers confidence about ordering online when they see you have the expertise and reliability of UPS shipping services behind your site.

When you open a UPS Account, you'll receive your UPS charges on one consolidated statement, and you can order selected UPS shipping supplies at no charge. (This includes free labels, boxes, and Tyvek envelopes for their premium services but, unlike the USPS Priority Mail, they do not provide boxes for ground services.) If you send at least 10 packages a week, you can qualify for a daily pickup. UPS also integrates with your *My eBay Page* so you can get detailed UPS tracking information 24 hours a day at eBay. Or request Quantum View Notify at www.UPS.com, and UPS will send you proactive e-mail updates about the status of your package.

UPS also integrates with the UPS shipping calculator that you can include in your auctions and can be linked to your end of auction message. If you use eBay's integrated UPS function, you can save time e-mailing potential buyers by posting a shipping calculator right in your auctions.

UPS integrates easily with your My eBay Page. You can …

- Quickly and conveniently print shipping labels.

- Manage in-transit UPS shipments via tracking.

- Pay for your shipments via PayPal or your UPS account.

Quantum View, the UPS tracking and notification system, is designed to provide proactive status information about UPS shipments. All Quantum View services are available at no cost. Quantum View Notify is a fee-based service that automatically notifies your customers of the progress of your shipments. UPS offers users two types of accounts. One is a daily pickup and the other is where you drop the goods off at a UPS Store or drop-off center. The drop-off service is less expensive, but if you have the volume, I'd pay the small extra charge to get pickup.

If you compare rates, USPS Priority Mail is much cheaper than UPS up to six pounds. Over six pounds, the rates are closer, but the Postal Service still beats UPS on packages weighing up to 10 pounds if you consider the cost of the box. Shipping boxes are expensive, so you really need to figure their cost into your calculations.

42.3 FedEx Ground

FedEx Ground has been gaining ground on UPS among eBay sellers. FedEx has put a lot of money into the company to compete with UPS and the Postal Service.

Like UPS, FedEx Ground charges a surcharge for residential delivery, but it is less than what UPS charges. They also have excellent automation support and, in my experience, they usually beat UPS door-to-door by one full day. They quote the same zone-to-zone delivery times on their website but almost always beat their quoted time by a full day.

The only service of its kind dedicated to residential customers, FedEx Home Delivery serves virtually 100 percent of the United States population. This residential-only network provides guaranteed delivery in the evenings, on Saturdays, and even by appointment. FedEx Ground Home Delivery Service offers a suite of automation tools that are completely web-based. However, they also offer a solution that is already built right into your QuickBooks program (another great reason for buying QuickBooks; see Chapter 5). QuickBooks Shipping Manager is the easiest way to integrate shipping with your accounting system, because you don't need a plug-in or additional software. QuickBooks Shipping Manager is built right into your QuickBooks software, and it's free.

With QuickBooks Shipping Manager, you can process shipments, print FedEx shipping labels, and even schedule pickups and track packages right in your QuickBooks software. The program prefills the shipping labels with the customer address information from your QuickBooks Invoice or Sales Receipt forms—no more handwriting labels and no need to enter data twice. It also enables you to ship via FedEx Express, FedEx Ground, and FedEx Home Delivery.

But here is the best news: QuickBooks users are qualified to receive up to 12 percent off select FedEx Ground services based on volume. Because FedEx Ground is already cheaper than UPS, this additional discount makes FedEx hard to beat.

If you use QuickBooks Basic Edition or earlier versions of QuickBooks, you can still easily integrate shipping with your accounting system. All you need to do is install ShipRush, a plug-in that integrates with QuickBooks. It automatically pulls the shipment address from your own databases, customer orders, or customer lists. When you buy QB, ShipRush is one of the QB downloads from their site.

42.4 Large Goods Shipping

If you sell very large merchandise, such as business and industrial equipment, motor scooters, or furniture, you'll need to use freight shippers to get your merchandise to your customers. Freight is pound for pound more expensive than using a shipping company, but if your merchandise weighs more than 150 pounds, you don't really have a choice.

If you sell a heavy yet standard product and you already have a good packaging solution, a standard shipping broker is probably the way to go. To find one near you, look in the Yellow Pages. If your items are unusual in size, very valuable, or otherwise difficult to pack and ship, you might be better served by Craters & Freighters or U-Ship.

42.4.1 Craters & Freighters

Craters & Freighters (www.cratersandfreighters.com) provides custom crating and shipping solutions for eBay sellers and other businesses with shipments too big, fragile, valuable, or uniquely shaped for traditional shippers. They are basically a network of specialty shippers who also provide crating and packaging services.

The Craters & Freighters website features e-Quote, a real-time, online quoting engine. CratersandFreighters.com is the only site that allows users to get immediate, full-service shipping estimates for one item or many at any time. According to company president, Diane Gibson, "With e-Quote, shipping large, odd-sized, or highly valued items is as easy as booking an airline ticket online."

e-Quote makes it possible for someone about to bid on your auction to go online and get a shipping quote to his zip code before he places a bid. Just place a link to the e-quote tool in your auction, and bidders can click it to get their quote.

42.4.2 U-Ship

U-Ship (www.uship.com; see Figure 42.4) is also very popular with eBay sellers who ship large or heavy merchandise.

Figure 42.4
U-Ship shipping service.

PowerSeller Tip

You can create links to your other auctions, your eBay store, and outside resources such as U-Ship by using a simple line of HTML code that looks like this:

<a href=*paste your link here*>Click Here</a> to get a shipping quote from U-Ship.</a>

The HTML code <a href=> is a command that tells the website what to do. In this case, we created a link to U-Ship. You could also invite someone to visit your eBay store like this: Please visit my <a href=your eBay store link goes here> eBay Store</a>. When someone views your auctions, he would see: Please visit my eBay Store. The underlined words eBay Store would appear in blue as a clickable link.

The U-Ship website is a shipping gateway for both buyers and sellers. When you sell an item and know the buyer's location, you list the item on the website and it is posted to a website. Drivers can check the website to identify shipments that coincide with their routes. I have only used U-Ship twice, but in both cases I had a bid back within two hours of posting it on the site, and the cost was almost one half of a standard freight quote. The shipments were delivered on time; the buyer was happy; and I received good feedback on both transactions.

U-Ship does not do any packaging, so you will have to prepare your goods for shipment. Most trucks have lift gates to get heavy cargo into the truck.

U-Ship also provides a portal for your buyers. You copy a snippet of HTML code from the U-Ship website and paste it into your auction. This will generate a small U-Ship banner in your auction that invites bidders to click the link to get a shipping quote for this item to their location. This way a prospective bidder can get a shipping quote before he bids, and you save time because prospective bidders can get a shipping quote directly from the shipper.

For more on shipping, see Sections 5.8 and 33.1.

chapter 43

Auction Management Software

As I mentioned in Chapter 41, you have two basic methods of automating your auction listings and customer communications. The first is with offline software that you install on your computer. The advantage of this method is that you can do your work offline and just go online when you want to upload your auctions or download your data. Also, in most cases the software is cheaper over the long run because it is a one-time purchase.

The other method is to use online systems. These are available directly from eBay as well as from several third-party auction management companies. This chapter covers the offline software by eBay and non-eBay offerings, and Chapter 44 covers web-based auction management services.

43.1 eBay Systems

eBay offers both auction management software and online systems. This chapter is mostly about offline software, but eBay's software offerings interface smoothly with eBay's online platform, and it makes sense to discuss them together.

The three solutions eBay offers are as follows:

- *Turbo Lister* is a free download available from eBay that enables you to create listings in your computer and launch them onto eBay. You can list multiple items at once and save listings to reuse again and again. You can access convenient HTML templates and easily create listings with a WYSIWYG (What You See Is What You Get) design editor. Turbo Lister can also schedule your listings to launch at a later time.

- *Blackthorne* comes in two versions: Basic and Pro. These are eBay's all-in-one, desktop-based listing and sales management tools designed to automate launching auctions. Blackthorne tools help medium- to high-volume sellers launch auctions on eBay without a constant Internet connection. Both versions offer many customizable features.

- *Selling Manager* and *Selling Manager Pro* are eBay's online (web-based, versus desktop-based) sales management tools. You access Selling Manager through your My eBay Page, which makes this tool very convenient. Selling Manager is for low- to high-volume listers and Selling Manager Pro is for high-volume listers.

  With Selling Manager you can relist multiple items at once; see a one-page snapshot of your business; track buying, selling, and account activities; create e-mails with custom templates; and print shipping labels and invoices.

Now let's explore each of these programs in detail.

43.1.1 Turbo Lister

Turbo Lister has been available since 2001, but eBay introduced a new version of it in 2005 and updated it in 2008 to match the new selling formats. The new version features an easy-to-learn interface and a much more reliable architecture. The program is very easy to learn and use; you simply create your listings and upload them to eBay. It also saves your listings for future use.

Using Turbo Lister is very similar to using the Sell Your Item (SYI) form on eBay. You start by creating an item of inventory just like you would create an auction listing.

Designing attractive listings is a breeze with eBay Turbo Lister. You can take advantage of eBay's themes and layouts and/or the built-in HTML editor to create compelling and professional item descriptions. You simply type your text into the box, and you can select bullets, bold, italic, and so on, just like a Microsoft Word document. When you click Save, the program creates the HTML code, and you can preview the listing before you launch it.

Turbo Lister offers you the choice of using eBay Picture Services for image hosting, or you can use your own web-hosting service. However, eBay's picture-hosting service is far too expensive for the high-volume seller. So you either need a website where you can store your photos and provide the URL to eBay, which can be very time-consuming, or you can use a photo-hosting service such as Image Host Plus (www.imagehostplus.com) at $4.95 per month or Smug Mug (www.smugmug.com) for $39.95 per year. Both offer unlimited hosting. There are some free photo-hosting websites, but I'd avoid them as they bomb you with advertising and aren't really adequate for the professional seller. (For more on image management, see Section 46.2.)

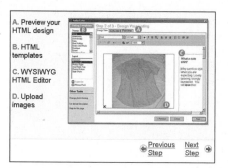

Figure 43.1
HTML Editor.

Next, specify your listing details such as shipping, payment, location, and so on. You can save basic information such as shipping address, payment policies, and instructions as defaults so they are automatically populated every time you create a new listing/inventory item. After you've created your listing, you're ready to upload to eBay.

Turbo Lister features an Item Inventory Screen, which becomes your control panel. The screen enables you to manage all the items you've created. You can create new items, edit existing items, and duplicate items to create new listings. Turbo Lister enables you to schedule your listings for a specific date and time. When you schedule a listing, eBay holds it in a pending state until the start time arrives (but they charge you 10 cents per listing to do this).

With the Inventory Control Panel, you can create folders to hold separate categories of merchandise. It features simple button interfaces to create new items, duplicate items, and manage your inventory. If you want to edit an item, simply click on it and the auction listing details come up so you can make changes.

When you select listings to send to eBay and click the **Add to Upload** button, Turbo Lister will show the listings to be uploaded in the **Listings Waiting to Upload** view. You can preview listing fees and confirm that your listings are correct before actually scheduling or launching them on eBay.

A really neat feature is the Pending Listing Page. If you schedule an item to launch and need to change any of the details, including the launch date and time, you simply click the listing from this page, and Turbo Lister will allow you to make any changes.

As you can see, Turbo Lister offers a variety of features to speed up your listing and launching of auctions, but in the end it still requires a lot of manual actions and only addresses part of the automation suite.

If you decide to try Turbo Lister, eBay offers a downloadable PDF file and an excellent online tutorial.

If you sell vehicles, parts, or automotive accessories on eBay Motors, eBay also provides a specialized version of Turbo Lister just for eBay Motors called CARad. This is a combination online and offline system that includes photo hosting and beautiful predesigned templates that reflect an automotive theme. The downside is the price. eBay charges $9.95 per listing or $299 per month for unlimited listings. They do have research that shows CARad auctions have higher closing rates and slightly higher final values. I sold a Porsche Boxster in early 2005 using CARad and thought paying $9.95 was pretty small compared to the selling price of an expensive car. However, if I were in the car business, I think I could find a less expensive solution, such as Vendio or ChannelAdvisor (see Chapter 44), to accomplish the same thing.

43.1.2 Blackthorne Basic and Blackthorne Pro

Blackthorne Basic and Pro are from Blackthorne software, now owned by eBay and available for purchase from the eBay Seller Central page. Blackthorne Basic and Pro are eBay's all-in-one, desktop listing and sales management tools designed to save time. It is basically an advanced version of Turbo Lister, doing everything Turbo Lister does and more, and is designed to help medium- to high-volume sellers manage their auctions without the need for a constant Internet connection. You might call it a Turbo Lister on steroids.

Beyond doing everything Turbo Lister does, Blackthorne also contains a bulk post-sale manager. You can track and manage your sales, send customizable e-mails, process feedback in bulk, print shipping labels and invoices, and keep sales records.

Many sellers like the idea of local data storage, so they can store all their listings and post-sales information on their own computers. Of course, this comes with a risk. You must be careful to back up your computer data frequently or you could lose valuable sales information, including ongoing transactions.

The Pro version is more appropriate for the larger-volume seller as it incorporates the following features:

- **Open Database:** Seller's Assistant's Microsoft Access database is open to the user, meaning you can fully integrate Blackthorne into your existing business processes.

- **Inventory Management:** This feature automatically adjusts inventory levels and sends restock alerts.

- **Monthly Sales Reports:** You can view sales reports such as Profit and Loss, Tax Collected, and Total Sales.

- **Image Management:** Upload photos and other images to your own web space for image hosting directly from Seller's Assistant Pro tool.

- **Multi-User Capability:** If you have multiple lines of business or employees, you can get up to five user profiles with each subscription.

If you really want a desktop-based program, Blackthorne Pro is an excellent solution. You still have the problem of image hosting, and because you must upload and download data, you are never working in real time. Having said all of this, many large PowerSellers use Blackthorne. Still, it's probably not the best solution for really large high-volume sellers who prefer online solutions (see Chapter 44).

You can try Blackthorne Basic or Blackthorne Pro for free for 30 days. After the trial period, eBay charges a monthly subscription fee of $9.99 for Blackthorne Basic and $24.99 a month for Pro. I always thought the point of paying for software was to own it, so I've never been a fan of renting software.

43.1.3 eBay Selling Manager

Now we turn to eBay's online system, Selling Manager (SM). This program performs most of the same tasks that Blackthorne Basic and Turbo Lister do. Some users like to combine Turbo Lister as their auction listing tool with Selling Manager for their auction and e-mail management.

The best thing about SM is that it operates right from your My eBay Page. Figure 43.2 shows a list of your auctions, how many (if any) bids they have, the number of bidders, and the number of watchers (people who usually wait until the last minute to bid). It also shows the time left and the quantity listed versus the quantity available, which is important for Dutch (multiple-item) auctions.

Figure 43.2
My eBay Selling page.

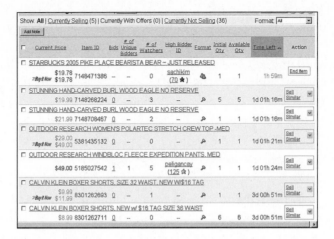

> **PowerSeller Tip**
>
> I especially like the number of watchers feature on eBay's Selling Manager. If you look at the second item, the Hand-carved Burl Wood Eagle, you see it had no bids with one day and one hour left to go, but it had three watchers. The next day, it had four watchers and still no bids. But within the last five minutes, three of those watchers began bidding, and the item ended up selling for over $45. Whenever I see an item with more than three people watching it, I know it should do pretty well. If I see an item with more than five people watching it, I immediately launch an identical item (if I have one) with a high starting price and a BIN price. Someone almost always snatches it up at the BIN price.

When you subscribe to Selling Manager, eBay activates the features so they work when you log into **My eBay.** After it is set up, you will be able to access these features:

- **Status columns:** Shows which post-sales activities (collect payment, ship, leave feedback, and so on) you've completed and what you still have to do.

- **E-mail and feedback templates:** Customized e-mail templates and stored feedback help you manage these tasks.

- **Bulk Relister:** Relist multiple sold and unsold listings at once.

- **Invoices and Shipping Labels:** Print labels and invoices directly from sales records.

- **Download Sales History:** Export your sales records to keep files on your computer. Unfortunately, this feature is not compatible with QuickBooks.

- **Bulk UPI and FVF:** File, track, and manage multiple unpaid items and final value fee requests.

- **Bulk Feedback:** Send feedback to multiple buyers all at one time.

Figure 43.3
My eBay Items Sold page.

As with Blackthorne, you'll want the Pro version of Selling Manager if you are a high-volume seller. Not only is Selling Manager Pro much more robust and sophisticated, it offers what I think is the most critical aspect of any automated solution: inventory management.

Seller Manager Pro comes with the following additional features:

- **Inventory management:** Tracks your inventory and alerts you when you are out of stock.

- **Listing statistics:** Helps you determine your products' success ratio and average selling prices.

- **Bulk features:** E-mail messages, send feedback, and print invoices to multiple buyers all at the same time.

- **Automatic time-savers:** Reduce your workload by automating some of your feedback and post-sales e-mails.

- **Reporting:** Generate monthly sales reports of all your eBay sales activities, including your fees. (The ability to track your eBay fees is very important, and this is one feature the third-party auction management systems lack.)

■ **Bulk NPB and FVF:** File, track, and manage multiple nonpaying bidders and final value fee requests.

■ **Free Listing Designer:** This is eBay's template designer, which is surprisingly good and easy to use. You get free HTML templates when you subscribe to Selling Manager Pro, regardless of which tool you use to list.

Selling Manager is $4.99 a month, but eBay gives it to you for free if you operate any level of eBay Store. Selling Manager Pro is $15.99 but is free if you are an eBay Premium or Anchor Store subscriber, or are also subscribed to Blackthorne Pro.

Given that most high-volume sellers are Premium or Anchor Store subscribers, the biggest advantage to Selling Manager Pro is that it's free. That is significant if you are a high-volume seller.

PowerSeller Tip

You can automatically place selected feedback comments from your feedback log into your auctions with a product called FAME—Feedback Admaker for eBay—from www.platinumpowerseller.com.

43.2 Third-Party Software

Dozens of software companies sell eBay management programs and solutions. (For a complete list, see Appendix C.) Spoonfeeder and Auction Genie (also works with Mac computers) are among the most popular. Both of them are easy-to-use and powerful, but they have shortcomings that are common to almost all offline auction management systems.

Spoonfeeder and Auction Genie operate in a very similar fashion to most of the systems on the market. And they are both similar to eBay's Turbo Lister if you combine it with Seller's Assistant. Unlike these other programs, Spoonfeeder provides image hosting.

Let's take a look at some of Spoonfeeder's features and benefits:

- Can quickly and easily generate professional-looking auction listings, using an easy-to-use template technology.
- Supports creating and posting listings to eBay auctions, eBay fixed-price listings, eBay Stores, and eBay Motors.
- Provides user control of font, size, color, and style, including bold, italic, underline, strike-through, marquee, slide, alternate, and scroll.
- Has an integrated spell checker and thesaurus.
- Manages a database of reusable phrases and descriptions to speed up the creation of numerous similar auctions.
- Easily includes and organizes photos of the item for sale and uploads photos automatically with integrated picture hosting. Picture hosting is free with the price.
- Enhances photos with resize, rotate, brightness, sharpen, crop, and adjust color saturation.
- Loads, saves, edits, and prints your item listings.
- Previews and quickly revises item listings.
- Formats with custom description footer for standard buyer instructions.
- Generates HTML web code for export to private websites or online shopping systems.
- Posts listings automatically and on-demand directly to major auction and commerce sites of your choice. (However, this is not that seamless when you go beyond eBay.)
- Schedules your listings to start automatically at any date and time (this feature saves you the eBay 10¢ scheduling fee).
- Starts standard auctions repetitively, according to your schedule with inventory integration.

The Deluxe edition has incorporated several new features that extend the automatic functions and versatility of the software, including the following:

- Tracks auction status from start through fulfillment.
- Automatically sends e-mail invoice and winning bidder notification within seconds of auction close.

- Automatically adds shipping charges to the invoice for both single-item and Dutch auctions.
- Provides a feedback database for easy selection.
- Automatically reciprocates on positive feedback.
- Automatically sends late payment notices by e-mail.
- Automatically files Unpaid Item disputes.
- Automatically files Final Value Credit Request to recover fees for incomplete auctions.

These last two features are especially valuable in controlling and reducing your eBay fees.

The control panel interface is where everything starts. From here (see Figure 43.4) you can control most aspects of launching and managing your auctions.

Figure 43.4

At the Spoonfeeder Operations panel, you can access all your automated functions.

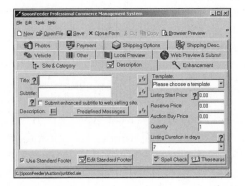

Both Spoonfeeder and Auction Genie are very powerful and easy to learn. As software programs go, they are both very popular. Both of these programs recently introduced powerful inventory editions whereby you start with an inventory item, photo, and description and create your listings from there. Older systems required you to create an auction listing first and it filed everything by the auction title rather than by your inventory item. The listing designer, photo hosting, and image management in both programs are excellent. In addition, the scheduler enables you to schedule recurring auctions that integrate into your inventory. The Spoonfeeder Photo Control feature (see Figure 43.5) allows you to manage and edit your images from one location.

When you launch an auction, it deducts the item from your inventory temporarily. If the item sells, the software deducts it permanently.

This is one of the very few auction management programs that gives you image control right in your management system. With most software and web-based auction management systems, you have to crop and resize your images in another program before you upload them.

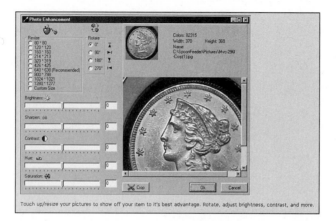

Figure 43.5
Spoonfeeder Photo Control screen.

Pricing for Spoonfeeder varies with the many options available. It starts around $19.95 for a basic license, but that license doesn't have enough features for the PowerSeller. If you are a serious seller and want all the features listed in this chapter, you'll need the full version at $99.95. I like the Spoonfeeder pricing model because you own the software after you pay for it. If you are going to do consignment sales as part of your eBay business, you want to review two other software programs: Liberty 4 at www.resaleworld.com and AuctionSound at www.auctionsound.com. Both of these systems operate similarly to Spoonfeeder but have the added ability to track consignors and consignment fees and commissions.

Finally, I must point out the most serious drawback of using software programs to manage and automate your auctions. These only work if you are selling on eBay. The trend today is for eBay sellers to diversify their business and sell on multiple channels, including Yahoo! and Amazon auctions, Yahoo! Stores, Overstock.com, and your own web store or website. The next chapter covers online auction management services, which provide the best automation solution if you're going to sell in multiple channels.

For more on using software to automate your processes, see Sections 5.2, 5.6, and 45.2.

chapter 44

Auction Management Services

There are several companies who provide complete, web-based, auction automation and management services which include all the features and benefits of the offline software systems (see Chapter 43). But instead of installing the program on your computer, you access it via the web, which I prefer for several reasons. Most importantly, as eBay makes changes on the platform, the auction management companies who are all registered third-party providers get advance notice so they can update their online systems and services. The updates are instantly incorporated into the web service, and I do not have to pay for upgrades. In addition, all the web-based services closely integrate picture hosting with their auction and inventory hosting features, making it very easy to add photos to my auctions. Image hosting is usually included in my fees, so although I'm paying a fee for the management and automation, I am saving money on picture hosting. If you use a lot of photos in your auctions, this savings—in both time and money—can be substantial.

These are the major players in auction management services. For a complete list of auction management services with descriptions of their offerings and how they set their fees, see Appendix C.

- **Auctiva** (www.auctiva.com) offers a basic suite of functions and services and is very highly rated by eBay sellers. They give a wide variety of plans to choose from so you can customize your services to your needs. Auctiva supports eBay US, eBay Canada, eBay UK, eBay Australia, eBay Parts and Accessories, and eBay Motors. They also have a consignment feature now as well as reports, and other features. Auctiva supports eBay and eBay Motors.

- **ChannelAdvisor** (www.channeladvisor.com) is one of the largest and most successful auction management companies. Their clients include 80 percent of the Fortune 100 companies that sell on eBay (Sears, IBM, Motorola, and more). ChannelAdvisor offers two automation products. Marketplace Advisor is an inventory-based automated selling service for eBay. Marketplace Advisor Premium automates listing and selling tasks for sellers who operate on multiple platforms including eBay, Amazon.com, and Overstock.com.

- **InkFrog** (www.inkfrog.com) is a great little company with super tools, but they only support eBay. Their users are almost cultish in their admiration for the service.

- **Kyozou** (www.kyozou.com) offers a very complete system with excellent warehouse inventory integration. eBay PowerSellers started Kyozou, and it is very well respected. Their system supports eBay, Overstock, Amazon, and several shopping engines.

- **Meridian** (www.noblespirit.com) is a fairly complete auction management system that is noted for its ease of use. They are the only system that offers an online solution for eBay consignment sellers (Trading Assistants). Currently they support eBay and Overstock.com.

- **Vendio** (www.vendio.com) is currently used by more than 100,000 eBay sellers (including myself). They offer a complete range of services and support eBay, eBay Motors, and eBay Canada. They also provide a web store and automated upsell features, such as a scrolling gallery in your listings so bidders can see the other products you have available.

Although dozens of other online services are available, these are the largest and most reliable. I'm not saying some of the newer services don't provide excellent solutions—it's just that they are not yet time-tested.

PowerSeller Tip

Automating your eBay business is one of the single best investments you can make. Setting up an automated system is like an employee you just pay once and then they work for free forever.

—Mike Enos, eBay guru, www.platinumpowerseller.com

I have elected to cover two systems in detail. The first is Vendio, which I have used for two years and have found to be very effective. The second is Channel-Advisor Merchant, a more complete solution that is aimed at high-volume sellers and sellers who want to market across as many channels as possible. Channel-Advisor Merchant is more expensive to set up but probably more cost-effective in the long run if you have a lot of volume. Additionally, it has some very sophisticated tools to more effectively take advantage of those selling sweet spots and to help you manage your inventory more effectively.

Let's look at Vendio first.

44.1 Vendio

Vendio is a good solution for medium- to large-scale sellers who don't need too many channels. Vendio currently supports eBay, eBay Motors, and eBay Canada, as well as Amazon Auctions.

Vendio also offers a third channel, Vendio Stores, which is essentially your own web store located on the Vendio site. Many sellers use these stores as their only websites. Vendio Stores open up additional fixed price sales channels by distributing your stores' items to Froogle (Google's shopping site) and Shopping.com at no additional charge. (For more on online stores, see Chapters 48 and 49.)

Vendio offers four solutions to manage your marketplace sales.

44.1.1 Sales Manager Merchandising Edition

Sales Manager Merchandising Edition (SMME) is Vendio's basic system, which includes automated listing to eBay, Vendio Stores, and shopping engines Shopzilla, Dealio, and Google product search. You can create attractive and professional item listings by choosing from a large selection of templates or by creating your own with their template creation utility. The basic price includes free image hosting supersized images that allows auction viewers to enlarge the image for a better look, a built-in HTML editor, and a very robust post-sale management system. The Merchandising Edition can be learned quickly and works very well for the average- to medium-size seller, particularly one with unique individual items; but if you are really planning to build a large business, you'll need more bulk creation capabilities and better inventory control.

44.1.2 Tickets Manager

Tickets Manager is a specialized solution developed in conjunction with eBay for the large-volume sellers who specialize in event and concert tickets. This is such a specialized area that I'm not going to cover this product here, but if you sell in this category, Tickets Manager is the best solution on the market.

44.1.3 Sales Manager Pro

Sales Manager Pro (SMPro) is a desktop Windows application that interfaces with Sales Manager online and provides all the listing features of Sales Manager Merchandising Edition in a PC application. The post-sale features are still online. The bulk creation capabilities and speed of a Windows application (rather than web pages) make SMPro the perfect application for those not always online or those on dial-up Internet access. SMPro also cuts listing time by enabling more bulk loading capabilities than those available directly in SMME.

44.1.4 Sales Manager Inventory Edition

Sales Manager Inventory Edition (SMIE) offers advanced selling automation for eBay and Vendio Stores that includes bulk item creation and editing, launch and repricing strategies, real-time inventory management, and the same cross-merchandising and post-sale features found in Sales Manager Merchandising Edition. Because Inventory Edition includes everything in the Merchandising Edition plus the added inventory control and re-pricing features, I want to cover this system in detail. SMIE is designed for sellers who list multiple quantities of the same items and enables you to automate and simplify inventory-based selling. SMIE includes bulk item creation and editing. You can create or edit up to 50 inventory items at once, then find and replace fields for multiple items later to optimize prices and quantities before launch.

SMIE also includes an intelligent launching and scheduling utility. You can schedule launches for hundreds of items at once and spread out related listings to give buyers multiple chances to purchase your items. This time spacing gives you great control over the perceived supply/demand position on eBay.

SMIE launches items automatically, all while maintaining tight control of the quantity at auction, as shown in Figure 44.1. You can also maximize sales by automating price and quantity changes for items depending on how well they are selling.

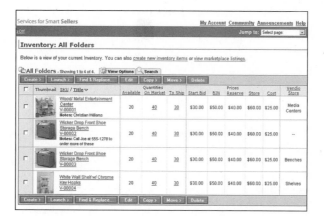

Figure 44.1
Vendio's inventory page.

SMIE's inventory management feature enables you to organize items into folders up to three levels deep so you can find, edit, and launch them quickly. Through a deep integration with eBay, the system automatically updates quantities as items launch or close successfully or unsuccessfully, so you can ensure that proper inventory levels are always maintained. If an item does not successfully sell, SMIE will automatically relist the item for you, taking advantage of the relist credit eBay offers.

For successful sales, the post-sale features monitor all the fulfillment steps you need to take. It first generates an automatic e-mail to auction winners. The e-mail contains a link that buyers click to check out. During the checkout process, the buyer is exposed to items in your Vendio Store, as shown in the example in Figure 44.2. This is a great tool for upselling your winning bidders. For example, if you sell a digital camera, you might offer flash cards, tripods, and camera bags in your Vendio store. The buyer could add these items onto her original order and pay for everything at once. Because you are not paying eBay fees on these additional items, your profit is greater and your eBay final value fee is spread over the larger actual final value.

Figure 44.2
Vendio Post-sale cross-selling tool shows buyers other items you have for sale.

The post-sale checkout is integrated with PayPal or (optionally) your merchant account to speed up the payment process by buyers. It also speeds up the shipping process by gathering the buyer's chosen carrier and exporting the shipping information to your preferred carrier, such as FedEx, UPS, or USPS, for label or postage printing. The buyer can even calculate the shipping using the shipping calculator shown in Figure 44.3. Finally, Vendio will also automatically post positive feedback when you receive it from buyers after the great experience you've given them.

One of the things I like about Vendio is if you are currently using another method or system when you sign up with Vendio, a utility automatically imports your ongoing auctions on eBay into their system so you don't have to start from scratch. All your ongoing auctions and eBay Store items will be imported into your inventory list, and all you have to do is go in and update the quantities.

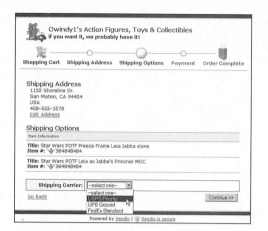

Figure 44.3
Vendio's post-sale shipping calculator.

SMIE shares the same merchandising features of Merchandising Edition, including custom templates and an HTML editor to make your listings stand out from others and inspire confidence from buyers (see Figure 44.4). Without having to know any HTML, you can create an infinite variety of templates to define the overall look and create a more professional listing. You can then type your description right into the HTML editor and use controls that look just like those in a Word document, such as insert table, bold, italic, bullets, etc., to polish off your description. There's no need to learn HTML—just type and launch!

Figure 44.4
Vendio's HTML editor.

Images are critical to merchandising your items, and Vendio offers some interesting image management features in their Image Hosting product, which is used in conjunction with all Sales Manager editions. You can store your images in folders that reflect your product categories, and you can use the Supersize option to let bidders click your images to enlarge them.

Vendio Image Hosting also addresses another issue on eBay, which is image theft. Some crooked eBay users will copy images from other people's auctions rather than take the time to make their own. Vendio Image Hosting addresses this issue with an image watermarking option. You can easily add a custom watermark to your images that a thief cannot remove, as in the example in Figure 44.5. If this doesn't prevent image theft in the first place, at least you'll be able to catch them easily and have their auctions shut down. (How would you know they were using your photos? Shame on you. Didn't we discuss how important it is for you to check your competitors' auctions?)

Figure 44.5

Vendio's water-marked image.

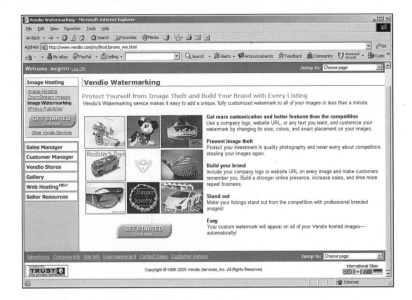

Vendio also offers several galleries to showcase additional listings after a buyer finds one of your eBay items. The Vendio Marquee Gallery, shown in Figure 44.6, for example, is a small filmstrip-size display of other listings that scrolls horizontally to catch buyers' attention. Vendio Gallery helps keep potential buyers on your items rather than clicking back to the main eBay search. According to a recent study conducted by Vendio, eBay PowerSellers using their Gallery doubled their hits, increased bids by 50 percent, and increased sell-through up to 18 percent, on average.

Figure 44.6
*Vendio Marquee
gallery.*

All in all, Vendio offers a very complete solution. Although other solutions are on the market, the average seller will be happy with Vendio's high level of auction launching automation, basic inventory management, and post-sale features. The biggest drawback to Vendio is the lack of additional sales channels, although I'd not be surprised if they added more channels soon. This seems to be the direction eBay sellers are going, and all the auction management companies will have to follow this trend if they want to keep their customers.

44.2 ChannelAdvisor—Marketplace Advisor

ChannelAdvisor offers the best overall solution for the really high-volume seller. Their inventory management is the most sophisticated of any on the web, and they have the most channels available to the seller. These include eBay, eBay Stores, eBay Motors, Yahoo! Stores, Amazon Shops, Overstock.com, and the ChannelAdvisor Store listings. Additionally, any inventory you list in the ChannelAdvisor Store is fed to the popular online shopping sites such as Froogle, CNET, Shopping.com, Shopzilla, BizRate, NexTag, and Price Grabber.

The ChannelAdvisor Marketplace Advisor (MA) and MarketPlace Advisor Premium (MAP) are used by some of the largest PowerSellers on eBay and include companies that sell their own merchandise on eBay, such as Motorola, Harman Audio, Crazy Ape, Orvis, Restaurant.com, and Digital Depot.

Both services operate basically the same. The major difference is that with the MA edition you can only list on eBay sites, and with the premium (MAP) edition you can also launch listings to the other shopping sites mentioned above. Since this book deals primarily with eBay, we will not go into much detail on the other launching services, but most of what is described here applies to both with minor variations.

The MA edition is organized into the following modules:

- Inventory
- E-Commerce Stores (MA Store)

- Scheduling and Relisting
- Merchandising
- Post-Sale Automation
- Order Processing and Checkout
- Yield Maximization
- Market Tracking and Performance History Review

What I like most about the MA service is that everything starts with inventory. Inventory management is the foundation of the Marketplace Advisor system, and this robust inventory management system enables you to manage more auctions more efficiently. You can automatically launch auctions when an item sells or even if an item reaches a specified bid point (see details below).

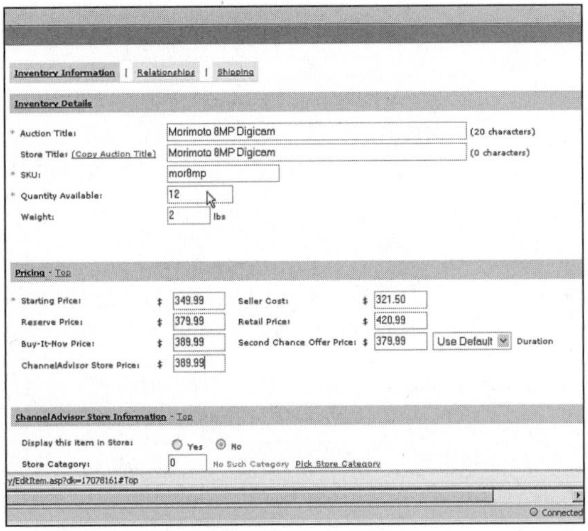

Figure 44.7

Create Inventory Item.

Inventory protection automatically tracks inventory as you post and close auctions and links to your e-commerce store so you never have to synchronize inventory manually again. The MA program provides flexible custom fields to track the data and product attributes that matter to you and your customers. Pre-filled item specifics and bulk upload and mapping capabilities streamline the transfer of inventory and images from spreadsheets or your inventory database to your inventory. After you create the standard information that is common to all your items (such as shipping and payment policy, warranty returns, and so on), this information is prefilled when you create an inventory item or upload from an offline database.

From the inventory page (see Figure 44.8), you can create auctions or launch items to your store, and the inventory page will not let you sell inventory via another method (such as an eBay store or your MA store) while an item is still at auction.

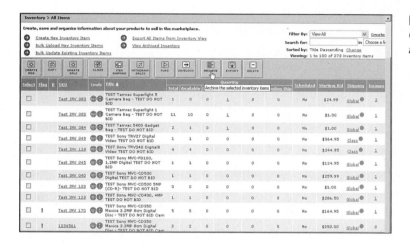

Figure 44.8
ChannelAdvisor inventory page.

Customized ad templates create a consistent look and feel. You can choose one of many professionally designed ad templates embedded in Marketplace Advisor or opt for a custom package. You can design your own, or ChannelAdvisor's designers will design them for you for a fee.

Sophisticated posting templates enable you to apply your selling strategy to individual classes of items through posting templates. You can set level cost and pricing data as a part of formulas (i.e., Product Cost × 1.2 = Minimum Bid) in posting templates that you create once and apply as often as you like.

The MA program allows for multiple users in a controlled environment. If you have employees, you can control how they access the system and what operations they are allowed to perform.

The ChannelAdvisor E-commerce Store is essentially a shopping cart–ready web store that is integrated with your auction function.

As you grow your business, you become increasingly dependent on up-to-date accuracy of your inventory. Without rigorous inventory management, costly mistakes can add up to big problems. That's why the ChannelAdvisor-hosted Store points to the same inventory database as your auctions.

Here is how the stores are used and how they integrate with your inventory and post-sales management, as well as how you can sell directly from them. This is as good as multi-channel selling gets:

- **Integrated Inventory System.** Store and marketplace inventory is managed from the same database, so you don't have to manually synchronize inventory data or risk inventory errors.

- **Combined Auction and Store Sales.** The integrated checkout enables you to combine invoices and leverage cross-selling.

- **Upsell Earlier in the Sales Cycle.** Shopping cart upsell capability is activated as soon as the customer puts the first item in the cart.

- **Category Trees.** You can customize your category tree for any unique product mix.

- **Customizable Store Titles and Descriptions.** Market your product differently on auctions or store listings.

- **Simple Set Up and Management.** Your settings and policies are automatically transferred into your store.

- **Design Center.** A choice of professionally designed templates and an easy-to-use Design Center make it simple for non-HTML experts to develop a great-looking design.

- **Web Hosting.** There is no additional fee for hosting; you can consolidate providers and keep your original domain name.

- **Meta Tags.** You retain full control of your meta tags—words that search engines look for when indexing your website or auctions—to leverage search engines to the fullest.

Using ChannelAdvisor's Advanced Scheduling and Relisting feature, you can prepare and schedule products for posting on multiple eBay marketplaces. If you use the premium (MAP) edition, you can also list on other marketplaces including Amazon and Overstock.com. The system allows you to automate at least 30 different considerations, such as posting time, quantity, category placement, and auction duration that are crucial to successful sales performance. By automating these practices, you can increase sales and productivity.

The Advanced Scheduling and Relisting feature enables you to set schedules that maintain a fluctuating number of listings pegged to the recovery rate that is being met by current auctions for the same SKU. The higher the prices, the more auctions are posted. If closing prices edge down, this schedule reduces the number of auctions it posts to match your preset formula.

The Distributed Scheduling feature enables you to evenly distribute your auctions throughout a set period of time, such as days, weeks, or even a full month, to eliminate downtime and ensure you always have active auctions.

Professional sellers use their About Me page as a focal point for incoming traffic and to feature current deals or auctions. ChannelAdvisor Merchant can help you publish your About Me page, manage the featured items and deals (such as free shipping) you are offering, and make sure the design of the page matches the brand you are promoting in your auctions, your CA Store, and the other channels you are selling in, such as Yahoo! Stores or Amazon.

Figure 44.9 shows an example of the branded ChannelAdvisor E-store run by shoe seller Grapevinehill. Their auctions reflect the same brand look and feel as you see in Figure 44.10.

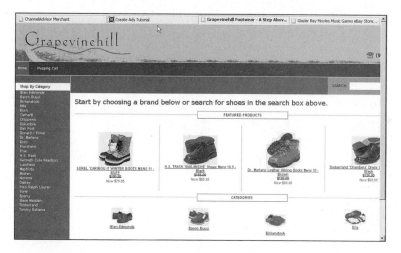

Figure 44.9
A ChannelAdvisor Store operated by Grapevinehill.

Notice the similar look and feel between the store and the auction listing. While you're at it, take a look at the size locator at the right of the photo. ChannelAdvisor's setup enables a user to click a size and see a listing of every shoe Grapevinehill has up for auction.

Figure 44.10
Grapevinehill auction for a pair of boots.

The really useful function of having a ChannelAdvisor store is the ability to upsell (or cross-sell) during the post-sale checkout process. If you sell different categories of goods, you can direct buyers to a specific category of store during the checkout process. For example, if you sell both men's and ladies' blue jeans and someone buys a pair of men's jeans, during the checkout process you could arrange to have him directed to the part of your store that lists women's jeans.

Another neat thing in the Merchant Edition's bag of tricks is the eBay Store Configurator. This option lets buyers dynamically configure products inside your eBay Storelisting. For example, if you sold the same shirt in several colors and sizes, a customer could configure their order to buy a different size even though it was not offered in the listing. This is a very sophisticated and advanced feature that requires a lot of setup and is only used by really large sellers. Sellers who take advantage of the Configurator, however, will be able to offer their customer a much more desirable model: get exactly what you want.

When a buyer opens a listing on eBay that features the Configurator, she will immediately see the difference. Inside that listing, the bidder can select options, see the price change in real time, and add on other products and accessories (e.g., a tripod for a camera). After the buyer completes the customization and presses the **Buy It Now** button, she is redirected to the newly created eBay Store Listing that features the exact specifications she selected. See Figure 44.11 for an example. The store is created and launched instantly by a Flash applet.

This feature is fantastic for anyone who sells items that come in different sizes or colors or items that you can add accessories to. This is another example of just how powerful automation can be for the auction seller. Without this feature you would have to work with this buyer by e-mail or telephone, or the buyer would have to click several of your auctions to build her final item.

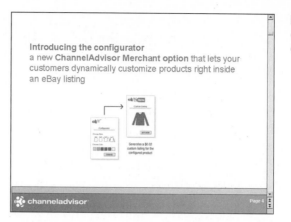

Figure 44.11
ChannelAdvisor Configurator page.

Now that you have made the sale—and possibly even an upsell—the post-sale automation module takes over. The post-sale process on eBay consists of notifying the winning bidder that she won an item, sending her instructions for payment, collecting the money, notifying her that the item has been shipped, and posting and receiving feedback. The post-sale process is one of the most time-consuming parts of the whole auction process and one where the most mistakes are made, which is why it's one of the most important parts of the process to automate. Automating these steps is a huge time-saver for any eBay seller.

Automated customer communications and management minimizes the drain on your resources and increases your productivity. In addition, customized communications help maintain an excellent feedback rating. Here is how the Merchant Advisor helps you achieve those goals:

- **Customer communications.** E-mail templates, automatic notifications, and correspondence tracking take the tedium out of this task.

- **Automated reminders.** Automatically generated e-mails let your customers know they have won and sends checkout reminders at preset intervals for a duration you establish. If the winner fails to check out within the time you set, the item is automatically returned to inventory and an automatic request for a listing fee refund is generated and sent.

- **Feedback management.** This ensures that you give—and get—prompt feedback. This feature monitors the feedback (+, –, or neutral) left by the buyer for you and automatically requests feedback from buyers if none is left within a specified time.

- **Manage unpaid items.** This feature supports eBay's Unpaid Item process, enabling you to automatically recover final value fees.

The other part of the post-sale function is order processing and checkout, another area that is prone to human error and one where automation can save time and prevent mistakes. This is also the area where you have an opportunity to capture the data your accounting system needs to track your business. The ChannelAdvisor MA Edition provides a high level of sophistication and features that enable you to manage the process and capture the data. Not every seller will need all these features, but they are available and become more important as you scale your business larger and larger. Selling in multiple channels can be challenging and confusing and requires close monitoring. It's no good to sell in an additional channel if you aren't making money in that channel.

When you are using an online payment and checkout system, you are dealing with very important data. Your customer must know her transaction will be secure and that her personal and financial information is protected.

Some of the processing and checkout features in both editions include …

- **Support for accounting and shipping.** This module supports QuickBooks, UPS, and FedEx file format reports for rapid processing throughout the process.

- **Checkout features.** Edits invoice details such as shipping costs, payment information, address, and method of payment. Merges auction or store invoices as a convenience to you and your buyers.

- **A transaction-processing module.** Uses the accounting report to create a file for direct download into your QuickBooks system. The shipping report can generate files that can be loaded into UPS Worldwide and FedEx and import tracking numbers back into Merchant. You can even process a payment reversal for a customer if needed.

- **Order process status.** Lets you view all stages of your orders as they move through the process. Helps you better manage your cash flow and money management.

- **More customization.** MA gives you the capability to customize shipping carriers, shipping zones, payment methods, fraud check, and data validation.

- **Automated payment processing.** Collects and processes data for credit cards and PayPal and supports shipping and tax calculations, all within a secure environment.

Yield maximization is ChannelAdvisor's term for all the little features that ensure you wring every last dollar out of the process. This includes automatically making Second Chance Offers (a Second Chance offer is a facility within eBay that allows you to offer an item to unsuccessful under-bidders at the price they bid if the price they bid was higher than the minimum you are willing to accept.) Other features of yield maximization include the upsell and cross-sell process and dealing with nonpaying bidders so you get your fees returned by eBay. This sounds like a small thing, but when you are listing and selling dozens or hundreds of items a week, this can be huge. Vendio and most of the other systems on the market provide a modest amount of automation in this area, but I still have to initiate each step. The truth is that most of the time I am just too busy with other things and forget to follow up on the fee refunds or make the Second Chance Offers. Automating this process solves this problem.

The last feature is Market Tracking and Performance History Review. We spend a lot of time on measuring your business metrics in Chapter 55, so here I'll just say that the key to understanding and measuring your business metrics is capturing the data in the first place. The market tracking and performance history tools in ChannelAdvisor make this task very easy.

Essentially your ChannelAdvisor system captures all of your cost, sales, and inventory performance data, as well as offering tools to measure your performance channel by channel. You can analyze the success of your marketplace strategy right down to a specific SKU. You can view an item with its posting and scheduling template, plus the number of hits, bids, and so on, for that product and that strategy. Figure 44.12 provides an overall view of your product performance detail.

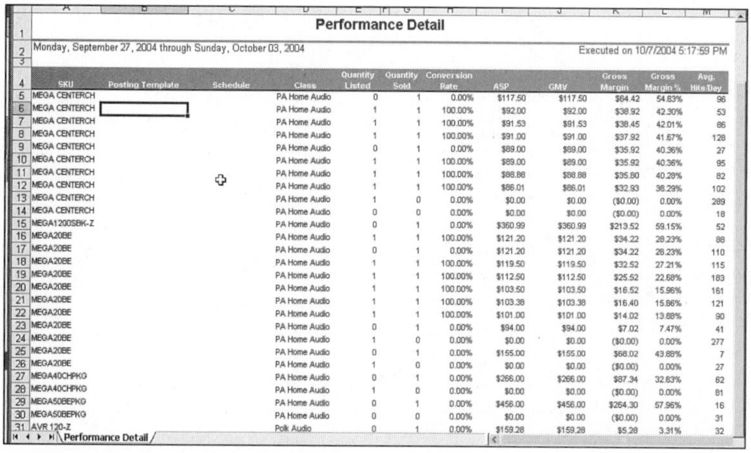

Performance Detail

Monday, September 27, 2004 through Sunday, October 03, 2004 — Executed on 10/7/2004 5:17:59 PM

SKU	Posting Template	Schedule	Class	Quantity Listed	Quantity Sold	Conversion Rate	ASP	GMV	Gross Margin	Gross Margin %	Avg. Hits/Day
MEGA CENTERCH			PA Home Audio	0	1	0.00%	$117.50	$117.50	$64.42	54.83%	96
MEGA CENTERCH			PA Home Audio	1	1	100.00%	$92.00	$92.00	$38.92	42.30%	53
MEGA CENTERCH			PA Home Audio	1	1	100.00%	$91.53	$91.53	$38.45	42.01%	86
MEGA CENTERCH			PA Home Audio	1	1	100.00%	$91.00	$91.00	$37.92	41.67%	128
MEGA CENTERCH			PA Home Audio	0	1	0.00%	$89.00	$89.00	$35.92	40.36%	27
MEGA CENTERCH			PA Home Audio	1	1	100.00%	$89.00	$89.00	$35.92	40.36%	95
MEGA CENTERCH			PA Home Audio	1	1	100.00%	$88.88	$88.88	$35.80	40.28%	82
MEGA CENTERCH			PA Home Audio	1	1	100.00%	$86.01	$86.01	$32.93	38.29%	102
MEGA CENTERCH			PA Home Audio	1	0	0.00%	$0.00	$0.00	($0.00)	0.00%	289
MEGA CENTERCH			PA Home Audio	0	0	0.00%	$0.00	$0.00	($0.00)	0.00%	18
MEGA1200SBK-Z			PA Home Audio	0	1	0.00%	$360.99	$360.99	$213.52	59.15%	52
MEGA20BE			PA Home Audio	1	1	100.00%	$121.20	$121.20	$34.22	28.23%	88
MEGA20BE			PA Home Audio	0	1	0.00%	$121.20	$121.20	$34.22	28.23%	110
MEGA20BE			PA Home Audio	1	1	100.00%	$119.50	$119.50	$32.52	27.21%	115
MEGA20BE			PA Home Audio	1	1	100.00%	$112.50	$112.50	$25.52	22.68%	183
MEGA20BE			PA Home Audio	1	1	100.00%	$103.50	$103.50	$16.52	15.96%	161
MEGA20BE			PA Home Audio	1	1	100.00%	$103.38	$103.38	$16.40	15.86%	121
MEGA20BE			PA Home Audio	1	1	100.00%	$101.00	$101.00	$14.02	13.88%	90
MEGA20BE			PA Home Audio	0	1	0.00%	$94.00	$94.00	$7.02	7.47%	41
MEGA20BE			PA Home Audio	1	0	0.00%	$0.00	$0.00	($0.00)	0.00%	277
MEGA20BE			PA Home Audio	0	1	0.00%	$155.00	$155.00	$68.02	43.88%	7
MEGA20BE			PA Home Audio	1	0	0.00%	$0.00	$0.00	($0.00)	0.00%	27
MEGA40CHPKG			PA Home Audio	0	1	0.00%	$266.00	$266.00	$87.34	32.83%	62
MEGA40CHPKG			PA Home Audio	1	0	0.00%	$0.00	$0.00	($0.00)	0.00%	81
MEGA50BEPKG			PA Home Audio	0	1	0.00%	$456.00	$456.00	$264.30	57.96%	16
MEGA50BEPKG			PA Home Audio	0	0	0.00%	$0.00	$0.00	($0.00)	0.00%	31
AVR 120-Z			Polk Audio	0	1	0.00%	$159.28	$159.28	$5.28	3.31%	32

Performance Detail

Figure 44.12
ChannelAdvisor's product performance detail report.

MarketTrack is ChannelAdvisor's exclusive analytics module. It evaluates trends in auction traffic so you can refine your marketing strategy. And this information can be presented digitally or graphically.

When I listed all the steps in the auction-sales process, I stressed the importance of finding an automated solution for as many of the steps as possible. Selecting an auction management company is as much a personal choice— you have to be comfortable with the system and how it integrates into your business—as it is a business decision—you want to find a system that is economical and matches your specific business needs. Paying for features you don't need can waste as much money as not using a system that saves you money.

ChannelAdvisor Marketplace Advisor is optimized for very large sellers. If you aren't that large of a seller, the time and investment to set up such a system could be prohibitive for your particular needs. In this case you might want to opt for InkFrog, Vendio, or one of the other auction management services. But realize there is no way you can grow a large, profitable eBay business without investing in some degree of automation.

For more on automating your standard tasks, see Section 5.8 and Chapters 43 and 54.

chapter 45

Humanizing the Automation Process for Profits

When you ask people why they don't buy products online, they typically give one of two reasons:

- They don't have confidence in the safety of the transaction. In other words, they are afraid of fraud.
- They don't like the lack of human interaction.

The best way to address the fear of fraud issue is to execute every transaction in a professional manner. This starts with the look and feel of your auction and how you brand and carries through to showing the buyer he has a secure way to pay.

The branding and the look and feel of your auction represent the first interaction with your customer. Compare the look and feel of the auction for shoes by Grapevinehill in Figure 45.1 with the auction description in Figure 45.2.

The first auction uses a template with a standard color scheme, good grammar, and a professional-looking photograph. The second has the shoes lying up against a white towel, uses a minimum of detail, and issues a warning about not paying within 10 days. In addition, the shipping cost of $5.50 by parcel post is excessive.

Figure 45.1
Grapevinehill auction for a pair of shoes.

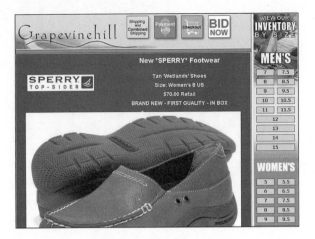

Figure 45.2
A nonbranded auction for a pair of shoes.

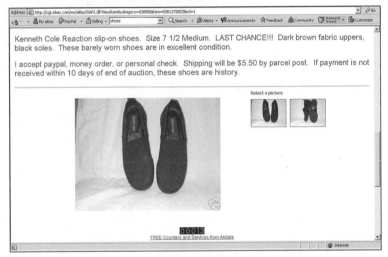

The best way to address concerns regarding lack of human interaction is to personalize your interactions with your customers as much as possible. The good news is that you can give your transactions a personal touch while still maintaining a high degree of automation.

45.1 Automated E-mails That Work

eBay users are a funny lot. The difference between eBay and other Internet e-commerce venues is the personal touch. Buyers want an e-mail from the seller with payment instructions or an e-mail from eBay with a payment link, even if an auction ends at 11 P.M. eBay and PayPal can generate such an e-mail if you turn those preferences on in your eBay and PayPal accounts. Sellers who use auction management software can generate those e-mails, but you have to log on and instruct the software to load and do its stuff. An online auction management system such as Vendio or ChannelAdvisor (and most others; see Chapter 44 and Appendix C), however, are always on and will generate your messages immediately.

PowerSeller Tip

Always include your phone number and e-mail address in all your auction correspondence. It makes you "real" and the buyer instantly gains more trust in you.

This brings us to a problem that plagues eBay sellers who use auction management services. That is the confusion between the eBay checkout messages and those generated by your system. When you set up an auction management system, you must be very careful to figure out how it integrates or even *if* it integrates with eBay and PayPal. Some systems require you to turn off the eBay/PayPal automation; others integrate seamlessly with it. If you don't do this right, it defeats the purpose of the automation, confuses the customer, and leaves you to respond to e-mails explaining what happened and giving further directions to the customer.

Most auction management services can be configured to generate e-mail messages either automatically or when an event occurs (such as the successful conclusion of an auction or a Buy It Now purchase), or you can generate a message with the manual click of a button when you perform a task such as shipping a package.

This is a typical sequence of events that occurs in the post-sale communications process with an auction management system:

1. When the auction ends, eBay sends a notice to the winner. If you have the checkout preference turned on, the e-mail will include a "Pay Now" link which starts the eBay Checkout process. If a checkout preference isn't selected, the message will instruct the buyer to contact the seller to arrange payment and shipping.

2. Your auction management system will generate a prewritten e-mail (you must first write the body of the e-mail and save it to your system) that contains a link for the buyer to click to access the checkout platform in your system.

3. Your buyer clicks the link that takes him to the checkout on your system's website. He gives either his PayPal or credit card information. For this process, let's assume he is paying through PayPal.

4. When the buyer pays, he is taken to a "thank you" page on the website thanking him for his payment and letting him know he will receive an e-mail when his item is shipped.

5. Later in the day or the next day you ship the item. Now you have to go into your post-sale manager control panel and click the item that sends an e-mail to the buyer saying the item has shipped. Most systems, such as those from Vendio and ChannelAdvisor, have a pop-up box where you can enter the package tracking number to include it in the e-mail.

6. The next step is to post feedback. This is no more than clicking another button on your control panel that will post prewritten positive feedback for the buyer. You can do this when you receive payment and shipping or wait a few days to make sure everything went okay. At this point you have a choice. You can just post the feedback and forget about it, or you can set the system to generate another e-mail telling the buyer you have posted positive feedback and asking him to respond if he is happy. Some systems now allow you to wait and see if a buyer posted positive feedback for you before you post feedback.

7. There is one additional step you can take, but not all systems are configured to do this with a button click. This is to send a follow-up message a few days after you ship the item asking if everything was received. It should say that if everything was not received, he should contact you, and if it was, that you have left positive feedback for him and a link he can click to leave feedback and Detailed Seller Ratings (DSRs) for you.

So let's take a look at the various post-sale steps and see how you can positively affect the outcome.

The first step is the winning bidder notice, but you cannot influence the content of eBay's winning bidder notice as it is sent by eBay to every auction winner. As stated above, however, unless your system integrates perfectly with eBay's system, you should turn off the preferences in eBay and PayPal so eBay's message simply tells the buyer to contact you. Usually within a few minutes your system will generate an e-mail giving the buyer payment instructions. This usually consists of a link the buyer clicks to access your payment gateway on your auction management system's website. The management service provides part of this e-mail, such as the link instructions, but you get to write the rest of it.

This is where the human touch comes in. It is very important that your form e-mail be warm and friendly yet provide very clear and precise directions.

I like to open my e-mail with a statement such as this:

> Congratulations and thank you for bidding on my auction for the *Best Handmade Steel Firepit Made in America*. (Note the words in italics are the auction title and are inserted automatically by your system.)
>
> My wife, Karen, and I have been selling on eBay for over nine years and are dedicated to making your transaction go smoothly in getting your item shipped to you in perfect condition and as fast as possible.
>
> We use the auction management company Vendio to help us track payment and shipping. This makes sure everything happens quickly and allows us to follow your order through the process until it arrives on your doorstep.
>
> Please click the link below. This will take you to our checkout page at Vendio.com where you can calculate shipping, purchase insurance, pay for your item, and track your order until it arrives.
>
> If you have any questions or concerns at any time or if there is something wrong with your purchase, please e-mail us immediately and give us a chance to fix the problem. We promise to do everything within our power to make your purchase a pleasant one. You can e-mail us by replying to this e-mail or using the contact form in the eBay auction you won or the Vendio checkout page. Please use whichever one you find convenient. You can also call us during the business day (Pacific time) at 360-555-5555.
>
> Best regards and good luck on eBay!
>
> Skip McGrath

Let's review why I designed this message the way I did. First, whenever a bidder wins something on eBay, he feels like a winner—I want to continue that good feeling by congratulating him. Then I personalize the message by letting bidders know there are two real people behind the auction. If you are a retailer or have employees helping you with fulfillment, you could mention their names. For example: *Bob and Susan in our customer service department will be following your order each step of the way. Please don't hesitate to contact them if you have any questions or should a problem arise.*

Next, I tell the customer *why* I want him to follow my payment gateway. I have received automated e-mails from sellers' systems with statements such as *Read these instructions very carefully, Click Here and follow the payment instructions exactly,* or sometimes just a note that says *You have agreed to purchase eBay item number 123456789. Please Click Here to make your payment.* These sound like they were generated by a computer. Why not take a little extra effort to humanize the process?

Finally, I reassure the buyer that I care about getting his item to him on time and in good condition and invite him to contact me if he has a question or experiences a problem (and give him multiple ways of getting hold of me).

Basically, anything you can do to personalize the process will give buyers confidence that they are dealing with real people who care about them. These sorts of friendly e-mails will also reduce problems and improve your feedback and DSR scores.

PowerSeller Tip

E-mail is a powerful tool, but many e-mails are sent in haste and without care. Here is a checklist for writing effective business e-mails to win and keep customers:

- *Make your e-mails concise.* E-mail messages are often more difficult to read than other printed matter, and long e-mails can quickly discourage recipients. Use an easy-to-read style. Paragraphs should be short, with blank lines between each paragraph. When making separate points, number them or use bullets so they can easily be identified.

- *Be direct.* Personal communications are driven by factors such as appearance and tone, but e-mail is based solely on written words. It can be very difficult to determine the sender's demeanor from the text of an e-mail, and subtleties of tone can easily be misunderstood.

  Make your points clearly and directly, and be obvious in your meanings. Remember this when reading e-mail as well—a tone that appears to be aggressive or derogatory might simply be the result of someone's haste in dashing off a reply. Reread messages to see if you might be misinterpreting the words.

- *Make the subject meaningful.* Use a subject heading that is meaningful to you and to the recipient. For example, if you're sending someone product information, write a subject field that has the actual name of the product instead of just product information. Similarly, the focus of the message thread might change over several e-mail responses. When that occurs, change the message field to reflect the shift—e.g., "Your 10/29 Order (Widget Information)" instead of "Re: Widget Information."

- *Keep threads relevant.* When responding to e-mails, use the Reply button instead of creating a new e-mail so the previous message is also included. Message threading helps ensure that your response can be read in context and the original sender won't have to remember the specifics of the original e-mail. But use threads carefully. Multiple threads can make the e-mail overly long and confuse the reader, especially when the original topic has shifted. Read over old threads and remove them when you feel they are no longer appropriate to the topic at hand.

- *Avoid unnecessary attachments.* Large attachments do more than just annoy recipients. They can bring down e-mail boxes (especially those that have an inbox size limitation) and slow down performance. In some cases, e-mail servers can delay delivery of large-size e-mails, causing urgent messages to arrive late.

- *Use a businesslike tone.* It is okay to warm up an e-mail with a personal greeting and a less-than-formal style, but stay away from online slang in business communications. Abbreviations such as LOL (laugh out loud) or BTW (by the way) are best avoided, as are smiley faces :-) and other emoticons.

- *Save high priority for the truly urgent.* Don't use your e-mail program's high-priority function indiscriminately. Flag e-mails this way only when you really need to alert the recipient that it requires immediate attention. Show similar caution with the words *urgent* or *important* when used in a message's subject field.

- *Proofread your e-mails.* Read over every e-mail you create before you send it out to be sure it conveys the message properly. Look at it through the eyes of the recipient to avoid any misunderstandings. Check spelling, grammar, and punctuation. Always use the spell-check function.

45.2 Integrating Automation with Customer Service

Designing your thank-you page is the next important area where you can positively influence the customer's experience. This page should have the same look and feel as your auctions or web store and should remind the buyers to contact you—don't forget to include contact information—if he has a problem. Some sellers post a phone number on their thank-you page. Our thank-you page even has a small photo of my wife and me. I have seen thank-you pages from large sellers that have a photo of their customer service people. Remember, you are trying to personalize and humanize what is essentially a totally electronic transaction.

The next message that goes out will be the notice that the buyer's item was shipped. Here again, you want to provide specific information, such as the date and method of shipment, a tracking number, and a reminder to contact you if there is a problem.

45.3 Automatic Feedback Posting

Finally we come to the issue of posting feedback. As noted in Chapter 29, the timing of posting feedback is controversial among eBay sellers. After you scale your business very large and your feedback numbers go into the thousands, it is virtually impossible to maintain a 100 percent positive feedback rating. Nevertheless, you want to do everything within your power to keep it as high as possible. When you are small and can maintain personal control over all aspects of the business, it is easier to take steps to maximize your feedback.

I believe in posting feedback immediately after the seller pays me. When the buyer sees I have done this, it helps give him confidence in me and the transaction. The downside to this is if the buyer receives the merchandise and is unhappy for some reason, he can still leave me negative feedback no matter what I do, even if I give him a full refund. Personally, I don't think this is a big problem. I have heard sellers complain about this, and when I checked their feedback, the comments were typically of a nature that showed poor customer service, such as comments about sloppy packaging, waiting too long to receive their item, gouging the buyer with excess shipping charges, or the seller not responding to e-mails. If you give good customer service, leaving feedback first isn't that risky.

If you have a large-scale business where you are shipping hundreds of items a week, then you might want to set your system not to leave feedback until a certain amount of time has elapsed—typically enough time for the shipment to arrive and the customer to make a complaint. Here is why that strategy is effective: if I receive something that is the wrong size or broken or not what I ordered, I will contact the seller and give her a chance to make it good. But some buyers are unreasonable or angry and go to the computer and fire off a negative comment, before they contact you. At that point the Tabasco sauce is out of the bottle, and there is no way to get it back in through that little tiny hole in the top.

In the old days, when sellers could leave negative feedback, they'd sometimes pause before doing this as they were afraid of a return negative being left by the buyer. But since May of 2008, eBay no longer permits sellers to leave neutral or negative feedback. So there really isn't much you can do when you run across one of these unreasonable people. Fortunately, transactions go smoothly the vast majority of the time. I set my system to send an automated e-mail five days after I ship an item. In this e-mail I ask the buyer if everything was received in good condition and if he is happy with his merchandise and the transaction, and I remind him that I have posted positive feedback for him. I tell him to contact me immediately if anything is wrong, and I ask him to post positive feedback for me. To make this easy, I provide the link from the eBay post feedback page. You can find this link in eBay's Feedback Forum in the Site Map.

For more on feedback, see Chapter 29.

For more on customer service, see Chapter 33.

chapter 46

A Picture Is Worth a Thousand Dollars

I overviewed auction photography in Chapter 5 from the standpoint of some of the equipment you will need. This chapter goes into much more detail on taking auction and website photographs. Taking photos for your auctions and websites and other selling venues is one challenge. Many sellers new to eBay are surprised to learn that an even larger challenge can be cataloging and managing their images. Fortunately, software is available to help you every step of the way. Let's look at the actual act of taking pictures first; later we will examine the various image management tools and resources.

46.1 Auction Photography

The ability to take good photos is an important skill for all eBay sellers. Photography is one of those skills that can take years to learn to do well, but fortunately, digital cameras, with their high level of automated features, have made this task much simpler.

46.1.1 Picking the Right Digital Camera

The first task in taking good auction photos is selecting a good digital camera with all the features you will need. Hundreds of digital cameras are on the market, and new models are coming out virtually every week. The trend today is toward higher and higher image quality, which is expressed in the number of pixels—or megapixels—a camera can resolve. In general, the more megapixels, the more expensive the camera. Fortunately you don't need extremely high resolution for your auction and website photography. In fact, large, high-resolution photos are undesirable because they take a long time to download when someone opens an auction.

eBay recommends that photo-file sizes be limited to 64 kilobytes (kb). Actually, you can go up to 75kb with no problem, and 64kb is the resolution you'll get on the e-mail setting on most digital cameras. So the first feature you need to look for when buying a camera is a low resolution or e-mail setting.

The e-mail/low resolution setting is okay for most digital photos if you are not going to crop them. When you do crop them, however, you lose detail. If you are selling a product where detail is important, then you want to shoot at a higher resolution, at least 1 megapixel, and crop or resize the photo using imaging software to lower the resolution to 64kb. Shooting at this higher resolution will preserve the detail when you crop or resize. Most cameras have three or four quality settings. The setting right above the e-mail, or lowest-quality setting, usually works well if you are going to crop a photo.

Look for these other features in a digital camera for eBay; I have included an explanation of the importance of each.

- **Tripod mount.** Almost all cameras have a standard tripod screw mount in the bottom. When taking auction photos, it is very important to use a tripod to avoid blurred images that occur when you handhold a camera.

- **Macro setting.** Macro is the photographic term for the ability to focus very close to an object. Typically the macro feature will allow you to focus as close as three or four inches from the subject. This is important when photographing small objects or getting up-close details—such as the original manufacturer's price tag—you might want to show on larger products.

- **White balance adjustment.** Basically, this is how you adjust a camera to account for different color temperatures of light. Almost all cameras have an automatic white balance, but you want to get one where you can manually select the white balance between daylight, fluorescent, and incandescent.

- **Manual focus.** The autofocus on digital cameras is often fooled, so you need to be able to manually focus on an object or a part of an object.

- **Exposure adjustment.** The light meter in a camera can be fooled by bright backgrounds. Because eBay sellers often shoot against a white background, especially when using a light tent, you need a camera that can adjust for this exposure.

- **Optical zoom.** Digital cameras come with both optical zoom and digital zoom. Digital zoom is very restrictive and difficult to work with. Make sure your camera has a basic optical zoom feature. You can tell if it does by pushing the zoom button and seeing if the lens actually moves in and out. If not, then the camera is using digital zoom.

- **Aperture priority setting.** The ability to select a small lens opening (aperture) enables you to achieve what is called "depth of field." This means those objects both close to you and far away are in focus.

Nikon, Sony, Panasonic, Fuji, Kodak, and Canon all make fairly low-cost cameras that fit these criteria. Digital camera models change so fast that I won't recommend any specific models. Just use the previous list as a checklist when you look at cameras for your eBay business. A feature that is nice to have but not really necessary is interchangeable lenses. Unfortunately, you must spend over $600 to get this feature. But if you want to go this way, then look at a Nikon D series or Canon Digital Rebel series—there are others but these are the most popular.

46.1.2 Digital Photo Tips

Rather than try to give you a complete course on digital photography, I've organized the most important information as a series of tips. If you want to read more about digital photography, several books on the market span the gamut from beginner to advanced. If you'd like a good basic book aimed at the auction photographer, I offer a free eBook titled *Online Auction Photography* on my website when you subscribe to our free monthly newsletter. You can subscribe at www.skipmcgrath.com/newsletters. For now, these tips should get you started:

- **Use a tripod.** Unless you are shooting outdoors or using a flash, digital cameras tend to use a very slow shutter speed. With a slow shutter speed, typically under $1/125$ of a second, most people cannot hold a camera steady enough to prevent blur. Putting your camera on a good tripod will enable you to shoot all the way down to $1/25$ of a second with good results. Make sure your tripod is sturdy and has an adjustable head that will rotate the camera both horizontally and vertically. A sturdy tripod can cost as much as $100, but I've found that most large photo stores often have good—even professional quality—tripods secondhand for as little as $20 to $30.

- **Focus carefully and correctly.** I see out-of-focus pictures on eBay every day. This is usually attributed to one of two things: autofocus malfunction or lack of depth of field. Most digital cameras project a laser or infrared beam onto the object being photographed and measure the reflection to determine the focus. This beam can often be fooled by large objects that allow the beam to spread out or something reflective on the object.

  The other issue is depth of field or the focal distance the camera will cover. The aperture or lens opening on a camera adjusts to allow more or less light into the camera. When the lens opening is large, the camera has a very narrow range of focus. When the opening is small, the focal length is longer.

  The aperture (lens opening) can be set manually on many digital cameras. Lens openings are marketed as a series of numbers that range from 3.5 to 16. The higher the number, the more depth of field the camera has. This is critical when shooting up close with the macro function as the macro function also limits the depth of field (for technical reasons I won't get into here). If I am shooting an object close up, I typically use a camera aperture setting of at least 8. Most cameras today have a setting called Aperture Priority. This is where you set the aperture, and the camera will set the corresponding shutter speed automatically. The advantage of setting your camera to Aperture Priority is the autofocus will not be fooled as easily if you use it.

- **Use soft lighting.** Sunlight or direct light from a bulb or a flash will create hot spots, harsh shadows, and reflections in your photos. If you are shooting outside, you want to shoot in bright shade or on a cloudy day. If you have a north-facing window, this can often produce very nice diffused light. If you are using lights, you can either purchase white plastic light covers to diffuse the light or use a light tent such as the EZcube (see Section 5.2).

  The EZcube, probably the most widely used system by eBay sellers, makes taking great photos easy. You simply place an object inside the light tent, shine the lights on the outside, and get very nice diffused light. This eliminates the glare and reflection from shiny objects. Also, it has a seamless background, and you can place colored paper or cloth in the background to get different effects.

- **Avoid clutter.** Try to photograph only the object you are shooting. Placing an object on a table with other things in the background will detract from your subject. If you are shooting a computer, for example, remove everything from the desk it's on, and hide the wires or any other distracting objects. If you are shooting a car, drive it to a park where you can shoot it with lawn and trees in the background instead of your garage or driveway.

  If you are shooting apparel, invest in a dress form or mannequin. Then place the mannequin against a wall draped with cloth to contrast the color and diffuse any shadows.

- **Avoid underexposure.** If you are shooting objects on a white or bright background or shooting outside in bright light, your camera's automatic light meter can often be fooled by trying to adjust to the surrounding bright light rather than the object. Most good digital cameras have over- and under-exposure compensation adjustment. If you are shooting on a white background such as in an EZcube, try setting your camera's exposure setting to +1, which will increase the amount of light on the subject. One way you can tell you are underexposing is if a white background appears gray in the photo. If this happens or if your objects are just too dark, try adjusting the exposure compensation until the white looks white.

- **Use the correct white balance.** Different types of light have different wavelengths. Without getting into a discussion of physics, this means you have to set the camera for the type of light you are using. If your camera is set on **Daylight** and you shoot with an ordinary household light bulb, your photos will appear yellow. If you shoot with a fluorescent light, your photos will appear blue-grey. You can purchase daylight bulbs at most camera stores—these are ordinary light bulbs that have the same wavelength as daylight. These are also available as compact fluorescent bulbs, which last much longer and don't get as hot as incandescent bulbs (very useful if you're shining the light through a diffuser).

- **Get close.** Getting close to your subject will produce a better photo. It is easier to focus accurately when you are close, and the image will show more of the object without the distracting clutter. If you cannot get close enough, then crop the photo so the object takes up at least 75 percent of the image area.

Study these tips and practice. With very little effort you can master these basics and end up with attractive auction photos.

PowerSeller Tip

If you sell clothes, buy a mannequin. If you sell Barbie Dolls, buy bubblegum pink cloth for a backdrop or just lay it next to the dolls. If you sell wooden ducks, buy some greenery at a local craft store and use it in your photo layout.

A cloudy day is your best friend. Take your best items outside and photograph them. You will love the results.

46.2 Image Management

Storing, managing, and inserting images into your auctions are critical functions, but you can waste a lot of time on these tasks if you don't have a good system in place. There are basically three ways to host and manage your photos: you can use eBay picture services, host them on your auction-management service, or host them on your web space. Let's look at each in turn.

46.2.1 The eBay Image Service

eBay offers two ways to manage your images. You can insert images from your computer's hard drive into your auctions one at a time. The first photo is free, and each additional photo costs 15¢, so if you used four photos in an auction, it would cost you 45¢ for every auction, whether the item sold or not. This is obviously too expensive if you are running hundreds of auctions a week. eBay does offer a discount package for sellers who use more photos in their auction called Picture Pack. Up to six photos costs 75 cents, or up to 12 costs $1. This service includes supersize (which enables the buyer to see a larger version of the picture).

eBay also offers a subscription hosting program based on the file size (number of photos) you host called Picture Manager. The cost is $9.95 for 50MB, $14.95 for 250MB, and $24.95 for 1GB. Discounts are available for Premium and Anchor Store subscribers. Free editing software is included in the price, but that's really not all that much of a bonus because there are dozens of free shareware editing programs you can download from www.tucows.com or www.shareware.com.

As for photo management, eBay offers very little. Basically you have to manage your images in folders on your hard drive. If you use eBay's Picture Manager you can organize them in a folder in My eBay. If you use an automated system such as Vendio, they offer sophisticated image management tools.

The only reason I can think of to use eBay's picture services is if you are using eBay Selling Manager Pro as your auction management tool and you want a service that easily integrates with it. The service is just not powerful and automated enough for the busy PowerSeller.

46.2.2 Auction Management Image Services

Almost all the popular auction management services, such as ChannelAdvisor, Vendio, and InkFrog, include image storage as part of their service (see Chapter 44). Most services include image storage as part of their basic fee, while others charge separately for this. Not all the services, however, include a management function. I've found that the savings I get from hosting my images on Vendio versus paying eBay picture services fees easily pays for my monthly subscription to Vendio's services.

In Vendio, for example, I can create my inventory items by category, such as men's apparel, women's apparel, and children's apparel. Then I can create image folders with the same category names and associate the image folders with the product folders. This way, when I'm creating an auction, I don't have to hunt through hundreds of images for nonrelated merchandise to find the image to attach to a specific product auction. This is a major timesaving feature and one that you should look for when selecting an auction management service.

The images are stored on the website of the auction management service. When you create an auction, you simply select the photo you want to use. The service inserts the URL of the particular image into your auction. When the auction launches, eBay locates the images and displays them in your auction. Your selected gallery image URL is fed constantly to eBay's website so it is always visible when members are searching, browsing, or perusing auctions with gallery photos (the little thumbnails that show up next to a listing). Note: You should always identify a gallery photo. It's free and buyers expect to see it. If you don't have one, you won't get nearly as many click-throughs to your auction.

Most of the auction management services do not offer image editing on the site, so you do have to crop, rotate, and resize your images before uploading them. You can do this with a program such as Photoshop CS or PhotoShop Elements; however, that is probably overkill as you will rarely use most of the advanced features.

Most digital cameras come with software you can use to upload, name, catalog, and edit your photos. The software from Kodak, Nikon, and Canon is excellent. Sony, which makes really excellent cameras, has the most limited photo editing software—it is designed more for making albums and slide shows for relatives and friends. If you own a Macintosh, the iPhoto program that comes pre-installed on every Mac is excellent and very easy to use. You can crop, rotate, resize, adjust contrast and brightness, and reduce red eye. Best of all, you can create product files by category and sort them before you start uploading, which saves a lot of time. Microsoft Office Picture Manager (which comes pre-loaded on many PCs) offers the same features as iPhoto, but you have to use Windows Photo Gallery to categorize the images.

If you go to shareware.com or Tucows.com and type **photo editing** into the search bar, you'll get a list of dozens of free shareware programs. The programs all have reviews and ratings by users. I first find the program with the features I want and then check the user reviews to select the one I want to try. I recently tried a program called PhotoMeister Professional that did almost everything iPhoto does. It is free to download for one month; after that you must pay a one-time fee of $39.95 if you want to keep it.

46.2.3 Storing Images on Your Own Website

Many eBay users store images on their own website if they have one. The obvious advantage of this is that because you already have a website, it doesn't cost anything more to store your images. Of course, you will have to be versed in the use of File Transfer Protocol (FTP) programs to upload your images, and you will have to configure a way to locate and manage all your images. Everytime you want to launch an auction, you have to navigate to your website, open the image, and copy the URL to paste into your auction description or auction management system or software. Frankly, this is a real pain, and I think the cost savings are outweighed by the time involved. The only advantage I can see of hosting your own photos is the availability of some specialized programs such as JPEG Magic from PlatinumPowerSeller.com, which can compress large photos for fast loading. These programs enable you to load lots of photos and very large photos very quickly. So if you are selling products, such as automobiles, that require the use of a lot of images, this might be something you want to explore.

46.2.4 Third-Party Image Hosting Services

The final option is to use a third-party image hosting service. I won't bother to name the various services here because they are too numerous. If you type **image hosting** into the Google or Yahoo! search bar, you find dozens of listings. Some of the services are free, but these sites are slow, are not very secure, and are peppered with advertising banners. Most of the paid services cost as little as $5 a month, which will get you enough storage to host over 1,000 images, and many of the sites include management tools such as folders, editing software, and the ability to e-mail photos right from the site.

Having reviewed all the possibilities, I strongly favor hosting your images on an auction management service. The various services, such as Channel Advisor, InkFrog, and Vendio, are inexpensive and offer a degree of automation and convenience that you simply cannot duplicate with offline software or the eBay picture services tools.

For more on auction photography, see Sections 5.4 and 5.5.

part 6

Beyond eBay

In the early days of eBay, an individual could make a good living by just selling on eBay. But over the past few years, eBay has had several fee increases, and greater competition has driven margins lower. Today almost every professional eBay seller uses multi-channel selling. This means that he sells not only on eBay but also on other venues such as Yahoo! shops, Amazon auctions and Amazon e-shops, Overstock.com, and most importantly from his own e-commerce websites. Indeed, the act of using eBay to capture a customer and then converting that customer off of eBay to one's own website has been raised to a high art. Combine this with learning the art of the upsell and cross-sell, and you have a winning combination for profits.

This part shows you how to expand your business into other platforms (channels) and then how to permanently capture customers as your own that you can sell to over and over again.

chapter 47

The eBay Store

An eBay Store is basically your personal website on eBay where you can sell products to eBay members at a fixed price. You can list your merchandise in an eBay Store for 30 days or on a permanent basis (called Good 'Til Cancelled, which renews every 30 days). Let's consider the advantages and features of using an eBay Store.

47.1 Why Set Up an eBay Store?

The first reason for setting up an eBay store is bigger profits. According to eBay's research, Store sellers see on average a 25 percent incremental increase in sales the first three months after opening their Store. As a Store seller, you'll save on listings fees—just 3¢ to 10¢ for each 30-day period.

An eBay Store can also spare you having to constantly re-list your items. Instead, you can stock your eBay Store with Store Inventory listings that last as long as you like with the Good 'Til Cancelled option.

A professional-looking Store gives you credibility as an online retailer—and makes shopping easier for your buyers. eBay includes a Business Resource Center where you can access tools, including templates for professional-looking business cards, to extend your Store brand. Such features help you build your brand on eBay and generate repeat business with your customers.

An eBay Store is essentially a website with its own URL, so you can drive buyers, both on and off eBay, directly to your Store. You control the look and feel of your Store. You can even optimize your web address so it shows up in search engine results.

All your Auction and Fixed Price listings also appear in your eBay Store as well as in their regular category, and eBay doesn't charge you anything extra. When a buyer clicks **View Seller's Other Items,** it will show both your Store Inventory listings and your auction listings.

47.2 eBay Store Fees and Promotional Options

eBay Stores have three kinds of fees:

- Monthly subscription fee
- Insertion and Final Value fees
- Listing upgrade fees

Let's take a look at each.

47.2.1 Subscription Fees

eBay charges all sellers a monthly subscription for their eBay Store. There are three subscription levels for eBay Stores, which have progressively more advanced features and benefits as the price increases:

- Basic—$15.95 month
- Premium—$49.95 month
- Anchor—$299.95 month

With a Basic Store subscription, you can …

- Showcase all your listings (Auction, Fixed Price, and Store Inventory) in a custom storefront that you design.
- Drive buyers to your custom URL.
- List an item in your Store for just 3¢ or 10¢ for each 30 days.
- Use the Cross-Promotion tool to cross sell your inventory on all your *Item, Bid Confirm*, and *Purchase Confirmation* pages.
- Receive free monthly Seller Reports on the performance of all your eBay sales.
- Receive free telephone support during business hours.

The Basic Store is okay for most small- to medium-size sellers, but lacks some of the more sophisticated features that many PowerSellers find useful.

With a Premium Store subscription, you get all the Basic Store benefits plus additional exposure, including …

- Priority inclusion in the Shop eBay Stores section on Search and Browse pages.
- Featured placement on the eBay Stores hub page (stores.ebay.com).
- Prime positioning in the top level Stores directory pages where you have items listed.
- Free monthly Seller Reports that include eBay marketplace data to benchmark your Store's performance against overall eBay performance.
- Marketplace data and sophisticated traffic stats reporting so you can see where your traffic is coming from.

At $49.95 per month, a Premium Store might seem expensive, but you also get free eBay Marketplace Research, a value of $4.95 per month, which lowers the cost a bit. eBay also promotes the Premium Stores in search, so you tend to get more visibility and this usually translates to greater sales.

If you sell products with high keyword potential—items frequently searched— you should seriously consider signing on to the Premium Store level.

With an Anchor Store subscription, you get all the Basic and Premium Store benefits, plus …

- One million impressions per month for your Store throughout eBay.com, including the eBay home page.
- Showcase placement of your logo within the eBay Stores hub page.
- Premium inclusion in the Shop eBay Stores section on the Search and Browse pages.

In general, only sellers who list more than 1,000 items opt for an Anchor Store because of the high monthly cost.

When you open a Store for the first time, eBay gives you the first 30 days of your Store subscription free. After that, they charge the normal monthly subscription fee.

47.2.2 Insertion Fees

Store Inventory listings are fixed-price listings that appear only within your eBay Store and Store Search pages, not in eBay's main search unless the buyer checks the "include Store inventory" box. The Insertion fee for these listings covers any quantity of items with a single listing, whether you list 1, 100, or 1,000 of the same item. The fees vary based on the price of the item, not on quantity.

Here are the insertion fees for eBay Stores:

eBay Store Insertion Fees

Item Price	Insertion Fee
$1.00-$24.99	3¢
$25.00-$199.99	5¢
$200.00 +	10¢

These fees are paid every 30 days on a Good 'Til Cancelled listing. The minimum price for Store Inventory Listings is $1.

47.2.3 Final Value Fees

In 2008, eBay raised their Final Value Fees for Store listings by about 10 percent. This caused a stir at the time, and a lot of small or marginal sellers closed their eBay Stores. However, savvy sellers realized the higher Final Value fees are far outweighed by the savings on listing fees. Also, eBay encourages sellers to promote their Store URLs outside of eBay and even assists them with this task. On any sale that originates in an eBay Store from outside of eBay (provided the right referral code is included in the link), eBay credits the seller 75 percent of the Final Value fee. Here is a breakdown of Final Value Fees for eBay Stores:

eBay Store Final Value Fees

Price	Final Value Fee
$1–$25.00	12% of the closing value.
$25.01–$100.00	12% of the initial $25 ($3), plus 8% of the remaining closing value balance.

$100.01–$1,000	12% of the initial $25 ($3), plus 8% of the initial $25.01–$100 ($6), plus 4% of the remaining closing value balance.
Over $1,000	12% of the initial $25 ($3), plus 8% of the initial $25.01–$100 ($6), plus 4% of the initial $100.01–$1,000 ($36), plus 2% of the remaining closing value balance.

Promoting your eBay Store through e-mail, printed materials, and on other websites can really boost your sales, plus you can combine it with the eBay Affiliate program and receive extra compensation on top of the Store Referral Credit.

47.2.4 Listing Upgrade Fees

eBay offers all the same listing upgrade options for Stores that they offer for auctions (see Chapter 36), but they cost less than in the auction format. eBay optional listing upgrade fees for your Store Inventory listings are as follows:

Feature	Fee
Gallery Plus	$0.35
Item Subtitle	$0.02
Listing Designer	$0.10
Scheduled Listing	$0.10
Bold	$1
Border	$3
Highlight	$5

Featured Plus Fee

Item Price	Fee
$1.00–$24.99	$9.95
$25.00–$199.99	$14.95
$200.00–$499.99	$19.95
$500.00 +	$24.95

eBay Store sellers receive monthly sales reports that outline their activity by category (monthly gross sales, conversion rates, number of buyers, and so on). This is valuable information for analyzing and understanding your business and controlling your fees. Additionally, if you have a Premium or Anchor Store, you'll also receive overall eBay marketplace data to benchmark your sales with other eBay sellers.

47.3 Promoting Your eBay Store

eBay provides a dedicated Search box within your eBay Store, so buyers can search through all your items to find exactly what they want.

In addition, eBay helps bring buyers to your Store by showing your Store's icon on all your listing pages and placing a link to the *Shop eBay Stores* box on all search and category pages on eBay.com and the Store's merchandising links on the eBay.com home page. eBay also submits Store listings to popular search engines and shopping sites such as Froogle and Shopping.com.

Setting up and branding your eBay Store is fairly easy and only takes a few minutes to set up a basic Store. Here are some ways you can control your Store's look and feel:

- Customize your Store's home page with open HTML.
- Select your color scheme for your header and left navigation bar.
- Insert your own custom graphics in your header.
- Choose the default option of how you want your items displayed.
- Create up to 20 custom categories within your Store.
- Provide additional information to your buyers, including descriptions about your Store, yourself, and your Store's policies.

Custom graphics are an important branding feature. If you don't have any experience creating online graphics, I recommend you find one of the many people on eBay who do this. Simply type **eBay Store graphics** into the eBay search engine, and you'll come up with dozens of listings for people who offer this service. Most sellers charge between $25 and $50 for a basic design, but you'll pay more for really sophisticated graphics.

Cross promotion is one of the most important features of an eBay Store. eBay Store sellers get cross-promotion placements on all of their Item, Bid, Confirm, and Purchase Confirmation pages. As a Store seller, you control exactly what items are cross-promoted to your buyers while they are viewing or bidding on any of your items. You can do this by building your own default rules that stipulate which items are displayed, based on your Store's custom categories. For example, if you are selling a camera, you might choose to display other cameras you are selling when bidders are on your Item page. After they bid, you might want to display complementary items, such as batteries or tripods, on the Bid confirm and Purchase confirmation pages. You also can override the default rules and manually select specific items. This feature enables you to cross-promote items in any listing format—stores, auctions, or fixed-price items.

With an eBay Store, cross-promoting items is very easy. The interface for manually selecting specific items is visually intuitive and fairly easy to use. You can learn how to use the cross-promote features from a tutorial located on the Manage Your Store page.

eBay automatically submits your Store URL to several search engines. Because of this, it's important to use keywords and search terms in your Store description and in each item description to increase the chances of hits from search engines.

If you have a large store with more than 50 listings of similar items that would show up in one keyword search, you might want to look into Google AdWords or Yahoo! Search Marketing (see Chapter 38). These pay-per-click search engines can drive traffic to your eBay auctions and Store.

Pay-per-click advertising can be particularly effective if you are selling a niche product. If you are selling DVDs or digital cameras, the cost of keyword bidding would be prohibitive. However, if you sell gardening gloves or pet beds, you can buy keywords very cheaply.

Store Referral Credit

When you set up the off-eBay links to your eBay Store, make sure to include the Store Referral Codes. If you sell a store inventory item through one of these links, eBay will credit you 75 percent of the Final Value fee you paid. However, you must use the correct code on the link, or you'll receive nothing.

The codes are specific to the page you send the buyer to:

- **Your eBay Store Main Page:** add **?refid=store** to your eBay store link. For example, my store referral link would look like this: www.stores.eBay. com/The-Auction-Sellers-Resource**?refid=store**.

- **Store Inventory Item:** Add **?refid=store** to the end of the link to that item: www.cgi.ebay.com/ws/eBayISAPI.dll?ViewItem&rd=1&item= 190172905080&ssPageName=STRK:MESE:IT&ih=009**?refid=store**.

- **Your About Me Page:** Add **&refid=store** to the end of your About Me Page link: www.cgi3.eBay.com/ws/eBayISAPI.dll?ViewUserPage&userid= mcgrrrrr**&refid=store**.

- **Category Page Within Your eBay Store:** Add **?refid=store** to the end of the link to that category page www.stores.eBay.com/ The-Auction-Sellers-Resource_EZ-Cube-Photo-Studio_ W0QQcolZ2QQdirZQ2d1QQfsubZ5QQftidZ2QQtZkm?refid=store.

For more information about the Store Referral Credit, go to the eBay help files and enter *Store Referral Credit* in the search box.

It is worth taking the time to add the correct codes because the fee credit adds up. For example, if you sell an item for $75, the Final Value fee would be $7. If the sale came from outside eBay using your referral code, you'd get $5.25 of that back and end up only paying $1.75.

47.4 Driving Sales from Your Auctions to Your eBay Store

Many of the really large PowerSellers on eBay generate most of their sales from their eBay Stores. The trick to doing this is to launch auctions that generate lots of interest and traffic and then convince everyone who looks at your auction to look at, and buy from, your eBay Store.

eBay uses two standard links to let bidders know you have an eBay Store. One is a little Store icon after your User ID. The other is a link in the Meet the Seller box in all your auctions that says **Visit seller's Store** and displays your eBay Store name. The problem with these two links is that very few bidders actually click them. The trick is to invite them to do so.

In my discussion of ChannelAdvisor in Chapter 46, I told you about an auction for Grapevinehill, an eBay shoe seller. Their auction sites have a size chart you can click on that will take you to a category of their eBay Store where you can look at all the listings for men's or women's shoes by a certain size. That is a good example of attracting traffic to your eBay Store.

This is probably a good time to discuss the eBay Store Categories. All subscription levels allow 300 customizable categories, which is very helpful if you are selling different types of products and want to direct your traffic to the correct Store. For instance, if you are selling men's, women's, and children's apparel, you could have a separate category for each. Similarly, if you sell aftermarket car accessories, you could have separate categories for all the popular car models, such as Nissan, Toyota, Honda, Mazda, and so on.

If you sell a niche product such as bird feeders and you also have other bird-related products, you might want to launch an auction for bird feeders and promote it with some of eBay's special features, such as Featured Plus, Home Page Featured, Bold, and Highlight. The idea is to run a few auctions that generate a lot of traffic. Be sure to run a paragraph that describes all the other bird-related items you sell in your store right under your product description. The paragraph should contain both an invitation and a clickable link to a specific category in your eBay Store. Here is an example:

> **If you love songbirds, please visit my eBay Store,** *<a href=www.your Store link goes here>* **BirdsForAll</a> where you will find a large selection of bird feeders, bird baths, bird houses, and books on birds and birding.**

The HTML code *<a href=XXX>* is the clickable link to your eBay Store. Only the words in bold will actually be shown. The word *BirdsForAll* will appear in blue and underlined, indicating to buyers that they can click the link to visit your Store.

Another way to attract visitors to your eBay Store is to offer free shipping. I often do this by putting a statement in my auctions such as:

FREE SHIPPING FOR MY EBAY STORE CUSTOMERS

You do not have to wait for the auction to end to buy this Garmin GPS unit. They are available in my eBay Store for immediate shipment. If you buy this item now from my eBay Store, I will ship it for FREE anywhere in the United States. If you are in Canada or overseas, I will give you a $5 credit toward the shipping cost. I also have several other Garmin models in my Store in different price ranges. *Click Here* to buy now or to see all the items in my Store.

After you get the bidders to your Store, make it as easy as possible for them to buy from you. First of all, direct them to the appropriate category. Also, make sure that the search box that enables them to search your Store is prominently featured. If you are selling apparel, you could invite them to search by size. If you sell different brands of cameras, you could place a message next to your search box inviting them to search by brand. Anything you can do to get the potential bidder to a product he is looking for as quickly as possible will produce the best results.

Another option is eBay Pro Stores. Unlike eBay Stores, eBay Pro Stores are actual e-commerce–enabled websites, which we cover in Chapter 49.

For more on eBay promotional options, see Chapter 36.

For more on making money with an eBay Store, see Chapter 49 and Sections 2.2 and 51.1.

chapter 48

Auction Management Service Web Stores

If you use an auction management company (see Chapter 44), you have to decide whether or not to use that service's integrated web store. Many large sellers prefer to direct traffic to their own websites rather than use their auction management service's store, while some sellers use both.

The biggest advantage of using an integrated store is the seamless connectivity to your checkout process. Most of the auction management companies' systems are designed so a customer is forced to see your other products as part of the checkout process. This will usually result in more upsold merchandise than if you direct them to your website. When directed to your website, buyers must click a link to view your products, whereas when they check out from your store, they will automatically see photos and titles of your web store products.

Some systems display everything in your stores during checkout while others allow you to target certain categories of product to display. If you plan to use an auction management service's web store, you should determine in advance whether they allow you to target which products are displayed.

Another advantage of having a web store through an auction management service is that you don't need to design, manage, and maintain your own website. The web store is integrated into your management system—you launch an item to your store much like you would launch an auction. The best services, including Vendio and ChannelAdvisor, integrate their store with their inventory system. This is very helpful because you can create an item in inventory and establish the quantity on hand. Your inventory record is debited in such a way that shows how many units you actually have and how many are at auction or in your store. When an item sells, your inventory is permanently debited.

For example, if you had a total of 10 widgets and you put one in your store, one on eBay at auction, one in an eBay store, and one on Amazon, your inventory would show as 10/4. That represents 10 units on hand, of which 4 are up for sale. After 2 of the units sell, the inventory record would change to 8/2, meaning you now have 8 units total on hand, of which 2 are up for sale.

Some systems allow you to automatically replace an item when it sells. This way you aren't showing lots of supply to a customer. No matter which venue he looks at—eBay, web store, or Amazon—he'd only see one item for sale in each of those venues. But you can direct the system to automatically launch a replacement item after someone makes a purchase.

When you are making the decision to sell on your website or use an auction management service web store, also consider cost and automation. If you already have an e-commerce–enabled website, it takes very little incremental cost to add items to it. But if the choice is to use a web store or set up a website, this is an entirely different cost model. The other factor to consider is automation. The advantage of using your service's web store is the high level of integration and automation. You might find you can automate the sales process from your website, but this could be a costly and time-consuming task to set up and maintain.

Of course, many sellers sell from a website as well as from their auction service's web store—as I do. For me the website is an additional sales channel where I can capture sales from people who do not visit eBay or Amazon. The challenge that most sellers face here is tracking and controlling their inventory between the two sites. I keep all my inventory on Vendio, so when I make a sale from the website, I simply go into Vendio and adjust the inventory manually. Unfortunately, I haven't found a way to automate this. However, if you are only selling dozens of items from your website each day, updating the inventory manually will take just a few minutes. If you are selling really high volumes, then you might have to go to a master inventory system that combines your website, eBay, and web store sales. In this event you would more than likely have an employee doing this for you.

For more on web stores, see Chapter 47.

chapter 49

The eBay Seller and the Merchant Website

In Chapter 48 I mentioned that many eBay sellers also sell from their own e-commerce–enabled website. The term *e-commerce–enabled* simply means you have a method of accepting orders and payment directly on your website, so people do not have to call in and place an order.

The requirements for an e-commerce website are pretty simple. You need a way to create web pages and upload product photos and descriptions, a shopping cart for buyers to select their items and quantities, and a payment gateway to accept payment. There are two basic types of payment gateways: PayPal or a merchant credit card account. The advantage of PayPal is that it enables you to accept immediate payment from the over 149 million PayPal members, plus PayPal provides sellers with a free shopping cart.

The advantage of a merchant credit card account is that you get more information on the client, such as his phone number and other data fields you can specify during the checkout process, which is helpful for building a customer database.

49.1 The Advantages of Selling from Your Own Website

eBay is only one venue for Internet-based marketing. It happens to be the largest venue, but if you are only selling on eBay, you are still only accessing part of the online market. I already talked about multiple-channel selling through sites like Yahoo!Stores, Amazon, Overstock.com, and others. Think of your own website as just one more channel. If properly branded, promoted, and marketed, it can be your most profitable channel.

The most significant advantage of selling from your own website is that you have no listing or selling fees. For this reason, most large eBay sellers use the eBay venue to capture customers and then market to them in the future directly from their websites.

There are fees associated with a website, but they tend to be very low compared with the fees you pay eBay or one of the other auction venues. The primary fee most website sellers pay is a hosting charge. There are two ways to host a website. You can lease or buy your own server, in which case you will need the technical knowledge to set up, run, and maintain that server. I don't recommend going this route because the time you spend maintaining your server you could better spend on marketing and sales. The other way is to rent server space from one of the hundreds of companies that provide this service. Here is a partial list of some of the more well-known companies:

www.register.com

www.godaddy.com

www.hosting.com

www.hostway.com

www.networksolutions.com

www.hostmysite.com

www.hostingleader.com

Each of these hosting companies offers a variety of service plans. You can elect to use a virtual server, where you share server capacity with other users, or have your own dedicated server. The dedicated server gives you total control and un-limited features, but this option is usually overkill for most simple e-commerce sites.

Here are some of the features you get with a typical hosting company on a virtual server. I selected GoDaddy as an example, but most of the listed server companies offer the same or similar services. The package described here from GoDaddy is $21.99 per month.

- Web Features

  50GB disc space

  2000GB bandwidth

  PayPal eCommerce integrated

  FrontPage extensions

  SSL secure server

  128-bit encryption

  99.9 percent uptime guarantee

- E-mail Features

  10 mailboxes

  Unlimited aliases

  Unlimited autoresponders

- Advanced Features

  ASP, PHP, Perl, Python

  Server Side Includes (SSI)

  Access to raw log files

  FTP account access

  Password-protected directories

- Hardware and Network

  Redundant Tier 1 backbone

  UPS battery backup

- Site Design

  Website Tonight Site Builder to build, edit, and maintain your website

- Marketing and Analysis

  Submit and optimize your site to improve its ranking on search engines

  Traffic Blazer website promoter

  Google AdWords $50 one-time free credit

  Web traffic stats

- Communications

  Online chat and E-mail Newsletters

  24/7 toll-free phone support

- Security

  Virus protection

  Spam filter

The other major costs associated with hosting a website are the design and the maintenance. All the companies I listed earlier offer web-based templates or a program called SiteBuilder, which allows people without web-design knowledge or programming skills to build a simple website. They also support the popular Microsoft program FrontPage, which is an easy-to-learn website design and content tool. A new free website design and uploading tool that has become very popular is PageBreeze at www.pagebreeze.com.

However, if you don't have much experience in web design and want a professional-looking site, I strongly encourage you to hire a professional to design a good, basic e-commerce website. Expect to pay between $500 and $1,000—even more if you want a lot of bells and whistles.

When shopping around for website designers, always ask for a portfolio of existing e-commerce websites they've done that are up and running, as well as references. I would not hire a designer who does not have at least five or ten websites up and running that he designed and can use as a portfolio.

After your site is designed and launched, you'll need to either hire a webmaster to do uploads and maintenance or do it yourself, using a program such as Microsoft FrontPage or Macromedia's Dreamweaver.

Template-based systems provide a wide variety of color and design choices, and most of the best ones have an HTML editor so you don't even have to learn HTML. You can personalize the site by uploading your logo so it doesn't really look like a template site. If you want to go the template route, I recommend www.register.com—their templates are attractive and the site is very intuitive and easy to use.

Register.com also has predesigned forms you can incorporate into your site, including order form, thank-you, and contact-us forms. You can also set up autoresponders to let browsers know you received their questions and that someone will get back to them within a specified time.

I have recently built two websites using the template services from PowerSellerBuilder at www.powersellerbuilder.com. Both of these were easy to implement and the resulting websites are very search engine friendly.

PowerSellerBuilder offers a large selection of design templates and hundreds of color combination choices. You can also upload your logo and any images you have to personalize and brand your site. PowerSellerBuilder gives excellent e-mail and telephone support and their website builder is optimized for search engines.

49.2 eBay Pro Stores

In January 2006 eBay launched their Pro Stores website service. Unlike a regular eBay Store, Pro Stores is hosted on eBay's servers, but you use your own unique URL. A Pro Store is just like a Register.com or PowerSellerBuilder template-based website, but it has the additional advantage of integrating your inventory with the inventory you have listed on eBay and in your eBay store. Also, you can launch auctions directly from your Pro Store onto eBay. The drawback to the Pro Store is that you cannot integrate or launch listings to competing services such as Overstock.com, Amazon, or Yahoo! Shops.

49.3 Free Websites: You Get What You Pay For

There is no such thing as a free lunch, and there is no such thing as free web space. I've seen dozens of advertisements for free web hosting, and all of them are running some type of scam or another. One type of site offers you free web space but bombards your site with garish advertising. The advertising is often targeted to keywords listed on your site, so in many cases visitors to your site will see ads from your competitors.

Another common scheme is an advertisement for free web space where you list your products in a predesigned shopping mall. However, when you click to sign up, you find there is a $199 setup fee and a 5 to 10 percent transaction fee on each sale you make. That is higher than eBay, but without the 85 million eBay members.

None of the so-called free website companies are really set up for you to run your business—they are mostly designed for you to run their business. They are simply not an option for the serious e-commerce entrepreneur.

49.4 Website Promotion: How to Get the Eyeballs

The term *getting the eyeballs* came out of the Internet stock boom of 1999 to 2000 when Internet companies with absolutely no profits were seeing total valuations greater than General Electric based solely on the number of visitors (traffic) their sites generated. The theory was that if a website got enough eyeballs it would eventually become successful. This theory was partially correct: you do need to get the eyeballs to sell your product. If no one sees it, no one will have an opportunity to buy. The problem was the business model. Most of the companies failed because they were burning cash to generate hits by purchasing expensive banner and television advertising. Unfortunately, they weren't converting the hits into sales.

There is a lesson here for every website entrepreneur. It is one thing to get the hits, but you also have to convert the visitor into a buyer. This goes back to your basic business proposition. Do you have a marketable product? Is it priced competitively—so you can get sales—but high enough so you can make a profit? Does your site look like a safe and trustworthy place to do business? I'll show you lots of ways to market your website and get the eyeballs, but you'll need to fill in the numbers on the other side of the equation to create a successful business formula.

49.4.1 Market to Your Customer Base

Website marketing is completely different from promoting your auctions and listings on eBay and somewhat more difficult, yet it can be more rewarding. On eBay you are selling in a city of 85 million people who are looking for you and your products. It is a safe, comfortable environment compared with the World Wide Web, which is still somewhat like the wild, wild West.

The easiest person to sell to is an existing customer, if, that is, he was pleased with his first transaction. Creating a customer database and marketing to that list by offering discounts is the cheapest and most effective form of direct marketing. To drive home my point, here's an example. A while back I received one of those coupon packets in the mail with discounts from local businesses in my town. Almost every restaurant in town had a coupon in the packet. Some of them were from my favorite restaurants, and some were from eateries I had never tried. The first thing I did was look for the coupons from my favorite places. After all, I knew the food and the service were good, and I could get a discount from a restaurant I would go to anyway.

I then took a minute to look through the other coupons and picked out a couple of places I might give a try. I wasn't that hot on them, but what the heck, buy-one-and-get-one-free is an okay deal.

In the end, both business owners won. I came back to my favorite places, spent money, and was pleased that I got the discount. Of the two new places I tried, I was really surprised that one of them was actually pretty good, and I will probably go there again. But I have been back to my two favorite places twice since then and still haven't tried the new place again, although I probably will some time. What is my point? Well, as I said at the beginning of this discussion, it is easier to sell to an existing satisfied customer than to capture a new customer.

You might think: *Why would I want to offer an existing customer a discount if he is already happy and will come back anyway?* Fair question. Now let me ask you: *How would I have felt if none of my favorite restaurants offered a discount, but these others ones were? Would I be inclined to try more of the ones I hadn't been to? What if I really liked one of the new restaurants and decided to become a regular there?* I think you get my point. Yes, it is easier to market to your existing customer base, but you must do it frequently if you are going to keep your customers coming back. Promotions and giveaways are not just to attract new customers; you need to use them to keep and build your existing customer base as well.

So how do you get your existing customers to visit your website? Through e-mail promotions and giveaways, that's how. Basically, you're going to do the same thing the restaurants in my town did: give something away or give a discount to keep your customers loyal and coming back.

The first thing you need to do is build a database of your existing customers and include what they bought so you know what to promote. If you sell various categories of products, then you will need several databases or, better yet, a master database that you can sort by product category.

The next task is to construct an offer. The expensive fire pit grills that I sell are heavy steel and really built to last, so it is unlikely I will sell another grill to the same person, but he just might buy one as a gift or refer me to a friend. Therefore, I want to stay in touch with these customers. One way to do that is to keep selling them things. When I sell the fire pit, during the checkout I offer the buyer a $29 plastic cover to keep his fire pit dry when it rains or snows. After a couple of weeks have gone by, I e-mail him with a link to my website where he can purchase packages of aromatic smoking woods such as hickory, alder, apple, and mesquite. I only get $9.95 for a single pack of wood, which is not a very big sale, so I offer him an electronic coupon where he gets 25 percent off if he buys three bags. Although I make less on each bag, the total sale is higher.

A month later I might e-mail him with a special offer of barbeque tools or an apron or some grilling rubs. Then at least twice a year I offer a discount on the fire pits themselves—again using an electronic promotional code—and I tell him that I know he doesn't really need another fire pit because his is so good, but if he will send the e-mail to a friend who buys, I will send him a free bag of aromatic smoking wood of his choice. You would not believe how well this works. I sent that offer to a list of 200 customers and sold 21 fire pits at $229 each within three days of doing the mailing. That is more than a 10 percent return from one small e-mailing.

49.4.2 Promoting Your Website

After you have secured your existing customer base, it's time to start finding additional customers on the web. eBay stats indicate that over 75 percent of customers find an item by searching. The rest use the browse feature. But on the web it is difficult to browse, so almost everyone finds what he is looking for by performing a keyword search on one of the major search engines such as Google, Yahoo!, AOL, or Alta Vista. This brings up a list of websites with relevant content.

The best thing you can do is to create a description at the top of every page on your website that accurately describes what is offered or contained on that page. Then put in the keywords that also reflect the products sold on that page, as well as other keywords you think people might type in if they were looking for your products.

The <title> section of your source code—in other words, what search engines see as the title of your page—should contain keywords that people search. If you sell designer ladies' shoes and the name of your site is Mission Hill Shoes Online, you don't want to make that the title of your page. Instead, make Mission Hill Shoes Online an image so the search engine doesn't see it. And then, under the image, write a line of text that customers see when they first come to the page. This is your title. For instance, you might write a keyword-rich title such as the following.

Discounts on famous designer and name brand ladies' shoes. Near wholesale prices on heels, pumps, boots, and loafers from Ferragamo, Anne Klein, Kenneth Cole, Marc Jacobs, and Michael Kors.

You would also type this statement into the <title> section of your source code. When a potential buyer searches for shoes, she will find a match to your site if she types in any of the following keywords:

wholesale shoes

discount shoes

famous designer shoes

Anne Klein

Ferragamo

Kenneth Cole

Marc Jacobs

Michael Kors

pumps

discount pumps

wholesale pumps

Now go to Google and Yahoo! and the other search engines, and type your keywords in to see what comes up. If one of your competitors comes in higher up the page than you, use the pull-down menu at the top of the page and select **view source.** This will display the source code for this site. Now you can see what description and keywords he is using that is resulting in the higher ranking. Use this information to refine your keywords and descriptions so you can achieve a higher ranking.

The next thing to do is submit your site to the search engines to make sure it gets seen. This is an awful lot of work, so you might want to pay someone to do it. My hosting company, GoDaddy.com, offers a submission service called Traffic Blazer for $29.99–$69.99 a year. This might sound like a lot of money for a submission service, but I saw my traffic increase dramatically after signing up for the service. Because each 1 percent increase in traffic delivers almost $1,000 in additional sales per year, the Traffic Blazer fee was a bargain.

You might also consider purchasing pay-per-click advertising on Google AdWords, Yahoo! Search Marketing, and Miva.com. See Chapter 38 for a thorough discussion of keyword advertising.

The final way to promote your website is to set up an affiliate program where you pay people who refer business to you. An affiliate puts a link to your website on his website, or he promotes your website with a link in his newsletter or e-mails. The link has a discreet code that identifies the affiliate, and it places a cookie in the computer of anyone who visits your site from that affiliate link. So even if someone visits your site and does not buy the first time, the cookie will generate an affiliate code every time he visits your site to make sure the affiliate gets credit for the sale if the person ever does buy.

The two largest affiliate systems are Commission Junction at www.cj.com and MyAp from www.Kowabunga.com. These services track your affiliate sales and give you reports at the end of the month so you can pay your affiliate commissions. It might seem expensive to pay a commission on every sale to an affiliate, but you don't pay for the traffic unless you make a sale.

You can also make money from your website as an affiliate for someone else. Several programs are available that place banners on your site for related, yet noncompetitive, products. When people visit your site and click one of those banners, they will be taken to the website you are affiliated with. If they buy something, you will earn a commission. Google AdWords also has a program where they will place AdWords on your site indexed to your site's content. When people click these, you will earn part of the cost-per-click for that ad. I have Google AdWords and several banners on my website for various affiliate programs and have earned as much as $3,000 per month in affiliate commissions from these links.

Only a small percentage of people actually purchase something when they visit your site, and selling ad space is a way to capture income from visitors even if they don't make a purchase.

49.5 Measuring Success

As we've seen, promoting your website requires some investment. The cost for pay-per-click advertising can be substantial. Therefore, it is important to track your visitors and sales and understand your return on any investment you make. Google AdWords and Yahoo! Search Marketing make this easy. They both have a built-in tracking tool so you can determine how many clicks turn into sales.

For more on websites, see Section 2.3.

For more on measuring success, see Chapter 55.

chapter 50

Electronic Payment Systems

We all like to make sales, but we can't spend our profits unless we get paid. Payment systems are not free—all of them charge a fee. So the one you select will have an impact on your profits. Selecting the best system is also important for two other reasons: security and customer convenience.

eBay requires "paperless payments." The only options currently allowed are PayPal, ProPay, or a direct credit or debit card payment using the seller's merchant credit card account. I recommend you offer all three. eBay is integrating all of these options into eBay Checkout and is phasing out Third-Party Checkout.

50.1 PayPal

PayPal is the largest payment service used by eBay sellers. With over 64 million customers worldwide, it has a large base of satisfied users.

PayPal was started by Peter Thiel in 1999. Peter, a Stanford alumnus, recruited many of his classmates to become the founding members and early employees of PayPal. At the time PayPal started, getting paid on eBay was somewhat problematic. Most people paid by check. I can even remember opening envelopes stuffed with cash for some of my early sales. PayPal was a very novel concept. In a world of finance controlled by banks, Peter spied a niche that wasn't being worked. People needed a method to send other people cash. When PayPal started, they hadn't really focused on eBay. Peter was thinking about a system where people could send money to their kids at school, pay for utilities, and pay for services electronically.

Within a few months of starting, however, some eBayers discovered PayPal, and PayPal discovered eBay.

In order to build his customer base, Peter introduced an affiliate program in which PayPal paid eBay sellers $10 for each customer they referred. I was one of the earliest users of PayPal. All of my auctions contained a link to PayPal with my affiliate code, and every e-mail I sent at the end of an auction invited the buyer to sign up and pay me with PayPal. I remember the excitement of receiving my first few PayPal payments. I would open my e-mail, and there would be e-mails with a subject line: *XYZ has sent you $37.00 with PayPal.* I would open the e-mail, and it would have all the details of the transaction. Then I could log into my PayPal account and see the money deposited to my account.

In the first three months after PayPal came onto eBay, I referred over 500 new customers who signed up, earning me just over $5,000 in the process. Shortly thereafter, PayPal lowered the commission to $5. As so many people on eBay were recommending PayPal, my sign-ups dropped off, but I still saw commission checks from PayPal of around $200 to $300 a month for the next year.

In the early days, the PayPal accounts were free. There was no transaction fee. PayPal made its money from interest on the float, the money in people's accounts waiting to be moved or withdrawn.

Eventually PayPal created the business account for professional users. They still offer a free account for occasional users, but if you do more than just a few transactions per month, you will need to get a professional account.

PayPal does not charge any fees to send money or to transfer money from your PayPal account into your bank account. The fee to receive money starts at 2.9 percent + 30¢ per transaction and goes down to as low as 1.9 percent + 30¢ per transaction for very large users (over $100,000 per month to qualify). Most professional eBay sellers fall into the $10,000 to $100,000 per month rate of 2.2 percent + 30¢.

eBay eventually bought PayPal and started expanding its business. PayPal soon developed the ability to accept credit cards on a website from someone who did not have a PayPal account—a move that brought it into direct competition with merchant credit cards. Soon PayPal developed WebAccept buttons, an easy way to create HTML code you could paste into your website or even in an e-mail. A buyer could simply click the button to pay. Next came a virtual shopping cart, a way to accept complex payments for multiple quantities of merchandise without the need to set up shopping cart software and a secure gateway on your own website. Other innovations, such as the PayPal money market account, soon followed. You could now earn market rate interest on your daily balance. PayPal next came out with a debit card that you can use to pay bills and pay your eBay fees. Every time you use the card, you get a 1.5 percent cash-back credit.

Now let's take a look at some of these services and how you can use them to make money with your auctions, web stores, and websites.

50.1.1 Web Accept Service

When you sell something on eBay, a link to PayPal is automatically inserted either into your end-of-auction e-mail or your auction-management service's checkout page.

PowerSeller Tip

If you use an auction management service, it is important to go into both your eBay preferences and your PayPal account setup and turn off the automatic payment request feature. If you don't, your customer will get two e-mails—one from eBay and another one from your auction management service—requesting payment. This can confuse new buyers, some of whom will pay twice, resulting in headaches and time lost refunding payments.

When you sell something on a website, you will need to create a payment button for the item. This is very easy. You simply log into your PayPal account and go to the **Merchant Services** tab. Select the **Buy Now Button** and you will be presented with a page similar to the one in Figure 50.1. Fill in the information about the product you're selling, including the shipping charge and sales tax rate if you wish. Click the **Create Button Now** button and PayPal will create a snippet of HTML code that you copy and paste onto your web page or into an e-mail. The entire process takes less than one minute.

When a buyer comes to your website and hits the **Buy Now** button, PayPal will determine if he has a PayPal account or not. If he does, the buyer will be presented with an invoice amount and all he has to do is enter his login password and hit **Send.** Bingo, the payment is made. If the buyer does not have a PayPal account, a screen will appear where the buyer types in their name, address, and credit card information. When the transaction is complete, PayPal immediately generates an e-mail to you with the payment information, the buyer's name and shipping address, and even a space for the buyer to write you a short note.

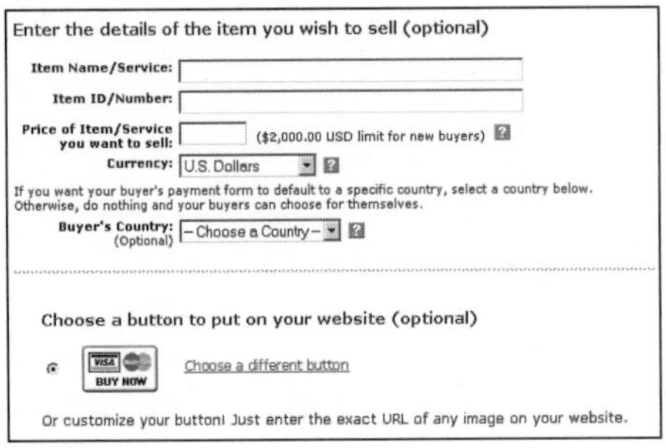

Figure 50.1
Example of a PayPal "Buy Now Button."

The really neat thing is that I can then copy/paste the shipping address from my PayPal e-mail into my Endicia Program, thereby creating a shipping label and an insurance record.

The Buy Now button is perfect for those situations where a buyer is likely to only purchase one item. But if you have the type of website where your buyers can perform multiple purchases, then you'll need to step up to a shopping cart.

PowerSeller Tip

I have my e-mail program set to recognize e-mail from PayPal with a sound notice. You guessed it! Whenever I receive an e-mail from PayPal, my computer goes *cha-ching*.

50.1.2 PayPal Shopping Cart

The PayPal shopping cart works much like the Buy Now button except that when you create a button and a buyer clicks it, she will be taken to a page on PayPal where all her items are displayed, and she will not check out until she is finished shopping.

You simply fill in the same information as you would on the **Buy Now** button, but you also get to pick a **View Cart** button that will appear on every page of the product portion of your website. You can use one of PayPal's standard buttons like the one shown in Figure 50.3, or you can create a custom button. PayPal has recently introduced Website Payments Pro for a flat $20 a month fee. This service includes the PayPal shopping cart on an unlimited number of websites and a virtual terminal to process credit cards.

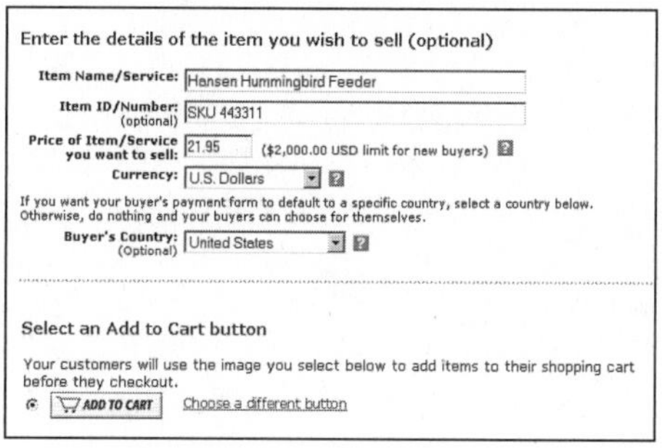

Figure 50.2
An example of PayPal's shopping cart button.

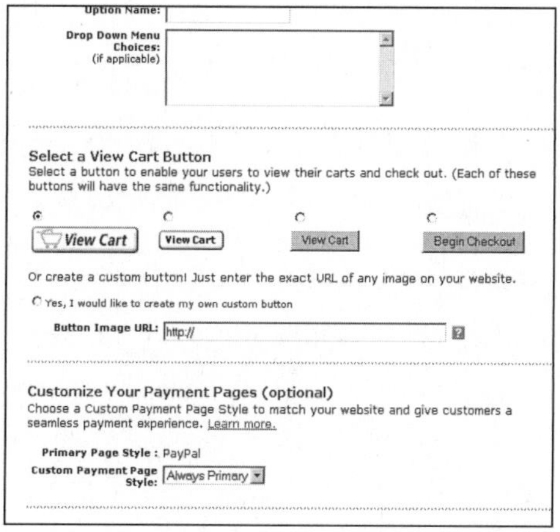

Figure 50.3
PayPal's shopping cart checkout page.

The main advantage of this system is that the shopping cart resides on PayPal's secure site, not on your website. Therefore, you do not have to purchase shopping cart software and worry about installing and uploading it to your website.

Whether you use the Buy Now button or the PayPal shopping cart, PayPal is also an excellent solution for international transactions. The system enables buyers to send and sellers to receive transactions in several major currencies, including the following:

Canadian Dollar	U.S. Dollar
Euro	Yen
Pound Sterling	Australian Dollar

Swiss Franc	Hong Kong Dollar
Singapore Dollar	Mexican Peso

Sellers can accept payments directly in their own currency. Furthermore, there are no currency exchange costs when you withdraw funds to your local bank account.

PayPal also offers fraud protection for both buyers and sellers. PayPal's Seller Protection Policy covers sellers for the full amount of any transaction that is fraudulent. In order to be eligible for 100 percent protection, PayPal sellers must adhere to the following requirements:

- Have a Verified Business or Premier account
- Refer to Transaction Details to confirm SPP eligibility
- Ship within seven calendar days of the payment
- Retain proof that the item was delivered to the required address
- Require a signature receipt for valuable items (over $250)
- Ship tangible goods (does not cover services or electronically delivered products)
- Accept your entire payment in a single transaction (partial payments not covered)
- Do not charge buyers an additional fee if they use PayPal
- Have your primary address (registered in PayPal) in the United States

Verifying your bank account is one of the most important steps both to ensure you are covered by the fraud protection policy and also to prove to potential buyers that you are a verified seller. Buyers are also covered by the PayPal Buyer Protection Policy as long as they purchase from a verified seller. If they see your account is not verified during the checkout process, a lot of buyers will cancel the transaction.

When you verify your account, it means you have added a bank account and confirmed the validity of that account through PayPal's simple "Verification" process. This makes your transaction safer and significantly reduces fraud risk. This is how PayPal verifies your bank account.

On your account page is a tab that says **Verify Your Account.** When you click that tab, it will take you to a page where you enter your bank account name and the routing and account numbers. After you send this information to PayPal, they will make two small deposits to your bank account. You either go online or call your bank to verify the date and the amount of the deposits. (You are not going to make much money from this. The deposits are usually under 15¢ each.) Now you go back to your PayPal account and fill out the verification form with the information; your account is now verified.

The other important issue on the fraud protection list is to retain proof of shipment. This is pretty much automatic with UPS or FedEx. But if you use the Post Office, then you must secure delivery confirmation. This costs 65¢ to 75¢ if you purchase it at the window but is free when you buy postage online either from the USPS or through a service such as Endicia or PayPal.

The final issue relates to chargebacks. A chargeback is when a customer complains he didn't get his goods or the goods were not what he ordered or just about any other complaint you can think of. Unlike the merchant credit card companies, PayPal actually helps you fight chargebacks. For example, they will suspend a payment for 45 days, and during that time they will require the customer to prove his allegation. If the customer cannot prove his complaint, PayPal will release the funds to you.

50.2 Third-Party Shopping Carts

If you use a merchant credit card account and PayPal or just a merchant credit card account, you will need a proprietary shopping cart. Dozens of companies design and sell shopping-cart software. If you have a merchant credit card account from some of the larger banks, they will provide software (for a fee). Here is a list of some of the more popular systems with their website addresses:

Storefront	www.storefront.net
Volusion	www.volusion.com
Shop Factory	www.shopfactory.com
X-Cart	www.x-cart.com
CartGenie	www.JStreetTech.com
1ShoppingCart	www.1shoppingcart.com
B-Net Online	www.bnetsoftware.com

Unless you are web-savvy, you'll need a web master to install and debug the software for you. Most of the systems listed above have been around a while and are pretty good. You will pay between $150 and $900 depending on the features and options you need. Some of the better ones come with inventory integration, reporting and analysis features, lead tracking, and marketing tools such as rebates, electronic coupons, and even automatically generated marketing-oriented e-mails.

50.3 Merchant Credit Card Accounts

Personally, I don't see the need for a separate merchant credit card account, because PayPal can fulfill all the functions, including taking credit cards from non-PayPal members. The only exception to this is if you need to be able to take orders over the phone or if you sell at shows or have a brick-and-mortar store where customers walk in. In these cases, you might want to use your merchant account to process all transactions and only use PayPal for auction transactions.

Accepting credit cards over the Internet requires putting a number of separate pieces together. You will have to deal with these various services:

- A bank that issues you a merchant credit card account
- A transaction clearinghouse designated by your bank
- Hardware or software gateway to the clearinghouse
- Secure processing software (This is usually integrated with your shopping cart, but not always. Sometimes you have to purchase this separately.)

If you find all of this overwhelming, there are brokers who will do all of this for you. They usually earn a fee from the bank or nonbank processor.

Almost any bank offers merchant credit card accounts and can provide the credit card processing machines. However, not all banks like to take web-based transactions, and some that do charge extra fees. So this is an area where it pays to shop around.

A lot of different fees are involved in merchant credit card processing. Here is an example of what one of the largest online providers charges:

Application fee	$195
Annual fee	$99
Payment gateway setup fee	$495
Sales receipts	$50 per 1,000
Amex setup fee	$75

Fraud screening	$0.50–$1.00 per transaction
Discount rate	2.85 percent
Transaction fee	50¢ per transaction
Monthly statement fee	$25 per month
Gateway fee	$35 per month
Card swipe machine rental	$18 per month

As you can see, the costs are not insignificant. (All of a sudden, PayPal with its 2.2 percent + 30¢ transaction fees looks pretty good.) You can beat these rates by shopping around, but your success at getting lower rates will depend on three factors: the product you are selling, your personal or business credit rating, and the monthly volume of sales. If you are selling more than $10,000 per month, you can really negotiate. Another factor is overseas sales. Selling overseas increases the risk of fraud for the credit card companies. If you do very many overseas transactions, your rates could be higher than those I listed.

Both banks and nonbank private companies offer merchant credit card accounts, although there is a bank in the background processing the transactions—you just might not know who they are. Banks tend to have the better rates, but non-bank private firms tend to understand website markets and marketing better and often offer more services, which tend to offset their higher fees.

These banks and nonbank private firms are active in website marketing services:

SecureNetShop.com	www.securenetshop.com
Wells Fargo Bank	www.wellsfargo.com
Citibank	www.citibank.com
VeriSign	www.verisign.com
Charge.com	www.charge.com
M Bank	www.mbankcard.com
BankOne	www.bankone.com
North American Bankcard	www.northamericanbankcard.com

The first company on the list, SecureNetShop.com, has a very sophisticated suite of services. They have a reasonable setup fee and frequently run promotions where they waive the setup fee for medium- to large-size accounts.

VeriSign and Charge.com are probably the largest and most well-known providers of web-based credit card services.

For more on PayPal and credit card fees, see Chapter 35.

chapter 51

The Art of the Upsell

Upselling and cross-selling are essentially the same thing, and the terms are used interchangeably by eBay sellers. It involves adding another product to an existing sale. If you go into Radio Shack and purchase an electronic item, the clerk always asks if you would like some extra batteries with your purchase. That is a basic upsell. While you are standing at the counter waiting for the clerk to process your credit card, you'll notice about a dozen or more gadgets and small items sitting in displays on or near the counter—this is just another form of upselling, impulse-buy items. The hope is that you'll pick one of them up and add it to your order.

There is no salesperson or counter to make the upsell when customers are checking out of your auction or website, so you need to find another way to ask the customer to add products to his order.

I like to do the basic upsell in my end-of-auction e-mail or on the order confirmation page of my website. When I am shopping for inventory items to sell on eBay, I always think of the upsell. If I buy an item, I ask myself what I can offer as an upsell item.

If I am selling clothing, I look for a fashion accessory. If I am selling shoes, I offer cleaning kits, shoelaces, or shoe trees. Cameras and electronic items offer all kinds of upsell opportunities in the form of accessories. If you sell books, you can offer books on related subjects or even bookmarks or book lights. You just need to use your imagination.

51.1 Upselling on eBay

After you know what you want to sell and have identified the upsell items, you need to develop a process to offer the item. Many eBay sellers do this in the e-mail they send out at the conclusion of the auction. This is easiest if you are only selling one category of product. If you sell multiple categories of product, you'll have to create separate e-mail messages to send your customers, and will have to send them manually rather than having them automatically sent for you.

The best way to drive upsells is to offer to combine the shipping, a shipping discount, or even free shipping if the customer buys a second item. Some sellers even go so far as to discount the second item. One large seller of blue jeans offers a 20 percent discount plus free shipping if a buyer purchases a second pair. This might seem like a large impact on your margin, but remember the concept of inventory turn. If you can increase your inventory turn rate by 20 percent, this will have a greater long-term impact on your profits than the 20 percent margin you lose on the incremental sale.

PowerSeller Tip

Despite what eBay tries to tell you, you *can* sell directly to your existing customers. In fact, if you don't, you are shooting yourself in the foot! When you send out marketing e-mails to your existing customers, you will see an immediate increase in sales, without having to pay eBay fees. Sweet!

—from Mike Enos, an eBay guru and Platinum PowerSeller. www.platinumpowerseller.com

---

There are three ways to work the eBay upsell. You can make an offer and have the buyer purchase the second item from your eBay store; you can direct the buyer to your web store; or you can make a direct offer in your e-mail or with a link to your website. This third option is the most profitable, as you are not paying eBay or web store fees, but it may have the lowest sell-through rate because the customer has to navigate to a separate site to make the purchase.

51.2 Upselling off of eBay

eBay insists that all sales that originate on eBay take place through eBay. However, it does agree that after you complete an auction and obtain a customer, you have the right to market to that customer directly. It is best if an upsell happens immediately, but it doesn't have to. Many sellers process their eBay auctions and ship the items and then work to entice customers to their website on the theory that a satisfied customer will buy from them again.

This type of upsell is usually done by e-mailing the buyer a few days after he receives his merchandise and inviting him to visit your website, where he can enter a promotional code (electronic coupon) to get a discount. If you are going to do this, you can use PayPal's promo code system. If you use a shopping cart and merchant credit card account, you have to make sure your software can handle electronic coupons.

Now that you have accomplished the initial upsell, you want to keep reselling to the customer. This is where newsletters and announcements come in. Some sellers create informational newsletters that customers can subscribe to. This works best if you are selling a product that is newsworthy or has tips and tricks associated with it. For example, if you are selling digital cameras, you can write articles about photo tips or new accessories and send out a quarterly newsletter. This would be harder to do with a product such as jeans or shoes. With those types of products, instead of a newsletter you might send out a monthly or quarterly electronic flyer with product specials.

51.3 How to Make an Extra $10 on Every eBay Sale

Almost everyone buys information. A very easy and clever technique to upsell for pure profit is to create an electronically delivered information product that would be of interest to someone buying your product. Depending on your product, you might have to use some imagination, but that's not all that hard to do.

If you sell hummingbird feeders, you could offer a booklet as a PDF file titled *How to Attract Hummingbirds to Your Yard*. If you sell digital cameras, you could write a short piece such as *20 Tips for Taking Great Digital Photos*. If you sell aftermarket car parts or accessories, you could put together a little manual on detailing cars. The possibilities are endless.

It is fairly easy to get the information to create a report or booklet. Plenty of information is available at your public library. Now you don't want to plagiarize something, but you can read up on the subject and then just write a 15- to 20-page report. If you really don't have any writing skills, you can hire an English major from your local college. You could probably get a project like this done for around $100. But if you consider you can sell hundreds of the same information product for $9.95, $100 is not much of an investment.

Another source of information is the Government Printing Office at bookstore. gpo.gov. Most (but not all) publications written and printed by the federal government have public domain copyrights that allow you to repackage and resell the information. There are thousands of such books on virtually any subject.

If you sell anything historical, such as antiques, collectibles, autographs, and items where historical information would be valuable to someone, you can reprint anything printed before 1923. Some of these old books are very hard to find. There are sellers who might pay a lot of money for an old book that is in high demand, scan it, and resell electronic copies to people who cannot find or cannot afford the high price of an original copy.

You could deliver it as a document, but most information sellers prefer PDF documents as they are less easy to copy.

Market your information product as an upsell in your end-of-auction e-mail. When you send out your invoice or shipping confirmation, simply put a note in your e-mail describing what you are offering, or place a link to your website where someone can read a sales letter about the product and order it online.

Creating an information product is also an opportunity to sell something to people who view your auctions but don't buy from you. If your report is perceived as valuable, you can mention it in your auction and provide a link to your eBay store where buyers can purchase it. Note, new eBay rules require you to print or burn the file to a disk and mail it, as eBay no longer allows electronically delivered information products.

For more on upselling, see Sections 44.1 and 44.2.

chapter 52

Driving Bidders from eBay to Your Website

In the early days of eBay, I made a lot of money by running auctions for products I also had for sale on my website. My auctions would get dozens of hits a day, but very few bids because I had a link to my website inviting bidders to visit me and buy the item directly. It didn't take long for eBay to realize that thousands of sellers were doing this, thereby subverting the sale on eBay and the collection of eBay fees. In 2002 eBay stopped the practice of allowing sellers to link from their auction to any website that sold the product. Over time, however, eBay modified and expanded the regulations. It is still possible to drive business from eBay to your website, but now you have to jump through some hoops to do so.

52.1 About Me Page Trick

One of the easiest ways to promote your website on eBay is to entice members to visit your About Me page. Here is eBay's rule about linking from your About Me page.

> The eBay About Me page may be used to describe the seller's business and may contain web addresses or links to the seller's individual website. It may not specifically promote off-eBay sales or sales of items prohibited on eBay, nor may it contain links to commercial websites where goods from multiple sellers are aggregated by a common search engine.

Notice the words "It may not specifically promote off-eBay sales …" You can have a link on your About Me page that describes your business, but you cannot put words to the effect that a person should "click here to buy your item now." eBay often changes its links policy—the policy that allows you to place links on eBay pages to outside websites. In general they try to discourage this. Despite what I say here, it is a good idea to check the current links policy before implementing any of these suggestions. Go to the bottom of any eBay page, and click on Policies. Then just type the word *links* into the search box that comes up, and you can read the current links policy.

A couple of years ago I wrote a document titled *99 Tips for Buying & Selling on eBay*. I have a note in my auction that says: "As a free gift for looking at my auction, please visit my <u>About Me Page</u> where you can download a copy of *99 Tips for Buying & Selling on eBay*." After a person visits the About Me page, he sees a description of my business and what I sell on my website. There is also a link to download the *99 Tips* document. That link takes the buyer to the download page on my website. When he goes there, he can see the navigation links to my other products. I know this works because I track visitors with my stats program. eBay is always one of my top ten source sites. When I went on vacation last year and took all my auctions down, I noticed that sales from my website dropped almost 20 percent.

The key to getting buyers to click your About Me page is to use the HTML *<a href=>* command to make the words *About Me page* a clickable link, or you can do this with the HTML editor in the eBay Sell Your Item form or the listing form in your auction management system.

52.2 The Image Trick

eBay's policy also allows you to link to a page with more images of the product you are selling. You can compose a sentence with a clickable link to your website that says something like **Click Here to view more images of this wonderful quilt** (or whatever product you are selling). Again, make the words *Click Here* an active hyperlink to the page. When the buyer gets to the page, you should have more images of the product, but you could have links on that page to your actual product pages. You have to be subtle. If you use any phrases such as *click here to purchase* or *click here to see our product catalog*, then eBay may end your listing.

52.3 The More Information Trick

You can do the same thing with information that you can do with photos. I sell Native American Eskimo Art when I can get it. Once I was selling some very expensive (over $2,000) Baleen Baskets. I had about a dozen of the baskets and did not want to put them all up on eBay at the same time, so I listed an auction for one and had a link in my auction that said **Click Here to read the full story about Baleen Basket making.** After the reader clicked the link, she was taken to my website where I had a page that talked about the history of Baleen Baskets. At the bottom of that page, I had a link to my product catalog that showed photos and prices of all the baskets. I managed to sell two baskets on eBay and five from my website over a six-week period.

For more on upselling and cross-selling, see Chapter 51.

chapter 53

Building on Your Brand

Your brand is the sum of everything you do. It encompasses the look and feel of your auctions, your store, and your website. It includes your feedback rating; your logo; your shipping, payment, and return policies; and the description of your goods. It even includes how you communicate with your customers. A brand gives people confidence, helps you capture a permanent customer, builds a relationship, and creates references and word-of-mouth sales.

53.1 Your Brand on eBay

The first thing a potential customer sees is your auction description. At the very least you should always use a listing designer template from eBay or one of the auction management services. Even better is to work with a web design specialist to create your own branded template like the one in Figure 53.1.

You can carry the design over to your eBay About Me page, your eBay Store, your web store, and your website. If you started with a website before you went onto eBay, then you should already have a design you can carry over.

When you scroll further down Apparel Specialty's listing, you also notice they have provided a size chart (see Figure 53.2) and well-defined shipping terms, payment terms, and a return policy (see Figure 53.3).

Figure 53.1
Auction Template showing a specialty in selling apparel.

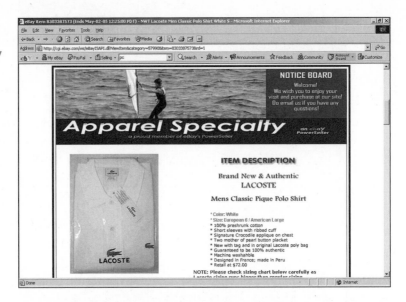

Figure 53.2
Size chart.

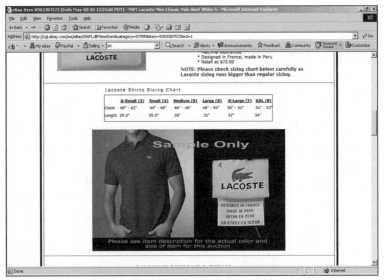

All this helps build your brand and lend credibility to your auctions.

Write your terms and conditions in clear, friendly language. Too many sellers make the mistake of writing their terms in legalese, or even worse, writing them as strict directions, such as the following.

You must e-mail us for permission to return an item, and the returns must be received within four days of our giving permission.

Wow—that sounds like my high school English teacher giving a homework assignment. Why not say instead:

If you have a problem, please contact us in advance if you wish to return an item so we can provide the correct shipping information. If you return your item quickly, there is a better chance we will have a replacement in stock.

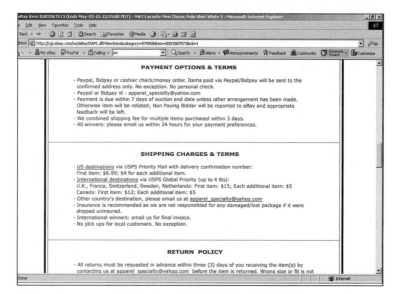

Figure 53.3
Seller's terms and conditions.

And when you ship your item, it will help if your packing information also contains your logo or artwork that reflects your brand design. Always, always put something in with your package such as an invoice, packing slip, or even a printed note thanking the customer for his business and giving contact information if something is wrong. If you ship insured, you should have an insurance stamp/label on the package or an insurance card inside. A lot of shippers, including myself, self-insure the first $100. I still put an insurance card in the package. Because I charge the customer for that insurance, they want to see that the package was insured. While eBay no longer allows self-insuring, I still do this for my website and sales on other venues such as Amazon.

53.2 Cross-Branding Between eBay and Your Website

Cross-branding is more involved than just having the same design. You should also carry the same policies and offer the same level of service. The advantage of cross-branding is that you can market to the customer in the future in such a way that he will prefer to buy from your website where he can make an immediate purchase and you will save the eBay fees.

Many sellers price their merchandise higher on their website than they sell for on eBay. Actually, this is okay as long as you offer your eBay buyers a discount in the form of a promotional code or an electronic coupon. If someone buys a blouse from you on eBay for $22.50 and then sees it on your website for $29, she will just go back to eBay and probably ignore your future e-mails and promotions. But if she visits your website with a coupon for $5 off, she might buy an item even though with the $5 she is still paying slightly more than on eBay because she still feels like she is getting a discount and doesn't have to bid on and risk losing the item.

53.3 Building a Newsletter List

Creating a newsletter is a great marketing tool and a superb way to build your brand. The purpose of building a brand is twofold: to instill trust in the customer and to drive repeat sales. You can't build a brand if a customer only buys from you once. The purpose of a newsletter is to bring the customer back to your auctions or your store or website so you can make a repeat sale. After you have made a second sale, it's much easier to make a third and fourth. Your goal should be to get customers to add you to their eBay favorite auctions and/or bookmark your website.

Your newsletter needs to have legitimate content. If all you do is send out advertisements, customers will tire of it. The idea is to weave subtle advertisements into your content. If you sell aftermarket car performance accessories, you can write a newsletter article of the top-three things you can do to increase performance. In the body of the article when you talk about exhaust systems, you can provide a hyperlink to your exhaust system products on the website.

You build a newsletter by offering something for free if people sign up. For example, I write a monthly newsletter for professional auction sellers. In my end-of-auction message to my customers, I have a statement that says: "Do you sell on eBay? Would you like to sell on eBay? If so, I publish a FREE monthly newsletter for auction sellers. Click here to sign up now, and I will send you a free eBook, *eBay Online Auction Photo Secrets*."

You could also offer an electronic coupon. If you sell designer fashions, you might send your buyers a note that says: "Click Here to subscribe to our free newsletter, *Designer Fashion News*, and we will send you a coupon for $10 off on your next purchase from our fashion web store."

53.3.1 Online Newsletter Services

You can keep your newsletter subscribers in a database, but you might find the services of an online newsletter subscription service helpful. The largest online newsletter service is Topica at www.topica.com. They work with large companies such as IBM and The GAP, but they also support thousands of small online entrepreneurs and even hobbyist and enthusiast newsletters.

Topica gives you the power and flexibility you need to create and manage professional-looking e-mail marketing campaigns. Some of the features include:

- Customizable HTML e-mail templates
- Custom branding
- Prescheduled delivery
- Recurring delivery
- Copy and paste back campaigns
- Support for text, HTML, and multipart formats
- Forward-to-a-friend link for viral list growth
- Test messages and routing
- Personalization on any database field
- Multiple list management
- Segmentation for testing
- Bounce and retry management
- Subscription confirmation (footer)
- PayPal integration
- Amazon integration
- eBay auction integration

Topica's e-mail templates allow you to carry your eBay template or website design over to your newsletter design, therefore extending your brand. One of the most important features is Topica's multiple list management. If you only sell one type or category of product, then you only need one list. But depending on what you sell, you may need different lists. If you sell both men's and women's apparel, you can separate your subscribers by gender. If you sell sporting gear, you could create separate lists for hunting, fishing, and camping. This allows you to tailor and target your mailing to a specific customer group.

Topica's CAN-SPAM compliance features meet all federal guidelines and conform to industry best practices, ensuring maximum deliverability of your messages. These features include:

- Bulk unsubscribe
- Integrated unsubscribe link
- Automated unsubscribe processing
- Never mail list
- Content checker

The thing I like best about Topica is that I can simply place a link to the Subscribe box in my e-mail or on my website. When a person clicks the link, it takes him to a page where he signs up and enters his demographic data. Collecting this data tells me more about my customers and enables me to better target market to them.

The other large newsletter management company is Quadra Mail at www. quadramail.com. I haven't tried them, but by looking at their website, their services appear similar to Topica's.

There are two ways to send out a newsletter. You can write the entire body of the newsletter and send it out via e-mail, or you can send the notice with a link to the newsletter where customers can read it on your website. I prefer the second method. If I mention a product or a special in my newsletter, customers might or might not be interested in that specific item. But if I can get them to visit my website, then they will be exposed to all my products.

53.3.2 Avoiding Spam Filters

Also, the shorter the message and the fewer key words it has in it, the easier time it will have getting through spam filters. Spam filters key on certain words such as *Viagra, vitamins, make money, mortgage, eBay success*, and so on. They also look for triggers such as overuse of all caps and multiple punctuation (!!!!!). You'll never know all the words and triggers spam filters are looking for because it is a closely guarded secret. So if you inadvertently use one of these words, there is an excellent chance your e-mail will be blocked. Spam filters also look for e-mails with hundreds or more addresses, which is another reason why you should use a service such as Topica, so your e-mails don't get blocked.

For the longest time, my newsletter was stalled at 30,000 subscribers. I would sign up about 500 new subscribers each month, but I'd also lose about 500 to spam filters. I finally got wise and signed up for a white list service from IronPort, who offers a Bonded Sender service. Under Bonded Sender, legitimate companies that want to send legitimate marketing e-mail to legitimate subscribers post a cash bond based on the size of their subscriber list, which IronPort reserves the right to keep if the sender breaks its anti-spam policies.

In return, the sender gets a backstage pass for some of the world's largest e-mail services. ISPs that subscribe to the service agree to let bonded senders send e-mails through their spam filters, on the basis that the user most likely requested the e-mail. Now more than 250 million e-mail accounts are using Bonded Sender, and the number of send-side customers has doubled since Microsoft Hotmail, AOL, and EarthLink joined the system. Since becoming a bonded seller, my monthly blocked e-mails have dropped below 100.

If you have a small newsletter, you'll be better served by purchasing a spam checking service. Dori Friend, the founder of Sonic Rocket Technology, is one of the leading experts on spam. He offers a great program for $197. You write your newsletter or marketing e-mail and simply paste it into his web page. Then you hit **Check e-mail,** and the program analyzes your e-mail for spam filter triggers and even suggests alternatives.

Use these don'ts to help get your newsletters and marketing e-mails through spam filters:

- Don't ever send more than 250 e-mails concurrently to AOL.
- Don't *ever* embed an image in an e-mail.
- Don't use all caps anywhere in your e-mail, especially in your subject line.
- Don't use words like FREE, F**E, or FR~EE, as the spam filter will look for these
- Don't use the word *remove*, use *unsubscribe*.

- Don't start your subject line with *Dear* ....
- Don't use your PC as a server.
- Don't forge headers.
- Don't put *ADV* in your subject line.
- Don't overuse punctuation (just one !).
- Don't leave headers blank.
- Don't use BCC to send e-mails (and certainly not CC).
- Don't overuse marketing phrases (order now, buy now, free bonus, etc.).
- Don't use the priority option.
- Don't change the time on your server so your e-mail stays on the top of the heap.
- Don't overuse hyperlinks.

Here are some do's to get your e-mail through the spam filters:

- Put a date in your e-mail subject line.
- Do be a newsletter.
- Send your e-mail from a trusted source such as Topica.
- Look and be legitimate.
- Send regular text e-mails.
- Have an unsubscribe link.
- Say *go here* instead of *click here*.
- Get on your customers' white lists.
- Personalize your e-mail with your customer's name.

Besides lining up subscribers from your customers and eBay bidders, you can also market your website directly to customers through e-mails. If you are going to do this, you must work with a legitimate e-mail broker who only sells what are called "opt-in" e-mail addresses. Better still, use a broker or service that will actually send out the e-mails so you won't be reported for spam violations if they break the rules. One of the best services is eeeMedia at www.eeemedia.com. They have been in the business for quite a while and have a very good reputation. Also, they offer an open guarantee, which is a guarantee of what percentage of e-mails will actually be opened and read.

You can buy millions of e-mail addresses for as little as $5 per million, but you are just getting junk. An e-mail campaign from a legitimate broker such as eeeMedia will cost a lot more than $5, but they have a proven track record and will allow you to perform a small, low-cost campaign first to evaluate the ROI before committing to a large and expensive campaign.

For more on building your brand, see Chapter 2.

part 7

Managing Your Business for Growth

After all the pieces of your business are in place and you have learned the techniques and strategies necessary for success, it is time to scale up your business.

You can grow in several ways. You can increase the number of products and product categories you sell into. You can expand your sales channels. Or you can do both. After you have established your products' niches, published your brand, and set up your business for a high degree of automation, growth is nothing more than finding more inventory to sell and launching more auctions.

But with this growth comes other challenges. Cost control becomes more important as pennies multiply with higher volumes. You might need one or more employees to produce more auctions and to ship more product. Bookkeeping systems and the ability to measure detailed business metrics become critical because things can get out of control as a business experiences rapid growth.

This part shows you how to address these challenges to prevent the business from running you and what to do when things do go wrong.

chapter 54

Putting Your Accounting and Bookkeeping Systems to Work for You

It is said that many businesses fail because they were underfunded to begin with. That's probably true, but I believe that more businesses fail because they don't know where their money is going. Understanding where your money is going is vital. The amount you spend on nondirect overhead is just as important as what you spend on eBay fees.

In Chapter 5, we discussed the various bookkeeping systems available, the major ones being QuickBooks, Peachtree Accounting, and MYOB. QuickBooks is by far the most popular, and therefore the easiest system to find help with. Most community colleges teach adult education classes in QuickBooks; it's easy to find bookkeepers who are familiar with this system; and it works very well for anything from a very small business to a medium-size business. Therefore I'll confine my discussion to QuickBooks, but if you decide on any of the other programs, they do essentially the same functions and operate much the same. But before you see how QuickBooks can help you understand and control your business, let's take a look at what it does.

54.1 The QuickBooks System

All QuickBooks' programs use the bank account as the platform for recording expenses and controlling your business. So the first thing you need to do is open a business bank account that is dedicated solely to your business. Make it a point never to spend personal money from this account, because it can really screw up your bookkeeping. If you need money from your business, you can pay yourself a salary, reimburse yourself for expenses, or declare a dividend if you are incorporated.

PowerSeller Tip

Keep *everything* organized electronically on the computer.

This allows you to use tools for indexing data. The result is that you and your employees can instantly access years' worth of data from anywhere!

—Mike Enos, an eBay Platinum level Power Seller (www.platinumpowerseller. com)

When you set up QuickBooks, start by entering your bank account information and the initial balance in your account. Next, set up your chart of accounts, which sounds a little technical but is really very simple. You have two kinds of accounts: Money In, which is your sales or amounts of money you fund the business with, and Money Out, which is your expenses. It is really no more complicated than that. Whenever you receive money from a customer, you make a deposit to your bank account that goes into your Sales Account (Money In). Whenever you pay a bill, the amount is debited from your expense account (Money Out). Your chart of accounts is really a list of subaccounts under those two headings.

On the income side, you can set up several income accounts to help you track where your money is coming from. These might include eBay sales receipts, website sales receipts, and a miscellaneous account for any other money you might earn. The expense side is a little more complex because you want to break down your expenses by category so you can see how much you are spending on each type of expense. I won't try to make a complete list here, but the following example shows some of the expenses you might want to track.

Cost of goods sold	This is what you pay for the merchandise you buy for resale. You could even break this down into subcategories so you can analyze your costs' product type. Be sure to include all your costs, such as insurance and inbound shipping.
eBay fees	Tracking these fees is very important.
PayPal fees	As with eBay fees, it's essential that you track all fees paid to PayPal.
Advertising	This includes money you spend on keyword advertising, banners, and so on.
Shipping and packing	Track shipping supplies separately from actual supplies and shipping costs.
Shipping costs	This is what you spend on UPS, FedEx, and the USPS and shipping insurance.
Rent and utilities	If you are incorporated and working out of your home, you can charge your personal corporation rent on your office in the home. You can include a portion of your utilities in this amount.
Labor	Keep track of all employees' salaries, including any salary you pay yourself. This account will have subcategories for payroll taxes.
Casual labor	This is money you pay to independent contractors or occasional labor. If you pay any one person more than $600 per year, then you must issue him an IRS 1099 form at the end of the year. Fortunately, QuickBooks will do this for you at the push of a button.
Travel and meals	This is any money you spend on business-related travel for yourself or your employees.
Entertainment	Entertainment is money you spend on others. Be careful. The IRS looks at this very carefully.
Office supplies	This can include small purchases of furniture and equipment that you are going to expense in one year.

Office furniture and equipment	This category is for more expensive equipment (over $1,000) that you will write off over several years.
Car expense	If you are incorporated, the corporation can buy your car. If you do this, you can use a corporate credit or debit card to pay for gas, oil, maintenance, etc. You can also make the car payments from your corporate bank account and put them in this expense category. If you are not incorporated, then you would file an expense report under the travel category and the company can reimburse you for mileage (check www.IRS.gov for the current mileage rate).
Insurance	This expense item can cover your business and liability insurance. Put employee medical insurance in a subcategory under Labor and your car insurance in the Car Expense account. This enables you to track those cost categories more accurately.
Legal and accounting	Put expenses for your attorney, CPA, and bookkeeper here.
Dues and subscriptions	Put any dues such as Chamber of Commerce membership, business magazines you subscribe to, or any other fees of that nature in this account.
Communications	Costs for your phone bills, cell phone, fax, and DSL or cable Internet fees go here.
Computer and website	This category includes monthly ISP fees and website hosting expenses or any monthly fees related to the computer side of your business.
Miscellaneous	This account catches everything else. If any expense occurs in this account more than two or three times a year, you should probably set up a separate account for that item.

After you set up your accounts, it's very easy to make entries into them since basically everything is based on your bank account. When you sit down at the computer to enter a deposit, QuickBooks will ask you to select an account to enter it into from a drop-down menu of your accounts. The same thing happens when you write a check to pay a bill or send someone an electronic payment. QuickBooks will present you with a list of the accounts and ask you which account to debit.

Every time you pay a vendor, QuickBooks will set that vendor up with all of the information you need to pay the bill, including their name, address, tax ID number, and so on. The next time you go to pay that vendor, instead of typing all that information in, QuickBooks will fill in the form for you. It can even generate invoices, print envelopes and labels, and enter the memo information on the checks.

QuickBooks will also calculate your local, state, and federal employment taxes and generate paychecks and W2 forms at the end of the year.

QuickBooks can also perform these other features:

- Track money in and money out. Nothing falls through the cracks, and you can find everything instantly.

- Create estimates, invoices, and sales receipts. It automatically fills in frequently used names and addresses for you, helping to reduce typos and saving time.

- Write checks, pay bills, record expenses. Work with everyday familiar forms including checks that look just like paper checks.

- Track customer payments. Automatically apply payments against specific invoices.

- Report tax totals instantly. It does all the math.

- Run business reports such as cash flow, profit and loss, balance sheet, expenses by category or account, and track the percentage of each expense as part of the total.

- Work with familiar, everyday forms. No bookkeeping or accounting knowledge is needed.

- Exchange data with Microsoft Excel and more than 325 other software applications.

- If you use an auction management service such as Vendio, or Channel-Advisor, you can download your sales data into your QuickBooks account.

- Use Microsoft Word to create and print letters and envelopes. Also turn an invoice into a personalized letter in a few clicks.

- Process UPS and FedEx shipments and print shipping labels directly from sales receipts and invoices.

- If your bank supports it, you can download your bank statement right into the system.

54.2 Controlling Your Costs

If you don't know what your costs are, you can't control them. Besides the level of automation and time saving, the greatest value of an accounting system is the ability to see how much money you are spending on various expenses. For example, you can set up your advertising accounts with several subaccounts where you could separately track Google Adwords advertising, Yahoo! Search Marketing, and banner ad buys. With this data broken out, you can judge the performance of those ads against sales on both a raw basis and on an adjusted basis that accounts for other factors.

QuickBooks enables you to pull a profit and loss report that shows the percentage of each expense account as part of the total expenses. This feature is especially valuable to spot expense trends when you compare the expenses on a month-to-month basis. If you see, for example, that your cost of goods sold is rising as a percentage of your total expenses, this could be a warning sign that your margins are eroding. Or perhaps your advertising is going up as a percentage of your costs, but your sales are not increasing to keep pace. This tells you there is a problem with your advertising performance.

Tax time is always a stressful time for small business owners. If you are persistent in always running all your business expenses through your QuickBooks program, however, tax time will be a snap. At the end of the year, all you have to do is pull a profit and loss report, a balance sheet, and generate your W-2s and 1099s. Most years I can do all this in a couple of hours.

54.3 Understanding Your Margins

Besides controlling your costs, QuickBooks also enables you to see and control your operating margins. You can look at your gross margins by running a report of your sales (money in) versus your cost of goods sold (direct expenses). Next, you can run a report of your sales versus expenses to determine your overhead—or your nondirect expenses. If shipping and insurance is a profit center for you, then you can include them in your cost of goods sold as a direct expense. This will enable you to see your real gross margins and prevents you from mixing direct with nondirect costs.

54.4 Tracking Cash Flow

In the final analysis, you must take more money in than goes out. This is called positive cash flow. QuickBooks can generate cash flow reports, which tell you how fast you are generating cash or how fast your cash is disappearing if you are in a negative cash flow situation. It is not unusual for businesses to experience negative cash flow for short periods of time—you just don't want it to go on for too long. For example, if you purchased a large amount of inventory, you might have a temporary negative cash-out balance until you can sell the inventory. The cash flow reporting feature will tell you how long it will take to turn your cash flow positive.

For example, if you spent $10,000 to purchase 400 pieces of merchandise at a cost of $25 each, you'd have a negative cash balance of $10,000 on day one. At the end of the month if you had sold 100 units of the item at $50 each, you'd have brought in $5,000 and your negative cash flow position would have been reduced to $5,000. Based on this sales data, you can run a report in QuickBooks that will tell you exactly when your cash flow will turn positive.

This is dynamic information, whereas a profit and loss statement and a balance sheet reflect only a snapshot in time. They can tell you how you have done, but they cannot predict the future. The ability to accurately predict your cash flow is essential to the smooth running of your business. If it turned out you were only getting $35 for the items you bought for $10,000, your cash flow statement would tell you that it will take a lot longer to turn positive. Because your cash flow report also takes things such as payroll, rent, and other expenses into account, it might point out that you will come up short next month and not have the cash to meet your payroll or pay your eBay fees unless you either raise your prices, cut your costs, speed up the rate at which you are selling the product, or all three. This is important information to find out in advance!

For more on accounting and bookkeeping systems, see Sections 1.2 and 5.2.

chapter 55

Understanding and Calculating Your Business Metrics

Metrics in the classical sense is the application of statistics and mathematical analysis to a field of study. More simply put, it's a standard of measurement. The term *business metrics* became popular at Harvard Business School sometime in the 1980s. B-School grads like to talk jargon and make the simple sound complicated. Business metrics is one of those terms that is meant to sound complicated: *you can't possibly understand it unless you have an MBA.* The reality is quite different. Subtract your cost from your selling price, and you have your gross margin. See, you just used a business metric.

55.1 If You Can't Measure It, You Can't Control It

Understanding your business metrics is essential to running a successful eBay business—or any online business for that matter. If you can't or don't measure the various elements that go into making your business successful, you will have no idea how or why you are making—or losing—money. When you understand where your profits are coming from, you can do more of the activity that produces them. When you see where you are losing money or not making very much money, you can reduce or eliminate that product, promotion, or marketing activity.

You must measure these important business metrics if you want to understand your eBay business:

- Gross merchandise sales
- Average selling price
- Conversion rate
- Buy It Now and Stores sales
- Fixed Price sales
- Fees to sales rate
- Upsell rate
- Nonpaying bidder rate
- Gross margin

Before we get into what these metrics are and how to measure them, we need to figure out what we will do with the data after we have it. I suggest you set up three Excel spreadsheets. One will measure monthly results on a month-to-date basis; one should combine the final monthly data into a quarterly report; and the other one should be year-to-date.

You should update your month-to-date report weekly, and always pick the same day of the week to enter your data. If you tend to end all or most of your auctions on Sunday evening, you should do your report on Monday. If your auctions all end at different times, then you could do a wrap-up report on Friday or Saturday.

I like to keep my spreadsheets on my desktop for easy access. Although I might only enter data in them once a week, I refer to them often.

If you use an auction management service, it is easy to calculate or even download the data into a separate calculation spreadsheet. Keep your spreadsheets simple, so you can see the metrics. Don't place all your sales and cost numbers in them—just your totals.

Now let's look at some of the individual metrics.

55.2 Gross Merchandise Sales

Gross Merchandise Sales (GMS) is nothing more than your raw total sales for the period you are measuring. By raw, I mean you should not factor in returns, refunds, or nonpaying bidders. There is a separate metric for Buy It Now and fixed-price sales. Some PowerSellers like to measure these two separately, but I prefer to show the true GMS and break the fixed-price sales out as a separate metric.

You only measure GMS when something sells. The key word is *sell*. Some sellers prefer to measure GMS when they get paid. They track getting paid as a "sale." The problem with this is that it makes it harder to measure the nonpaying bidder rate, which is also a very important statistic. Instead, you should track all sales. So if you were measuring your eBay sales for the month of March, you'd measure all auctions that closed successfully during March whether you got paid or not. If you list something in March and it sells in April, that item will go into your April GMS.

You need to track your GMS because this is the largest measure that can tell you if your business is growing or not. It also allows you to look at your sales period by period to see if any outside factors are influencing your sales. This could include elections, SuperBowl week, seasonal slowdowns, increased sales around Christmas or back-to-school periods, and so on.

55.3 Average Selling Price

The Average Selling Price (ASP) is simply your GMS divided by the number of items sold over a specific period of time (week, month, year, etc.). This will give you your average price per item of merchandise sold. You want to combine all your items—fixed-price, auction, web store, and so on—as well as looking at these items individually.

55.4 Conversion Rate

Your conversion rate is the rate at which your items are selling expressed as a percentage of the items listed. (Some auction management services call this sell-through rate [STR]. This means the same thing). To measure your conversion rate, simply divide the number of items sold in a given period (week, month, and so on) by the number of items listed in the same period. Once again, we are looking at raw sales—don't worry if the items were paid for or not.

If you listed 140 items in a week and you sold 98, your conversion rate would be 98 ÷ 140, which equals .7 or 70 percent. Conversion rate is one of the most important statistics to watch because it dramatically affects your profit margin. Every time you list an auction that doesn't sell, you still have to pay the eBay Insertion fee. If your conversion rate is only 50 percent, then you are paying fees on the other 50 percent of auctions that didn't sell. Paying eBay fees for auctions that don't convert (sell) is like buying advertising that doesn't work.

One of the best ways to use the conversion rate is to test promotions. If you run a series of auctions one way—say using the Bold listing upgrade—and a series of identical auctions without this feature, you can calculate the conversion ratios to see if the promotion worked. You can then go back and look at the ASP of those items and see if the ASP went up by more than the cost of the fee.

55.5 Buy It Now Fixed Price and eBay Store Sales

eBay has three fixed-price formats: the fixed-price listing, eBay Store, and Buy It Now added to an auction. It is important to track these sales separately because they have different fee structures than regular auctions, and products tend to sell at higher prices in fixed-price formats. Also, people usually find eBay Stores from links in your auctions and from advertising using Google AdWords and Yahoo Search Marketing. Because these are fairly expensive promotional tools, you want to track these sales separately.

55.6 Fees to Sales Rate

The fees-to-sales-rate (F/S) is simply a measure of the percentage of your eBay fees divided by your GMS for a given period. I usually measure these on a monthly basis because eBay generates my fee invoice at the end of the month. You can see your fees about two weeks before eBay sends you an invoice by clicking the **My Account** link on your **My eBay** page.

If your GMS for the month was $34,200 and your fees were $3,855, your F/S Rate would be $3,855 \div 34,200 = 11.3$ percent.

Your fees-to-sales rate is a very important number to track. After material costs (or cost of goods sold, COGS) and shipping costs, eBay fees are one of your largest expenses. If your F/S rate is rising, it is probably because your conversion rate is falling. This is why you want to watch your conversion rate weekly. After your fee invoice comes in, it's too late to make changes. But if you notice during the middle of the month that your conversion rate is falling, you can take some action to fix the problem before a whole month goes by.

55.7 Upsell Rate

The upsell rate (UR) is the rate at which customers add something to their original order during the checkout process (see Chapter 51). You can only measure this if you do it. So unless you have a web store or an e-mail system that offers the customer an upsell before you ship, this rate is not important. Having said this, upselling is very important; if you are not doing it, you should be. Let me show you why:

If you listed a Ralph Lauren Polo Shirt for $19.99 and it sold for $39, the eBay Insertion fee would be 55¢ and the final value fee would be $2.68, for a total of $3.23. If you added the Bold Option for $1, your total would be $4.23. This works out to 10.8 percent of your selling price. If you upsold the customer a Ralph Lauren baseball cap for $15, your total sale is now $54, so your fees now represent 7.8 percent of your sale.

The purpose of measuring your upsell rate is so you can evaluate what promotions and communications are working to improve it.

55.8 Nonpaying Bidder Rate

The nonpaying bidder rate (NPB) is the percentage of your GMS, in dollars, that are never paid for. Here is the formula:

Take the total dollar amount of all the auctions that were not paid for during the month and divide it by your GMS in dollars for the same period. If you had $2,945 worth of auctions that were not paid for out of total sales of $33,000, your NPB rate would be 2,945 ÷ 33,000 = 8.9 percent.

There are two ways to measure this rate. You can measure the raw rate, which is helpful in determining whether you have problems. If you do, perhaps editing your terms would help, or maybe your shipping costs are not fully explained and people are not paying because they are surprised when they get the total bill. The other way to measure the NPB is to base it on the NPB dollars left after you have reclaimed your fees from eBay, which is your final NPB.

55.9 Gross Margin

Your gross margin (or gross profit) is simply your gross merchandise sales less your cost of goods sold (COGS). If you ship your goods at cost, then calculate this number without adding in your shipping costs. If, however, shipping and insurance is a profit center (you add a handling charge), then calculate your GMS to include your shipping charges and subtract both your shipping cost and your COGS from the GMS to get your gross margins.

The importance of gross margin cannot be understated. This is ultimately where all your profit comes from. The higher you can drive your gross margins, the greater your profit will be in the end. Gross margin is much harder to control than below-the-line expenses such as advertising, rent, labor, utilities, and so on. It's a large gross margin that allows you to afford these other expenses.

You can increase your gross margin in two ways. You can either get higher prices for your products or pay less for your inventory. So if you see your gross margins shrinking, look at one of those two items.

55.10 Net Margin

Net margin is your net profit. *Net* means minus all expenses (gross margin – expenses = net). This is the figure that comes up at the bottom of your profit and loss statement when you do a P&L report using QuickBooks. You start with your gross margin and subtract all of your expenses except taxes. You want to look at your net profit before taxes so you can measure it from period to period. This is because tax rates change, and you can't really do anything about them. Your true net margin or profit is what you have left after taxes, but it is helpful to see the number both before and after.

Where do I get all these numbers? If you go to your My eBay Page and click the link that says **Subscriptions** under **My Account** (see Figure 55.1), it will bring up your sales report. If you have not yet subscribed to Sales Reports, you will see a list of eBay products you can subscribe to. Next to **Sales Reports Plus** click **Subscribe**. It's free. If you look at Figure 55.2, you can see all the items eBay tracks for you. This information is also presented graphically, as in Figure 55.3.

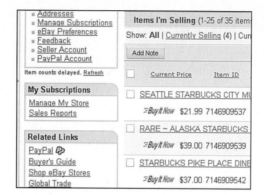

Figure 55.1
Subscriptions link on My eBay Page.

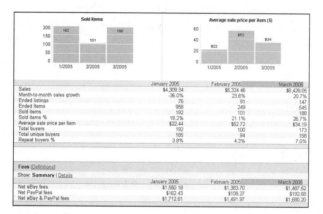

Figure 55.2
Summary Sales Report.

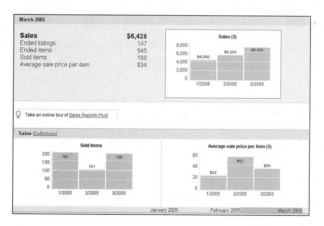

Figure 55.3
Sales Reports presented as a graph.

eBay breaks down the following information:

- Sales—This is your total GMS.

- Month-to-month sales growth—This compares the previous two months' sales.

- Ended listings—These are listings that didn't sell. Unfortunately, eBay does not show how many listings you did, so you cannot calculate your conversion ratio from this list. You will have to take that data from your eBay invoice or your auction management system or software.

- Ended items—These are the number of individual items—as opposed to listings—that didn't sell. The reason this number is so high is because this seller probably runs a lot of Dutch (multiple-item) auctions. This also skews the report because there is no additional cost to run the extra items.

- Sold items—This is the number of total items (not auctions that closed successfully).

- Sold items percentage—This is sort of a measure of conversion ratio. If this seller only ran single-item auctions, this would be the true conversion ratio.

- Average sale price per item—This is your average sale price, or ASP.

- Total buyers—This is the number of sales per username.

- Total unique buyers—This is the number of individual buyers. The difference between these two numbers is the number of people who bought more than one item, probably through upsells.

- Repeat buyers percentage—This is your upsell rate from your eBay store. It does not include any upsells from e-mail or your auction management web store because eBay does not have that data.

This data is very useful, but it is not complete. To get a complete financial picture, you have to combine this with data from your web store, QuickBooks, and any website sales you made.

In this discussion, I have focused mostly on eBay, but you should be selling in multiple channels. If you are also selling on Overstock.com, for example, you will also want to create a spreadsheet for that venue. This will enable you to compare your sales channels to see which are more profitable. Another reason to open new channels is supply and demand. If you buy a large quantity of product to sell on eBay, you have to either list it slowly over a long period of time to keep from driving the prices down or list it all at once and accept a lower gross margin. If you can also list some of it on Overstock, some on Amazon, some on eBay, and some on your website or in your web store, you will help preserve the illusion of low supply, which should result in your moving the merchandise more quickly.

The other value of measuring your business metrics is their value as goal-setting targets. If you have good data, you can make projections based on it and set goals that are realistic and attainable. Most sellers focus solely on GMS when they are setting their goals, but you should also focus on subsets of your business to see which areas can help you become more profitable.

Looking at all the individual parts of your business in this fashion will help you understand what you need to do to scale your business or expand into new selling channels. You will know exactly how much investment and resources you will need to accomplish each step toward your growth.

55.11 Tracking Hits

The final metric you want to follow is your hit ratio.

If you subscribe to an eBay store, go to the link to Manage My Store on your My eBay page. Click on the icon that says Traffic Reports and you can see exactly how many hits each of your listings gets. If your auctions are not getting hits, you might have a problem with your headline or keywords. Tracking hits is the best way to test your headlines (auction titles) and the value of promotional options such as bold, highlight, or category featured.

If you are getting a lot of hits, but very low bids, then your headline and keywords are working, but you might have a problem with your pricing or your auction description.

For more on monitoring your business, see Chapters 7 and 10.

chapter 56

Using Business Metrics to Manage Your Inventory

In Chapter 16 I stressed the importance of managing and controlling your inventory. And doing this is easier than it sounds. Understanding your business metrics can be a valuable tool for helping control inventory.

In the previous chapter I talked about macro metrics: the metrics of your total business—the large view. But when it comes to inventory control, you need to take a micro look at using those same metrics.

56.1 Product Profit Margins

Just as your overall business has a profit margin, so does each individual product. But the total profit margin is not always the whole story. If you simply contrast one product that sells for $40 with a 50 percent margin against a $20 product that earns only a 20 percent margin, you might think "I don't want to carry any more of that $20 product." But if you sell 25 of the $20 product every week and only sell one of the $40 products during that same period, the vast majority of your profits are actually coming from the $20 product.

My point is that you cannot always look at the profit potential of a single product in a vacuum—you have to examine the total picture. If you keep detailed sales records, you should easily be able to determine which products are making you money on a total basis as opposed to an individual basis.

56.2 Product Conversion Rates

When you look at your macro business, you are measuring your overall sell-through rate (conversion rate). This is very important data. But individual products have a conversion rate as well. If you sell dozens of different products, it can be very time-consuming to track your individual product conversion rate. In this case you might want to break your products down by categories. If you see that one category is not performing, then you might want to analyze all the products in that one category to remove your nonperforming or poorly performing inventory.

Measuring these metrics is important, but running a business is more than just math. You should consider other factors as well. Are there products you must carry so your customers will see your business as a total source? Digital camera flash cards are so competitive that it is virtually impossible to make a good margin on them. But if you sell digital cameras and you don't offer flash cards as an option, your customer might go to another seller who does. If you sell rhythm and blues CDs and you don't carry the obscure artists, will you drive your repeat customers to a competitor? These are the kinds of business decisions you must make that go beyond the math of metrics.

When you run into these sorts of situations, you might want to get a little creative. Perhaps it is more profitable in the long run to include an extra or larger flash card as part of your digital camera package. Or if you are only making a small margin on those obscure CDs, maybe you can offer free shipping if a customer buys two or three at a time. This way your individual product margin is no greater, but the total sale is larger and you are moving two or three pieces of inventory at a time instead of one.

56.3 Optimizing Product Selection

Tracking your macro and micro business metrics can help you optimize your product selection. Of course, when you measure a metric, you are looking at history, but you can use that history to help predict the future. Stock market gurus do it all the time. For instance, 100 years of history shows that stocks rise when interest rates fall. Likewise, you can look at the history of your sales to spot trends and patterns.

When you look back at your sales and see margins eroding over a period of time, this can be a warning that a product is moving into a new phase of the selling cycle. It can be an early warning to start cutting prices and dumping inventory before the price falls too far. You can only do this, however, if you look at the metrics within each category. Just like the biologist who has to look deep within a cell to understand the whole organism, you have to drill down into your product categories to understand what is happening with your business. Doing so will help you maximize your margins by putting your capital into the best performing products and quickly eliminating inventory before it becomes nonperforming.

Online automation systems such as Vendio or ChannelAdvisor make it easy for you to collect data to make these sorts of decisions. (The ChannelAdvisor system is probably a little more sophisticated in this regard because it offers built-in analysis tools.)

Whether you use Vendio, ChannelAdvisor, or another system, make sure you can download your inventory and sales performance data into an Excel spreadsheet. With Excel you can sort data column by column. If you create a spreadsheet of your products listing their cost versus the selling price and including a column that calculates your gross margin, it is very simple to find your best- and worst-performing products by sorting the gross margin column from high to low.

For more on managing your inventory, see Chapter 16.

chapter 57

Controlling Fulfillment Costs

Packaging and shipping materials can be a major cost center, but the shipping and handling service can also be a profit center. Large eBay sellers ship hundreds of packages a week, and making an extra 50¢ to a dollar on each package can really add up over the year. Conversely, spending too much on shipping and packaging can seriously cut into profits over time.

The whole area of packing and shipping is called fulfillment. Depending on the size and weight of what you are selling, fulfillment costs can be a major part of your expenses. If you sell collectible sports cards, fulfillment costs might be no more than an envelope and a first-class stamp. But if you sell framed art prints, the packaging and shipping becomes a much more costly part of the operation.

57.1 Shipping as a Profit Center

Most large eBay sellers use shipping as a profit center. This is a controversial issue with many buyers and sellers because a handful of sellers have gouged buyers with shipping prices. Buyers have a way to express their displeasure with the Detailed Seller Rating system that eBay introduced in 2007. The Shipping and Handling Cost is a factor in your item's placement in the Best Match search results order, so you do want to be judicious in your use of these strategies.

There is nothing wrong with trying to recover all your material and shipping costs as well as adding a small charge to cover handling (the labor to package and label the items). If you add a handling charge to your shipments, the best strategy is to disclose this to the buyers in your auction description or in the shipping policy section of your auction. Here's an example of a simple but effective statement:

> Shipping and handling for this package is $7.90. This amount includes a small charge to cover packaging, handling, and the cost of packaging materials. We pack all items professionally using only new shipping materials to make sure your package arrives in the same condition we sent it.

If you are a volume shipper and you have negotiated shipping discounts, it's totally acceptable to keep the savings. For instance, if the standard UPS shipping rate for a given package is $6.90 and you get a 30 percent discount, you can still charge $6.90, which is the price a buyer would see if he looked it up on the UPS site, but you would be making a $2.07 handling charge.

Another advantage of having a UPS or FedEx account is the ability to generate shipping labels that do not show the actual shipping charge. If you use the U.S. Postal Service, you can also do this with Endicia's Stealth Postage feature (see Chapter 42).

Insurance is another moneymaker. The Post Office charges $1 per $100 of value for insurance. UPS and FedEx give you the first $100 of insurance free but then charge rates similar to the Post Office. I've worked with a company called Discount Shipping Insurance (DSI) for several years. DSI is a private insurance carrier that offers insurance rates as much as 70 percent below USPS and UPS rates. You can make a lot of money selling this kind of insurance to your customers.

If you sell goods with ASPs under $100, you can offer insurance as an option. I charge $1.20 to insure items, and about 20 percent of the buyers on items that cost less than $100 take me up on it. If I ship via UPS or FedEx, the insurance costs me nothing. If I ship with USPS with delivery confirmation, the first $100 of insurance through DSI costs me only 40¢, so I make 80¢.

For items with ASPs of over $100, I don't give the customers a choice. I show in the auction that I charge $1.20 per $100 for insurance. I rarely get any kickback from customers—in fact, most of them seem to appreciate having the coverage. Because I make as much as 80¢ per $100 on insurance, this can be a nice margin generator on expensive merchandise.

When you insure a package with UPS or the USPS, they place an insurance stamp or label on the outside of the box. You do not get this when you use private insurance. Therefore, you should include a note on the packing slip that your package was insured with a private carrier. DSI actually supplies little cards you can insert into the box that says they covered the item and gives the buyer a web link to click if he wants to make a claim.

57.2 Handling Returns

Your return policy is important to your branding and your overall image, and eBay now includes having a stated return policy as part of the algorithm they use to rank your listings in Best Match search results. How you handle returns can also impact your costs and profits. The first decision you have to make is whether you are going to pay for the return shipping. Most sellers do not, although a few do.

Endicia offers a return service via the U.S. Postal Service. With Endicia you can avoid $625 in annual USPS accounting/permit fees for Merchandise Return service. Instead, you choose the mail class and print return shipping labels for your customers prepaid from your Endicia postage account (see Figure 57.1).

Figure 57.1
Endicia shipping return label.

If you are going to use this service, then you must insert return instructions into your package. It is important customers know they need to call you and get a return authorization label before returning the item.

One of the biggest annoyances as an online retailer is receiving returns without notice. It is amazing that people will return items with nothing in the box except the item: no name, no auction number—nothing. The best way to avoid this scenario is to clearly state your return policy in your auction and once again on the packing slip or with an insert in the package.

For more on shipping and fulfillment costs, see Sections 5.7 and 5.8.

chapter 58

When Things Go Wrong

I have started seven companies over the years. Some were very successful; a few were moderately successful; and two failed. Every venture has a risk. Some ventures are just bad ideas to start with and never have a chance of succeeding. Others are great ideas but are never properly executed. And sometimes businesses fail for reasons that are just beyond the owner's control. Business bankruptcies jumped over 200 percent in the months following 9/11 and have been increasing since the mortgage lending crisis started in 2008.

Over the last nine years, I have seen eBay sellers come and go for many reasons. Sometimes it was just lousy product selection. Not everything sells successfully on the Internet. There are still some products that customers prefer to touch and feel before they buy. Competition is now a huge factor on eBay. Hundreds of sellers who were very successful in the early days of eBay failed in the face of increased—and in some cases massive—competition.

The Internet is one of the fastest-moving and most rapidly changing marketplaces in the history of business. It is so easy to open an eBay account or a Yahoo! store or to launch an Internet site. Unlike a brick-and-mortar store, the investment is minimal. If I come up with a new or innovative idea in the morning, I could sign on to a template Internet site such as PowerSellerBuilder.com and have a website launched by mid-afternoon. My total investment would be $29.95. The secret to surviving on eBay and the Internet is constant vigilance—staying on top of every aspect of your business and your competition and being able to quickly and nimbly respond to competition and changes in the market.

58.1 Reducing Risk

Every time you buy inventory, you take a risk. Deciding what to buy and how much to pay for it is probably the most important decision a seller makes on a regular basis. If your inventory doesn't perform, you are guaranteed to lose money. If you do this too often, you will be out of business. Watching your business metrics will not only allow you to maximize your Return on Investment (ROI) on inventory, but it will also help you reduce risk. Spotting problems or declining pricing trends early will give you room and time to maneuver. It also can help you predict if a new product will be successful. Two other things you can do to reduce risk are research and test, test, test.

Other risks can befall a seller. I know one large eBay seller who was operating out of his house when he should have been in a commercial location. His house burned down, and his homeowner's insurance did not cover the over $80,000 worth of inventory he had stored in his garage. Taking risks like this are just foolish. He could have kept a small amount of inventory in his home and the bulk in a commercial storage location where he could have easily purchased insurance for it.

Fraud is another risk eBay sellers face. If you have employees, you must be constantly vigilant for employee theft and fraud. And if you're in the business very long, you're sure to come across customers who will attempt to defraud you. When my wife and I were in the antiques business, I cannot tell you how many times a customer wrote me and said the item was received broken or had a small chip or flaw that was not there when I shipped the item. The real reason was the buyer probably got excited and paid too much when bidding or had a case of buyer's remorse. In one case I shipped an original porcelain figurine to a customer. He immediately wrote back that the item was a fake. I said okay, return it to me. When it was returned, it was indeed a cheap fake. Unfortunately, it was not the same piece I sent him. At that time my feedback was very low, and I didn't want to risk a negative feedback, so this con artist ended up with the original figure and a full refund. I spent the next two days in a blue funk.

Other types of fraud are common on eBay. After they've been used a few times, experienced sellers can spot them pretty easily, but new ones pop up all the time. Many of them are thwarted if you stick to eBay's payment policies which require electronic payments (fake cashier's checks used to be a popular scam on eBay).

A current popular scam is the escrow scam. A scam artist will set up a website that looks like a legitimate escrow company. Now you sell a very expensive item on eBay—perhaps a piece of diamond jewelry. The buyer, who is usually overseas, sends you an e-mail saying that because of the high value of the item, he would like to use an escrow company and he sends you a link to the company. You go and register and inform the buyer that you have done so. Now the buyer sends you an e-mail saying that he has made the payment to the escrow company, and soon thereafter the escrow company sends you a very official-looking e-mail informing you that payment has been received and it is okay to ship the package to the buyer. A few days go by, and you get delivery confirmation that the buyer received the package. Now you go back to the escrow website, and it is gone! Your e-mails get no response, and you are hit with the sudden reality that you have been totally and thoroughly conned.

eBay is an incredibly safe environment as far as Internet sites go. Both eBay and PayPal have large aggressive fraud departments and work closely with state and federal law enforcement. Nonetheless, all eBay sellers must be on a constant lookout for fraud. A lot of people make the mistake of thinking that eBay is somehow responsible when they are defrauded, but this is not the case. eBay is a shopping platform—they are not in the middle of the transaction and the courts have already held that they are not responsible when one member defrauds another. Having said this, eBay does much to prevent fraud, but ultimately it is you, the buyer or seller, who must be vigilant.

58.2 Coping with Adversity

Things will go wrong. Some of them will be your fault; some will be caused by the realities of the marketplace. How you deal with adversity will have a lot to do with your eventual or continuing success.

The first thing to remember is that this is a business—it's not your life! Sure, it might be your baby, but investing too much emotional energy into your business can be a fatal flaw. When you make decisions based on emotion instead of cold, hard reason, you usually make bad decisions.

When I was young and started to play the stock market, I did a lot of research and carefully evaluated any investment before I made it. When I bought a stock, I watched it every day and followed all the news on the company. As is typical with any investor, some of my stocks went up and some went down. My problem was that I could never bring myself to sell the ones that went down. I held on to those dogs because I just knew the market was wrong and the company would bounce back any day. The problem was I was emotionally involved with my stock. Professional investors call this "falling in love with your stock picks." I saw the same thing happen to several relatives and friends when the Internet bubble burst. They had bought Pets.com at $112 a share and just couldn't bring themselves to sell it even when it fell below $50. One friend of mine kept buying as the stock fell—all the way to $2 a share. The company no longer exists, and the domain was bought by PetSmart.

Over time I learned to take an unemotional approach and let the market make my decisions for me. Today I place an automatic stop-loss order on every stock I buy. If the market stops me out, I'm out.

You have to take the same approach to your business. Just as I did with stocks, I've seen eBay sellers purchase inventory that they are convinced will sell. When it doesn't, they refuse to stop listing it and keep incurring eBay fees trying to sell it at a price where they can make a profit. They refuse to sell it at or below cost to get some money back so they can move on to other things.

When I find myself stuck with nonperforming inventory, I might try to sell it once or twice at a price that will generate a profit. If it doesn't work, it goes up the next week for $1 with no reserve. If I get back 50¢ on the dollar, that's fine. I can use that money to buy something else that will sell.

If you find yourself struggling with several aspects of your business, the problem might be your business model. Sometimes it pays to step back and look at what you are doing. If you can't tell what the problem is, then get help. A number of eBay doctors—Internet business consultants—can help; one place to find them is at www.keane.com. There are also companies that offer mentoring and coaching programs, which I've listed on the Resources section of the website for this book at www.skipmcgrath.com/titanium. Your local county business development organization might be able to put you in touch with local business owners who can help. There is also an organization called the Service Corps of Retired Executives (SCORE), which is administered by the Small Business Administration. SCORE executives are usually retired former business owners who volunteer their time helping other small business owners and entrepreneurs. Don't worry if they do not have specific eBay or Internet experience—it can be valuable for someone without intimate knowledge to take a fresh look at your business.

Most of all, don't stress out when things go wrong. This won't help. When you make mistakes or misjudgments, don't beat yourself up about it. Worry, doubt, and self-incrimination are wasted emotions. You cannot change the past—all you can do is plan, change, and adapt to the new reality.

If you want to start or grow a large eBay business, then you qualify as an entrepreneur. Webster's dictionary defines *entrepreneur* as "one who organizes, manages, and assumes the risks of a business or enterprise." The key words in that definition are *assumes the risk*. That is the whole point. Short of walking through the woods and stumbling over a log only to find a fortune in cash hidden inside, you can't make money without accepting some risk. So going into the venture knowing that you are taking on risk is the key to your success.

But just how much risk should one take? That is a very personal question. I know both successful and unsuccessful entrepreneurs who risked everything they owned to start their venture. They took out a second mortgage on their house, sold their car, and borrowed to the max on dozens of credit cards. When you hear about someone who did that and was successful, you call them brilliant and courageous. But what is your reaction when you hear about another person who did the same thing and failed, losing everything? People usually call him stupid or worse. Yet he could have been the same individual. In fact, many entrepreneurs have lost everything more than once before becoming successful. I don't suggest you expose yourself to so much risk, however. I'd be very uncomfortable advising someone to take out a second mortgage on his house or borrow money on credit cards to buy inventory. Most people who put themselves in that position lack the emotional discipline to make good business decisions when the consequences of failure are so severe.

This book is about building a large eBay business, but you don't have to do it overnight. Never take on a level of risk that you cannot tolerate. If you are having trouble sleeping at night because you are worrying about the business, then your level of risk is too high. Professional investors have another saying that is very germane to entrepreneurs: liquidate down to the sleeping point.

If you want to grow your business and you need capital, re-read Chapter 6. There are plenty of professional investors—risk-takers, who want to loan or invest money in the hopes of making a good return on their investment. If you are just starting out, it might be difficult to convince those people to work with you, but if you take your time and prove your business concept, they will come around.

58.3 Coping with Failure

It always sounds trite to encourage people not to give up when they are failing. So at the risk of sounding trite: don't give up if you are failing. eBay is replete with thousands of people who gave up too soon. You can see their posts on the eBay message boards every day. They bought some product, put it on eBay, and it didn't sell—or it sold for too little money to recover their costs. Obviously, you can sell on eBay and make money—over 600,000 people in the United States do it every day. So how do you join those 600,000?

If your business plan isn't working, stop and reassess what you are doing. Get some help, but make sure the help comes from positive people. Ignore all those who say you will fail and no one can make money on eBay. Surround yourself with positive people who believe in you.

Over the years I have developed a sort of checklist for success on eBay. I keep it posted on the wall near my computer and refer to it when I am having a problem. Invariably, if I am having trouble with my auctions, I find I have broken one of my own rules:

- **Pay attention to the basics.** You would think that after an athlete made it to the NFL or the NBA, he would have mastered the basics, but professional coaches drill their players in the basics all the time. What are your basics? Writing good titles and descriptions, taking good photographs, having clearly-defined shipping and payment policies, and making your auctions look clean, professional, and attractive.

- **Research, test, research.** Instead of taking one big risk, take lots of little risks. You can recover from small mistakes, but large mistakes can be financially devastating.

- **Set goals and measure your progress.** Don't go through your day reacting to events. Have a plan for success. Set reasonable and reachable goals, and write down a plan for meeting them.

- **Get and stay organized.** This is a business where it pays to be organized. Organize your office, your shipping area, your inventory, and your day.

- **Exercise patience and control.** Things will go wrong. When they do, just take a deep breath and treat it like the business problem it is. If a customer complains or threatens you with negative feedback, it's not personal. This person doesn't know you. Communicate with customers with patience, understanding, and good humor, no matter how stupid or idiotic their questions or complaints are.

- **Communicate with your customers.** Check your e-mail at least three or four times a day. Make an effort to get back to customers and potential bidders as quickly as possible.

- **Don't be foolishly frugal.** Don't be afraid to spend money if it will make you more effective or efficient. Wasting your time performing manual tasks that you can automate is a drain on your business.

- **Never stop learning.** Read books; visit the eBay message boards and forums; attend eBay's online workshops; attend eBay Live and network with other sellers.

- **Take pains to understand your business and your competitors.** Measure your metrics and your performance, and stay on top of your business on a daily basis. A pilot can safely put his plane on autopilot while he checks his charts or eats a sandwich, but he doesn't go to the back of the plane and take a nap.

- **Set aside some time for yourself and your family.** Any business involving e-mail and computers is easy to get sucked into. You are working away, and all of a sudden it's dark outside and your dinner is cold. You need the support of your family to be successful in business—and they need your support to be successful as a family.

The best advice I can give you is to make sure you have built a business that you can enjoy. If you don't love your business, you won't enjoy it, and you won't be able to cope with problems when things go wrong. If you find you are not having fun, then stop and take stock of what you are doing. Make sure you are in the right business.

For more on investing in your business, see Chapter 6.

For more on business planning and goals, see Chapters 7 and 10.

chapter 59

You Can't Do This Alone

How large do you want your business to grow? If you just want a small part-time business, you probably would have bought one of the many basic eBay books on the market. But you bought this book, so you are most likely interested in growing a full-time business. Maybe you are still working and want to fire your boss. Maybe you just lost your job and need a new career—or maybe you are just fascinated with the potential of eBay and the Internet and see this as an opportunity to make a ton of money. Whatever your motivation, the first thing you have to decide is how large a business you want to have. That decision will determine if you can do it alone, with your spouse, or with paid employees.

The amount of gross merchandise sales (GMS) you can do in a month is determined by two factors: the average selling price (ASP) of your products and the number of auctions you launch. If you are selling $10,000 diamond rings, you can become a Titanium PowerSeller by selling only 15 rings a month. But if you sell clothing and your typical ASP is $75, then you need to successfully close over 2,000 auctions a month. You could easily work completely alone to launch 15 to 30 auctions a month in the first example. But could you launch, communicate about, sell, and ship 2,000 items a month by yourself?

If you are highly automated, you could handle the launching of 2,000 auctions with a system such as Vendio or ChannelAdvisor, but that's the easy part. The more time-consuming part is communicating with buyers, tracking payments, and packing, labeling, and shipping merchandise. At some point you will need help. Unless you have a large family, this usually means employees.

PowerSeller Tip

In order to have a successful eBay business, your goal should be to hire a trustworthy employee as soon as possible! You MUST offload all of the manual work to someone else so you can focus as much of your time on finding product to sell and growing and improving the business.

—Mike Enos, eBay guru and Platinum PowerSeller (www.platinumpowerseller. com)

59.1 When and How to Hire Employees

You should take extreme care when considering whether to hire employees. One of the big appeals of eBay is that you can run your business from your home with a minimum of investment and without having to deal with too many government regulations. But as soon as you hire an employee, all of this changes.

The first decision you'll need to make is whether to move your business out of your home (where most eBay sellers start) and into some commercial space. I strongly advise doing this. If you are going to hire an employee, you have all sorts of regulatory, legal, and liability issues related to an employee working in the home. Insurance is a very big issue. It is almost impossible to get insurance for a business operating out of a home, unless your home is also zoned for commercial use.

But avoid renting expensive space. Unless you are opening a storefront to do consignment sales, you don't need to be in an expensive high-traffic area. Your priorities should be security, storage, and adequate comfortable working space. Security is important for two reasons: a theft or vandalism can really interrupt your business even if everything is insured. Also, insurance companies rate locations and types of buildings when they determine their rates. Space in an industrial part in the suburbs will cost a lot less to insure than a space in the inner city.

Your space will need adequate storage for merchandise and room to build shelves so you can organize your inventory for quick access. You will also need room for a shipping station and a photo studio.

When it comes to hiring employees, I would avoid hiring a friend or family member unless you are absolutely sure you can manage the relationship. I once hired a close friend and had to fire her. Because she was a friend, I kept her on longer than I should have; and when it came time to fire her, it ruined the friendship.

You will need to decide what you want an employee to do. When you're first starting out, I suggest you look into hiring someone to do the low-value tasks that free up your time for more important work. This would include stocking shelves, packing and shipping, and perhaps sending out the shipping notice e-mails. Later you might want to train a person to take photographs and upload them. Eventually, as your business grows, you might want to hire a highly skilled customer service person who can handle phone calls and e-mails to customers.

We all want to trust people. I always operate on the principle that I trust people until they do something to misplace that trust. But when it comes to employees, I use Ronald Regan's philosophy when he was dealing with the Soviet Union over disarmament, "Trust but verify."

It's very easy these days to check criminal, DMV, and employment records on the Internet. If you are going to hire an employee, spend the few dollars it takes to check out his background in official records. If an employee is going to operate a company-owned vehicle, check his driving record with the DMV.

You can purchase a background check on a prospective employee at these websites. The fees range from $14.95 for a basic check to $75 for a more comprehensive report:

www.yourownprivateeye.com/backgroundcheck.htm

www.intelligentinvestigations.com

www.backgroundnow.com

www.peoplefinders.com

It also pays to check employees' references. Many companies will not comment on past employees for liability reasons, but some will. Sometimes the fact that a company will not comment says enough. A small mail order company in our community went through a downsizing, and several of the employees applied with us for a job. I made one call to get a reference on a woman I will call Sally. The person who answered the phone said: "Sally was great—we really hated to lose her." The next day I called about another fellow I'll call Greg. The same person whom I spoke with about Sally now said this: "We have a long-standing policy about commenting on former employees. All I can do is verify his dates of employment." That raised a red flag, and I decided to pass on Greg.

When you hire employees, you have to manage them. If you do not have any experience in the workplace supervising employees, this is an area where you should get some help and some advice. This is the sort of skill that the Service Corps of Retired Executives (SCORE) can help with (see Appendix B for details).

After you hire employees, you need set up and communicate your employment policies. Personnel Policies, Inc. runs a great website at www.ppspublishers. com/articles. They have free employment policies you can download and tailor to your needs. You can download these free policies:

- Attendance
- Behavior of Employees
- COBRA Requirements
- Dress Code
- Drugs/Narcotics/Alcohol
- Employee Classification
- FLSA Compliance
- FMLA Checklist
- Workplace Smoking
- Workplace Safety
- Holiday and Vacation Policy
- Internet/E-mail Communication
- Military Leave
- Pay Procedures
- Rest Breaks
- Sexual Harassment

Hiring and training a new employee is always a time-consuming chore and entails some risk that the employee will not work out. So do everything you can within reason to keep a great employee when you find one. Sometimes paying a little higher than the local scale for the skill level can save you a lot of money in the long run.

Last but not least, always follow all the local, state, and federal labor laws. Not doing so can get you in a lot of trouble and cost you a fortune in lawsuit defense, higher insurance rates, and fines. The best resource is your local Department of Labor. They have plenty of books and publications that explain the labor laws, safety regulations, and worker's compensation insurance issues. They can also supply you with all the posters and legal notifications you are required to post.

59.2 Employee Leasing

Let's face it, dealing with employees can be difficult and time-consuming. One way to avoid most of the hassles of having employees but still reap the majority of benefits is to lease your employees from a professional employee organization (PEO). When PEOs first started, they only offered their services to companies with a dozen or more employees. Now there are PEOs who will work with you even if you only have one or two employees. Some PEOs will even act as a hiring agency to help you find employees, but most of them prefer you hire the employees first.

PEOs actually hire your employees and rent or lease them back to you. You are responsible for their daily supervision, job performance, and management, including hiring and firing. But the PEO provides all of the nonmanagement employee services, such as taking care of payroll, providing benefits, filing reports and forms, and so on. A typical PEO can provide some of these services:

- Payroll checks
- Federal deposits (FICA, W/H, Federal Unemployment)
- Quarterly deposits (941 and State Unemployment)
- Government payroll audits
- Federal payroll summaries
- Year-end W-2s
- Health-care benefits

- Section 125 Cafeteria Plan
- 401(k) plan
- Voluntary insurance products
- Safety inspections
- OSHA compliance
- Employment and wage verifications
- Personnel files
- Terminations and garnishments
- EEO claims

And the cost for these services is surprisingly affordable. Some PEOs charge a percentage of the employee's salary; others charge a monthly fee for each employee. When you consider the time you would spend performing all of these functions and the risk of making a mistake, paying a small fee to have someone do all this for you seems a bargain.

59.3 Working With Independent Contractors

An independent contractor is someone who works for you who is not an employee. You pay him an hourly rate or a fixed fee to perform a specified task, but he pays his own taxes, benefits, and normal costs. This sounds like a good solution to the employee problem, but you need to make sure you and the IRS see eye-to-eye on whether the person you hire really should be classified as an independent contractor.

First of all, the contractor must be truly independent. You cannot treat him as you would an employee. A general rule is that you, the payer, have the right to control or direct only the result of the work done by an independent contractor and not the means and methods of accomplishing the result.

The IRS requires you to file information returns to report payments made to independent contractors during the year. For example, you must file Form 1099-MISC, Miscellaneous Income, to report payments of $600 or more to persons not treated as employees (i.e., independent contractors) for services performed for your trade or business. (For details about filing Form 1099, go to www.irs. gov/forms. You can read the regulations and download a copy of the form from this site.)

Carefully follow the rules as they relate to independent contractors. Because if the IRS finds that you are paying someone to do work as an independent contractor who is really an employee, they can force you to pay back withholding taxes and fines.

Generally, if you hire someone to perform a specific task and he can come and go when the task is complete, then you can qualify and pay the person as an independent contractor. For example, suppose you hire a student to come in every day after school to package, address, and ship your merchandise. This is a specific task, and you pay the student a fixed rate per package or a set daily fee. When he finishes shipping your merchandise, he can leave. You cannot ask him to sweep the floors or stock shelves or do other duties an employee might do.

You can also hire independent contractors to do specific technical tasks such as take digital photos, update your website, come in and count inventory, and perform similar specific tasks. A lot of small businesses do this today; they hire the minimum number of actual employees they need to accomplish the daily tasks of their business and then pay for other services such as website design, bookkeeping, janitorial service, and so on from independent contractors.

For more on employees, see Section 4.4.

chapter 60

Bringing It All Together

As you know by now, building and running a large-scale eBay and Internet business involves many elements. Some of the information might seem overwhelming, and the various processes can be somewhat intimidating, but the key is to take it one step at a time.

As I pointed out in Chapter 58, the first step is to have a plan and master the basics. After you write your business plan and set your goals, the best thing you can do is sit down and write out a list of tasks to accomplish. When you break the processes into small steps, it becomes a simple matter of attacking each task as an individual item, checking it off your list, and then moving on to the next one.

Some people bought this book because they already have an eBay business and want to scale it to new heights; others might be going into this for the first time. What you do and the order you do it in will depend on where you are in the process.

If you are an existing eBay seller, start by completely reexamining your business model. Look at where you are and where you want to go. Depending on how far along in your business you are, you might just need to modify your processes. Another, whose eBay business is struggling, might want to examine every aspect of his business from the beginning. If so, ask yourself these questions:

- What business am I in?
- Does my business model lend itself to eBay?
- Is there growth potential in my product line?

- Are there additional products or product categories I can expand into?
- Where do I stand competitively?
- Can I reach my sales goals just selling on eBay, or is it time to expand into additional channels?
- How much am I investing in my business now, and what resources would I need to double or triple my business?

These are the sorts of tough questions you should ask yourself before deciding where you want to go and how much and how fast you want to grow your business.

If you have an existing eBay business, one of the first things you should do is put the systems and software in place to understand your business to ensure you are working with good data. If you do not yet have a bookkeeping system, get set up with QuickBooks and hire a bookkeeper to enter all your financial information so you can see exactly where your money is going, understand your costs and margins, and examine your business from a detailed financial perspective.

After you really understand where your business is, you can start doing research and writing a new business plan. You should also review the first 10 chapters of this book, which are related to setting up and organizing your business. Getting the tools, systems, and processes in place before you start rebuilding your business will save you time and help you stay organized as you go through the process.

If you are a new eBay seller, setting up a first-time business, start with product research. Determining what to sell is really the first and most difficult step to running a successful eBay business—and the one task that will have the greatest long-term impact on the success of your business model. Next, write your business plan, and set your goals. This will help you determine the level of money and resources you'll need to start and grow your business. After you've done this, it's simply a matter of breaking your plan down into tasks and performing the tasks in a logical manner.

A few words about business plans: General George Patton once said, "Planning is critical to the success of a battle, but no plan ever survives first contact with the enemy." In other words, you need a plan of action so you know what the objective is, how you will get there, and what logistical supplies and support you will need to achieve the objective. However, the plan has to allow for changes and reactions to unexpected events. Business planning today stresses having the ability to react to changes in the marketplace and putting the resources into place to react to those changes. Although having a well-thought-out business plan is essential to your success, make sure you can adapt to challenges, competition, and changes in the marketplace, updating your business plan as you go.

Start small, and take it one step at a time. Be careful of diving in too fast. In my seminars and adult education classes, I've met dozens of eBay sellers who started their businesses without proper research and preparation. Invariably they lost money and became discouraged. In almost every case, they had gotten excited and started selling without doing the research and preparation necessary to succeed.

After you have researched your product and product category, it's time to test it. Research, test, refine your research, and test again until you are satisfied you are on the right track. You might lose a little money during this phase, but don't let that discourage you. Expending a small amount of resources in the beginning will help you avoid making large mistakes in the future.

Don't wait until you are struggling to get help. Even if things are going along smoothly, keep looking for help and ideas to further refine your business model. eBay and the Internet change rapidly. This means you must stay on top of things. Subscribe to newsletters; stay on top of the eBay announcements; look for new books; and attend seminars to keep your knowledge base up-to-date.

There are several PowerSeller boards on eBay, and these are great places to post questions and run ideas and concepts by other PowerSellers. I belong to a group called the Professional eBay Seller's Alliance (PESA). When this group first started, it was limited to the top 500 sellers on eBay, but since then they have opened up their membership to any PowerSeller. The group is dedicated to networking and helping each other. In addition to their own member message board, they also meet twice a year. These meetings are also attended by executives from eBay, Amazon.com, and Overstock.com as well as other vendors who support eBay sellers. The seminars are excellent, but the real benefit is the opportunity to meet other top sellers and exchange ideas and techniques. You can get information about PESA at www.gopesa.org.

Don't neglect your own continuing education. You are the only renewable resource, besides your employees, that your business has. You might be a master at getting the most out of your other resources, but how are you doing with you?

As I pointed out, the Internet and technology-based businesses are characterized by rapid change. Keeping up on innovations in your business and new business strategies is crucial for long-term success. However, most small business owners do not invest any time or money into developing themselves. The less you know, the more time, money, and energy you will waste in the future.

Many small businesses perish because the entrepreneur simply lacks the know-how in a particular aspect of business. This is particularly true for sole proprietors and personal corporation owners who must learn how to wear many hats. Maybe you're great launching auctions, but you might need help in setting up your accounting system or managing your inventory. The key to winning this game is continual self-education and knowing when to get help.

Do not be satisfied knowing just the basics of the software and systems you use to run your business. There might be many time-saving options in those programs if you take time to find them. Here's an easy strategy that will take about 15 minutes a day. Take your favorite program (accounting, mail, auction management system, or shipping software) and access the Help menu. Try to learn just one new feature, tool, or function of that program per day. A few minutes of your time now could yield big returns in the future.

I also keep an idea notebook in my office. In this special hard-bound notebook, I write down ideas I have heard about or thought of during the week. And once a week I set aside an hour for random brainstorming. This time is sacrosanct; I get out of the office, turn off my cell phone, and find a quiet place to work and think. I bring along my idea notebook and just spend some time thinking about my business and doing some creative brainstorming. It's amazing what I can come up with when I get away from the working environment.

I got this idea when I visited Microsoft's offices in Kirkland, Washington. As I walked through the halls with my escort, I kept noticing rooms with beanbag chairs on the floor and nothing else. Inside these rooms Microsoft employees were sprawled out on the chairs. Some were just staring at the ceiling; some were reading; and others were furiously writing in notebooks. None of them, however, had a computer or cell phone—these were not allowed in the room. Even Bill Gates, before he retired from Microsoft, used to take one week a year and hide out in a cabin in a remote location in the Pacific Northwest where he did nothing but think and plan.

Time management is another challenge faced by eBay sellers. The nature of the business is one of constant interruptions. You need to resist this. Set aside specific time frames to answer e-mails, launch auctions, and perform other important tasks. Plan your tasks in small increments. I keep a notebook handy with sections marked *product, systems, promotions,* and *customers,* and I make notes as thoughts and ideas come to me during the day. At the end of the day, I take a few minutes to create a "to-do" list for the next day and place the actions that will yield the highest returns at the top of the list.

Pay constant attention to your marketing and promotion. It is easy to get caught up in the daily minutia of running your business. Launching auctions, monitoring inventory, communicating with customers, and shipping orders can become all-consuming. Then one day you look up and wonder what happened to the business.

Marketing and promotion are all about the future of your business. If you want a long-term successful business, don't neglect the marketing and promotion. Every week you should set aside a couple of hours to measure the results of your promotions and plan new ones.

The assessment of your marketing and promotion efforts should include deciding to expand an existing product line, dumping unprofitable products or adding new products, determining where your advertising can generate the biggest return for the investment, and testing and planning future promotions. These are crucial functions to your success, and they can come back and bite you if you neglect them.

The last piece of advice I can give you is to have fun. This really is a fun business. eBay is a great community founded on the principal that all people are basically good. I have found this to be true over the years. Sure, there is the occasional idiot you have to deal with, and yes, there is a small amount of fraud on eBay, but these are minor annoyances in the overall enjoyment of your business. eBay and other Internet sites have created stunning new business opportunities for hundreds of thousands of entrepreneurs.

I have talked to dozens of people who think it's all been done and no more opportunities are available on eBay. This is just plain wrong. On almost any day I can go on eBay or the Internet and find new products and services that were not available a few weeks ago and new ways of selling existing products. The Internet today is about where aviation was when Lindberg crossed the Atlantic just a few short years after the Wright brothers first demonstrated powered flight. There will be millions of new businesses started and fortunes made during your lifetime. With a little creativity, hard work, and a plan to reach your goals, you can be one of them.

For more on mastering the basics, see Chapter 1.

eBay Terminology

Over the years, eBay has developed its own slang, jargon, and abbreviations, which you will often see in auction descriptions and e-mails. I suggest you use care with abbreviations as they can often cause confusion or misunderstandings with newbies, and I've placed them here in case you come across a term you're not familiar with.

A/O   Acronym for all original. Auction term used to describe the condition of an item on auction. Usually used in the auction title to save space.

active user   An eBay member who has bought or sold at least once in the prior 12 months.

ADDY   E-mail address.

AG   About Good, a term used to describe the condition of an item.

AKA   Acronym for also known as.

AOL   America Online.

AOV   Acronym for average order value.

as is   Items that are sold at auction without warranties as to the condition of the property. Item might be damaged or have missing parts.

ASAP   Acronym for as soon as possible.

ASP   Acronym for average selling price.

ATM   Acronym for at the moment.

B&W   Acronym for black and white.

BC   Acronym for back cover.

bid increment   The amount by which you must increase your bid over the current high bid. The bid increment is established by the former bid price. For example, if eBay sets a bid increment of 50¢ and the current bid is $9.35, your new bid must be at least $9.85.

bid rigging   The unlawful practice whereby two or more people agree not to bid against one another so as to deflate value.

BIN   Acronym for Buy It Now. A price set by the seller whereby buyers can end the auction immediately by paying the buy-it-now price.

BIN rate   The percentage of your items sold that were sold with BIN or any fixed-price format.

blocked bidders   eBay feature that enables sellers to create a list of specific eBay members who are not allowed to bid on or buy items they sell. A person on the list will be blocked from participating in all the seller's auctions.

BRB   Acronym for be right back.

BTW   Acronym for by the way.

caveat emptor   A Latin term meaning Let the buyer beware! A legal maxim stating that the buyer takes the risk.

CC   Acronym for carbon copy.

COA   Acronym for Certificate of Authenticity. Auction term used to describe an item as genuine (usually certified by an expert).

CIB   Acronym for cartridge instructions/box (as in computer equipment).

CONUS   Acronym for continental United States, not including Alaska and Hawaii.

CR   Acronym for conversion rate.

DBA   Acronym for doing business as.

deadbeat bidder   One who wins an auction and fails to complete a transaction.

DOA   Acronym for dead on arrival (the item you bought doesn't work out of the package).

Dutch auction   Auction format for selling multiple quantities of identical items in one auction. Bidders choose the number of items they want and how much they want to bid. The final price is determined by the lowest bid among all the winning bidders. The highest bidders win, but pay the lowest bid price.

DSL   High-speed Internet connection through a special phone line.

emoticon   A specific group of characters used to form a facial expression in e-mails. For example, :-) is a smiley face.

escrow   Third-party company that holds payment in trust until the seller makes delivery of merchandise to the buyer.

FAQ   A list of frequently asked questions and answers.

FB   Acronym for feedback.

flame   An angry message or feedback sent many times.

flameout (a.k.a. crash and burn)   Slang for when you don't follow the advice in this book and your eBay business fails.

FTP   Acronym for File Transfer Protocol; a method for uploading pages to the Internet.

FV   Acronym for final value; the price something sells for on eBay, not including shipping.

FVF   Acronym for final value fee that eBay charges for selling.

FWIW   Acronym for for what it's worth.

gently used   Used but with little wear.

GMS   Acronym for gross merchandise sales.

HP   Acronym for home page.

HTML   Acronym for hypertext markup language. The computer programming language that tells web pages what to do. HTML commands are indicated by the < and > marks. For example, the command <B> will turn all the type that follows it into boldface type. You end the command by placing a slash in front of the command such as </B>.

IE   Acronym for Internet Explorer. A popular Internet browser made by Microsoft.

IMHO   Acronym for in my humble opinion.

IMO   Acronym for in my opinion.

INIT   Acronym for initials.

ISP   Acronym for Internet service provider.

JPG   Preferred file format for pictures on eBay (pronounced *jay-peg*).

keyword spamming   The practice of placing a keyword in an auction title that is not related to or exactly what you are selling. An example would be *Italian Loafers Just Like Gucci.*

link   Hyperlink; a clickable photo or text on a web page that takes you to another page on the Internet.

LOL   Acronym for laughing out loud.

Lot or Lots   Similar items sold in quantities. Lots are normally sold at discount or wholesale prices.

LTD   Acronym for limited edition.

MIB   Acronym for mint in box.

MIMB   Acronym for mint in mint box.

MIMP   Acronym for mint in mint package.

mint   In perfect condition (a subjective term).

MIP   Acronym for mint in package.

MNB   Acronym for mint no box.

MOC   Acronym for mint on card.

My eBay   A page that displays your ongoing auctions, status, and auction history.

MYOB   Acronym for mind your own business.

NARU   Acronym for not a registered user (suspended user).

NBW   Acronym for never been worn.

NC   Acronym for no cover.

newbie   Someone recently new to eBay.

NM   Acronym for near mint.

NO RESERVE   *See* NR.

NPB   Acronym for nonpaying bidder (*see* deadbeat bidder).

NR   Acronym for no reserve price on auction. *See* reserve.

NRFB Acronym for never removed from box.

NWT Acronym for new with tag.

OEM Acronym for original equipment manufacturer.

OOP Acronym for out of print.

OTOH Acronym for on the other hand.

PayPal Verified User A PayPal user who has confirmed his or her address and account information through PayPal.

phishing *See* spoofs.

pink Slang for eBay employees who post on the eBay message boards. Because they are employees, their User IDs are displayed in the color pink.

PPC Acronym for pay per click.

PM Acronym for Priority Mail.

Primail Priority Mail.

private auction An auction in which neither the buyers' nor the sellers' identities are disclosed.

proxy bidding A bidder enters the maximum amount he is willing to spend on an item, and eBay will automatically continue incremental bidding until either he is the high bidder or his maximum is reached.

relisting Process of again listing an item that did not sell on auction.

Reserve Auction An auction in which the seller reserves a minimum acceptable price. Sellers sometimes disclose the reserve price to perspective bidders, but they do not have to.

Reserve Not Met Auction term that means no bid is high enough to match the minimum price the seller will accept.

Reserve Price The minimum price a seller is willing to accept for an item to be sold at auction.

River (The River) The code name for Amazon.com used on the message boards so eBay won't delete your posts.

RMA Acronym for return merchandise authorization.

ROFL Acronym for rolling on floor laughing; *see also* LOL.

RSVP   Acronym for "Respondez S'il Vous Plait," a French phrase that means please respond.

SCO   Acronym for second chance offer.

shilling   Fraudulent bidding by an associate of the seller in order to inflate the price of an item. Also known as *bid rigging* or *collusion.*

SIG   Signature.

siphoning   Other sellers contacting bidders and offering to sell them the same item they are currently bidding on, thus drawing bidders away from the legitimate seller's auction.

SKU   Acronym for stock-keeping unit—essentially a stock number.

snail mail   Ordinary postal mail.

sniping   Bidding at the last possible moment.

SNR   A listing that starts at $1 with no reserve.

spam   Unwanted e-mail; eBay will discipline you for sending e-mail to bidders in auctions you are not involved in.

spamming the category   Placing auctions in popular, but unrelated, categories. eBay might suspend your auctions if they catch you doing this.

spoofs   A spoofed website that is typically made to look like a well-known, branded site (such as eBay, PayPal, or Amazon) with a subtly different URL. A spoofed e-mail looks like it came from eBay, PayPal, or your bank. However, the link leads you to the fake website. It is used to deceive online shoppers into disclosing their credit card numbers, bank account information, Social Security numbers, passwords, and other personal information.

TA   Acronym for Trading Assistant. Experienced eBay sellers who meet eBay requirements and will sell another person's items on eBay for a fee or commission. Also known as an eBay consignment Seller.

TM   Acronym for trademark.

unwanted bid   A bid that does not meet the seller's terms stated in the auction. For example, if a seller states in an auction that he will only ship items to U.S. locations and the bidder is located overseas, the seller can cancel the bid.

UPS   Acronym for United Parcel Service.

URL   The address that identifies a website. The acronym stands for Uniform Resource Locator.

USPS   Acronym for United States Postal Service.

VERO   Acronym for eBay's Verified Rights Owners program for copyright and trademark enforcement.

VHTF   Acronym for very hard to find.

Western Union Auction Payments (formally called BidPay)   An online auction payment service owned by Western Union.

Winning Bidder Notification (WBN)   Notification sent at end of auction to the winning bidder. It might be sent by eBay, PayPal, the seller, or the seller's auction management system.

WTMI   Acronym for way too much information.

WYSIWYG   Acronym for what you see is what you get.

Yahoo! Shops   A shopping portal run by Yahoo! (separate from Yahoo! auctions).

Reader Website Support

Throughout the book I've mentioned several times how rapidly eBay and the Internet can change. Just in the time it takes to edit, print, and distribute this book, changes will take place, and new resources will come along. Rarely will changes make the strategies and tips in this book obsolete, but they can change some of the relevant facts, tactics, and statistics. Therefore, I have created a website just for you readers where I can update information, list resources, and provide a list of linkable resources that I can update frequently.

The plan is for this website to become a continuing resource for my readers. It is located at www.skipmcgrath.com/titanium. When you first visit the website, fill out the form to subscribe to my twice-monthly newsletter, as this is where I update news and information for sellers. The newsletter is free and is just for you. I will not rent, sell, or share your information with any other party. After you subscribe, be sure to look in your e-mail for a link that you must click on to confirm your subscription. If you do not see this e-mail within a few minutes, check your spam or junk e-mail filter, as it can occasionally end up there.

A lot of companies sell information, services, software, and tools for eBay and Internet sellers, and I have contacted a number of these companies and arranged for valuable discounts and electronic coupons for the readers of this book. By checking the website often, you can access the valuable discounts as they are offered.

I also conduct eBay boot camps throughout the year. These two-day intensive training sessions are held twice a year in Las Vegas—usually in conjunction with a major wholesale sourcing trade show. The cost of tuition and lodging runs between $1,999 and $2,499, depending on the event and the time of year. I often offer early-bird discounts to my readers, which I announce in the newsletter.

Online Business Resources

This appendix contains links to online informational services, business assistance websites, and other resources to help entrepreneurs and start-up businesses.

Some of the URLs can be quite long to type; therefore, in many cases I have used a service called Tiny URL to generate short, easy-to-type links. Tiny URL is a free service you can access at www.tinyurl.com. You simply type in a long URL and hit the button to instantly create a short URL. This is a useful feature for creating links on your website, business cards, or in auctions.

The Service Corps of Retired Executives (SCORE)

SCORE is located online at www.score.org. SCORE is a nonprofit association affiliated with the U.S. Small Business Administration (SBA). The SCORE website contains a wealth of information for small business owners and links to contact SCORE counselors in your area.

SCORE's extensive national network of 10,500 retired and working volunteers are experienced entrepreneurs and corporate managers/executives. These volunteers provide free business counseling and advice as a public service to all types of businesses, in all stages of development.

The SCORE website contains free business plan templates you can download to help build your business plan. After you write the plan, you can e-mail SCORE counselors to have them review the plan and give you their comments and advice.

In addition to a business plan template, SCORE also provides several other types of forms and templates for running your business. This partial list gives you some of the resources available online at the SCORE website:

- A Business Plan for a Start-up Business
- A Business Plan for an Established Business
- Bank Loan Request for Small Business
- Break-Even Analysis
- Competitive Analysis
- Financial History & Ratios
- Loan Amortization Schedule
- Nondisclosure Agreement
- Opening Day Balance Sheet
- Personal Financial Statement
- Projected Balance Sheet
- Start-Up Expenses
- 4-Year Profit Projection
- 12-Month Cash Flow Statement
- 12-Month Profit and Loss Projection
- 12-Month Sales Forecast

The SCORE website also contains hundreds of business articles on subjects of interest to entrepreneurs and start-up businesses.

Welcome Business USA

Welcome Business USA (www.welcomebusiness.com) is an excellent website with tons of free resources for start-up and entrepreneurial small businesses. One of the neatest things is their seven checklists for business success, which can help you make sure you are not missing important steps in starting and running your business:

- Start-up Checklist
- General Business Checklist
- Operations Checklist
- Human Resources Checklist

- Marketing/Advertising/Sales Checklist
- Accounting & Bookkeeping Checklist
- Start-Up Financing Checklist
- Website Checklist

The U.S. Small Business Administration (SBA)

The SBA, which has been around since the 1960s, is the government organization devoted to helping small businesses succeed and grow. You can access the website at www.sba.gov. The SBA is a great place to start if you need to raise financing for an existing business, although they rarely fund start-up businesses. The SBA website also contains a wealth of information for entrepreneurs.

The heart of the website is their start-up guide. This small business guide serves as a road map for starting a business and is both comprehensive and easy to use. It also includes numerous electronic links for additional information. You can use this powerful interactive tool, with many supporting resources, to help you start a successful business.

The SBA also offers free online courses in subjects such as a basic course in entrepreneurship, building a business plan, financing a business, and buying a franchise. Another asset is their online plain language law library. The SBA Law Library contains valuable legal and business information and also includes small business research and statistical information.

International Council of Online Professionals (iCop)

iCop is sort of a Better Business Bureau for online businesses, which sets ethical standards for business transactions and privacy issues. Membership includes a seal you can use in your auctions and the opportunity to network with other Internet professionals. The website is located at www.i-cop.org.

All Business, Inc.

All Business, Inc. at www.allbusiness.com is a great small business resource website. They feature daily blogs and weekly newsletters on topics of interest to entrepreneurs. This is another location where you can download tons of free forms and templates; this partial list shows some of the useful information they offer.

- Confidentiality & Nondisclosure Agreements
- Consultants & Independent Contractors
- Domain Name Purchase Agreements
- Employment Policies & Termination
- Letters of Intent
- Promissory Notes & Loan Agreements
- Protecting Ideas & Information
- Raising Capital
- Real Estate Leases
- Venture Capital Agreements

GE Business Services

GE Business Services is a division of General Electric Capital, one of the largest commercial lenders in the country. GE Business Services has a program for eBay sellers called the GE Premier Line of Credit, an unsecured credit program with interest rates as low as 7 percent.

GE also offers a secured credit line (inventory financing) for eBay sellers who sell new, nonperishable consumer goods, purchased directly from a manufacturer or wholesale distributor.

For those who qualify for secured credit, GE Business Credit Services pays the manufacturer or distributor invoices while providing the business with flexible repayment terms. GE Business Credit Services can also provide qualified eBay sellers other financing solutions, depending on the business's needs. You can get more information and apply for a loan online at their website, www.gebcs.com.

American Express Small Business Network

American Express runs an excellent small business resource website at tinyurl.com/5xyda. American Express actively courts small businesses with a wide range of services from credit to investments, to cash flow management tools. Their small business website contains a wealth of information and resources for small business owners. Lately, American Express has been courting eBay entrepreneurs with advertising on eBay and by exhibiting at eBay Live.

Entrepreneur.com

Entrepreneur.com, at www.entrepreneur.com, is the online presence of *Entrepreneur Magazine.* This website is loaded with hundreds of free articles on all aspects of starting and running a small business. They have a very powerful search engine. So for example, if you are searching for articles on cash flow, you just type *cash flow* into the search box and find several articles on the topic.

One of the neatest features of this website is the free online calculators to help you measure different aspects of your business, to use as tools to refine your business plan, or to write a request for raising capital. Here is a sampling of some of the calculators available:

- Break-Even Calculator. Break-even analysis is an expected component of most business plans, especially for start-up companies. This calculator shows how much revenue you need to cover both fixed and variable costs.

- Cash Flow Calculator. This cash calculator shows you how advertising and promotion, carrying inventory, and rapid growth can absorb a business's money.

- Investment Offering Calculator. Use this calculator to view both sides of the investment table. See what an investor gets and what a company gives up, all in one easy tool.

- Starting Costs Calculator. Calculate the start-up costs of your new business before you get going. This calculator helps you evaluate how much capital you'll need to start your business.

- Website Conversion Rate Calculator. This calculator enables you to see the impact improving your website conversion rate has on your total online sales. Enter your visitors and total orders, and you can see what an increase in conversion can do.

- E-mail Return on Investment (ROI) Calculator. Use this calculator to determine the ROI for your e-mail campaigns. Based on your marketing campaign results and expected results, your ROI will be automatically calculated. Use this tool to test different scenarios and see results.

- Pay-Per-Click ROI Calculator. Use this calculator to determine the ROI for your pay-per-click advertising campaigns.

Start-up Journal: *The Wall Street Journal* for Entrepreneurs

The Wall Street Journal launched a website devoted to information and resources just for entrepreneurs in late 2005 at www.startupjournal.com. This website is loaded with articles, resources, and links to all types of information for start-up business owners. Although the site is aimed at all types of entrepreneurs, it heavily favors online marketing.

Auction Management Software

The following table includes all the major desktop-based software solutions for selling on eBay and other auction channels. Most of the programs are Windows-based, although two options, AuctionGenie and e-Lister, also offer Mac versions.

This list of auction software providers and the list of auction management companies in the following appendix is provided by AuctionBytes and used with their permission. You can link to all of these companies at www.auctionbytes.com. AuctionBytes updates this list three or four times a year, so going there to link to the various sites will provide the latest up-to-date pricing and information.

Name	Online Venues Supported	Cost	Platforms Supported
AuctionGenie tinyurl.com/8b5qu	eBay	$40/year	Windows and Mac OSX
Auction Sage www.auctionsagesoftware.com	eBay	$69.95	Windows
AuctionSubmit www. auctionsubmit.com	eBay, Yahoo!, Amazon, and Shoporium	Free	Windows
Auction Tamer www.auctiontamer.com	eBay, Yahoo!, Amazon, BidVille, and most foreign eBay sites	$99/year or $270 one-time purchases	Windows
Blackthorne	eBay	$24.99/month	Windows
Auction Wizard 2000 www.auctionwizard2000.com	eBay & Yahoo!	$76 for first year and $50 annual renewal	Windows
DEK Auction Manager www.dekauctionmanager.com	eBay	$39.95/month	Windows
eBay Seller's Assistant and Seller's Assistant Pro www.tinyurl.com/dy63p	eBay, eBay Motors	$9.95/month or $24.99/month for Pro	Windows
e-Lister www.blackmagik.com/elister.html	eBay	$29.95/ six months	Windows and Mac
Foo Dog www.foodogsoftware.com	eBay U.S., UK, CA, and AU	$49.95	Windows
Liberty 4 Trading Assistant www.resaleworld.com	All eBay U.S. and International sites	$60/month	Windows
Sold www.timbercreeksoftware.com	eBay and eBay Motors	$79.85	Windows
Yahoo! Seller's Manager www.auctions.yahoo.com Auctions	Yahoo! Auctions	Free with Yahoo!	Windows

Online Auction Management Services

Online services vary widely in their offerings. Some only provide listing and launching tools; some are just image management and storage solutions; and others provide the full range of services. I have listed only the complete providers because the partial solutions are just that—partial solutions that are not useable for the full-time seller. This list is taken from AuctionBytes (www.auctionbytes.com) with their permission; however, the comments in the remarks section are mine.

Name/Website	Venues Supported	Monthly Cost	Remarks
Auctiva www.auctiva.com	eBay and Amazon	$109.95, including unlimited image hosting	Auctiva provides the standard auction management services but lacks inventory management tools and integration with offline systems.
ChannelAdvisor www.channeladvisor. com	eBay, Yahoo!, Overstock.com, Amazon, Shopzilla, Shopping.com, MSN, BizRate, C-Net, and Froogle	$99.95 includes 2,000 closed auctions	ChannelAdvisor is the largest and probably the most comprehensive auction management service. One of its greatest advantages is the large number of channels it supports.
eBay Selling Manager Pro www.eBay.com	eBay and eBay Motors	$15.99	This is an excellent tool fully integrated with the My eBay Dashboard.
InkFrog www1.inkfrog.com/ index.php		$9.95	Very good tool. Not as powerful as Vendio or ChannelAdvisor, but InkFrog has a large and loyal following
Infopia Marketplace Manager www. marketplacemanager. com	Amazon Auctions, Amazon ZShops, Bidway.com, BizRate, Catalog City, CNET Auctions, eBay Network, eBay Stores, Dealtime, Overture, sell.com, Yahoo! Auctions, and Yahoo! Shopping	$99 and up, based on inventory size and customization	Infopia is one of ChannelAdvisor's leading competitors in the advanced multi-channel venue. It also offers Configurator and a new system called Trade In, where eBay buyers can trade in old merchandise for new.
InkFrog	eBay	Basic $9.95	This full-featured auction management system includes image hosting.
Meridian www.noblespirit. com	eBay and Overstock.com	$39.95 for 3,000 listings	Meridian is a full-featured service with no extra image-hosting fees. It also offers the only online service platform for consignment selling.

Name/Website	Venues Supported	Monthly Cost	Remarks
Spoonfeeder www.spoonfeeder.com	eBay only	One-time fee of $99 + $19.95 for 2,000 completed auctions	This includes a full suite of services but unfortunately only supports eBay.
Vendio www.vendio.com	eBay, Overstock, and Amazon	$12.95 + 20¢ per listing	Excellent service—one of my personal favorites. It has great inventory management features and is easy to learn and use for new sellers.
Zoovy www.zoovy.com	eBay, Yahoo!, Amazon, ePier, and Ubid	$100 + 5¢ per completed auction + $300 for training	This very complete service has special solutions for apparel and jewelry sellers. Very nice branding package and excellent training.

Promotional and Timesaving Tools for the Professional Online Seller

A wealth of services is available for online sellers. Many are free or charge nominal fees, and others are quite expensive. You have to evaluate which of these are right for you. All of the resources listed here are also available to link to from the www.skipmcgrath/titanium website.

Some of these links are quite long and some others offer promotions or other discounts if you use special links, so I have used TinyURL links to allow you to access these.

HammerTap (www.hammertap.com)

HammerTap's research tool sifts through the masses of auctions to help you pinpoint the hottest-selling items up for bid in your particular niche. This helps you determine how likely specific products are to sell. The tool gives you the ability to drill down and narrow your search to find the most successful brand or product feature within a given list of products.

HammerTap uncovers the market trends that lead to higher auction success rates. Discover which day of the week to end your auction listing; find out whether or not to use a reserve; choose starting prices that attract more bids; and much more. HammerTap provides a wealth of data to discover how to maximize your auction listings and final values. If you use the link www.hammertap.com/skip, they offer a discount to readers of this book.

Terapeak Research Service (www.terapeak.com)

Terapeak is one of the leading research services for eBay sellers. They offer all the features of HammerTap, plus a new keyword analysis tool. You can now get most of Terapeak's services within eBay as part of eBay Marketplace Analysis available for a fee or free to premium eBay store subscribers.

Terapeak information includes ...

- Average sales price
- Total sales for your item
- Total listings
- Success rate
- Total bids received
- Demand for your item
- Prices realized on eBay
- Time of day to sell
- Top-ranked sellers
- Total bids they receive
- Total sales market share
- Sell-through rate

Terapeak also enables you to download the data to Excel for further offline analysis.

Auction Niches (www.tinyurl.com/9fymy)

Auction Niches is a monthly service that researches the hot keywords used in over 100 narrow product niches. This is a great tool for finding new niches and for targeting the best keywords for any niches you select.

AuctionBytes (www.auctionbytes.com)

AuctionBytes, run by David and Ina Steiner, is the authoritative news source for eBay and the online auction community. They publish a daily newsletter for the online auction community and a weekly wrap-up with longer stories, advice, and articles by online auction experts. The site also contains several free resources and links to hundreds of Internet services.

eBay Keyword Hotlist (http://pulse.ebay.com/)

eBay publishes a monthly hot list on the eBay Pulse page. The list shows all the hot products and keywords by category and which keywords are driving the highest hit-to-bid ratio. There are also other good seller resources on the eBay Pulse page.

Seller's Voice (www.sellersvoice.com)

Seller's Voice is a program that easily adds audio to your eBay auctions. Research has shown that adding audio can increase bids by 30 percent and final values by 19 percent.

Worldwide Brands (www.worldwidebrands.com)

Worldwide Brands publishes two online directories used by thousands of eBay sellers. One is the Wholesale Drop Ship Source Directory that can connect you with actual manufacturers who will drop ship to your customers. The other product is the Light Bulk Wholesale Directory that lists wholesalers who will sell in small to medium volumes. If you use the link www.worldwidebrands.com/skipmcgrath, they offer a $20 discount on their service to my readers.

My Corporation (www.tinyurl.com/bkglc)

My Corporation offers online incorporating service and other services such as forming an LLC, setting up DBAs, trademarks, copyrights, and corporate filings.

BuySafe (www.buysafe.com)

BuySafe is a bonding company that provides your buyers protection against fraudulent transactions on eBay and the Internet. This is useful if you sell high-priced merchandise, as it gives your customers confidence in you.

Suggested Reading List

A number of books and training resources are available to help you develop your Internet marketing and eBay skills. I have listed some of the best ones here.

The *Internet Marketing Course*, by Derek Ghel, is the oldest and most comprehensive Internet marketing training program available today. It is available on the web at www.tinyurl.com/8vbqs.

Turn eBay Data into Dollars, by Ina Steiner, shows sellers how to use the eBay search engine and third-party research services to increase their profits by showing the best keywords to use and the best times and days to launch their auction listings.

eBay Strategies: 10 Proven Methods to Maximize Your eBay Business, by Scot Wingo, teaches the Five P's—Product, Promotion, Placement, Price, and Performance—to help you think strategically about your eBay Business.

eBay Power Seller Secrets: Insider Tips from eBay's Most Successful Sellers, by Debra and Brad Schepp, contains interviews of dozens of top eBay sellers gathered for this excellent guide.

The Official eBay Bible, by Jim "Griff" Griffith. Griff is an early eBay employee who now hosts eBay Radio and is the Dean of eBay University. His book is the official eBay reference text.

The Complete eBay Marketing System, by Skip McGrath. This is my complete basics to advanced-sellers guide. You can order it from my website at www. skipmcgrath.com.

How and Where to Locate the Merchandise to Sell on eBay, by Dan W. Blacharski. This book gives insider information you need to know from the experts who do it every day.

index

Numbers

$1 No Reserve start, 116
2%/30, 248
10-day Duration option, 316
99 Tips for Buying & Selling on eBay, 446

A

A&A Customs Brokers, 238
ABCD approach to inventory, 145-146
About Me page, 445-446
accounting software, 27, 31
   QuickBooks, 462-466
accrual method of inventory counting, 62
Adobe Acrobat Reader, 101
Adobe Photoshop CS, 36
Adobe Photoshop Elements 3.0, 36
adversity, coping with, 489-492
advertising for goods, 222-223
all caps in headline, 269
Anchor Store subscription, 411
AND NOT in searches, 98
angels, 44
anti-virus software, 31
antiques, 77, 85-86, 92
   advertising for, 222-223
   auctions, 219-220

estate sales, 217-218
importers, 223-225
pricing, 216
tag sales, 217-218
toys, 134
wholesalers, 223-225
yard sales, 216-217
aperture setting on camera, 400
appliances, 84-85
Armstrong Auctions, 194
art, 85-86
   advertising for, 222-223
   auctions, 219-220
   branding and, 451
   definition of, 215
   estate sales, 217-218
   tag sales, 217-218
   yard sales, 216-217
ASP (Average Selling Price), 86, 471
Auction Genie, 364, 366
auction management service web stores, 419-420
auction management services
   Auctiva, 370
   ChannelAdvisor, 370, 377-386
   InkFrog, 370
   Kyozou, 370
   Meridian, 370
   Vendio, 370-371
      SMIE (Sales Manager Inventory Edition), 372-376

C

D

S

X–Y–Z